WELCOME TO
FUNDAMENTALS OF STRATEGY

Strategy is a fascinating subject. It's about the overall direction of all kinds of organisations, from multinationals to entrepreneurial start-ups, from charities to government agencies, and many more. Strategy raises the big questions about these organisations – how they grow, how they innovate and how they change. As a manager of today or of tomorrow, you will be involved in influencing, implementing or communicating these strategies.

Our aim in writing *Fundamentals of Strategy* is to give you a clear understanding of the fundamental issues and techniques of strategy, and to help you get a great final result in your course. Here's how you might make the most of the text:

- Focus your time and attention on the fundamental areas of strategy in just **10 carefully selected chapters**.

- Read the **illustrations** and the **case examples** to clarify your understanding of how the concepts of strategy translate into an easily recognisable, real-world context.

- Follow up on the **recommended key readings** at the end of each chapter. They're specially selected as accessible and valuable sources that will enhance your learning and give you an extra edge in your course work.

Fundamentals of Strategy is available with **MyStrategyLab**, and you can register at **www.mystrategylab.com*** to find essential student learning material including:

- **The Strategy Experience Simulation**, which gives you practical hands-on experience of strategic decision-making in organisations. As a Director of the Board, you must deal with opportunities as they arise, and your decisions will affect the company'sperformance. Choose wisely!

- A **personalised study plan** based on feedback that identifies your strengths and weaknesses, then recommends a tailored set of resources that will help to develop your understanding of strategy.

- **Audio** and **video resources**, including case studies on IKEA, Land Rover and the Eden Project, that put a spotlight on strategy in practice.

We want *Fundamentals of Strategy* to give you what you need: a clear and concise view of the subject, an ambition to put that into practice, and – of course – success in your studies. We hope that you'll be just as intrigued by the key issues of strategy as we are!

So, read on and good luck!

Gerry Johnson
Richard Whittington
Kevan Scholes

* P.S. In order to log in to the website, you'll need to register with the access code included in the access card, or you can purchase access online at www.mystrategylab.com.

Gerry Johnson, BA, PhD is Emeritus Professor of Strategic Management at Lancaster University Management School and a Senior Fellow of the UK Advanced Institute of Management Research (AIM). He has also taught at Strathclyde Business School, Cranfield School of Management, Manchester Business School and Aston University. He is the author of numerous books and his research has been published in many of the foremost management research journals in the world. He also serves on the editorial boards of the *Academy of Management Journal*, the *Strategic Management Journal* and the *Journal of Management Studies*. He is a partner in the consultancy partnership Strategy Explorers (see www.strategyexplorers.com) where he works with senior management teams on issues of strategy development and strategic change.

Richard Whittington MA, MBA, PhD is Professor of Strategic Management at the Saïd Business School and Millman Fellow at New College, University of Oxford. He is author or co-author of nine books and has published many journal articles. He serves on the editorial boards of *Organization Science*, *Organization Studies*, the *Strategic Management Journal* and *Long Range Planning*, amongst others. He has had full or visiting positions at the Harvard Business School, HEC Paris, Imperial College London, the University of Toulouse and the University of Warwick. He is a partner in Strategy Explorers and active in executive education and consulting, working with organisations from across Europe, the USA and Asia (see www.strategyexplorers.com). His current research is focused on strategy practice and international management.

Kevan Scholes MA, PhD, DMS, CIMgt, FRSA is Principal Partner of Scholes Associates – specialising in strategic management. He is also Visiting Professor of Strategic Management and formerly Director of the Sheffield Business School, UK. He has extensive experience of teaching strategy to both undergraduate and postgraduate students at several universities. In addition, his corporate management development work includes organisations in manufacturing, many service sectors and a wide range of public service organisations. He has had regular commitments outside the UK – including Ireland, Australia and New Zealand. He has also been an advisor on management development to a number of national bodies and is a Companion of The Chartered Management Institute.

FUNDAMENTALS OF STRATEGY

SECOND EDITION

GERRY JOHNSON
Lancaster University Management School

RICHARD WHITTINGTON
Saïd Business School, University of Oxford

KEVAN SCHOLES
Sheffield Business School

**Financial Times
Prentice Hall
is an imprint of**

Harlow, England • London • New York • Boston • San Francisco • Toronto
Sydney • Tokyo • Singapore • Hong Kong • Seoul • Taipei • New Delhi
Cape Town • Madrid • Mexico City • Amsterdam • Munich • Paris • Milan

Pearson Education Limited

Edinburgh Gate

Harlow

Essex CM20 2JE

England

and Associated Companies throughout the world

Visit us on the World Wide Web at:
www.pearsoned.co.uk

First published 2009
Second edition published 2012

ISBN: 978-0-273-75725-2

British Library Cataloguing-in-Publication Data
A catalogue record for this book is available from the British Library

Library of Congress Cataloging-in-Publication Data
Johnson, Gerry.
    Fundamentals of strategy / Gerry Johnson, Richard Whittington, Kevan Scholes. -- 2nd ed.
      p. cm.
    ISBN 978-0-273-75725-2 (pbk.)
    1. Business planning. 2. Strategic planning. 3. Business planning--Case studies.
4. Strategic planning--Case studies. I. Whittington, Richard, 1958- II. Scholes, Kevan. III. Title.

HD30.28.J6495 2012
658.4′012--dc23

                                                            2011033616

10 9 8 7 6 5 4 3 2 1
15 14 13 12 11

Typeset in 9.5/13.5pt Photina by 35
Printed and bound by Rotolito Lombarda, Italy

FUNDAMENTALS OF STRATEGY ONLINE

A wide range of supporting resources are available at:

PEARSON mystrategylab

Register to create your own personal account using the access code supplied with your copy of the book,* and access the following teaching and learning resources:

Resources for students

- **A dynamic eText** of the book that you can search, bookmark, annotate and highlight as you please
- **Self-assessment questions** that identify your strengths before recommending a personalised study plan that points you to the resources which can help you achieve a better grade
- **Key concept audio summaries** that you can download or listen to online
- **Video cases** that show managers talking about strategic issues in their own organisations
- **Revision flashcards** to help you prepare for your exams
- **A multi-lingual online glossary** to help explain key concepts
- Guidance on **how to analyse a case study**
- **Links** to relevant sites on the web so you can explore more about the organisations featured in the case studies
- **Classic cases** – over 30 case studies from previous editions of the book
- **The Strategy Experience Simulation** gives you hands-on experience of strategic analysis and putting strategy into action

Resources for instructors

- **Instructor's manual**, including extensive teaching notes for cases and suggested teaching plans
- **PowerPoint slides**, containing key information and figures from the book
- **Secure testbank**, containing over 600 questions
- Support for **The Strategy Experience Simulation** with guidance on the aims and objectives of the simulation, and instructions on how to set up simulation groups that enable you to monitor your student's performance

For more information, please contact your local Pearson Education sales representative or visit **www.mystrategylab.com**

* If you don't have an access code, you can still access the resources by purchasing access online. Visit **www.mystrategylab.com** for details. A sample selection of these resources is also available at **www.pearsoned.co.uk/fos2**

CONTENTS

ABOUT *FUNDAMENTALS OF STRATEGY*

Based on the ninth edition of the market-leading *Exploring Strategy*, this book concentrates on the fundamental issues and techniques of strategy. The book will particularly suit those on short courses in strategy focused on strategy analysis, or studying strategy as part of a wider degree, perhaps in the sciences or engineering. Students can be sure that they have the essential materials in this book, while knowing that they can easily go deeper into particular topics by referring to the complete *Exploring Strategy*. There they will find extended treatments of the issues covered here, as well as greater attention to issues of strategy development and change and the role of the strategist. *Exploring Strategy* also offers more cases and deeper exploration of issues through 'key debates', 'strategy lenses' and 'commentaries'. A brief contents of *Exploring Strategy* can be found on pp. xiv and xv.'

Teachers familiar with *Exploring Strategy* will find that the definitions, concepts and the content of *Fundamentals of Strategy* are entirely consistent, making it easy to teach courses using the different books in parallel.

Fundamentals of Strategy has ten chapters, with the emphasis on what *Exploring Strategy* terms the 'strategic position' and 'strategic choices' facing organisations. Under 'strategic position', *Fundamentals* introduces environmental analysis, strategic capability and strategic purpose (which includes a discussion of culture and strategy). Under 'strategic choices', the book addresses business-level strategy, corporate-level strategy, international strategy, strategy innovation and mergers and acquisitions. The final tenth chapter, 'Strategy in action', raises implementation issues such as organisational structure, management processes and strategic change. There is also an appendix providing the bases of strategy evaluation.

We believe that *Fundamentals of Strategy* brings the proven benefits of *Exploring Strategy* to the growing number of students on shorter courses. We hope that you will enjoy using it too.

A guide to getting the most from all the features and learning materials of *Fundamentals of Strategy* follows this preface.

Gerry Johnson
Richard Whittington
Kevan Scholes
May 2011

GETTING THE MOST FROM
FUNDAMENTALS OF STRATEGY

Fundamentals of Strategy builds on the established strengths of *Exploring Strategy*, proven over nine best-selling editions. A range of in-text features and supplementary resources have been developed to enable you and your students to gain maximum added value to the teaching and learning of strategy.

- **Outstanding pedagogical features**. Each chapter has clear learning outcomes, definitions of key concepts in the margins, practical questions associated with real-life Illustrations, and concise end-of-chapter case examples through which students can easily apply what they have learnt.

- **Up-to-date materials**. *Fundamentals of Strategy* is based on the latest 9th edition of *Exploring Strategy*. Our references are up to date, so that you can easily access the latest research. Cases and examples are fresh and engage with student interests and day-to-day experience.

- **Range of examples**. This edition maintains the wide range of examples used in the text, Illustrations and cases. We draw from all over the world, with no bias to North America, and use examples from the public and voluntary sectors as well as the private.

  Fundamentals of Strategy does not include any longer cases. If you wish to supplement the book with any of the case studies included in *Exploring Strategy*, please consult your local Pearson Education representative to find out what their Custom Publishing programme can do for you.

- **Attractive text layout and design**. We make careful use of colour and photography to improve clarity and ease of 'navigation' through the text. Reading the text should be an enjoyable and straightforward process.

- **Teaching and learning support**. If you are using *MyStrategyLab* you and your students can access a wealth of resources at **www.mystrategylab.com**, including the following:

  Resources for students
  - A dynamics eText
  - Self-assessment questions
  - Key concept audio summaries
  - Video cases
  - Revision flashcards
  - A multi-lingual glossary
  - Links to relevant websites
  - Classic cases
  - The Strategy Experience Simulation

  Resources for lecturers
  - Instructor's manual
  - Powerpoint slides
  - A testbank of assessment questions

This book is available with an access card for *MyStrategyLab*, but if your book did not come with an access card you can purchase access online at **www.mystrategylab.com**. There is also a companion website available at **www.pearsoned.co.uk/fos2** which contains a sample selection of these materials.

- **Video resources on DVD**. A DVD has been specially created for in-class use and contains briefings on selected topics from the authors, and material to support some of the case studies in *Exploring Strategy*. Some of this material may also be relevant for users of *Fundamentals of Strategy*.

  1 'With the experts' (the authors explain key concepts)
     Strategy in different contexts
     Porter's five forces
     Core competences
     Strategic drift and the cultural web

  2 Case Study organisations
     SAB Miller – international development
     eBay – success and sustainability
     Amazon.com – business level strategy
     Manchester United – football club or business?
     easyJet – competitive strategy
     Marks & Spencer – two CEOs on managing turnaround

  You can order and find out more about these resources from your local Pearson Education representative (**www.pearsoned.co.uk/replocator**).

- **Teachers' workshop**. We run an annual workshop to facilitate discussion of key challenges and solutions in the teaching of strategic management. Details of forthcoming workshops can be found at **www.pearsoned.co.uk/strategyworkshop**.

- **Complementary textbooks**. *Exploring Strategy* provides deeper and more extensive coverage of the theory and practice of strategy. A brief table of contents from the ninth edition is listed below:

  1 Introducing strategy
     Commentary The strategy lenses

  Part I THE STRATEGIC POSITION

  2 The environment
  3 Strategic capabilities
  4 Strategic purpose
  5 Culture and strategy
     Commentary on Part I The strategic position

  Part II STRATEGIC CHOICES

  6 Business strategy
  7 Corporate strategy and diversification
  8 International strategy

GUIDED TOUR

→ Setting the scene

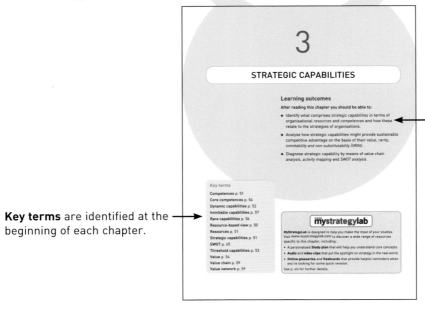

Learning outcomes enable you to check that you have understood all the major areas by the end of the chapter.

Key terms are identified at the beginning of each chapter.

→ Strategy in the real world

Illustrations showcase the application of specific strategic issues in the real world so that you can identify and relate theory to practice.

The **case example** at the end of each chapter allows exploration of topics covered in the chapter.

→ Checking your understanding

Chapter summaries recap and reinforce the key points to take away from the chapter.

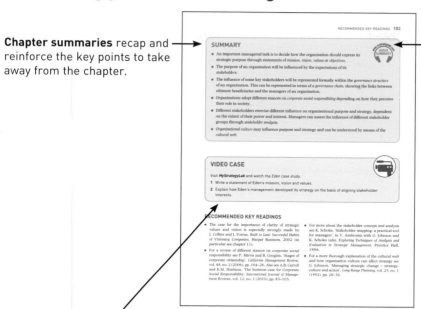

Audio icons in the text direct you to *MyStrategyLab* where you can reinforce your understanding of key concepts.

Video cases enable you to engage with and learn from the experience of senior managers responsible for determining and implementing strategy.

→ **Check your understanding with** mystrategylab*

Key terms are included in the **Glossary**, found in *MyStrategyLab*. (The Glossary is also translated into Chinese, Dutch, French, Norwegian and Swedish.) You can test your understanding of these key terms using **Flashcards** on the website.

Need a little extra help? **Self-assessment tests** will help you to identify the areas where you need to improve . . .

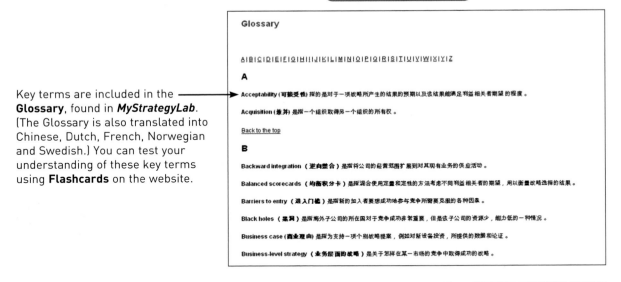

. . . and the **Personalised study plan** will direct you to the specific resources that can help you achieve a better grade.

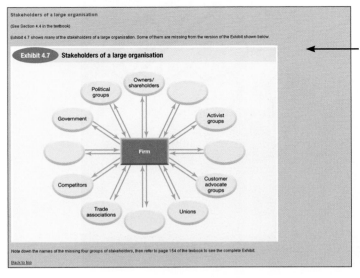

***Don't forget to register using your access code at: www.mystrategylab.com**

THE STRATEGY EXPERIENCE SIMULATION

The Strategy Experience Simulation included in *MyStrategyLab*, puts you in the position of a strategic decision maker. You are the Director of the Board at WRSX Group, a global advertising and marketing communications business.

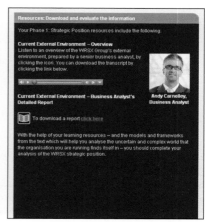

Multimedia resources and briefing documents help you to build an understanding of the WRSX Group's strategic position, as well as the choices that are available to the organisation.

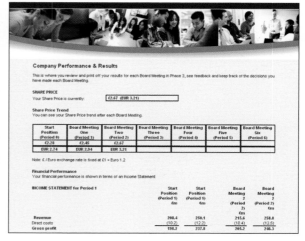

You apply your knowledge in the boardroom, where you are faced with a number of scenarios. Here you must make tough decisions that will shape the company's future.

Success will depend on how well you understand and can apply the concepts that are covered in *Fundamentals of Strategy*. Choose wisely!

1

INTRODUCING STRATEGY

Learning outcomes

After reading this chapter you should be able to:

- Explain what 'strategy' is about.

- Summarise the strategy of an organisation in a *'strategy statement'*.

- Identify key issues for an organisation's strategy according to the *Exploring Strategy* model.

- Distinguish between *corporate*, *business* and *operational* strategies.

PEARSON mystrategylab

MyStrategyLab is designed to help you make the most of your studies. Visit **www.mystrategylab.com** to discover a wide range of resources specific to this chapter, including:

- A personalised **Study plan** that will help you understand core concepts.

- **Audio** and **video clips** that put the spotlight on strategy in the real world.

- **Online glossaries** and **flashcards** that provide helpful reminders when you're looking for some quick revision.

See p. xiv for further details.

(1.1) INTRODUCTION

Strategy is about key issues for the long-term future of organisations. For example, how should Google – originally a search company – manage its expansion into the mobile phone industry? Should universities concentrate their resources on research excellence or teaching quality or try to combine both? How should a small video games producer relate to dominant console providers such as Nintendo and Sony? What should a rock band do to secure revenues in the face of declining CD sales?

All these are strategy questions. Naturally, they concern entrepreneurs and senior managers at the top of their organisations. But these questions matter more widely. Middle managers also have to understand the strategic direction of their organisations, both to know how to get top management support for their initiatives and to explain their organisation's strategy to the people they are responsible for. Anybody looking for a management-track job needs to be ready to discuss strategy with their potential employer. Indeed, anybody taking a job should first be confident that their new employer's strategy is actually viable. There are even specialist career opportunities in strategy, for example as a strategy consultant or as an in-house strategic planner, often key roles for fast-track young managers.

This book takes a broad approach to strategy, looking at both the economics of strategy and the people side of managing strategy in practice. The book is also relevant to any kind of organisation responsible for its own direction into the future. Thus the book refers to large private-sector multinationals and small entrepreneurial start-ups; to public-sector organisations such as schools and hospitals; and to not-for-profits such as charities or sports clubs. Strategy matters to almost all organisations, and to everybody working in them.

(1.2) WHAT IS STRATEGY?[1]

In this book, **strategy is the long-term direction of an organisation**. Thus the long-term direction of Nokia is from mobile phones to mobile computing. The long-term direction of Disney is from cartoons to diversified entertainment. This section examines the practical implication of this definition of strategy; distinguishes between different levels of strategy; and explains how to summarise an organisation's strategy in a 'strategy statement'.

1.2.1 Defining strategy

Defining strategy as the long-term direction of an organisation implies a more comprehensive view than some influential definitions. Figure 1.1 shows the strategy definitions of three leading strategy theorists: Alfred Chandler and Michael Porter, both from the Harvard Business School, and Henry Mintzberg, from McGill University, Canada. Each points to important but distinct elements of strategy. Chandler emphasises a logical flow from the determination of goals and objectives to the allocation of resources. Porter focuses on deliberate choices, difference and competition. On the other hand, Mintzberg uses the word 'pattern' to allow for the fact that strategies do not always follow a deliberately chosen and logical plan, but can emerge in more

Figure 1.1 **Definitions of strategy**

'the determination of the long-run goals and objectives of an enterprise and the adoption of courses of action and the allocation of resource necessary for carrying out these goals'

Alfred D. Chandler

'Competitive strategy is about being different. It means deliberately choosing a different set of activities to deliver a unique mix of value'

Michael Porter

'a pattern in a stream of decisions'

Henry Mintzberg

'the long-term direction of an organisation'

Exploring Strategy

Sources: A.D. Chandler, *Strategy and Structure: Chapters in the History of American Enterprise*, MIT Press, 1963, p. 13; M.E. Porter, 'What is strategy?', *Harvard Business Review*, 1966, November–December, p. 60; H. Mintzberg, *Tracking Strategy: Toward a General Theory*, Oxford University Press, 2007, p. 3.

ad hoc ways. Sometimes strategies reflect a series of incremental decisions that only cohere into a recognisable pattern – or 'strategy' – after some time.

All of these strategy definitions incorporate important elements of strategy. However, this book's definition of strategy as 'the long-term direction of an organisation' has two advantages. First, the long-term direction of an organisation can include both deliberate, logical strategy and more incremental, emergent patterns of strategy. Second, long-term direction can include both strategies that emphasise difference and competition, and strategies that recognise the roles of cooperation and even imitation.

The three elements of this strategy definition – the long term, direction and organisation – can each be explored further. The strategy of News Corporation,* owner of social networking company MySpace, illustrates important points (see Illustration 1.1):

● *The long term*. Strategies are typically measured over years, for some organisations a decade or more. The importance of a long-term perspective on strategy is emphasised by the 'three horizons' framework in Figure 1.2. **The three horizons framework suggests that every organisation should think of itself as comprising three types of business or activity, defined by their 'horizons' in terms of years.** *Horizon 1* businesses are basically the current core activities. In the case of News Corporation, Horizon 1 businesses include the original print newspapers. Horizon 1 businesses need defending and extending, but the expectation is

---

* The enquiries into News Corporation's involvement in telephone 'hacking' and its associated governance implications were just under way as this edition of the book was going to press.

ILLUSTRATION 1.1

MySpace becomes part of a bigger network

Social networking site MySpace presents opportunities and challenges for the global media conglomerate News Corporation.

The social networking site MySpace was founded in California in 2003 by MBA graduate Chris DeWolfe and rock musician Tom Anderson. From the first, the networking site was strong on music, and helped launch the careers of the Arctic Monkeys and Lily Allen. By 2005, it had 22 million members, with more page views than Google. That was the point when the multinational media conglomerate News Corporation bought it for $580m (€406m).

News Corporation started in Australia in the newspaper business, acquiring the *Times* newspaper group in the United Kingdom and the *Wall Street Journal* in the United States. It also diversified into television (for example Fox News and BSkyB) and film, including 20th Century Fox, responsible for the hit film *Avatar*. Its chairman is Rupert Murdoch, whose family owns a controlling interest: Rupert Murdoch's son James is expected to succeed him at the top.

In 2005, with media audiences increasingly moving to the internet, Rupert Murdoch declared his ambition to create 'a leading and profitable internet presence'. The acquisition of MySpace seemed a good fit. Chris DeWolfe and Tom Anderson were retained at the head of MySpace, but within a new division providing oversight for all News Corporation's internet interests. Ross Levinsohn, long-time News Corporation insider and head of the new division, told the *Financial Times*: 'The MySpace guys were really freaked out that we were going to come in and turn it into Fox News. One of the things we said was: "We're going to leave it alone"'.

Some adjustments had to be made. Tom Anderson told *Fortune* magazine: 'Before, I could do whatever I wanted. Now it takes more time to get people to agree on things. All the budget reviews and processes. That can be a pain. But it's not stopping us.' News Corporation was able to fund a more robust technology platform to cope with the thousands of new users MySpace was getting each day. In 2006, MySpace signed a three-year advertising contract with Google worth $900m, which paid for the original acquisition with money left over. Executives summed up MySpace's distinctive positioning by saying: 'Your mom uses Facebook'.

But business then got tougher. Facebook overtook MySpace in terms of unique visitors in 2008. News Corporation executives complained about the excessive new initiatives at MySpace and the failure to prioritise: DeWolfe and Anderson were even considering launching their own film studio. Then Rupert Murdoch announced a target of $1bn in advertising revenues for 2008, without consulting DeWolfe. MySpace missed the target by about 10 per cent. The push from News Corporation to increase advertisements on MySpace, and a reluctance to remove pages with advertising from the site, began to make MySpace increasingly less attractive for users.

During 2009, MySpace's share of the social networking market fell to 30 per cent, from a peak of 66 per cent. The company missed the online traffic targets set by the Google contract. Losses were expected to be around $100m. In March, Chris DeWolfe was removed as Chief Executive of MySpace. The new Chief Executive was Alan Van Natta, from Facebook. Van Natta told the *Financial Times* that MySpace was no longer competing with Facebook: 'we're very focused on a different space . . . MySpace can foster discovery [of music, films and TV] in a way that others can't'.

Sources: M. Garnham, 'The rise and fall of MySpace', *Financial Times*, 4 December 2009; P. Sellers, 'MySpace Cowboys', *Fortune*, 29 August 2006; S. Rosenbusch, 'News Corp's Place in MySpace', *Business Week*, 19 July 2005.

Questions

1 How valuable is MySpace's distinctive position in the social networking market?

2 How should News Corporation have managed MySpace?

Figure 1.2 Three horizons for strategy

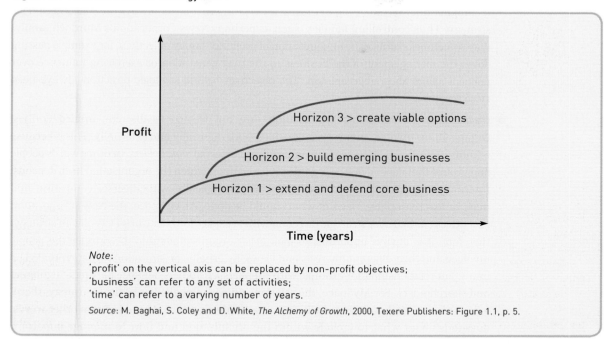

Note:
'profit' on the vertical axis can be replaced by non-profit objectives;
'business' can refer to any set of activities;
'time' can refer to a varying number of years.

Source: M. Baghai, S. Coley and D. White, *The Alchemy of Growth*, 2000, Texere Publishers: Figure 1.1, p. 5.

that in the long term they will likely be flat or declining in terms of profits (or whatever else the organisation values). *Horizon 2* businesses are emerging activities that should provide new sources of profit. In News Corporation, those include the various internet initiatives, principally MySpace. Finally, there are *Horizon 3* possibilities, for which nothing is sure. These are typically risky Research & Development (R&B) projects, start-up ventures, test-market pilots or similar, some of which may fuel growth in the future even if most are likely to fail. For a fast-moving internet organisation like MySpace, *Horizon 3* might only be a couple of years from the present time. In a pharmaceutical company, where the R&D and regulatory processes for a new drug take many years, *Horizon 3* might be a decade ahead. While times-cales might differ, the basic point about the 'three horizons' framework is that managers need to avoid focusing on the short-term issues of their existing activities. Strategy involves pushing out Horizon 1 as far as possible, at the same time as looking to Horizons 2 and 3.

● *Strategic direction*. Over the years, strategies follow some kind of long-term direction or trajectory. The strategic direction of News Corporation is from print to internet media, as represented by MySpace. Sometimes a strategic direction only emerges as a coherent pattern over time. Typically, however, managers and entrepreneurs try to set the direction of their strategy according to long-term *objectives*. In private-sector businesses, the objective guiding strategic direction is usually maximising profits for shareholders. Thus Rupert Murdoch's acquisition of MySpace was driven by the objective to create a leading and profitable presence on the internet. However, profits do not always set strategic direction. First, public-sector and charity organisations may set their strategic direction according to other objectives: for example, a sports club's objective may be to move up from one league to a higher one. Second, even in the private sector, profit is not always the sole criterion for strategy. Thus controlling families (such as perhaps News Corporation's Murdoch family) may sometimes sacrifice the maximisation of profits for family objectives, for example passing down the management of the business to the next generation or exercising influence over political affairs and public opinion. The objectives behind strategic direction always need close scrutiny.

● *Organisation*. In this book, organisations are not treated as discrete, unified entities. Organisations involve complex relationships, both internally and externally. This is because organisations typically have many internal and external *stakeholders*, in other words people and groups that depend on the organisation and upon which the organisation itself depends. Internally, organisations are filled with people, typically with diverse, competing and more or less reasonable views of what should be done. At MySpace, the News Corporation executives clashed over strategic direction with MySpace founder Chris DeWolfe. In strategy, therefore, it is always important to look *inside* organisations and to consider the people involved and their different interests and views. Externally, organisations are surrounded by important relationships, for example with suppliers, customers, alliance partners, regulators and shareholders. For MySpace, the relationship with Google was critical. Strategy, therefore, is also crucially concerned with an organisation's external *boundaries*: in other words, questions about what to include within the organisation and how to manage important relationships with what is kept outside.

Because strategy typically involves managing people, relationships and resources, the subject is sometimes called 'strategic management'. This book takes the view that managing is always important in strategy. Good strategy involves understanding the managerial context and consequences of strategy, not just the strategic decisions themselves.

1.2.2 Levels of strategy

Inside an organisation, strategies can exist at three main levels. Again they can be illustrated by reference to MySpace and News Corporation (Illustration 1.1):

● **Corporate-level strategy is concerned with the overall scope of an organisation and how value is added to the constituent businesses of the organisational whole.** Corporate-level strategy issues include geographical scope, diversity of products or services, acquisitions of new businesses, and how resources are allocated between the different elements of the organisation. For News Corporation, diversifying from print journalism into television and social networking are corporate-level strategies. Being clear about corporate-level strategy is important: determining the range of businesses to include is the *basis* of other strategic decisions.

● **Business-level strategy is about how the individual businesses should compete in their particular markets** (for this reason, business-level strategy is often called 'competitive strategy'). These individual businesses might be stand-alone businesses, for instance entrepreneurial start-ups, or 'business units' within a larger corporation (as MySpace and Fox are inside

News Corporation). Business-level strategy typically concerns issues such as innovation, appropriate scale and response to competitors' moves. In the public sector, the equivalent of business-level strategy is decisions about how units (such as individual hospitals or schools) should provide best-value services. Where the businesses are units within a larger organisation, business-level strategies should clearly fit with corporate-level strategy.

- **Operational strategies are concerned with how the components of an organisation deliver effectively the corporate- and business-level strategies in terms of resources, processes and people.** For example, MySpace engineers had to keep developing enough processing capacity to cope with the strategy of rapid growth. In most businesses, successful business strategies depend to a large extent on decisions that are taken, or activities that occur, at the operational level. Operational decisions need, therefore, to be closely linked to business-level strategy. They are vital to successful strategy implementation.

This need to link the corporate, business and operational levels underlines the importance of *integration* in strategy. Each level needs to be aligned with the others.

1.2.3 Strategy statements

David Collis and Michael Rukstad[2] at the Harvard Business School argue that all entrepreneurs and managers should be able to summarise their organisation's strategy with a 'strategy statement'. **Strategy statements should have three main themes: the fundamental *goals* that the organisation seeks, which typically draw on the organisation's stated mission, vision and objectives; the *scope* or domain of the organisation's activities; and the particular *advantages* or capabilities it has to deliver all of these.** These various contributing elements of a strategy statement are explained as follows, with examples in Illustration 1.2:

- *Mission.* This relates to goals, and refers to the overriding purpose of the organisation. It is sometimes described in terms of the apparently simple but challenging question: '*What business are we in?*' The mission statement helps keep managers focused on what is central to their strategy.

- *Vision.* This too relates to goals, and refers to the desired future state of the organisation. It is an aspiration which can help mobilise the energy and passion of organisational members. The vision statement, therefore, should answer the question: '*What do we want to achieve?*'

- *Objectives.* These are more precise and, ideally, quantifiable statements of the organisation's goals over some period of time. Objectives might refer to profitability or market share targets for a private company, or to examination results in a school. Objectives introduce discipline to strategy. The question here is: '*What do we have to achieve in the coming period?*'

- *Scope.* An organisation's scope or domain refers to three dimensions: customers or clients; geographical location; and extent of internal activities ('vertical integration'). For a university, scope questions are twofold: first, which academic departments to have (a business school, an engineering department and so on); second, which activities to do internally themselves (vertically integrate) and which to externalise to subcontractors (for example, whether to manage campus restaurants in-house or to subcontract them).

ILLUSTRATION 1.2
Strategy statements

Both Nokia, the Finnish telecommunications giant, and University College Cork, based in the West of Ireland, publish a good deal about their strategies.

Nokia vision and strategy

Our vision is a world where everyone can be connected. Our promise is to help people feel close to what is important to them.

The businesses of Nokia

- Compelling consumer solutions with devices and services
- Strong infrastructure business with Siemens Networks

Our competitive advantage is based on scale, brand and services

- Scale-based assets and capabilities
- Leading brand
- Build further competitive advantage by differentiating our offering through services

Our business strategy

- Maximize Nokia's lifetime value to consumer
- Best mobile devices everywhere
  - Take share and drive value across price brands and geographies
  - Enhance and capture market growth in emerging markets
- Context-enriched services
  - Take share of the internet services market by delivering winning solutions
  - Take share of business mobility market

University College Cork (UCC), Strategic Plan 2009–2012

University College Cork (UCC) . . . is sited in Ireland's second city . . . UCC's motto *'Where Finbarr taught let Munster learn'* binds us to the sixth-century monastery and place of learning established by St. Finbarr . . . UCC was established in 1845 as one of three Queen's Colleges . . . The campus today is home to over 18,000 students including 2,000 international students from

93 countries. . . . A third of our staff are from overseas. Our strategic alliances with world-ranking universities in Asia, Europe and North America ensure that we learn from and contribute to the best standards of teaching, learning and research.

Vision

To be a world-class university that links the region to the globe.

Mission

In an environment which gives parity of esteem to teaching, learning and research and where students are our highest priority, the University's central roles are to create, preserve and communicate knowledge and to enhance intellectual, cultural, social and economic life locally, regionally and globally.

Targets by 2012 (selected from 'Teaching, Learning and the Student Experience')

- Achieve a first year retention rate of 93 per cent or greater
- Increase the proportion of students at postgraduate level from 19 per cent to 30 per cent
- Increase flexible/part-time provision to 15 per cent of undergraduate entrants

Sources: www.nokia.com; www.ucc.ie.

Questions

1 Construct short strategy statements covering the goals, scope and advantage of Nokia and University College Cork. How much do the different contexts matter?

2 Construct a strategy statement for your own organisation (university or employer). What implications might this statement have for your particular course or department?

● *Advantage*. This part of a strategy statement describes how the organisation will achieve the objectives it has set for itself in its chosen domain. In competitive environments, this refers to the *competitive* advantage: for example, how a particular company or sports club will achieve goals in the face of competition from other companies or clubs. In order to achieve a particular goal, the organisation needs to be better than others seeking the same goal. In the public sector, advantage might refer simply to the organisation's capability in general. But even public-sector organisations frequently need to show that their capabilities are not only adequate, but superior to other rival departments or perhaps to private-sector contractors.

Collis and Rukstad suggest that strategy statements covering goals, scope and advantage should be no more than 35 words long. Shortness keeps such statements focused on the essentials and makes them easy to remember and communicate. Thus for News Corporation, a strategy statement might be: 'to build a leading and profitable presence in both old and new media, drawing on competitive advantages in terms of the scale, diversity and international range of our businesses'. The strategy statement of American financial advisory firm Edward Jones is more specific: 'to grow to 17,000 financial advisers by 2012 by offering trusted and convenient face-to-face financial advice to conservative individual investors through a national network of one-financial adviser offices'. Of course, such strategy statements are not always fulfilled. Circumstances may change in unexpected ways. In the meantime, however, they can provide a useful guide both to managers in their decision-making and to employees and others who need to understand the direction in which the organisation is going. The ability to give a clear strategy statement is a good test of managerial competence in an organisation.

As such, strategy statements are relevant to a wide range of organisations. For example, a small entrepreneurial start-up will need a strategy statement to persuade investors and lenders of its viability. Public-sector organisations need strategy statements not only for themselves, but to reassure external clients, funders and regulators that their priorities are the right ones. Voluntary organisations need to communicate persuasive strategy statements in order to inspire volunteers and donors. Thus organisations of all kinds frequently publish materials relevant to such strategy statements on their websites or annual reports. Illustration 1.2 provides published materials on the strategies of two very different organisations: the technology giant Nokia from the private sector and the medium-sized University College Cork from the public sector.

(1.3) THE *EXPLORING STRATEGY* MODEL

This book is structured around a three-part model that encompasses issues of economics and people equally. **The *Exploring Strategy* Model includes understanding *the strategic position of an organisation; assessing *strategic choices* for the future; and managing *strategy in action*.** Figure 1.3 shows these elements as overlapping circles, each closely interlinked with the others. However, because this book is about the *fundamentals* of strategy, it concentrates on the first two elements of position and choice. There is less emphasis on the management issues of strategy in action: on these, the book focuses just on key issues such as managing strategic change and putting in structures and systems to deliver the chosen strategy. Other issues to do

Figure 1.3 The *Exploring Strategy* Model

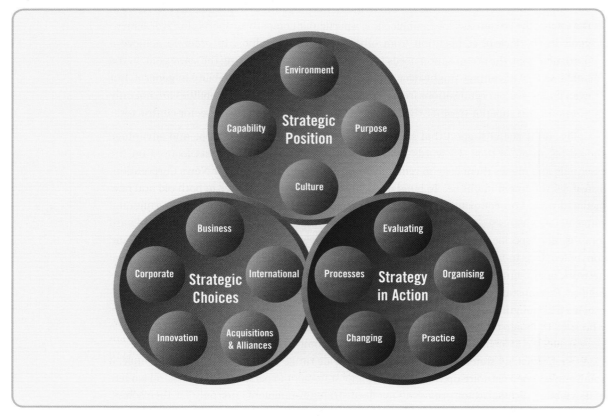

with strategy in action – such as strategic planning and the practice of strategy – are covered more fully in *Exploring Strategy*.[3]

It is important to understand why the *Exploring Strategy* Model is drawn as interlinked circles. Figure 1.3 could have shown the model's three elements in a linear sequence – first understanding the strategic position, then making strategic choices and finally turning strategy into action. Indeed, this logical sequence is implicit in the definition of strategy given by Alfred Chandler (Figure 1.1) and many other textbooks on strategy. However, as Henry Mintzberg recognises, in practice the elements of strategy do not always follow this linear sequence. Choices often have to be made before the position is fully understood. Sometimes too, a proper understanding of the strategic position can only be built from the experience of trying a strategy out in action. The real-world feedback that comes from launching a new product is often far better at uncovering the true strategic position than remote analysis carried out in a strategic planning department at head office.

The interconnected circles of Figure 1.3 are designed to emphasise this potentially non-linear nature of strategy. Position, choices and action should be seen as closely related, and in practice none has priority over another. It is only for structural convenience that this book follows a sequence with its subject matter; the book is not meant to suggest that the process of strategy must follow a logical path of distinct steps. The three circles are overlapping and non-linear, just as strategy often is in real life. Strategy rarely occurs in tidy ways and it is better not to expect it to do so.

However, the *Exploring Strategy* Model does provide a comprehensive and integrated framework for analysing an organisation's position, considering the choices it has and putting strategies into action. Each of the chapters can be seen as asking fundamental strategy questions and providing the essential concepts and techniques to help answer them. Working systematically through questions and answers provides the basis for persuasive strategy recommendations.

1.3.1 Strategic position

Strategic position

The **strategic position** is concerned with the impact on strategy of the external environment, the organisation's strategic capability (resources and competences), the organisation's goals and the organisation's culture. Understanding these four factors is central for evaluating future strategy. These issues, and the fundamental questions associated with them, are covered in Chapters 2–4 of this book:

- *Environment.* Organisations operate in a complex political, economic, social and technological world. These environments vary widely in terms of their dynamism and attractiveness. The fundamental question here relates to the *opportunities* and *threats* available to the organisation in this complex and changing environment. Chapter 2 provides key frameworks to help in focusing on priority issues in the face of environmental complexity and dynamism.

- *Strategic capability.* Each organisation has its own strategic capabilities, made up of its *resources* (e.g. machines and buildings) and *competences* (e.g. technical and managerial skills). The fundamental question on capability regards the organisation's *strengths* and *weaknesses* (for example, where is it at a competitive advantage or disadvantage?). Are the organisation's capabilities adequate to the challenges of its environment and the demands of its goals? Chapter 3 provides tools and concepts for analysing such capabilities.

- *Strategic purpose.* Although sometimes unclear or contested, most organisations claim for themselves a particular purpose, as encapsulated in their *vision*, *mission* and *objectives*. The strategic purpose is a key criterion against which strategies must be evaluated. This strategic purpose is influenced by both the *governance structure* of the organisation and its *culture*. The third fundamental question therefore is: what is the organisation's strategic purpose; what does it seek to achieve?

Applying the *Exploring Strategy* Model to the positioning of News Corporation (Illustration 1.1) raises the following issues. News Corporation was threatened by an environmental shift from print to the internet. It also lacked the capabilities to develop a social networking business on its own. The company was determined to grow its internet business fast, setting demanding objectives that MySpace struggled to meet. Finally, there appeared to be culture clashes between the traditional family-owned conglomerate and the young entrepreneurial start-up.

1.3.2 Strategic choices

Strategic choices involve the options for strategy in terms of both the *directions* in which strategy might move and the *methods* by which strategy might be pursued. For instance, an organisation might have a range of strategic directions open to it: the organisation could diversify into new products; it could enter new international markets; or it could transform its existing products and markets through radical innovation. These various directions could be pursued by different methods: the organisation could acquire a business already active in the product or market area; it could form alliances with relevant organisations that might help its new strategy; or it could try to pursue its strategies on its own. Typical strategic choices, and the related fundamental questions, are covered in Chapters 5 to 9 of this book, as follows:

- *Business strategy*. There are strategic choices in terms of how the organisation seeks to compete at the individual *business level*. Typically these choices involve strategies based on *cost* (for example, economies of scale) or *differentiation* (for example, superior quality). Crucial is deciding how to win against competitors (for this reason, business strategy is sometimes called 'competitive strategy'). The fundamental question here, then, is how should the business unit compete? Key dilemmas for business-level strategy, and ways of resolving them, are discussed in Chapter 5.

- *Corporate strategy and diversification*. The highest level of an organisation is typically concerned with corporate-level strategy, focused on questions of portfolio scope. The fundamental question in corporate-level strategy is therefore which businesses to include in the portfolio. This relates to the appropriate degree of *diversification*, in other words the spread of products and markets. Corporate-level strategy is also concerned both with the relationship between the various businesses that make up the corporate portfolio of the business and with how the corporate 'parent' (owner) adds value to the individual businesses. Chapter 6 provides tools for assessing diversification strategies and the appropriate relationships within the corporate portfolio.

- *International strategy*. Internationalisation is a form of diversification, but into new geographical markets. It is often at least as challenging as product or service diversification. Here the fundamental question is: where internationally should the organisation compete? Chapter 7 examines how to prioritise various international options and identifies key methods for pursuing them: export, licensing, direct investment and acquisition.

- *Innovation strategies*. Most existing organisations have to innovate constantly simply to survive. Entrepreneurship, the creation of a new enterprise, is an act of innovation too. A fundamental question, therefore, is whether the organisation is innovating appropriately. Chapter 8 considers key choices about innovation and entrepreneurship, and helps in selecting between them.

- *Mergers, acquisitions and alliances*. Organisations have to make choices about methods for pursuing their strategies. Many organisations prefer to grow 'organically', in other words by building new businesses with their own resources. Other organisations might develop through mergers and acquisitions or strategic alliances with other organisations.

The fundamental question here, then, is whether to buy another company, ally or to go it alone. How to choose between these alternative methods is discussed in Chapter 9.

Again, issues of strategic choice are live in the case of News Corporation and MySpace (Illustration 1.1). The *Exploring Strategy* Model asks the following kinds of questions here. Should MySpace compete against Facebook by emphasising its music strengths? Should a newspaper company diversify into the new social networking market and, if it does, is an acquisition the best method? How should News Corporation add value to its entrepreneurial new business? And should MySpace be allowed to continue to innovate in its old, loosely disciplined style?

1.3.3 Strategy in action

Strategy in action is concerned with how chosen strategies are actually put into practice. Chapter 10 covers three key issues for strategy in action:

- *Structuring* an organisation to support successful performance. A key question here is who is in charge and who is accountable.

- *Systems* are required to control the way in which *strategy is implemented*. The issue here is how to ensure that strategies are implemented according to plan.

- Managing *strategic change* is typically an important part of putting strategy into action. How should change be led?

Strategy in action issues loom large in the MySpace case (Illustration 1.1). For example, should the new business have been integrated into a larger division within News Corporation? Was it appropriate to impose big company systems on a new social networking company? Chapter 10 is an introduction to such important issues of strategy in action. There is also the question of *evaluating* the strategy behind the MySpace acquisition: Appendix 1 to this book provides a guide to evaluating strategic options, which should be useful for checking recommendations on case analyses or assignments generally. All these issues, and related ones to do with strategic planning and practice, are dealt with more extensively in Johnson, Whittington and Scholes' *Exploring Strategy*.

 STRATEGY DEVELOPMENT PROCESSES

The previous section introduced strategic position, strategic choices and strategy in action. However, strategies do not always develop in a logical sequence of analysis, choice and action. There are two broad explanations of strategy development:

- The *rational–analytic view* of strategy development is the conventional explanation. Here strategies are developed through rational and analytical processes, led typically by top managers. There is a linear sequence. First, the strategic position is analysed; then options are weighed up and choices are made; finally, structures, processes and change procedures are put in place to allow effective implementation. Often formal strategic planning systems are important to the analysis and formulation of the strategy. In this view, strategies are *intended*, in other words the product of deliberate choices. This rational–analytical view is associated with theorists such as Alfred Chandler and Michael Porter, in Figure 1.1.

● The *emergent strategy* view is the alternative broad explanation of how strategies develop. In this view, strategies often do not develop as intended or planned, but tend to emerge in organisations over time as a result of ad hoc, incremental or even accidental actions. Good ideas and opportunities often come from practical experience at the bottom of the organisation, rather than from top management and formal strategic plans. Even the best laid plans may need to be abandoned as new opportunities arise or the organisation learns from the marketplace. This is a view associated with Henry Mintzberg, referenced in Figure 1.1.

The two views are not mutually exclusive. Intended strategies can often succeed, especially in stable markets where there are few surprises. Moreover, an organisation's key stakeholders – employees, owners, customers, regulators and so on – will typically want to see evidence of deliberate strategy-making: it is rarely acceptable to say that everything is simply emergent. The tools and concepts throughout the book are particularly helpful in this deliberate strategy-making. But it is wise to be open as well to the possibilities of emergence. Inflexible plans can hinder learning and prevent the seizing of opportunities. Moreover, strategic choices do not always come about as a result of simple rational analysis: *cultural and political processes* in organisations can also drive changes in strategy, as will become apparent in the discussions in Chapter 4.

This book allows for *both* the rational–analytical view and the emergent view. Indeed, the interconnected circles of the *Exploring Strategy* Model in Figure 1.3 deliberately underline the possibly non-linear aspects of strategy. It is not just a matter of putting strategic choices into action in a logical sequence leading from strategy formulation to strategy implementation. Strategy in action often creates the strategic choices in the first place, as new opportunities and constraints are discovered in practice. Implementation can lead to formulation as well.[4]

SUMMARY

● Strategy is the long-term direction of an organisation. A 'strategy statement' should cover the *goals* of an organisation, the *scope* of the organisation's activities and the *advantages* or *capabilities* the organisation brings to these goals and activities.

● *Corporate-level strategy* is concerned with an organisation's overall scope; *business-level strategy* is concerned with how to compete; and *operational strategy* is concerned with how resources, processes and people deliver corporate- and business-level strategies.

● The *Exploring Strategy* Model has three major elements: understanding the *strategic position*, making *strategic choices* for the future and managing *strategy in action*.

RECOMMENDED KEY READINGS

It is always useful to read around a topic. As well as the specific references below, we particularly highlight:

- Three accessible introductory articles on the nature of strategy are M. Porter, 'What is strategy?', *Harvard Business Review*, November–December 1996, pp. 61–78; F. Fréry, 'The fundamental dimensions of strategy', *MIT Sloan Management Review*, vol. 48, no. 1 (2006), pp. 71–75; and D. Collis and M. Rukstad, 'Can you say what your strategy is?', *Harvard Business Review*, April 2008, pp. 63–73.

- For contemporary developments in strategy practice, business newspapers such as the *Financial Times*, *Les Echos* and the *Wall Street Journal* and business magazines such as *Business Week*, *The Economist*, *L'Expansion* and *Manager-Magazin*. See also the websites of the leading strategy consulting firms: www.mckinsey.com; www.bcg.com; www.bain.com.

REFERENCES

1. The question 'What is strategy?' is discussed in R. Whittington, *What is Strategy – and Does it Matter?*, International Thomson, 1993/2000 and M.E. Porter, 'What is strategy?', *Harvard Business Review*, November–December 1996, pp. 61–78.
2. D. Collis and M. Rukstad, 'Can you say what your strategy is?', *Harvard Business Review*, April 2008, pp. 63–73.
3. G. Johnson, R. Whittington and K. Scholes, *Exploring Strategy*, 9th edition, Pearson, 2010.
4. The classic discussion of the roles of rational strategy formulation and strategy implementation is in H. Mintzberg, 'The design school: reconsidering the basic premises of strategic management', *Strategic Management Journal*, vol. 11 (1991), pp. 171–95 and H.I. Ansoff, 'Critique of Henry Mintzberg's The Design School', *Strategic Management Journal*, vol. 11 (1991), pp. 449–61.

Glastonbury – from hippy weekend to international festival

Steve Henderson, Leeds Metropolitan University

Glastonbury Festival has become a worldwide attraction for music fans and artists alike. In 2009, Bruce Springsteen was added to the long list of acts (from Paul McCartney to Oasis) that have appeared at the festival. It started in 1970 when 1,500 hippy revellers gathered on a farm near Glastonbury Tor to be plied with free milk and entertainment from a makeshift stage. Now, Glastonbury is a major international festival that attracts over 150,000 attenders. Without any knowledge of the line-up, the tickets for the 2010 Festival sold out in days.

In those early days, the Festival was developed by local farmer, Michael Eavis, whose passion for music and social principles led to a weekend of music as a means of raising funds for good causes. It was a social mission rooted in the hippy counter-culture of the 1960s and events such as Woodstock. Today, the Glastonbury Festival attender finds that those early days of hippy idealism are a long way off. The scale of the organisation demands strong management to support the achievement of the festival's social aims.

At first, the statutory requirements for an event held on private land were minimal. Jovial policemen looked over hedges while recreational drugs were sold from tables near the festival entrance as if this was just a slightly unusual village fête. Needless to say, the festival began to attract the attention of a number of different groups, especially as legislation around the running of events tightened. Eavis struggled with local residents who hated the invasion of their privacy; with hippy activist groups who felt that their contribution in helping at the festival gave them a sense of ownership; with drug dealers carrying on their activities on the fringes of the festival; and fans climbing over the fences to get free access.

The festival's continued expansion has resulted in a festival with over ten stages covering jazz, dance, classical, world music and other genres. Added to this, there is comedy, poetry, circus, theatre and children's entertainment alongside more esoteric street theatre

Source: Getty Images.

performances. Much of this is organised into specific grassy field areas where, for example, the Dance Village uses a number of tents dedicated to different types of dance music. Indeed, such is the range of entertainment on offer that some attenders spend the whole weekend at the festival without seeing a single live music act. Though the Eavis family remain involved with the main programme, much of the other entertainment is now managed by others. Reflecting this shift towards more diverse entertainment, the name of the festival was changed from Glastonbury Fayre (reflecting the ancient cultural heritage of the area) to the Glastonbury Festival for Contemporary Performing Arts.

In some years, the festival is forced to take a year off to allow the farmland to recover from the trampling of thousands of pairs of feet. Not only is this wise on an agricultural front but also gives the local residents a rest from the annual invasion of festival goers. Despite this, the festival has met with a number of controversies such as when a large number of gatecrashers spoilt the fun in 2000. This caused the festival to be fined due to exceeding the licensed attendance and excessive noise after the event. Furthermore, health and safety laws now require the event management to have a 'duty of care' to everyone on the festival site. To address these health and safety concerns, support was sought from Melvin Benn who ran festivals for the Mean Fiddler organisation. With a steel fence erected around the perimeter, Melvin Benn helped re-establish the festival in 2002 after a year off.

Ownership of the festival remained with the Eavis family but Melvin Benn was appointed Managing Director. However, concerns arose in 2006 when his employer, Mean Fiddler, was taken over by major music promoters, Live Nation and MCD Productions. In a worrying move, Live Nation announced that they would entice a number of major artists to appear on the weekend normally used by Glastonbury at a new UK festival called Wireless. Based in London, this seemed set to offer a city-based alternative to Glastonbury. At much the same time, Live Nation announced that they would launch their own online ticket agency to support the sales of their music events. This shift in power between the major music promoters indicated not only their interest in the ownership of key events but their desire to control income streams.

Elsewhere in the world of live entertainment, the success of Glastonbury had not gone unnoticed and the festival market showed considerable growth. Some of the other festivals tried to capitalise on features that Glastonbury could not offer. For example, Glastonbury was famous for its wet weather with pictures of damp revellers and collapsed tents being commonplace. Live Nation's city-based Wireless festival offered the opportunity to sleep under a roof at home or hotel, as opposed to risking the weather outdoors. Alternatively, Benicassim in southern Spain offered a festival with an excellent chance of sunshine and top acts for the price of a low cost airline ticket. Other festivals noted that Glastonbury attenders enjoyed the wider entertainment at the event. In doing this, they realised that many festival goers were attracted by the whole social experience. So, sidestepping major acts and their related high fees, smaller festivals were created for just a few thousand attenders. These offered entertainment in various formats, often in a family-friendly atmosphere. Sometimes described as boutique festivals, Freddie Fellowes, organiser of the Secret Garden Party, describes this type of festival as a chance 'to be playful, to break down barriers between people and create an environment where you have perfect freedom and perfect nourishment, intellectually and visually'. Festival Republic, the rebranded Mean Fiddler, created a boutique festival on a larger scale with their Latitude festival. Similarly, Rob da Bank, a BBC DJ, put together Bestival on the Isle of Wight where the attenders are encouraged to join in the fun by appearing in fancy dress. Quite clearly, audiences are now being presented with a wide range of festivals to consider for their leisure time entertainment.

Many of these festivals attract sponsors with some becoming prominent by acquiring naming rights on the festival. Others have low profile arrangements involving so-called 'contra' deals as opposed to sponsorship payments. For example, Glastonbury has official cider suppliers who typically boost their brand by giving the festival a preferential deal on their products in exchange for publicity. Though these commercial relationships are sometimes spurned by the smaller festivals that see the branding as an intrusion on their fun environment, larger festivals often need such relationships to survive. In order to attract sponsors, large festivals are turning to radio and television broadcasters as a means to expand the audience and offer wider exposure for the sponsor. Indeed, in 2009, the BBC sent over 400 staff members down to Glastonbury for broadcasting aimed at satisfying the interest of the armchair viewer/listener.

With such huge demand for their talents, artists can have a lucrative summer moving between festivals. Similarly, audiences can make lengthy treks to their favourite festivals. For some, this has caused environmental concerns with Glastonbury's rural location, poor transport links and large audience being cited as a specific problem. On the other hand, artists are not only finding that the festivals offer a good source of income but that private parties and corporate entertainment have emerged as alternative, often greater, income opportunities. One newspaper claimed that George Michael pocketed more than £1.5m (~€1.65m; ~$2.25m) to entertain revellers at the British billionaire retailer Sir Philip Green's 55th birthday party in the Maldives. Hence, for many artists, the summer has become a case of 'cherry picking' their favourite festivals or seeking out the most lucrative opportunities.

Over time, the shift from small, homespun event to corporate-controlled festival has provided awkward situations for Michael Eavis – from the difficulties with establishment figures who felt the event was out of control to the demands of counter-cultural groups such as the travelling hippies. However, along the way, the festival has maintained its aim of supporting charities like CND and, later, Greenpeace, Oxfam and a number of local charities. In the mind of the audience, this helps position the festival as a fun event with a social conscience. The continued expansion and shift in management of the festival has freed Michael Eavis to be the figurehead for the event and to pursue the original social mission of the festival.

Given this growing and increasingly competitive market, there is much to consider for the festivals involved. In recent years, Glastonbury has sold all its tickets and made donations to its favoured causes, confirming the financial viability of its current business model. Indeed, the festival's iconic status has traditionally meant that it is a rite of passage for many young music fans. Yet, in 2008, Eavis publicly registered concern over the age of the Glastonbury audience suggesting that selling tickets by phone would help attract a younger audience. Maybe Eavis was concerned by comments such as those in *The Times* newspaper that cruelly declared Glastonbury as suited to the 'the hip-op generation' and questioned whether young people thought it was 'cool' to go to the same music events as their parents. On the other hand, their parents belong to the 'baby boomer' generation that grew up with popular music and festivals like Glastonbury. So, there is no real surprise that they would enjoy this eclectic event. Whatever disturbed Eavis, he announced that Jay-Z, an American rap artist, was to headline in order to help attract a younger audience. With sales slower compared with previous sell-out years, he later stated 'We're not trying to get rid of anybody. The older people are fantastic, but we do need young people coming in as well.' Then, reflecting on the 2008 festival in 2009, Michael Eavis displayed concerns over the future of the festival saying 'Last year I thought that maybe we'd got to the end and we'd have to bite the bullet and fold it all up. A lot of the bands were saying Glastonbury had become too big, too muddy and too horrible.'

With such an established festival as Glastonbury, one would expect the management might be looking to leverage its brand with, for example, further events. Yet, the comments of Michael Eavis suggest not only a lack of clarity about the target audience but also concern over whether it can persist. Furthermore, Eavis seems nervous about the festival's appeal to artists who have lots of opportunities to make appearances over the summer. Audiences and artists are the two key factors that underpin financial success at these events, as successful festival promoters are well aware.

Sources: The history of Glastonbury is charted on its website (http://www.glastonburyfestivals.co.uk/history) while ownership and finances are available through Companies House.

Most of the background to the festival and related market has been drawn from online news resources such as the BBC, Times Online and the *Guardian*, or industry magazines such as *Music Week*.

More information on UK Festivals is available from Mintel.

Questions

1 Sticking to the 35-word limit suggested by Collis and Rukstad in section 1.2.3, what strategy statement would you propose for the Glastonbury Festival?

2 Carry out a 'three horizons' analysis (section 1.2.1) of the Glastonbury Festival, in terms of both existing activities and possible future ones. How might this analysis affect their future strategic direction?

3 Using the headings of environment, strategic capability and strategic purpose seen in section 1.3.1, identify key positioning issues for the Glastonbury Festival and consider their relative importance.

4 Following on from the previous question and making use of section 1.3.2, what alternative strategies do you see for the Glastonbury Festival?

5 Converting good strategic thinking into action can be a challenge: examine how the Glastonbury Festival has achieved this by considering the elements seen in section 1.3.3.

2

THE ENVIRONMENT

Learning outcomes

After reading this chapter, you should be able to:

● Analyse the broad macro-environment of organisations in terms of political, economic, social, technological, environmental ('green') and legal factors (*PESTEL*).

● Identify key drivers in this macro-environment and use these key drivers to construct alternative *scenarios* with regard to environmental change.

● Use *Porter's five forces* analysis in order to define the attractiveness of industries and sectors and to identify their potential for change.

● Identify successful *strategic groups*, valuable *market segments* and attractive *'Blue Oceans'* within industries.

● Use these various concepts and techniques in order to recognise *threats* and *opportunities* in the marketplace.

Key terms

Barriers to entry p. 28

Blue Oceans p. 40

Buyers p. 29

Critical success factors p. 40

Industry p. 25

Key drivers for change p. 21

Market p. 25

Market segment p. 38

PESTEL framework p. 21

Porter's five forces framework p. 25

Rivals p. 30

Strategic customer p. 39

Strategic groups p. 36

Strategy canvas p. 40

Substitutes p. 28

Suppliers p. 30

Value curves p. 40

Value innovation p. 40

(2.1) INTRODUCTION

The environment is what gives organisations their means of survival. It creates opportunities and it presents threats. For example, the success of Apple's iPhone created rich market opportunities for the writers of mobile phone apps. On the other hand, the rise of the free online news content has severely threatened the survival of many traditional newspapers, who can no longer count on customers paying for their daily print editions. Although the future can never be predicted perfectly, it is clearly important that entrepreneurs and managers try to analyse their environments as carefully as they can in order to anticipate and – if possible – influence environmental change.

This chapter therefore provides frameworks for analysing changing and complex environments. These frameworks are organised in a series of 'layers' briefly introduced here and summarised in Figure 2.1.

- *The macro-environment* is the highest-level layer. This consists of broad environmental factors that impact to a greater or lesser extent on almost all organisations. Here, the PESTEL framework can be used to identify how future issues in the *political, economic, social, technological, environmental ('green') and legal* environments might affect organisations. This PESTEL analysis

Figure 2.1 Layers of the business environment

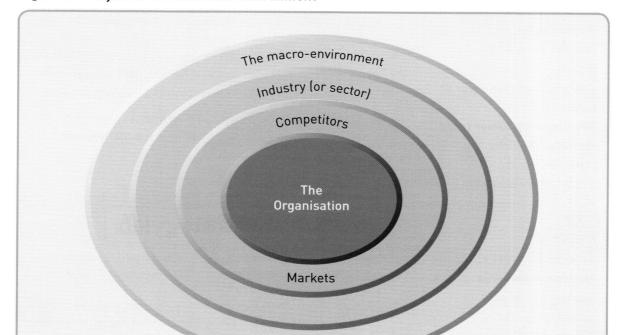

provides the broad 'data' from which to identify *key drivers of change*. These key drivers can be used to construct *scenarios* of alternative possible futures.

● *Industry, or sector*, forms the next layer within this broad general environment. This is made up of organisations producing the same products or services. Here the *five forces* framework is particularly useful in understanding the attractiveness of particular industries or sectors and potential threats from outside the present set of competitors.

● *Competitors and markets* are the most immediate layer surrounding organisations. Here the concept of *strategic groups* can help identify different kinds of competitors. Similarly, in the marketplace, customers' expectations are not all the same. They have a range of different requirements the importance of which can be understood through the *concepts of market segments* and *critical success factors*.

This chapter works through these three layers in turn, starting with the macro-environment.

2.2 THE MACRO-ENVIRONMENT

The three concepts in this section – PESTEL, key drivers and scenarios – are interrelated tools for analysing the broad macro-environment of an organisation. *PESTEL* provides a wide overview; *key drivers* help focus on what is most important; and *scenarios* build on key drivers to explore different ways in which the macro-environment might change.

2.2.1 The PESTEL framework

The **PESTEL framework** categorises environmental influences into six main types: political, economic, social, technological, environmental and legal. Thus PESTEL provides a comprehensive list of influences on the possible success or failure of particular strategies.[1] In particular, Politics highlights the role of governments; Economics refers to macro-economic factors such as exchange rates, business cycles and differential economic growth rates around the world; Social influences include changing cultures and demographics, for example ageing populations in many Western societies; Technological influences refer to innovations such as the internet, nano-technology or the rise of new composite materials; Environmental stands specifically for 'green' issues, such as pollution and waste; and finally Legal embraces legislative constraints or changes, such as health and safety legislation or restrictions on company mergers and acquisitions. Illustration 2.1 provides examples of PESTEL factors for the airline industry.

PESTEL framework

For managers, it is important to analyse how these factors are changing, drawing out implications for their organisations. Many of these factors are linked together. For example, technology developments may simultaneously change economic factors (for example, creating new jobs), social factors (facilitating more leisure) and environmental factors (reducing pollution). As can be imagined, analysing these factors and their interrelationships can produce long and complex lists.

Rather than getting overwhelmed by a multitude of details, it is necessary to step back eventually to identify the key drivers for change. **Key drivers for change are the environmental**

ILLUSTRATION 2.1

PESTEL analysis of the airline industry

Environmental influences on organisations can be summarised within six categories. For the airline industry, an initial list of influences under the six PESTEL analysis categories might include the following:

Political

- Government support for national carriers
- Security controls
- Restrictions on migration

Economic

- National growth rates
- Fuel prices

Social

- Rise in travel by elderly
- Student international study exchanges

Technological

- Fuel-efficient engines and airframes
- Security check technologies
- Teleconferencing for business

Environmental

- Noise pollution controls
- Energy consumption controls
- Land for growing airports

Legal

- Restrictions on mergers
- Preferential airport rights for some carriers

Questions

1 What additional environmental influences would you add to this initial list for the airline industry?

2 From your more comprehensive list, which of these influences would you highlight as likely to be the 'key drivers for change' for airlines in the coming five years?

factors likely to have a high impact on the success or failure of strategy. Typical key drivers will vary by industry or sector. Thus a retailer may be primarily concerned with social changes driving customer tastes and behaviour, for example forces encouraging out-of-town shopping, and economic changes, for example rates of economic growth and employment. Identifying key drivers for change helps managers to focus on the PESTEL factors that are most important and which must be addressed as the highest priority. Many other changes will depend on these key drivers anyway (for example, an ageing population will drive changes in retail clothing markets). Without a clear sense of the key drivers for change, managers will not be able to take the decisions that allow for effective action.

2.2.2 **Building scenarios**

When the business environment has high levels of *uncertainty* arising from either complexity or rapid change (or both), it is impossible to develop a single view of how environmental influences might affect an organisation's strategies – indeed it would be dangerous to do so. Scenario analyses are carried out to allow for different possibilities and help prevent managers from closing their minds about alternatives. Thus scenarios offer plausible alternative views of how the business environment might develop in the future, based on key drivers for change about which there is a high level of uncertainty.[2] Scenarios typically build on PESTEL analyses and key drivers for change, but do not offer a single forecast of how the environment will change. The point is not to predict, but to encourage managers to be alert to a range of possible futures.

Illustration 2.2 shows an example of scenario planning for the global financial system to 2020. Rather than incorporating a multitude of factors, the authors focus on two key drivers which (i) have high potential impact and (ii) are uncertain: geo-economic power shifts and international coordination on financial policy. Both of these drivers may produce very different futures, which can be combined to create four internally consistent scenarios for the next decade. The authors do not predict that one will prevail over the others, nor do they allocate relative probabilities. Prediction would close managers' minds to alternatives, while probabilities would imply a spurious kind of accuracy.

Scenario analyses can be carried out as follows:[3]

- *Identifying the scope* is an important first step. Scope refers to the subject of the scenario analysis and the time span. For example, scenario analyses can be carried out for a whole industry globally, or for particular geographical regions and markets. They can be for a decade or so (as in Illustration 2.2) or for just three to five years ahead.

- *Identifying key drivers for change* comes next. Here PESTEL analysis can be used to uncover issues likely to have a major impact upon the future of the industry, region or market.

- *Selecting opposing key drivers* is crucial in order to generate a range of different but plausible scenarios. Typically scenario analyses select from the various key drivers for change two key drivers which both have high uncertainty and have the potential for producing significantly divergent or opposing outcomes. In the oil industry, for example, political stability in the oil-producing regions is one major uncertainty; another is the capacity to develop major new oilfields, thanks to new extraction technologies or oilfield discoveries.

- *Developing scenario 'stories'*: as in films, scenarios are basically stories. Having selected opposing key drivers for change, it is necessary to knit together plausible 'stories' that incorporate both key drivers and other factors into a coherent whole. Thus in Illustration 2.2, the Fragmented protectionism scenario brings together in a consistent way failure to achieve international coordination and a slow rate of geo-economic shift: nationalistic protectionist measures in the West would prevent coordination at the same time as delaying the rise of the Asian economies. But completing the 'story' of Fragmented protectionism would also

ILLUSTRATION 2.2

Scenarios for the global financial system, 2020

Founded in 1971, the World Economic Forum (www. weforum.org) is a not-for-profit organisation based in Geneva and dedicated to developing new thinking amongst political, business and society leaders from countries worldwide. Participants at its famous annual Davos meetings have included German Chancellor Angela Merkel, Microsoft founder Bill Gates and South African President Nelson Mandela. As the world wrestled with the financial crisis of 2008–09, the World Economic Forum proposed to the 2009 Davos meeting four long-range scenarios for how the global financial system might develop to 2025. These scenarios were developed through eight separate workshops involving over 250 financial executives, regulators, policy-makers and senior academics.

The scenarios were based on two key drivers, each governed by a great deal of uncertainty. The first key driver was the pace of geo-economic power shifts, in particular from the traditional centres of economic power in the United States and Europe to the emerging ones in Asia and elsewhere. The second key driver was the degree of international coordination of financial policy, referring to issues such as banking regulation and currency policies. It was the upsides and downsides of these key drivers that defined the following four scenarios.

Re-engineered Western-centrism proposes a world in which the power-shift from the West is reasonably slow and policy-makers manage to coordinate a stable financial framework in which to navigate change. This is a comforting scenario for many Western companies. The *Rebalanced multilateralism* scenario envisages a more rapid shift from the West, but none the less policy-makers are able to coordinate change. For most Western companies, this is challenging but manageable, with Asia continuing to value their participation. More limiting is the *Financial regionalism* scenario. Here policy-makers are unable to find global agreement and the world splits into three major blocs, an American one, a European one and an increasingly powerful Asian one. Western companies are obliged to adopt very different strategies and structures for each of the three main blocs. The final scenario of *Fragmented protectionism* is daunting. Here nationalistic protectionism slows the shift from the West, but also reduces economic growth and leads to the collapse of the integrated Eurozone. All kinds of international business suffer from volatility, conflict and controls.

The World Economic Forum made no forecast about which scenario was more probable. But in presenting the alternatives, it aimed to get policy-makers to see the need for serious action, at the same time as warning business leaders that 'business as usual' was not a likely prospect.

Source: http://www.weforum.org/pdf/scenarios/TheFutureoftheGlobalFinancialSystem.pdf.

	Slow geo-economic shift	Rapid geo-economic shift
Harmonised financial coordination	Re-engineered Western-centrism	Rebalanced multilateralism
Discordant financial coordination	Fragmented protectionism	Financial regionalism

Question

Over which of the two drivers – the geo-economic power shift and policy coordination – do companies have the most influence? How should they exercise this influence?

involve incorporating other consistent factors: for example, slow economic growth resulting from barriers to trade; possible military conflicts due to lack of international cooperation; and illiberal domestic politics associated with nationalism.

- *Identifying impacts* of alternative scenarios on organisations is the final key stage of scenario building. Fragmented protectionism would obviously have a very negative impact for most multinational corporations. Rebalanced multilateralism on the other hand would favour multinationals, especially those from the rising Asian economies. It would be important for an organisation to carry out *robustness checks* in the face of each plausible scenario and develop *contingency plans* in case they happen.

(2.3) INDUSTRIES AND SECTORS

The previous section looked at how forces in the macro-environment might influence the success or failure of an organisation's strategies. But the impact of these general factors tends to surface in the more immediate environment through changes in the competitive forces surrounding organisations. An important aspect of this for most organisations will be competition within their industry, sector or market. **An industry is a group of firms producing products and services that are essentially the same.**[4] Examples are the automobile industry and the airline industry. Industries are also often described as 'sectors', especially in public services (for example, the health sector or the education sector). Industries and sectors are often made up of several specific markets. **A market is a group of customers for specific products or services that are essentially the same (for example, a particular geographical market).** Thus the automobile industry has markets in North America, Europe and Asia, for example.

This section concentrates on industry analysis, starting with Michael Porter's *five forces framework* and then introducing techniques for analysing the *dynamics* of industries. However, while the following section will address markets in more detail, this section will refer to markets and most of the concepts apply similarly to markets and industries.

2.3.1 Competitive forces – the five forces framework

Porter's five forces framework helps identify the attractiveness of an industry in terms of five competitive forces: the threat of entry, the threat of substitutes, the power of buyers, the power of suppliers and the extent of rivalry between competitors. These five forces together constitute an industry's 'structure' (see Figure 2.2), which is typically fairly stable. For Porter, an attractive industry structure is one that offers good profit potential. His essential message is that where the five forces are high, industries are not attractive to compete in. There will be too much competition, and too much pressure, to allow reasonable profits.

Porter's five forces framework

Although initially developed with businesses in mind, the five forces framework is relevant to most organisations. It can provide a useful starting point for strategic analysis even where profit criteria may not apply. In the public sector, it is important to understand how powerful suppliers can push up costs; amongst charities, it is important to avoid excessive rivalry within the same market. Moreover, once the degree of industry attractiveness has been understood,

Figure 2.2 The five forces framework

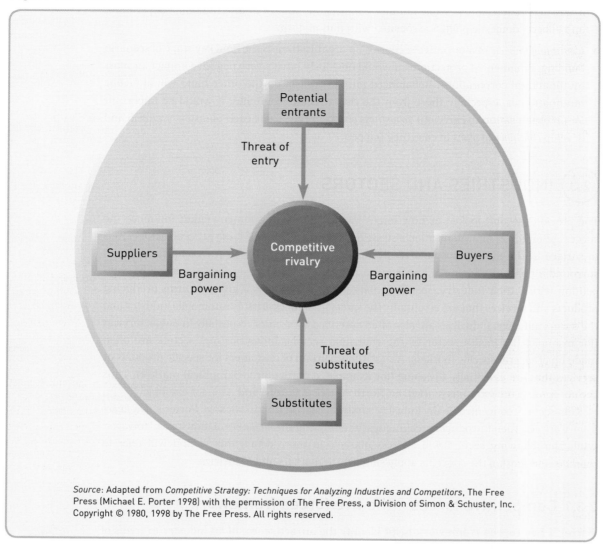

the five forces can help set an agenda for action on the various critical issues that they identify: for example, what should be done to control excessive rivalry in a particular industry? The rest of this section introduces each of the five forces in more detail. Illustration 2.3 on the evolving steel industry provides examples.

The threat of entry

How easy it is to enter the industry obviously influences the degree of competition. The greater the threat of entry, the worse it is for incumbents (existing competitors) in an industry. An attractive industry has high barriers to entry in order to reduce the threat of new competitors.

ILLUSTRATION 2.3

The consolidating steel industry

Five forces analysis helps understand the changing attractiveness of an industry.

For a long time, the steel industry was seen as a static and unprofitable one. Producers were nationally-based, often state-owned and frequently unprofitable – the early 2000s saw 50 independent steel producers going into bankruptcy in the United States alone. But recent years have seen a turnaround. During 2006, Mittal Steel paid $35bn (~€24.5bn) to buy European steel giant Arcelor, creating the world's largest steel company. The following year, Indian conglomerate Tata bought Anglo-Dutch steel company Corus for $13bn. These high prices indicated considerable confidence in the prospects of a better industry structure.

New entrants

In the last two decades, two powerful groups have entered world steel markets. First, after a period of privatisation and reorganisation, Russia had become the world's second largest steel exporting country (behind Japan) in 2009, led by giants such as Severstal and Evraz. China too had become a major force. Between the early 1990s and 2009, Chinese producers have increased their capacity six times. Although Chinese share of world capacity reached over 40 per cent in 2009, most of this was directed at the domestic market. China was the word's fourth largest steel exporter in 2009.

Substitutes

Steel is a nineteenth-century technology, increasingly substituted for by other materials such as aluminium in cars, plastics and aluminium in packaging and ceramics and composites in many high-tech applications. Steel's own technological advances sometimes work to reduce need: thus steel cans have become about one-third thinner over the last few decades.

Buyer power

The major buyers of steel are the global car manu-facturers. Car manufacturers are sophisticated users, often leading in the technological development of their materials. In North America at least, the decline of the once dominant 'Big Three' – General Motors, Ford and Chrysler – has meant many new domestic buyers, with companies such as Toyota, Nissan, Honda and BMW establishing local production plants. Another important user of steel is the metal packaging industry. Leading can producers such as Crown Holdings, which makes one-third of all food cans produced in North America and Europe, buy in large volumes, coordinating purchases around the world.

Supplier power

The key raw material for steel producers is iron ore. The big three ore producers – Vale, Rio Tinto and BHP Billiton – control about 70 per cent of the market for internationally traded ore. Iron ore prices had multiplied four times between 2005 and 2008, and, despite the recession, were still twice the 2005 level in 2010.

Competitive rivalry

The industry has traditionally been very fragmented: in 2000, the world's top five producers accounted for only 14 per cent of production. Companies such as Nucor in the US, Thyssen-Krupp in Germany as well as Mittal and Tata responded by buying up weaker players internation-ally. By 2009, the top five producers accounted for 20 per cent of world production. New steel giant ArcelorMittal alone accounted for about 10 per cent of world produc-tion, with one-fifth of the European Union market. None the less, despite a cyclical peak in 2008 and a slump in 2009, the world steel price was basically the same in 2010 as in 2005.

Questions

1 In recent years, which of the five forces has become more positive for steel producers, which less so?

2 Explain the acquisition strategies of players such as Mittal, Tata and Nucor.

3 In the future, what might change to make the steel industry less or more attractive?

Barriers to entry are the factors that need to be overcome by new entrants if they are to compete in an industry. Typical barriers are as follows:

● *Scale and experience.* In some industries, *economies of scale* are extremely important: for example, in the production of automobiles or the advertising of fast-moving consumer goods. Once incumbents have reached large-scale production, it will be very expensive for new entrants to match them and until they reach a similar volume they will have higher unit costs. This scale effect is increased where there are high *investment requirements* for entry, for example research costs in pharmaceuticals or capital equipment costs in automobiles. Barriers to entry also come from *experience curve* effects that give incumbents a cost advantage because they have learnt how to do things more efficiently than an inexperienced new entrant could possibly do (see section 5.2.1). Until the new entrant has built up equivalent experience over time, it will tend to produce at higher cost.

● *Access to supply or distribution channels.* In many industries manufacturers have had control over supply and/or distribution channels. Sometimes this has been through direct ownership (vertical integration), sometimes just through customer or supplier loyalty. In some industries this barrier has been overcome by new entrants who have bypassed retail distributors and sold directly to consumers through e-commerce (for example, Dell Computers and Amazon).

● *Expected retaliation.* If an organisation considering entering an industry believes that the retaliation of an existing firm will be so great as to prevent entry, or mean that entry would be too costly, this is also a barrier. Retaliation could take the form of a price war or a marketing blitz. Just the knowledge that incumbents are prepared to retaliate is often sufficiently discouraging to act as a barrier. Thus the history of fierce retaliation in the Atlantic airline market helps deter potential new entrants.

● *Legislation or government action.* Legal restraints on new entry vary from patent protection (e.g. pharmaceuticals), to regulation of markets (e.g. pension selling), through to direct government action (e.g. tariffs). Of course, organisations are vulnerable to new entrants if governments remove such protection, as has happened with deregulation of the airline industry.

● *Differentiation.* Differentiation means providing a product or service with higher perceived value than the competition; its importance will be discussed more fully in section 5.2.2. Cars are differentiated, for example, by quality and branding. Steel, by contrast, is by-and-large a commodity, undifferentiated and therefore sold by the ton. Steel buyers will simply buy the cheapest. Differentiation reduces the threat of entry because of increasing customer loyalty.

The threat of substitutes

Substitutes are products or services that offer a similar benefit to an industry's products or services, but by a different process. For example, aluminium is a substitute for steel in automobiles; trains are a substitute for cars; television and videogames are substitutes for each other. Managers often focus on competitors in their own industry, and neglect the threat posed by substitutes. Substitutes can reduce demand for a particular type of product as customers switch to alternatives – even to the extent that this type of product or service becomes obsolete. However, there does not have to be much actual switching for the substitute threat to have an effect. The simple risk of substitution puts a cap on the prices that can be charged in an industry. Thus, although Eurostar has no direct competitors in terms of train services from Paris to London, the prices it can charge are ultimately limited by the cost of flights between the two cities.

There are two important points to bear in mind about substitutes:

- *The price/performance ratio* is critical to substitution threats. A substitute is still an effective threat even if more expensive, so long as it offers performance advantages that customers value. Thus aluminium is more expensive than steel, but its relative lightness and its resistance to corrosion give it an advantage in some automobile manufacturing applications. It is the ratio of price to performance that matters, rather than simple price.

- *Extra-industry effects* are the core of the substitution concept. Substitutes come from outside the incumbents' industry and should not be confused with competitors' threats from within the industry. The value of the substitution concept is to force managers to look outside their own industry to consider more distant threats and constraints. The higher the threat of substitution, the less attractive the industry is likely to be.

The power of buyers

Buyers are the organisation's immediate customers, not necessarily the ultimate consumers. If buyers are powerful, then they can demand cheap prices or insist on costly improvements in products or services.

Buyer power is likely to be high when some of the following conditions prevail:

- *Concentrated buyers.* Where a few large customers account for the majority of sales, buyer power is increased. This is the case with items such as milk in the grocery sector in many European countries, where just a few retailers dominate the market. If a product or service accounts for a high percentage of the buyers' total purchases, their power is also likely to increase as they are more likely to 'shop around' to get the best price and therefore 'squeeze' suppliers than they would be for more trivial purchases.

- *Low switching costs.* Where buyers can easily switch between one supplier and another, they have a strong negotiating position and can squeeze suppliers who are desperate for their business. Switching costs are typically low for weakly differentiated commodities such as steel.

- *Buyer competition threat.* If the buyer has the capability to supply itself, or if it has the possibility of acquiring such a capability, it tends to be powerful. In negotiation with its suppliers, it can raise the threat of doing the suppliers' job themselves. This is called *backward vertical integration* (see section 6.4.1), moving back to sources of supply, and might occur if satisfactory prices or quality from suppliers cannot be obtained. For example, some steel companies have gained power over their iron ore suppliers as they have acquired iron ore sources for themselves.

It is very important that *buyers* are distinguished from *ultimate consumers*. Thus for companies like Procter & Gamble or Unilever (makers of shampoo, washing powders and so on), their buyers are retailers such as Carrefour or Tesco, not ordinary consumers (see discussion of the 'strategic customer' in 2.4.2). Carrefour and Tesco have much more negotiating power than an ordinary consumer would have. The high buying power of such supermarkets has become a major source of pressure for the companies supplying them.

The power of suppliers

Suppliers **are those who supply the organisation with what it needs to produce the product or service.** As well as fuel, raw materials and equipment, this can include labour and sources of finance. The factors increasing supplier power are the converse to those for buyer power. Thus *supplier power* is likely to be high where there are:

- *Concentrated suppliers.* Where just a few producers dominate supply, suppliers have more power over buyers. The iron ore industry is now concentrated in the hands of three main producers, leaving the steel companies, still relatively fragmented, in a weak negotiating position for this essential raw material.

- *High switching cost.* If it is expensive or disruptive to move from one supplier to another, then the buyer becomes relatively dependent and correspondingly weak. Microsoft is a powerful supplier because of the high switching costs of moving from one operating system to another. Buyers are prepared to pay a premium to avoid the trouble, and Microsoft knows it.

- *Supplier competition threat.* Suppliers have increased power where they are able to cut out buyers who are acting as middlemen. Thus airlines have been able to negotiate tough contracts with travel agencies as the rise of online booking has allowed them to create a direct route to customers. This is called *forward vertical integration*, moving up closer to the ultimate customer.

Most organisations have many suppliers, so it is necessary to concentrate the analysis on the most important ones or types. If their power is high, suppliers can capture all their buyers' own potential profits simply by raising their prices. Star football players supply their labour at astronomical cost, with the result that even the leading football clubs – their 'buyers' – struggle to make money.

Competitive rivalry

These wider competitive forces (the four arrows in the model in Figure 2.2) all impinge on the direct competitive rivalry between an organisation and its most immediate rivals. Thus low barriers to entry increase the number of rivals; powerful buyers with low switching costs force their suppliers to high rivalry in order to offer the best deals. The more competitive rivalry there is, the worse it is for incumbents within the industry.

Competitive rivals **are organisations with similar products and services aimed at the same customer group (i.e. not substitutes).** In the European airline industry, Air France and British Airways are rivals; trains are a substitute. As well as the influence of the four previous forces, there are a number of additional factors directly affecting the degree of competitive rivalry in an industry or sector:

- *Competitor balance*. Where competitors are of roughly equal size there is the danger of intensely rivalrous behaviour as one competitor attempts to gain dominance over others, through aggressive price cuts for example. Conversely, less rivalrous industries tend to have one or two dominant organisations, with the smaller players reluctant to challenge the larger ones directly (for example, by focusing on niches to avoid the 'attention' of the dominant companies).

- *Industry growth rate*. In situations of strong growth, an organisation can grow with the market, but in situations of low growth or decline, any growth is likely to be at the expense of a rival, and meet with fierce resistance. Low growth markets are therefore often associated with price competition and low profitability. The *industry life cycle* influences growth rates, and hence competitive conditions: see section 2.3.2.

- *High fixed costs*. Industries with high fixed costs, perhaps because requiring high investments in capital equipment or initial research, tend to be highly rivalrous. Companies will seek to spread their costs (i.e. reduce unit costs) by increasing their volumes: to do so, they typically cut their prices, prompting competitors to do the same and thereby triggering price wars in which everyone in the industry suffers. Similarly, if extra capacity can only be added in large increments (as in many manufacturing sectors, for example a chemical or glass factory), the competitor making such an addition is likely to create short-term over-capacity in the industry, leading to increased competition to use capacity.

- *High exit barriers*. The existence of high barriers to exit – in other words, closure or disinvestment – tends to increase rivalry, especially in declining industries. Excess capacity persists and consequently incumbents fight to maintain market share. Exit barriers might be high for a variety of reasons: for example, high redundancy costs or high investment in specific assets such as plant and equipment that others would not buy.

- *Low differentiation*. In a commodity market, where products or services are poorly differentiated, rivalry is increased because there is little to stop customers switching between competitors and the only way to compete is on price.

Some analysts add a 'sixth force' to Porter's five forces, organisations supplying complementary products and services. For example, suppliers of microprocessors (such as Intel) and suppliers of software (such as Microsoft) are *complementors* to each other in the sense that the value of one of their products depends on the effectiveness of the other (good software needs good microprocessors). The profitability of an industry can be affected by the effectiveness of complementors. For example, personal computer makers depend on Microsoft to drive demand for their products. Better software may increase the market for more advanced computers.

2.3.2 The dynamics of industry structure

Industry structure analysis can easily become too static: after all, structure implies stablility.[5] However, scenario analysis raises the issue of how competitive forces may change *over time*.

ILLUSTRATION 2.4

Chugging and the structure of the charity sector

Industry structure contributes to inefficiency and aggression in the United Kingdom's charity sector.

The charity sector has become controversial in the United Kingdom. The aggressive fund-raising of some charities is epitomised by workers soliciting donations from shoppers on a commission basis. Such is their perceived aggression that these charity workers are known as 'chuggers', compared with the violent street-crime of 'muggers'.

In 2008, there were 189,000 charities registered in England and Wales, 95 per cent having annual incomes of less than £500,000. However, about 80 per cent of all charity income is raised by the largest twenty charities, headed by Cancer Research UK (2008 income, £355m (~€390m; ~$532m)). According to *Charity Market Monitor*, in 2008, the top 300 charities averaged a 0.9 per cent increase in income, but the largest 10 managed income growth of 2.3 per cent (excluding impact of mergers).

The United Kingdom government introduced the 2006 Charities Act with the specific intention of assisting mergers between independent charities. This had followed a report of the Charity Commission, the regulator for charities in England and Wales, that had commented on the charity sector thus:

> Some people believe that there are too many charities competing for too few funds and that a significant amount of charitable resource could be saved if more charities pooled their resources and worked together . . .
>
> The majority of charities are relatively small, local organisations that rely entirely on the unpaid help of their trustees and other volunteers. They may have similar purposes to many other charities but they are all serving different communities. The nature of these charities suggests that there are less likely to be significant areas of overlap . . . It is the much larger, professionally run, charities which, because of their size, tend to face charges of duplication, waste and over-aggressive fund-raising. Whilst there are some clear advantages to be had from a healthy plurality of charities, which are constantly refreshed by new charities pursuing new activities, there are also big benefits of public confidence and support

to be had from showing collaborative, as opposed to over-competitive, instincts.

Local authorities in particular were frustrated by duplication and waste, as they increasingly commission local charities to deliver services. With respect to small charities, local authority budgets are relatively large. One charity sector chief executive, Caroline Shaw, told *Charity Times* as she pursued more cooperation between local charities:

> 'Without a doubt there is increased competition when it comes to [local authority] commissioning . . . Our driving force has really been to try to create a more effective service for front line organisations; to offer more projects, more diverse services, more effective services. There's a huge amount [of charities] all fighting for funding. I really think that people should be looking at working more closely together.'

During 2008, more than 230 charity mergers were registered with the Charity Commission. As the recession began to put pressure on charitable donations throughout the sector, early 2009 saw the merger of two well-established charities helping the elderly in the United Kingom, Help the Aged and Age Concern. The new charity, Age UK, has a combined income of around £160 million, including £47 million a year raised through fundraising, and over 520 charity shops.

Sources: 'RS 4a – Collaborative working and mergers: Summary', http://www.charity-commission.gov.uk/publications/rs4a.asp; *Charity Times*, 'Strength in Numbers', August 2007; *Charity Market Monitor*, 2009.

Questions

1 Which of Porter's five forces are creating problems for the United Kingdom's charity sector?

2 What type of industry structure might the charity industry be moving towards? What would be the benefits and disadvantages of that structure?

The key drivers for change are likely to alter industry structures and scenario analyses are useful for analysing possible impacts. An illustration of changing industry structure, and the competitive implications of this, is provided by Illustration 2.4 on the UK charity sector. This section examines two additional approaches to understanding change in industry structure: the *industry life cycle* concept and *comparative five forces analyses*.

The industry life cycle

The power of the five forces typically varies with the stages of the industry life cycle. The industry life cycle concept proposes that industries start small in their development stage, then go through a period of rapid growth (the equivalent to 'adolescence' in the human life cycle), culminating in a period of 'shake-out'. The final two stages are first a period of slow or even zero growth ('maturity'), and then the final stage of decline ('old age'). Each of these stages has implications for the five forces.[6]

The *development stage* is an experimental one, typically with few players, little direct rivalry and highly differentiated products. The five forces are likely to be weak, therefore, though profits may actually be scarce because of high investment requirements. The next stage is one of high *growth*, with rivalry low as there is plenty of market opportunity for everybody. Buyers may be keen to secure supplies of the booming new product and may also lack sophistication about what they are buying, so diminishing their power. One down-side of the growth stage is that barriers to entry may be low, as existing competitors have not built up much scale, experience or customer loyalty. Another potential downside is the power of suppliers if there is a shortage of components or materials that fast-growing businesses need for expansion. The *shake-out stage* begins as the growth rate starts to decline, so that increased rivalry forces the weakest of the new entrants out of the business. In the *maturity stage*, barriers to entry tend to increase, as control over distribution is established and economies of scale and experience curve benefits come into play. Products or service tend to standardise. Buyers may become more powerful as they become less avid for the industry's products or services and more confident in switching between suppliers. Market share is typically crucial at the maturity stage, providing leverage against buyers and competitive advantage in terms of cost. Finally, the *decline stage* can be a period of extreme rivalry, especially where there are high exit barriers, as falling sales force remaining competitors into dog-eat-dog competition. Figure 2.3 summarises some of the conditions that can be expected at different stages in the life cycle.

It is important to avoid putting too much faith in the inevitability of life-cycle stages. One stage does not follow predictably after another: industries vary widely in the length of their growth stages, and others can rapidly 'de-mature' through radical innovation. The telephony industry, based for nearly a century on fixed-line telephones, de-matured rapidly with the introduction of mobile and internet telephony. Anita McGahan of Toronto University warns of the 'maturity mindset', which can leave many managers complacent and slow to respond to new competition.[7] Managing in mature industries is not necessarily just about waiting for decline. However, even if the various stages are not inevitable, the life-cycle concept does remind managers that conditions are likely to change over time. Especially in fast-moving industries, five forces analyses need to be reviewed quite regularly.

Figure 2.3 The industry life cycle

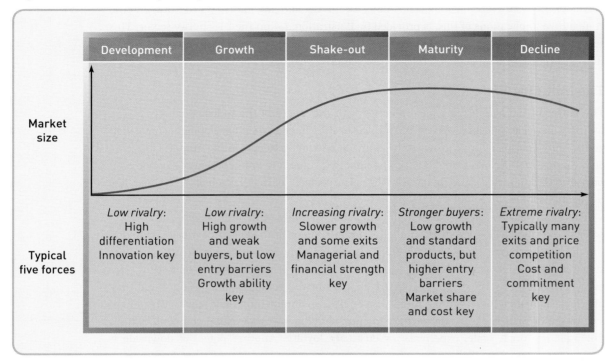

Comparative industry structure analyses

The industry life cycle underlines the need to make industry structure analysis dynamic. One effective means of doing this is to compare the five forces over time in a simple 'radar plot'.

Figure 2.4 provides a framework for summarising the power of each of the five forces on five axes. Power diminishes as the axes go outwards. Where the forces are low, the total area enclosed by the lines between the axes is large; where the forces are high, the total area enclosed by the lines is small. The larger the enclosed area, therefore, the greater is the profit potential. In Figure 2.4, the industry at Time 0 (represented by the light blue lines) has relatively low rivalry (just a few competitors) and faces low substitution threats. The threat of entry is moderate, but both buyer power and supplier power are relatively high. Overall, this looks like only a moderately attractive industry to invest in.

However, given the dynamic nature of industries, managers need to look forward – here five years represented by the green lines in Figure 2.4. Managers are predicting, in this case, some rise in the threat of substitutes (perhaps new technologies will be developed). On the other hand, they predict a falling entry threat, while both buyer power and supplier power will be easing. Rivalry will reduce still further. This looks like a classic case of an industry in which a few players emerge with overall dominance. The area enclosed by the green lines is large, suggesting a relatively attractive industry. For a firm confident of becoming one of the dominant players, this might be an industry well worth investing in.

Figure 2.4 Comparative industry structure analysis

Comparing the five forces over time on a radar plot thus helps to give industry structure analysis a dynamic aspect. Similar plots can be made to aid diversification decisions (see Chapter 6), where possible new industries to enter can be compared in terms of attractiveness. The lines are only approximate, of course, because they aggregate the many individual elements that make up each of the forces into a simple composite measure. Notice too that if one of the forces is very adverse, then this might nullify positive assessments on the other four axes: for example, an industry with low rivalry, low substitution, low entry barriers and low supplier power might still be unattractive if powerful buyers were able to demand highly discounted prices. With these warnings in mind, such radar plots can none the less be both a useful device for initial analysis and an effective summary of a final, more refined analysis.

(2.4) COMPETITORS AND MARKETS

An industry or sector analysis may be at too high a level to provide a detailed understanding of competition. The five forces can impact differently on different kinds of players in an industry. Thus Hyundai and Porsche may be in the same broad industry (automobiles), but they are positioned differently: they are protected by different barriers to entry and competitive moves by one are unlikely to affect the other. It is often useful to disaggregate. Many industries contain a range of companies, each of which has different capabilities and competes on different bases. These competitor differences are captured by the concept of *strategic groups*. Customers too can differ significantly and these can be captured by distinguishing between different *market segments*.

Thinking in terms of different strategic groups and market segments provides opportunities for organisations to develop highly distinctive positionings within broader industries. The potential for distinctiveness is further explored through 'Blue Ocean' thinking, the last topic in this section.

2.4.1 Strategic groups[8]

Strategic
groups

Strategic groups **are organisations within an industry or sector with similar strategic characteristics, following similar strategies or competing on similar bases.** These characteristics are different from those in other strategic groups in the same industry or sector. For example, in the grocery retailing industry, supermarkets, convenience stores and corner shops each form different strategic groups. There are many different characteristics that distinguish between strategic groups, but these can be grouped into two major categories (see Figure 2.5). First, the *scope* of an organisation's activities (such as product range, geographical coverage and range of distribution channels used). Second, the *resource commitment* (such as brands, marketing spend and extent of vertical integration). Which characteristics are relevant differs from industry to industry, but typically important are those characteristics that separate high performers from low performers.

Strategic groups can be mapped on to two-dimensional charts – for example, one axis might be the extent of product range and the other axis the size of marketing spend. One method for choosing key dimensions by which to map strategic groups is to identify top performers (by

Figure 2.5 Some characteristics for identifying strategic groups

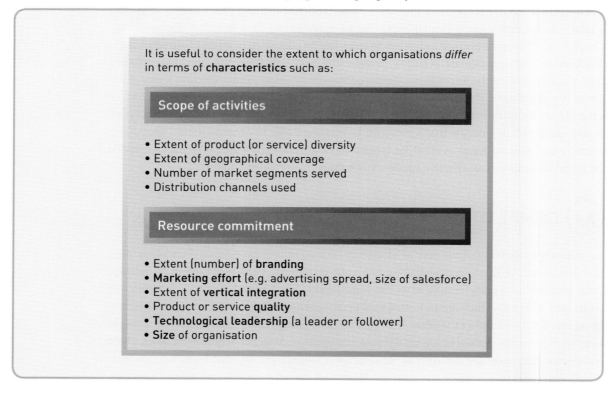

It is useful to consider the extent to which organisations *differ* in terms of **characteristics** such as:

Scope of activities

- Extent of product (or service) diversity
- Extent of geographical coverage
- Number of market segments served
- Distribution channels used

Resource commitment

- Extent (number) of **branding**
- **Marketing effort** (e.g. advertising spread, size of salesforce)
- Extent of **vertical integration**
- Product or service **quality**
- **Technological leadership** (a leader or follower)
- **Size** of organisation

growth or profitability) in an industry and to compare them with low performers. Characteristics that are shared by top performers, but not by low performers, are likely to be particularly relevant for mapping strategic groups. For example, the most profitable firms in an industry might all be narrow in terms of product range, and lavish in terms of marketing spend, while the less profitable firms might be more widely spread in terms of products and restrained in their marketing. Here the two dimensions for mapping would be product range and marketing spend. A potential recommendation for the less profitable firms would be to cut back their product range and boost their marketing.

Figure 2.6 shows strategic groups amongst Indian pharmaceutical companies, with research and development intensity (R&D spend as a percentage of sales) and overseas focus (exports and patents registered overseas) defining the axes of the map. These two axes do explain a good deal of the variation in profitability between groups. The most profitable group is the Emergent Globals (11.3 per cent average return on sales), those with high R&D intensity and high overseas focus. On the other hand, the Exploiter group spends little on R&D and is focused on domestic markets, and only enjoys 2.0 per cent average return on sales.

Figure 2.6 Strategic groups in the Indian pharmaceutical industry

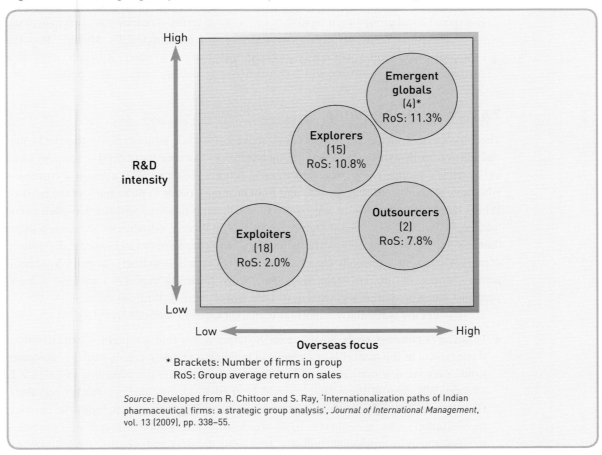

* Brackets: Number of firms in group
RoS: Group average return on sales

Source: Developed from R. Chittoor and S. Ray, 'Internationalization paths of Indian pharmaceutical firms: a strategic group analysis', *Journal of International Management*, vol. 13 (2009), pp. 338–55.

This strategic group concept is useful in at least three ways:

- *Understanding competition.* Managers can focus on their direct competitors within their particular strategic group, rather than the whole industry. They can also establish the dimensions that distinguish them most from other groups, and which might be the basis for relative success or failure. These dimensions can then become the focus of their action.

- *Analysis of strategic opportunities.* Strategic group maps can identify the most attractive 'strategic spaces' within an industry. Some spaces on the map may be 'white spaces', relatively under-occupied. In the Indian pharmaceutical industry, the white space is high R&D investment combined with focus on domestic markets. Such white spaces might be unexploited opportunities. On the other hand, they could turn out to be 'black holes', impossible to exploit and likely to damage any entrant. A strategic group map is only the first stage of the analysis. Strategic spaces need to tested carefully.

- *Analysis of mobility barriers.* Of course, moving across the map to take advantage of opportunities is not costless. Often it will require difficult decisions and rare resources. Strategic groups are therefore characterised by 'mobility barriers', obstacles to movement from one strategic group to another. These are similar to barriers to entry in five forces analysis. Although movement from the Exploiter group in Indian pharmaceuticals to the Emergent Global group might seem very attractive in terms of profits, it is likely to demand very substantial financial investment and strong managerial skills. Mobility into the Emergent Global group will not be easy. As with barriers to entry, it is good to be in a successful strategic group into which there are strong mobility barriers, to impede imitation.

2.4.2 Market segments

The concept of strategic groups discussed above helps with understanding the similarities and differences in terms of competitor characteristics. The concept of market segment looks at the other side, differences in customer needs. A **market segment**[9] **is a group of customers who have similar needs that are different from customer needs in other parts of the market.** Where these customer groups are relatively small, such market segments are often called 'niches'. Dominance of a market segment or niche can be very valuable, for the same reasons that dominance of an industry can be valuable following five forces logic. However, dominance of market segments is typically less secure than that of a whole industry, as entry from competitors in adjacent market segments is likely to be relatively easy. For long-term success, strategies based on market segments must keep customer needs firmly in mind.

Three issues are particularly important in market segment analysis, therefore:

- *Variation in customer needs.* Focusing on customer needs that are highly distinctive from those typical in the market is one means of building a secure segment strategy. Customer needs vary for a whole variety of reasons – some of which are identified in Table 2.1. Theoretically, any of these factors could be used to identify distinct market segments. However, the crucial bases of segmentation vary according to market. In industrial markets, segmentation is often thought of in terms of industrial classification of buyers: steel producers might segment by automobile industry, packaging industry and construction industry, for example. On the other hand, segmentation by buyer behaviour (for example, direct buying

Table 2.1 Some bases of market segmentation

Type of factor	Consumer markets	Industrial/organisational markets
Characteristics of people/organisations	Age, sex, race Income Family size Life-cycle stage Location Lifestyle	Industry Location Size Technology Profitability Management
Purchase/use situation	Size of purchase Brand loyalty Purpose of use Purchasing behaviour Importance of purchase Choice criteria	Application Importance of purchase Volume Frequency of purchase Purchasing procedure Choice criteria Distribution channel
Users' needs and preferences for product characteristics	Product similarity Price preference Brand preferences Desired features Quality	Performance requirements Assistance from suppliers Brand preferences Desired features Quality Service requirements

versus those users who buy through third parties such as contractors) or purchase value (for example, high-value bulk purchasers versus frequent low-value purchasers) might be more appropriate. Being able to serve a highly distinctive segment that other organisations find difficult to serve is often the basis for a secure long-term strategy.

- *Specialisation*. Within a market segment, this can also be an important basis for a successful segmentation strategy and is sometimes called a 'niche strategy'. Organisations that have built up most experience in servicing a particular market segment should not only have lower costs in so doing, but also have built relationships which may be difficult for others to break down. Experience and relationships are likely to protect a dominant position in a particular segment. However, precisely because customers value different things in different segments, specialised producers may find it very difficult to compete on a broader basis. For example, a small local brewery competing against the big brands on the basis of its ability to satisfy distinctive local tastes is unlikely to find it easy to serve other segments where tastes are different, scale requirements are larger and distribution channels are more complex.

- *Strategic customers*. It is crucial to understand whose needs matter. The **strategic customer is the person(s) at whom the strategy is primarily addressed because they have the most influence over which goods or services are purchased.** As above, for a food manufacturer, it is the retailers' needs that matter most directly, not simply the ultimate consumers of the food. It is retailers who pay the manufacturer and decide what to stock. Retailers care about price and quality because consumers do, so the manufacturer must take these needs into account, but retailers also care about delivery convenience and reliability. For a food manufacturer, therefore, the strategic customer is the retailer: the retailer's needs, not just the ultimate consumers' needs, should shape strategy. In the public sector, the strategic customer is very often the agency that controls the funds or authorises use, rather than the user of the service. In public health care, therefore, it is hospitals, not patients, that are the strategic customers of pharmaceutical companies.

2.4.3 Blue Ocean thinking

The more differentiated views of competitors and customers embodied in strategic groups and market segments can be taken a step further by 'Blue Ocean' thinking. As developed by W. Chan Kim and Renée Mauborgne at INSEAD, **Blue Oceans** **are new market spaces where competition is minimised**.[10] Blue Oceans contrast with 'Red Oceans', where industries are already well defined and rivalry is intense. Blue Oceans evoke wide empty seas. Red Oceans are associated with bloody competition and 'red ink', in other words financial losses.

Blue Ocean thinking therefore encourages entrepreneurs and managers to be different by finding or creating market spaces that are not currently being served. Strategy here is about finding *strategic gaps*, opportunities in the environment that are not being fully exploited by competitors. The strategy canvas is one framework that can effectively assist this kind of Blue Ocean thinking. A **strategy canvas** **compares competitors according to their performance on key success factors in order to develop strategies based on creating new market spaces**. Figure 2.7 shows a strategy canvas for three engineering components companies, highlighting the following three features:

- **Critical success factors** (CSFs) **are those factors that are either particularly valued by customers or which provide a significant advantage in terms of cost**. Critical success factors are therefore likely to be an important source of competitive advantage or disadvantage. Figure 2.7 identifies five established critical success factors in this engineering components market (cost, after-sales service, delivery reliability, technical quality and testing facilities). Note there is also a new sixth critical success factor, design advisory services, which will be discussed under the third subhead, value innovation.

- **Value curves** **are a graphic depiction of how customers perceive competitors' relative performance across the critical success factors**. In Figure 2.7, companies A and B perform well on cost, service, reliability and quality, but less well on testing. They do not offer any design advice. Company C has a radically different value curve, characteristic of a 'value innovator'.

- **Value innovation** **is the creation of new market space by excelling on established critical success factors on which competitors are performing badly and/or by creating new critical success factors representing previously unrecognised customer wants**. Thus in Figure 2.7, company C is a value innovator in both senses. First, it excels on the established customer need of offering testing facilities for customers' products using its components. Second, it offers a new and valued design service advising customers on how to integrate their components in order for them to create better products.

Company C's strategy exemplifies two critical principles in Blue Ocean thinking: *focus* and *divergence*. First, Company C focuses its efforts on just two factors, testing and design services, while maintaining only adequate performance on the other critical success factors where its

Figure 2.7 Strategy canvas for electrical components companies

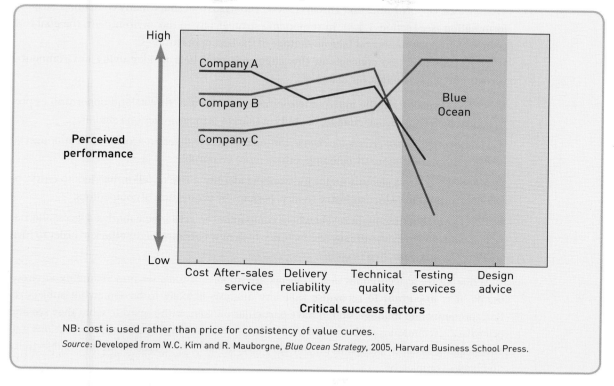

NB: cost is used rather than price for consistency of value curves.

Source: Developed from W.C. Kim and R. Mauborgne, *Blue Ocean Strategy*, 2005, Harvard Business School Press.

competitors are already high performers. Second, it has created a value curve that significantly diverges from its competitors' value curves, creating a substantial strategic gap, or Blue Ocean, in the areas of testing and design services. This is shrewd. For Company C, beating Companies A and B in the areas where they are performing well anyway would require major investment and likely provide little advantage given that customers are already highly satisfied. Challenging A and B on cost, after-sales service, delivery or quality would be a Red Ocean strategy. Far better is to concentrate on where a large gap can be created between competitors. Company C faces little competition for those customers who really value testing and design services, and consequently can charge good prices for them.

2.5 OPPORTUNITIES AND THREATS

The concepts and frameworks discussed above should be helpful in understanding the factors in the macro-, industry and competitor/market environments of an organisation. However, the critical issue is the *implications* that are drawn from this understanding in guiding strategic decisions and choices. The crucial next stage, therefore, is to draw from the environmental analysis specific strategic opportunities and threats for the organisation. Identifying these opportunities and threats is extremely valuable when thinking about strategic choices for the future (the subject of Chapters 5 to 9). Opportunities and threats forms one half of the Strengths, Weaknesses, Opportunities and Threats (SWOT) analyses that shape many companies' strategy formulation (see section 3.4.3). In responding strategically to the environment, the goal is to reduce identified threats and take advantage of the best opportunities.

The techniques and concepts in this chapter should help in identifying environmental threats and opportunities, for instance:

- a *PESTEL analysis* of the macro-environment might reveal threats and opportunities presented by technological change, or shifts in market demographics and similar;
- identification of *key drivers for change* can help generate different scenarios for managerial discussion, some more threatening, others more favourable;
- a *Porter five forces analysis* might for example identify a rise or fall in barriers to entry, or opportunities to reduce industry rivalry, perhaps by acquisition of competitors;
- *Blue Ocean* thinking might reveal where companies can create new market spaces; alternatively it could help identify success factors which new entrants might attack in order to turn 'Blue Oceans' into 'Red Oceans'.

While all these techniques and concepts are important tools for understanding environments, it is important to recognise that any analysis is likely to be somewhat subjective. Entrepreneurs and managers often have particular blinkers with regard to what they see and prioritise.[11] Techniques and concepts can be helpful in challenging existing assumptions and encouraging broader perspectives, but they are unlikely to overcome human subjectivity and biases completely.

SUMMARY

- Environmental influences can be thought of as layers around an organisation, with the outer layer making up the *macro-environment*, the middle layer making up the *industry or sector* and the inner layer *strategic groups* and *market segments*.
- The macro-environment can be analysed in terms of the *PESTEL factors*, from which *key drivers of change* can be identified. Alternative *scenarios* about the future can be constructed according to how the key drivers develop.
- Industries and sectors can be analysed in terms of the *Porter five forces* – barriers to entry, substitutes, buyer power, supplier power and rivalry. Together, these determine industry or sector attractiveness.
- Industries and sectors are dynamic, and their changes can be analysed in terms of the *industry life cycle* and *comparative five forces radar plots*.
- In the inner layer of the environment, *strategic group* analysis, *market segment* analysis and the *strategy canvas* can help identify strategic gaps or opportunities.
- *Blue Ocean* strategies characterised by low rivalry are likely to be better opportunities than *Red Ocean* strategies with many rivals.

VIDEO CASE

Visit *MyStrategyLab* and watch the *Hiscox* case study.

1 Describe recent environmental changes in the insurance industry in terms of Porter's five forces. What else needs to be factored into an environmental analysis?

2 Assess Hiscox's strategic position in this environmental context.

RECOMMENDED KEY READINGS

- There is a good summary of industry analysis in M.E. Porter, 'The five competitive forces that shape strategy', *Harvard Business Review*, vol. 86, no. 1 (2008), pp. 58–77.

- For approaches to how environments change, see K. van der Heijden, *Scenarios: The Art of Strategic Conversation*, 2nd edition, Wiley, 2005, and the work of Michael Porter's colleague, A. McGahan, *How Industries Evolve*, Harvard Business School Press, 2004.

REFERENCES

1. PESTEL is an extension of PEST (Politics, Economics, Social and Technology) analysis, taking more account of environmental ('green') and legal issues.

2. For a discussion of scenario planning in practice, see K. van der Heijden, *Scenarios: The Art of Strategic Conversation*, 2nd edition, Wiley, 2005. For how scenario planning fits with other forms of environmental analysis such as PESTEL, see G. Burt, G. Wright, R. Bradfield and K. van der Heijden, 'The role of scenario planning in exploring the environment in view of the limitations of PEST and its derivatives', *International Studies of Management and Organization*, vol. 36, no. 3 (2006), pp. 50–76.

3. Based on P. Schoemaker, 'Scenario planning: a tool for strategic thinking'. *Sloan Management Review*, vol. 36 (1995), pp. 25–34.

4. See M.E. Porter, *Competitive Strategy: Techniques for Analysing Industries and Competitors*, Free Press, 1980, p. 5.

5. There is a good discussion of the static nature of the Porter model, and other limitations, in M. Grundy,

'Rethinking and reinventing Michael Porter's five forces model', *Strategic Change*, vol. 15 (2006), pp. 213–29.

6. An overview of the industry life cycle is A. McGahan, 'How industries evolve', *Business Strategy Review*, vol. 11, no. 3 (2000), pp. 1–16.

7. A. McGahan, 'How industries evolve', *Business Strategy Review*, vol. 11, no. 3 (2000), pp. 1–16.

8. For an example of strategic group analysis, see G. Leask and D. Parker, 'Strategic groups, competitive groups and performance in the UK pharmaceutical industry', *Strategic Management Journal*, vol. 28, no. 7 (2007), pp. 723–45.

9. A useful discussion of segmentation in relation to competitive strategy is provided in M.E. Porter, *Competitive Advantage*, Free Press, 1985, Chapter 7.

10. W.C. Kim and R. Mauborgne, 'How strategy shapes structure', *Harvard Business Review*, September 2009, pp. 73–80.

11. P. Schoemaker and G. Day, 'How to make sense of weak signals', *Sloan Management Review*, vol. 50, no. 3 (2009), pp. 81–89.

Global forces and the Western European brewing industry

Mike Blee and Richard Whittington

This case is centred on the European brewing industry in Western Europe and examines how the increasingly competitive pressure of operating within global markets is causing consolidation through acquisitions, alliances and closures within the industry. This has resulted in the growth of the brewers' reliance upon super-brands.

In the early years of the 21st century, European brewers faced a surprising paradox. The traditional centre of the beer industry worldwide and home to the world's largest brewing companies, Europe, was turning off beer. Beer consumption was falling in the largest markets of Germany and the United Kingdom, while burgeoning in emerging markets around the world. In 2008, Europe's largest market, Germany, ranked only 5th in the world, behind China, the United States, Brazil and Russia. China, with 12 per cent annual growth between 2003 and 2008, had become the largest single market by volume, alone accounting for 23 per cent of world consumption (Euromonitor, 2010).

Table 1 details the overall decline of European beer consumption. Decline in traditional key markets is due to several factors. Governments are campaigning strongly against drunken driving, affecting the propensity to drink beer in restaurants, pubs and bars. There is increasing awareness of the effects of alcohol on health and fitness. Particularly in the United Kingdom, there is growing hostility to so-called 'binge drinking', excessive alcohol consumption in pubs and clubs. Wines have also become increasingly popular in Northern European markets. However, beer consumption per capita varies widely between countries, being four times higher in Germany than in Italy, for example. Some traditionally low consumption European markets have been showing good growth.

The drive against drunken driving and binge drinking has helped shift sales from the 'on-trade' (beer consumed on the premises, as in pubs or restaurants) to the off-trade (retail). Worldwide, the off-trade increased from 63 per cent of volume in 2000 to 67 per

Source: Picturesbyrob/Alamy.

Table 1 European beer consumption by country and year (000 hectolitres)

Country	1980	2000	2003	2007
Austria	7651	8762	8979	9100
Belgium	12945	10064	9935	9137
Denmark	6698	5452	5181	4840
Finland	2738	4024	4179	4073
France	23745	21420	21168	18781
Germany‡	89820	103105	97107	91000
Greece	N/A	4288	3905	4600
Ireland	4174	5594	5315	5193
Italy	9539	16289	17452	17766
Luxembourg	417	472	373	429
Netherlands	12213	13129	12771	12910
Norway*	7651	2327	2270	2670
Portugal	3534	6453	6008	6200
Spain	20065	29151	33451	35658
Sweden	3935	5011	4969	4900
Switzerland*	4433	4194	4334	4489
UK	65490	57007	60302	51300

* Non-EU countries; ‡ 1980 excludes GDR. Figures adjusted.

Source: Based on information from www.Brewersofeurope.org.

cent in 2008. The off-trade is increasingly dominated by large supermarket chains such as Tesco or Carrefour, who often use cut-price offers on beer in order to lure people into their shops. More than one-fifth of beer volume is now sold through supermarkets. German retailers such as Aldi and Lidl have had considerable success with their own 'private-label' (rather than brewery-branded) beers. Pubs have suffered: in the United Kingdom, an estimated 50 pubs closed per week during the recessionary year 2009. However, although on-trade volumes are falling in Europe, the sales values are generally rising, as brewers introduce higher-priced premium products such as non-alcoholic beers, extra cold lagers or fruit-flavoured beers. On the other hand, a good deal of this increasing demand for premium products is being satisfied by the import of apparently exotic beers from overseas (see Table 2).

Brewers' main purchasing costs are packaging (accounting for around half of non-labour costs), raw material such as barley, and energy. The European packaging industry is highly concentrated, dominated by international companies such as Crown in cans and Owens-Illinois in glass bottles. In the United Kingdom, for example, there are just three can makers: Ball Packaging Europe, Crown Bevcan and REXAM.

Acquisition, licensing and strategic alliances have all occurred as the leading brewers battle to control the market. There are global pressures for consolidation due to over-capacity within the industry, the need to contain costs and benefits of leveraging strong brands. For example, in 2004, Belgian brewer Interbrew merged with Am Bev, the Brazilian brewery group, to create the largest brewer in the world, InBev. In 2008, the new InBev bought the second largest brewer, the American Anheuser-Busch, giving it nearly 20 per cent of the world market. In 2002, South African Breweries acquired the Miller Group (USA) and Pilsner Urquell in the Czech Republic, becoming SABMiller. SABMiller in turn bought Dutch specialist Grolsch in 2007. Smaller players in the fast-growing Chinese and Latin American markets are being snapped up by the large international brewers too: in 2010, Dutch Heineken bought Mexico's second largest brewery, FEMSA. On the other hand, medium-sized Australian brewer Fosters has withdrawn from the European market. The European Commission fined Heineken and Kronenbourg in 2004 for price-fixing in France, and Heineken, Grolsch and Bavaria in 2007 for a price-fixing cartel in the Dutch market.

Table 3 lists the world's top ten brewing companies, which accounted for about 60 per cent of world beer volumes in 2009. However, there remain many specialist, regional and microbreweries, for example Greene King (see below). Germany, with its pub-brewing tradition (the Brauhaus), still has 1319 separate breweries owned by 583 separate brewing companies. None the less, market concentration has increased in Western Europe: in 2000, the top two players (Heineken and Interbrew) had 19.3 per cent of the market; in 2009, the top two players, Heineken and Carlsberg, held 28.5 per cent of the Western European market, with A-B InBev accounting for a further 10.6 per cent.

Three brewing companies

The European market contains many very different kinds of competitor: this section introduces the world's largest brewer and two outliers.

Table 2 Imports of beer by country

Country	Imports 2002 (% of consumption*)	Imports 2008 (% of consumption)
Austria	5.1	6.6
Belgium	4.74	12.8
Denmark	2.6	10.5
Finland	2.3	10.1
France	23	31.4
Germany	3.1	7.6
Greece	4.1	6.5
Ireland	NA	16.8
Italy	27.2	33.5
Luxembourg	NA	43.1
Netherlands	3.2	18.6
Norway	5.4	3.7
Portugal	1.1	0.6
Spain	11.7	8.6
Sweden	NA	23.4
Switzerland	15.4	17.6
United Kingdom	10.9	17.7

Note: Import figures do not include beers brewed under licence in home country; also countries vary in measuring per cent of consumption.

Source: Based on information from www.Brewersofeurope.org.

Table 3 The world's top ten brewery companies by volume: 2000 and 2009

2000		2009	
Company	Share global volume %	Company	Share global volume %
Anheuser-Busch (US)	8.8	A-B InBev (Belgium)	19.5
AmBev (Brazil)	4.6	SABMiller (UK)	9.5
Heineken (Dutch)	4.3	Heineken (Dutch)	6.9
Interbrew (Belgium)	4.0	Carlsberg (Danish)	5.9
Miller (US)	3.6	China Resources (China)	4.5
SAB (South Africa)	3.3	Tsingtao (China)	3.1
Modelo (Mexico)	2.7	Modelo (Mexico)	2.9
Coors (US)	2.0	Molson Coors (US)	2.8
Asahi (Japan)	2.0	Beijing Yanjing (China)	2.5
Kirin (Japan)	1.9	FEMSA (Mexico)	2.3

Source: Euromonitor International, 2010.

Anheuser-Busch InBev (Belgium)

A-B InBev has roots going back to 1366, but has transformed itself in the last decade with a series of spectacular mergers. First, InBev was created in 2004 from the merger of Belgian InterBrew and Brazilian AmBev. As well as making it the second largest brewing company in the world, this merger gave it a significant position in the Latin American soft drinks market. Then in 2008 InBev acquired the leading American brewer Anheuser-Busch for $52bn (~€36.4bn), making the company indisputably the world leader. The company now has nearly 300 brands, led by such well-known international beers as Beck's, Budweiser and Stella Artois. The company has nearly 50 per cent share of the US market, and owns 50 per cent of Mexico's leading brewer, Modelo, famous for its global Corona brand. In 2008, the new A-N InBev had four of the top ten selling beers in the world, and a number one or number two position in over 20 national markets. However, the company has been reducing its stake in the Chinese market in order to raise funds to pay for the Anheuser-Busch acquisition and to meet local monopoly authority concerns. It also sold its Central and Eastern beer operations in 2009.

The company is frank about its strategy: to transform itself from the biggest brewing company in the world to the best. It aims to do this by building strong global brands and increasing efficiency. Efficiency gains will come from more central coordination of purchasing, including media and IT; from the optimisation of its inherited network of breweries; and from the sharing of best practice across sites internationally.

A-B InBev is now emphasising organic growth and improved margins from its existing business. Its declared intention is to be 'The Best Beer Company in a Better World'.

Greene King (United Kingdom)

Established in 1799, Greene King is now the largest domestic British brewer, owner of famous brands such as Abbot, IPA and Old Speckled Hen. It has expanded through a series of acquisitions including Ruddles (1995), Morland (1999) and Hardys and Hansons (2006). Acquisition is typically followed by the closure of the acquired brewery, the termination of minor brands and the transfer of major brand production to its main brewery in Bury St Edmunds. This strategy has led to critics calling the company 'Greedy King'. IPA is the UK's top cask ale, with over 20 per cent of the on-trade market, and Old Speckled Hen is the top premium UK ale with more than one-eighth of the multiple retailer market. Greene King is unusual among contemporary breweries in operating many of its own pubs, having added to its original chain several acquisitions (notably Laurels with 432 pubs and Belhaven with 271). Greene King now operates nearly 2000 pubs across the United Kingdom, with a particularly dominant position in its home region of East Anglia. The company is also active in restaurants. Business is effectively confined to the UK market. In 2009, Greene King raised £207m (~€228m; ~$310m) on the financial markets in order to fund further acquisitions. Greene King explains its success formula in brewing thus: 'The Brewing Company's continued out-performance is driven by a consistent, focused strategy: most importantly, we brew high quality beer from an efficient, single-site brewery; [and] we have a focused brand portfolio, minimising the complexity and cost of a multibrand strategy.'

Tsingtao (China)

Tsingtao Brewery was founded in 1903 by German settlers in China. After state ownership under Communism, Tsingtao was privatised in the early 1990s and listed on the Hong Kong Stock Exchange in 1993. In 2009, the Japanese Asahi Breweries held 19.9 per cent of the shares, purchased from A-B InBev (which also sold the remainder of its original stake – 7 per cent – to a Chinese private investor). Tsingtao has 13 per cent market share of its home market but has long had an export orientation, accounting for more than 50 per cent of China's beer exports. Tsingtao Beer was introduced to the United States in 1972 and is the Chinese brand-leader in the US market. A bottle of Tsingtao appeared in the 1982 science fiction film *Blade Runner*. Tsingtao set up its European office in 1992 and its beer is now sold in 62 countries. The company has described its ambition thus: 'to promote the continuous growth of the sales volume and income to step forward (sic) the target of becoming an international great company'.

Sources: Ernst & Young, The Contribution Made by Beer to the European Economy, 2009; Euromonitor International, Global Alcoholic Drinks: Beer – Opportunities in Niche Categories, April, 2009; Euromonitor, Strategies for Growth in an Increasingly Consolidated Global Beer Market, February 2010.

Questions

1 Using the data from the case (and any other sources available), carry out for the Western European brewing industry (i) a PESTEL analysis and (ii) a five forces analysis. What do you conclude?

2 For the three breweries outlined above (or breweries of your own choice) explain:

 a how these trends will impact differently on these different companies; and

 b the relative strengths and weaknesses of each company.

3

STRATEGIC CAPABILITIES

Learning outcomes

After reading this chapter you should be able to:

- Identify what comprises *strategic capabilities* in terms of organisational *resources* and *competences* and how these relate to the strategies of organisations.

- Analyse how strategic capabilities might provide sustainable competitive advantage on the basis of their *value*, *rarity*, *inimitability* and *non-substitutability (VRIN)*.

- Diagnose strategic capability by means of *value chain analysis*, *activity mapping* and *SWOT analysis*.

PEARSON
mystrategylab

MyStrategyLab is designed to help you make the most of your studies. Visit **www.mystrategylab.com** to discover a wide range of resources specific to this chapter, including:

- A personalised **Study plan** that will help you understand core concepts.
- **Audio** and **video clips** that put the spotlight on strategy in the real world.
- **Online glossaries** and **flashcards** that provide helpful reminders when you're looking for some quick revision.

See p. xiv for further details.

(3.1) INTRODUCTION

Chapter 2 outlined how the external environment of an organisation can create both strategic opportunities and threats. However, manufacturers of saloon cars compete within the same market and within the same technological environment, but with markedly different success. BMW has been relatively successful consistently. Ford and Chrysler have found it more difficult to maintain their competitive position. And others, such as Rover in the UK, have gone out of business. It is not so much variations in the environment which explain these differences in performance, but the differences in their *strategic capabilities* in terms of the *resources and competences* they have or have tried to develop. It is the strategic importance of such capabilities that is the focus of this chapter.

The key issues posed by the chapter are summarised in Figure 3.1. Underlying these are two key concepts. The first is that organisations are not identical, but have different capabilities. The second is that it can be difficult for one organisation to obtain or copy the capabilities of another. For example, competitors cannot readily obtain or access a successful business's experience built up over decades of success. The implication for managers is that they need to understand how their organisations are different from their rivals in ways that may be the basis of achieving competitive advantage and superior performance. These concepts underlie what has become known as the **resource-based view** (RBV) of strategy[1] (though it might more appropriately be labelled the 'capabilities view'): **that the competitive advantage and superior performance of an organisation is explained by the distinctiveness of its capabilities**. RBV has become very influential in strategy and this chapter draws on it a good deal. It should be borne in mind, however, that there are different treatments of the topic. So, whilst the terminology and concepts employed here align with RBV, readers will find different terminology used elsewhere.

Figure 3.1 Strategic capabilities: the key issues

The chapter has four further sections:

- Section 3.2 discusses the foundations of *strategic capability*; in particular what is meant by *resources, competences* and the related concept of *dynamic capabilities*. It also draws a distinction between *threshold capabilities* required to be able to compete in a market and *distinctive capabilities* that may be a basis for achieving competitive advantage and superior performance.

- Section 3.3 explains the ways in which distinctive capabilities may contribute to the *developing and sustaining of competitive advantage* (in a public-sector context the equivalent concern might be how some organisations sustain relative superior performance over time). In particular, the importance of the *Value, Rarity, Inimitability* and *Non-substitutability (VRIN)* of capabilities is explained.

- Finally section 3.4 moves on to consider different ways in which strategic capability might be analysed. These include *value chain analysis* and *activity system mapping*. The section concludes by explaining the use of *SWOT* analysis as a basis for pulling together the insights from the analyses of the environment (explained in Chapter 2) and of strategic capabilities in this chapter.

(3.2) FOUNDATIONS OF STRATEGIC CAPABILITY

Given that different writers, managers and consultants use different terms and concepts it is important to understand how concepts relating to strategic capabilities are used in this book. Here **strategic capabilities** means **the capabilities of an organisation that contribute to its long-term survival or competitive advantage**. What follows in the rest of this section is an explanation of the components of such capabilities and the characteristics of those components.

3.2.1 Resources and competences

There are two components of strategic capability: resources and competences. **Resources are the assets that organisations have or can call upon** (e.g. from partners or suppliers); **competences are the ways those assets are used or deployed effectively**. A shorthand way of thinking of this is that resources are 'what we *have*' and competences are 'what we *do well*'. Other terms are common. For example, Gary Hamel and C.K. Prahalad refer to *core competences* and many writers use the term *intangible assets* as an umbrella term to include intangible resources such as brands and business systems as well as competences.

Typically, all strategic capabilities have elements of both resources and competences as Table 3.1 shows. Resources are certainly important, but how an organisation employs and deploys its resources matters at least as much. There would be no point in having state-of-the-art equipment if it were not used effectively. The efficiency and effectiveness of physical or financial resources, or the people in an organisation, depend, not just on their existence, but on the systems and processes by which they are managed, the relationships and cooperation between people, their adaptability, their innovatory capacity, the relationship with customers and suppliers and the experience and learning about what works well and what does not.

Table 3.1 Components of strategic capabilities

Strategic capability		
Resources: what we have, e.g.		**Competences: what we do well, e.g.**
Machines, buildings, raw materials, products, patents, data bases, computer systems	Physical	Ways of achieving utilisation of plant, efficiency, productivity, flexibility, marketing
Balance sheet, cash flow, suppliers of funds	Financial	Ability to raise funds and manage cash flows, debtors, creditors etc.
Managers, employees, partners, suppliers, customers	Human	How people gain and use experience, skills, knowledge, build relationships, motivate others and innovate

Long-term survival and competitive advantage

3.2.2 Dynamic capabilities[2]

If they are to provide a basis for long-term success, strategic capabilities cannot be static; they need to change. University of Berkeley economist David Teece has introduced the concept of **dynamic capabilities**, by which he means **an organisation's ability to renew and recreate its strategic capabilities to meet the needs of changing environments**. He argues that the capabilities that are necessary for efficient operations:

> maintaining incentive alignment, owning tangible assets, controlling costs, maintaining quality, optimizing inventories – are necessary but . . . are unlikely to be sufficient for sustaining superior performance.[3]

Moreover he acknowledges the further danger that capabilities that were the basis of competitive success may over time be imitated by competitors, become common practice in an industry or become redundant as its environment changes. Harvard's Dorothy Leonard-Barton also warns of the danger that, despite a changing environment, such capabilities can become 'rigidities'.[4] So, the important lesson is that if capabilities are to be effective over time they need to change; they cannot be static.

Dynamic capabilities may take the form of relatively formal organisational systems, such as recruitment and management development processes, or major strategic moves, such as acquisitions or alliances, by which new skills are learned and developed. For example, Stanford's Kathy Eisenhardt[5] has shown that successful acquisition processes can bring in new knowledge to organisations. However, this depends on high-quality pre- and post-acquisition understanding of how the acquisition can be integrated into the new organisation so as to capture synergies and bases of learning from that acquisition. As Teece acknowledges, then, dynamic capabilities are likely to have foundations in less formal, behavioural aspects of organisations, such as the way in which decisions get taken, personal relationships, and entrepreneurial and intuitive skills.

3.2.3 Threshold and distinctive capabilities

A distinction also needs to be made between strategic capabilities that are at a threshold level and those that might help the organisation achieve competitive advantage and superior performance. Table 3.2 summarises these distinctions.

Threshold capabilities are those needed for an organisation to meet the necessary requirements to compete in a given market and achieve parity with competitors in that market. Without such capabilities the organisation could not survive over time. Indeed, many start-up businesses find this to be the case. They simply do not have or cannot obtain the resources or competences needed to compete with established competitors. Identifying threshold requirements is, however, also important for established businesses. By the end of the first decade of the 21st century, BP faced declining oil output in countries such as the US, the UK and Russia. BP's board regarded securing new sources of supply as a major challenge. There could also be changing *threshold resources* required to meet minimum customer requirements: for example, the increasing demands by modern multiple retailers of their suppliers mean that those suppliers have to possess a quite sophisticated IT infrastructure simply to stand a chance of meeting retailer requirements. Or they could be the *threshold competences* required to deploy resources so as to meet customers' requirements and support particular strategies. Retailers do not simply expect suppliers to have the required IT infrastructure, but to be able to use it effectively so as to guarantee the required level of service.

While threshold capabilities are important, they do not of themselves create competitive advantage or the basis for superior performance. These are dependent on an organisation having distinctive or unique capabilities that are of value to customers and which competitors find difficult to imitate. This could be because the organisation has *distinctive resources* that critically underpin competitive advantage and that others cannot imitate or obtain – a long-established brand, for example. Or it could be that an organisation achieves competitive advantage because it has *distinctive competences* – ways of doing things that are unique to that organisation and effectively utilised so as to be valuable to customers and difficult for competitors to obtain or imitate. Gary Hamel and C.K. Prahalad[6] argue that the distinctive competences that are especially important are likely to be: 'a bundle of constituent skills and technologies

Table 3.2 Threshold and distinctive capabilities

	Resources	Competences
Threshold capabilities Required to be able to compete in a market	Threshold resources	Threshold competences
Distinctive capabilities Required to achieve competitive advantage	Distinctive resources	Distinctive competences

rather than a single, discrete skill or technology'. They use the term **core competences** to emphasise **the linked set of skills, activities and resources that, together, deliver customer value, differentiate a business from its competitors and, potentially, can be extended and developed.** Core competences may extend and develop as markets change or new opportunities arise. There are, then, also similarities here to Teece's conceptualisation of dynamic capabilities.

Bringing these concepts together, a supplier that achieves competitive advantage in a grocery retail market might have done so on the basis of a distinctive resource such as a powerful brand, but also by distinctive competences such as the building of excellent relations with retailers. However, it is likely that what will be most difficult for competitors to match and will therefore be the basis of competitive advantage will be the multiple and linked ways of providing products, high levels of service and building relationships – its core competence.

Illustration 3.1 shows how executives in the medical technology business of Sandvik explain the importance of its resources and capabilities.

Section 3.3 that follows discusses in more depth the role played by distinctive resources and competences in contributing to long-term, sustainable competitive advantage. Section 3.4 then explores further the importance of linkages of activities.

3.3 'VRIN': STRATEGIC CAPABILITIES AS A BASIS FOR COMPETITIVE ADVANTAGE

How, then, does a strategist consider on what bases organisational capabilities might be the foundation for sustainable competitive advantage and superior economic performance? As argued above, this is unlikely if the organisation is no different from its rivals and therefore has nothing that provides a basis for earning greater profits. Threshold capabilities may achieve parity with competitors, but not advantage over those competitors. Jay Barney, a leading proponent of RBV proposes four key criteria by which capabilities can be assessed in terms of their providing a basis for achieving such competitive advantage: Value, Rarity, Inimitability and Non-substitutability – or *VRIN*.[7]

3.3.1 V – value of strategic capabilities

Strategic capabilities are of **value** when they provide potential competitive advantage in a market at a cost that allows an organisation to realise acceptable levels of return (in the case of the private sector). There are four components here:

- *Taking advantage of opportunities and neutralising threats.* The most fundamental question is whether the capabilities provide the potential to address the opportunities and threats that arise in the organisation's environment.

- *Value.* It may seem an obvious point to make that capabilities need to be of value both to customers and to the well being of the organisation itself. In practice this can be overlooked or poorly understood. For example, managers may seek to build on capabilities that *they* may see as valuable but which do not meet customers' critical success factors (see section 2.4.3).

ILLUSTRATION 3.1

Sandvik's strategic capabilities

Strategic capabilities are central to the search for competitive advantage.

Swedish-based global industrial group, Sandvik, manufactures products for companies operating in a wide range of industries including medical technology. In a 2009 press release, it announced it had:

> invested in a technologically advanced direct metal laser sintering machine (DMLS) in order to provide rapid production capabilities to its customers, unique amongst contract manufacturers.
>
> Sandvik is now significantly reducing the time required to cost-effectively develop working prototypes, which means its customers can bring new innovations to market far more quickly than was previously possible. Sandvik is also exploiting the powder-based technique used by the DMLS machine to manufacture to almost any design, thereby removing limitations previously imposed on design teams within medical device OEMs (original equipment manufacturers). In an industry where innovation and speed to market are crucial differentiators, these benefits represent a real commercial advantage to OEMs.
>
> Through this investment and the enhanced capabilities it brings, Sandvik has further strengthened its position as a strategic partner to medical technology companies, helping them improve their competitiveness.

Tord Lendau, President of Sandvik MedTech, explained:

> Medical device OEMs operate in a highly competitive market. We want to leverage Sandvik's long experience within powder metallurgy to deliver real value to OEMs and so must continuously introduce new manufacturing techniques, which is why we have made this significant investment . . . Medical device manufacturers can now capitalise on enhanced capabilities and improve the speed to market of their new designs and innovations.

The press release continued:

> The new capabilities provided by the DMLS machine are ideal for the production of working prototypes of medical devices and for complex custom-made instruments.

It quoted John Reynolds, a special projects manager at Sandvik:

> Prototyping is an important stage in the creation of a new device, since it provides the opportunity to explore the design and make the necessary adjustments prior to full production. However, most rapid prototyping processes do not produce a working model, while those that do are time consuming and more expensive . . . By using the DMLS machine we can bring to bear rapid production techniques that enable us to quickly and cost-effectively manufacture a working prototype. This means our customers can present a working model to their customers in a fraction of the time it would take with conventional manufacturing techniques and bring the final design to market far quicker . . . We can also now manufacture almost any design the OEM can create, irrespective of the complexity of the geometry. This means our customers' design teams are not constrained by the manufacturing limitations previously typical in the industry. They have the flexibility to respond with precision to the individual preferences of any one surgeon or the specific needs of a patient.

The press release concluded:

> By enhancing its capabilities through this significant investment and combining it with its materials and manufacturing expertise, Sandvik is helping OEMs achieve real competitive advantage in a challenging market.

Source: www.smt.sandvik.com/sandvik. © AB Sandvik Materials Technology.

Questions

1 Categorise Sandvik's range of capabilities in terms of section 3.2. and Tables 3.1 and 3.2.

2 Assess the bases of Sandvik's strategic capabilities using the VRIN criteria (section 3.3).

3 Which are the key strategic capabilities which provide, or could provide, Sandvik with sustainable competitive advantage?

Or they may see a distinctive capability as of value simply because it is distinctive. Having capabilities that are different from other organisations is not, of itself, a basis for competitive advantage. So the discussion in sections 3.3.2 and 3.3.3 and the lessons it draws are important here.

- *Providing potential competitive advantage.* The capabilities do, nonetheless, need to be capable of delivering a product or service that competitors do not currently have or do not currently emphasise.

- *Cost.* The product or service needs to be provided at a cost that still allows the organisation to make the returns expected of it (e.g. by investors). The danger is that the cost of developing the capabilities to deliver what customers especially value is such that products or services are not profitable.

Managers should therefore consider carefully which of their organisation's activities are especially important in providing such value and which are of less value. Value chain analysis and activity mapping explained in sections 3.4.1 and 3.4.2 can help here.

3.3.2 R – rarity

If competitors have similar capabilities, they can respond quickly to the strategic initiative of a rival. This has happened in competition between car manufacturers as they have sought to add more accessories and gadgets to cars. As soon as it becomes evident that these are valued by customers, they are introduced widely by competitors who typically have access to the same technology. **Rare capabilities**, on the other hand, **are those possessed uniquely by one organisation or by a few others**. Here competitive advantage might be longer-lasting. For example, a company may have patented products or services that give it advantage. Service organisations may have rare resources in the form of intellectual capital – perhaps particularly talented individuals. Some libraries have unique collections of books unavailable elsewhere; a company may have a powerful brand; or retail stores may have prime locations. In terms of competences, organisations may have unique skills developed over time or have built special relationships with customers or suppliers not widely possessed by competitors. However, there are two important points to bear in mind about the extent to which rarity might provide competitive advantage:

- *Meeting customer need.* Again rarity, of itself, is of little value unless the resources or capabilities lead to outputs in the form of products or services that meet customer needs and are therefore of value to them.

- *Sustainability.* Rarity could be temporary. For example, uniquely talented individuals may be an advantage but can also be a risk. In 2009, and again in 2011, the financial press reported increasing concerns about Apple, given the health of its CEO Steve Jobs, with headlines such as: 'Can Apple survive without Steve Jobs?'[8] Moreover, it may be dangerous to assume that resources and capabilities that are rare will remain so. If an organisation is successful on the basis of something distinctive, then competitors will very likely seek to imitate or obtain that distinctiveness. So it may be necessary to consider other bases of sustainability.

3.3.3 I – inimitability

It should be clear by now that the search for strategic capability that provides sustainable competitive advantage is not straightforward. Having capabilities that are valuable to customers and relatively rare is important, but this may not be enough. Sustainable competitive advantage also involves identifying **inimitable capabilities** – **those that competitors find difficult to imitate or obtain**.

At the risk of over-generalisation, it is unusual for competitive advantage to be explainable by differences in the tangible resources of organisations, since over time these can usually be acquired or imitated. Advantage is more likely to be determined by the way in which resources are deployed and managed in terms of an organisation's activities; in other words on the basis of competences.[9] For example, it is unlikely an IT system will improve an organisation's competitive standing of itself, not least because competitors can probably buy something very similar in the open market. On the other hand, the capabilities to manage, develop and deploy such a system to the benefit of customers may be much more difficult to imitate. This is likely to be so if two conditions are met.

- *Superior performance*. The capabilities lead to levels of performance of product or service that are significantly better than competitors'.
- *Linked competences*. If the capability integrates activities, skills and knowledge both inside and outside the organisation in distinct and mutually compatible ways. It is, then, the *linkages* of the activities that go to make up capabilities that can be especially significant.

There are four reasons that may make capabilities particularly difficult for competitors to imitate.

Complexity

The capabilities of an organisation may be difficult to imitate because they are complex. This may be for two main reasons.

- *Internal linkages*. There may be linked activities and processes that, together, deliver customer value. The discussion of activity systems in section 3.4.2 below explains this in more detail and shows how such linked sets of activities might be mapped so that they can be better understood.
- *External linkages*. Organisations can make it difficult for others to imitate or obtain their bases of competitive advantage by developing activities together with the customer such that the customer becomes dependent on them. For example, an industrial lubricants business moved away from just selling its products to customers by coming to an agreement with them to manage the applications of lubricants within the customers' sites against agreed targets on cost savings. The more efficient the use of lubricants, the more both parties benefited. Similarly software businesses can achieve advantage by developing computer programs that are distinctively beneficial to specific customer needs.

Causal ambiguity[10]

Another reason why capabilities might be difficult to imitate is that competitors find it difficult to discern the causes and effects underpinning an organisation's advantage. This is called *causal ambiguity*. This might be for at least two reasons. First, because the capability itself is difficult to discern or comprehend, perhaps because it is based on tacit knowledge based on people's experience. For example, the know-how of the buyers in a successful fashion retailer may be evident in the sales achieved for the ranges they buy, but it may be very difficult for a competitor to see just what that know-how is. Second, because competitors may not be able to discern which activities and processes are dependent on which others to form linkages that create core competences. The expertise of the fashion buyers is unlikely to be lodged in the one individual or even one function. It is likely that there will be a network of suppliers, intelligence networks to understand the market and links with designers.

Culture and history

Competences may become embedded in an organisation's culture. So coordination between various activities occurs 'naturally' because people know their part in the wider picture or it is simply 'taken for granted' that activities are done in particular ways. We see this in high-performing groups or sports teams that work together to combine specialist skills, but also in how some firms integrate different activities in their business to deliver excellent customer service.

Change

The concept of dynamic capabilities is relevant here. If an organisation builds a basis of competitive advantage on resources or capabilities that change as the dynamics of a market or the needs of customers change, they will be more difficult for competitors to imitate. Indeed, arguably, organisations that wish to be market leaders, to innovate and create new markets, must do so on the basis of dynamic capabilities. They are, in effect, continually seeking to stay ahead of their competitors by evolving new bases for doing so.

3.3.4 N – non-substitutability[11]

Providing value to customers and possessing competences that are rare and difficult to imitate may mean that it is very difficult for organisations to copy them. However, the organisation may still be at risk from substitution. Substitution could take two different forms:

- *Product or service substitution.* As already discussed in Chapter 2 in relation to the five forces model of competition, a product or service as a whole might be a victim of substitution. For example, increasingly e-mail systems have substituted for postal systems. No matter how complex and culturally embedded were the competences of the postal service, it could not avoid this sort of substitution.

- *Competence substitution.* Substitution might, however, not be at the product or service level but at the competence level. For example, task-based industries have often suffered because of an over-reliance on the competences of skilled craft workers who have been replaced by expert systems and mechanisation.

In summary and from a resource-based view of organisations, managers need to consider whether their organisation has strategic capabilities to achieve and sustain competitive

Figure 3.2 VRIN

V	**Value:** Do capabilities exist that are valued by customers and provide potential competitive advantage?
R	**Rarity:** Do capabilities exist that no (or few) competitors possess?
I	**Inimitability:** Are capabilities difficult for competitors to imitate?
N	**Non-substitutability:** Is the risk of capability substitution low?

Increasing bases of sustainable competitive advantage

advantage – to do so they need to consider how and to what extent it has capabilities which are (i) valuable to buyers, (ii) rare, (iii) inimitable and (iv) non-substitutable.

As Figure 3.2 shows, there is an additive effect here. Strategic capabilities provide sustainable bases of competitive advantage the more they meet all four criteria. If such capabilities for competitive advantage do not exist, then managers need to consider if they can be developed.

3.4 DIAGNOSING STRATEGIC CAPABILITIES

So far, this chapter has been concerned with explaining concepts associated with the strategic significance of organisations' resources and capabilities. This section now explains ways in which strategic capabilities can be understood and diagnosed.

3.4.1 The value chain and value network

The **value chain** describes the categories of activities within an organisation which, together, **create a product or service.** Most organisations are also part of a wider **value network, the set of inter-organisational links and relationships that are necessary to create a product or service.** Both are useful in understanding the strategic position of an organisation.

KEY CONCEPT

www.mystrategylab.com

Value chain and value network

The value chain

If organisations are to achieve competitive advantage by delivering value to customers, managers need to understand which of the activities their organisation undertakes are especially important in creating that value and which are not. It can, then, be used to model the value system of an organisation. The important point is that the concept of the value chain invites the strategist to think of an organisation in terms of sets of activities. There are different frameworks for considering these categories: Figure 3.3 is a representation of a value chain as developed by Michael Porter.[12]

Primary activities are directly concerned with the creation or delivery of a product or service, for example, for a manufacturing business.

Figure 3.3 The value chain within an organisation

- *Inbound logistics* are activities concerned with receiving, storing and distributing inputs to the product or service including materials handling, stock control, transport etc.

- *Operations* transform these inputs into the final product or service: machining, packaging, assembly, testing etc.

- *Outbound logistics* collect, store and distribute the product to customers; for example, warehousing, materials handling, distribution.

- *Marketing and sales* provide the means whereby consumers or users are made aware of the product or service and are able to purchase it. This includes sales administration, advertising and selling.

- *Service* includes those activities that enhance or maintain the value of a product or service, such as installation, repair, training and spares.

Each of these groups of primary activities is linked to *support activities* which help to improve the effectiveness or efficiency of primary activities.

- *Procurement*. Processes that occur in many parts of the organisation for acquiring the various resource inputs to the primary activities. These can be vitally important in achieving scale advantages. So, for example, many large consumer goods companies with multiple businesses none the less procure advertising centrally.

- *Technology development*. All value activities have a 'technology', even if it is just know-how. Technologies may be concerned directly with a product (e.g. R&D, product design) or with processes (e.g. process development) or with a particular resource (e.g. raw materials improvements).

- *Human resource management*. This transcends all primary activities and is concerned with recruiting, managing, training, developing and rewarding people within the organisation.

- *Infrastructure*. The formal systems of planning, finance, quality control, information management and the structure of an organisation.

The value chain can be used to understand the strategic position of an organisation in three ways.

- As a *generic description of activities* it can help managers understand if there is a cluster of activities providing benefit to customers located within particular areas of the value chain. Perhaps a business is especially good at outbound logistics linked to its marketing and sales operation and supported by its technology development. It might be less good in terms of its operations and its inbound logistics.

- In *analysing the competitive position of the organisation* using the VRIN criteria as follows:

  V Which value-creating activities are especially significant for an organisation in meeting customer needs and could they be usefully developed further?

  R To what extent and how does an organisation have bases of value creation that are *rare*? Or conversely are all elements of their value chain common to their competitors?

  I What aspects of value creation are difficult for others to *imitate*, perhaps because they are *embedded* in the activity systems of the organisation (see section 3.4.2 below)?

  N What aspects of the value chain are or are not vulnerable to substitution?

- To *analyse the cost and value of activities*[13] of an organisation. This could involve considering the following steps:

  - *Relative importance of activity costs internally*. Does the significance of the costs align with the strategic significance of the activities? Which activities most add value to the final product or service (and in turn to the customer) and which do not? For example, organisations that have undertaken such analyses often find that central services have grown to the extent that they are a disproportionate cost to internal sets of activities and to the customer.

  - *Relative importance of activities externally*. How does value and the cost of a set of activities compare with the similar activities of competitors? For example, although they are both global oil businesses, BP and Shell are different in terms of the significance of their value chain activities. BP has historically outperformed Shell in terms of exploration; but the reverse is the case with regard to refining and marketing.

  - *Where and how can costs be reduced?* For example, can costs be reduced in some areas without affecting the value created for customers? Can some activities be outsourced, for example, those that are relatively free-standing and do not add value significantly? Can cost savings be made by increasing economies of scale or scope; for example, through central procurement or consolidating currently fragmented activities (e.g. manufacturing units)?

The value network

A single organisation rarely undertakes in-house all of the value activities from design through to the delivery of the final product or service to the final consumer. There is usually specialisation of roles so, as Figure 3.4 shows, any one organisation is part of a wider *value network.* There are questions that arise here that also build on an understanding of the value chain.

● *What are the activities and cost/price structures of the value network?* Just as costs can be analysed across the internal value chain, they can also be analysed across the value network: Illustration 3.2 shows how value network analysis was used by Ugandan fish farmers as a way of identifying what they should focus on in developing a more profitable business model.

● *The 'make or buy'* or *outsourcing* decision for a particular activity is critical given some of the above questions. Increasingly, outsourcing is becoming common as a means of lowering costs. Of course, the more an organisation outsources, the more its ability to influence the performance of other organisations in the value network may become a critically important capability in itself and even a source of competitive advantage. For example, the quality of a cooker or a television when it reaches the final purchaser is not only influenced by the

ILLUSTRATION 3.2

A value chain for Ugandan chilled fish fillet exports

Even small enterprises can be part of an international value chain. Analysing it can provide strategic benefits.

A fish factory in Uganda barely made any profit. Fish were caught from small motorboats owned by poor fishermen from local villages. Just before they set out they would collect ice and plastic fish boxes from the agents who bought the catch on their return. The boxes were imported, along with tackle and boat parts. All supplies had to be paid for in cash in advance by the agents. Sometimes ice and supplies were not available in time. Fish landed with insufficient ice achieved half of the price of iced fish, and sometimes could not be sold to the agents at all. The fish factory had always processed the fillets in the same way – disposing of the waste back into the lake. Once a week, some foreign traders would come and buy the better fillets; they didn't say who they sold them to, and sometimes they didn't buy very much.

By mapping the value chain it was clear that there were opportunities for capturing more value along the chain and reducing losses. Together with outside specialists, the fish factory and the fishing community developed

a strategy to improve their capabilities, as indicated in the figure, until they became a flourishing international business, The Lake Victoria Fish Company, with regular air-freight exports around the world. You can see more of their current operations at http://www.ufpea.co.ug/, and find out more about the type of analytical process applied at www.justreturn.ch.

(The approximate costs and prices given represent the situation before improvements were implemented.)

Questions

1 Draw up a value chain for another business in terms of the activities within its component parts.

2 Estimate the relative costs and/or assets associated with these activities.

3 What are the strategic implications of your analysis?

Figure 3.4 The value network

Source: Adapted from *Competitive Advantage: Creating and Sustaining Superior Performance* (Michael E. Porter 1998) with the permission of The Free Press, a Division of Simon & Schuster Adult Publishing Group, Copyright © 1985, 1998 by Michael E. Porter. All rights reserved.

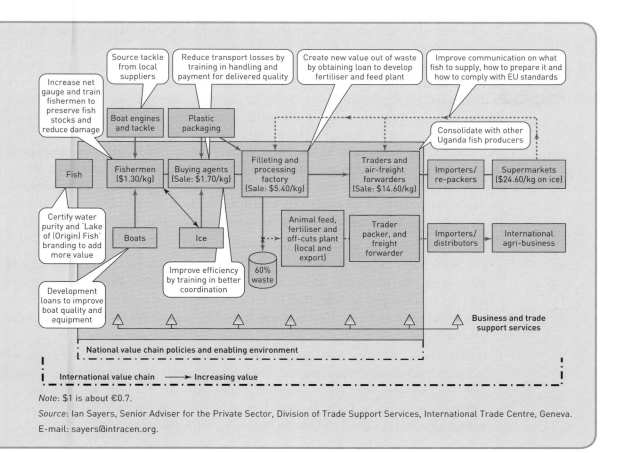

Note: $1 is about €0.7.

Source: Ian Sayers, Senior Adviser for the Private Sector, Division of Trade Support Services, International Trade Centre, Geneva. E-mail: sayers@intracen.org.

activities undertaken within the manufacturing company itself, but also by the quality of components from suppliers and the performance of the distributors. There is, of course, the converse question: which activities most need to be part of the internal value chain because they are central to achieving competitive advantage?.

- *Partnering.* Who might be the best partners in the parts of the value network? And what kind of *relationships* are important to develop with each partner? For example, should they be regarded as suppliers or should they be regarded as alliance partners (see section 9.4),

3.4.2 Activity systems

The discussion so far highlights the fact that all organisations comprise sets of capabilities, but that these are likely to be configured differently across organisations. It is this variable configuration of capabilities that makes an organisation and its strategy more or less unique. So for the strategist, understanding this matters a good deal.

Value chain analysis can help with this, but so too can understanding the activity systems of an organisation. So it is important to identify what these activities are, why they are valuable to customers, how the various activities fit together and how they differ from those of competitors.

A number of the writers,[14] including Michael Porter, have written about the importance of mapping activity systems and shown how this might be done.

The starting point is to identify what Porter refers to as 'higher order strategic themes'. In effect, these are the ways in which the organisation meets the critical success factors in the market. The next step is to identify the clusters of activities that underpin each of these themes and how these do or do not fit together. The result is a picture of the organisation represented in terms of activity systems such as that shown in Illustration 3.3. This shows an activity systems map for the Scandinavian strategic communications consultancy, Geelmuyden.Kiese.[15] At the heart of its success is its knowledge, built over the years, of how effective communications can influence 'the power dynamics of decision making processes'. However, as Illustration 3.3 shows, this central theme is related to other higher-order strategic themes, each of which is underpinned by clusters of activities. Four points should be emphasised here:

- *The importance of linkages and fit.* An activity systems map emphasises the importance of different activities that create value to customers pulling in the same direction and supporting rather than opposing each other. So the need is to understand (a) the fit between the various activities and how these reinforce each other and (b) the fit externally with the needs of clients.

- *Relationship to VRIN.* It is these linkages and this fit that can be the bases of sustainable competitive advantage. In combination they may be *valuable* to clients, truly distinctive and therefore *rare.* Moreover, while individual components of an activity system might be relatively easy to imitate, in combination they may well constitute the complexity and causal ambiguity rooted in culture and history that makes them *difficult to imitate.*

- *Disaggregation.*[16] Useful as an activity map is, the danger is that, in seeking to explain capabilities underpinning their strategy, managers may identify capabilities at too abstract a level. If the strategic benefits of activity systems are to be understood, greater disaggregation is likely to be needed. For example, managers may talk of 'innovation' or 'putting the customer first' as a basis for 'good service'. These terms are, however, generic descriptors of activities that exist at an even more operational level than those shown in the activity map. If an activity map is to be useful for the purposes of managing activities then managers need to identify specific activities at an operating level that are manageable. To take an example from Illustration 3.3, there is the recognition that the mentoring of junior staff by partners is important; but the map itself does not show specifically how this is done.

- *Superfluous activities.* Just as in value chain analysis, but at a more detailed level, the question can be asked: are there activities that are not required in order to pursue a particular strategy? Or how do activities contribute to value creation? If activities do not do this, why are they being pursued by the organisation? Whether Ryanair used activity mapping or not, they have systematically identified and done away with many activities that other airlines commonly have. They are also continually seeking further activities that can be eliminated or outsourced to reduce cost.

3.4.3 SWOT[17]

It can be helpful to summarise the key issues arising from an analysis of the business environment and the capabilities of an organisation to gain an overall picture of its strategic position. **SWOT summarises the strengths, weaknesses, opportunities and threats likely to impact on strategy development** that arise from such analyses. This can also be useful as a basis against which to generate strategic options and assess future courses of action.

The aim is to identify the extent to which strengths and weaknesses are relevant to, or capable of dealing with, the changes taking place in the business environment. Illustration 3.4 takes the example of a pharmaceuticals firm (Pharmcare). It assumes that key environmental impacts have been identified from analyses explained in Chapter 2 and that major strengths and weaknesses have been identified using the analytic tools explained in this chapter. A scoring mechanism (+5 to −5) is used as a means of getting managers to assess the interrelationship between the environmental impacts and the strengths and weaknesses of the firm. A positive (+) denotes that the strength of the company would help it take advantage of, or counteract, a problem arising from an environmental change or that a weakness would be offset by that change. A negative (−) score denotes that the strength would be reduced or that a weakness would prevent the organisation from overcoming problems associated with that change.

Pharmcare's share price had been declining because investors were concerned that its strong market position was under threat. This had not been improved by a merger that was proving problematic. The pharmaceutical market was changing, with new ways of doing business, driven by new technology, the quest to provide medicines at lower cost and politicians seeking ways to cope with soaring healthcare costs and an ever more informed patient. But was Pharmcare keeping pace? The strategic review of the firm's position (Illustration 3.4(a))

ILLUSTRATION 3.3

Activity systems at Geelmuyden.Kiese

The strategic capabilities of an organisation can be understood and analysed in terms of linked activities (an activity system)

Geelmuyden.Kiese is a Scandinavian strategic communications consultancy – an extension of what has traditionally been known as public relations services (PR). Their clients include organisations in the financial, oil, energy, pharmaceuticals and healthcare sectors. These clients typically approach Geelmuyden.Kiese when they have a problem, the solution for which critically depends on effective external or internal communication. In this context, Geelmuyden.Kiese's services include facilitation of contacts with public agencies, officials and government, investor relations, media relations, communication campaigns for new product launches, crisis management and in-company communication on key strategic issues.

At the heart of the company's success is the knowledge they have built up since their founding in 1989 of the dynamics of decision-making processes, often within influential bodies such as government and, linked to this, 'how effective communication may move power within those decision making processes'. This knowledge is underpinned by some key aspects in the way in which they do business, summarised here and shown as an activity system opposite.

- They seek to *work at a strategic level* with their clients, prioritising those clients where such work is especially valued. Here they employ their own in-house methodology, developed on the basis of their years of experience, and systematically review the assignments they undertake both internally and on the basis of client surveys.

- They take a clear stance on *integrity of communication*. They always advise openness of communication rather than suppression of information and only deal with clients who will accept such principles. They also take a stance on this approach often in controversial and high profile issues in the public domain.

- Staff are given high degrees of *freedom*, but with some absolute criteria of *responsibility*. In this regard there are strict rules for handling clients' confidential information and strict sanctions if such rules are broken.

- *Recruitment* is based on ensuring that such responsibility can be achieved. It is largely on the basis of values of openness, integrity but also humour. The emphasis tends to be on recruiting junior personnel and developing them. Geelmuyden.Kiese has learned that this is a better way of delivering its services than recruiting established 'high profile' consultants. Combined with its mentoring system for competence development of junior staff, they therefore believe that it offers the *best learning opportunities* inScandinavia for young communications consultants.

- Geelmuyden.Kiese also offers *strong financial incentives* for top performance within the firm. Such performance includes rewards for the development of junior personnel, but is also based on the internal evaluation of leadership qualities and performance.

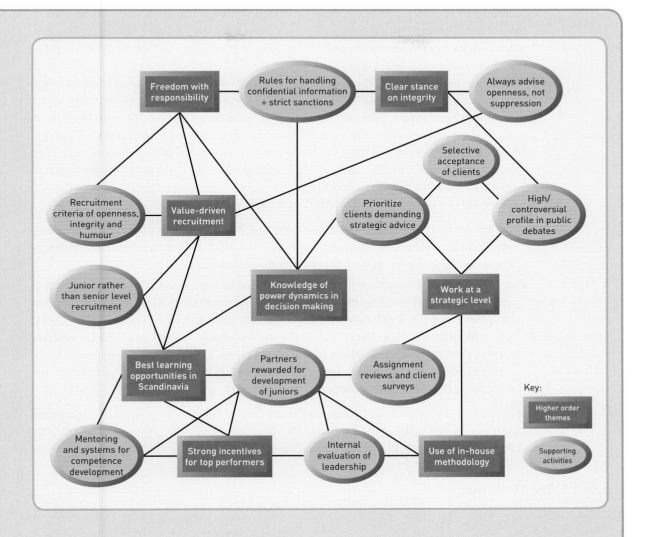

Questions

1 Assuming Geelmuyden.Kiese managers are correct that they have capabilities that provide competitive advantage:
   a What would competitors find difficult to imitate and why?
   b Are there any activities that could be done away with without threatening that advantage?

2 If disaggregation (see section 3.4.2) is important, suggest what even more specific activites underpinning those in the activity map that might be important.

confirmed its strengths of a flexible salesforce, well-known brand name and new healthcare department. However, there were major weaknesses, namely relative failure on low-cost drugs, competence in information and communication technology (ICT) and a failure to get to grips with increasingly well-informed users.

However, in the context of this chapter, if this analysis is to be useful, it must be remembered that the exercise is not absolute but relative to its competitors. So SWOT analysis is most useful when it is comparative – if it examines strengths, weaknesses, opportunities and threats in relation to competitors. When the impact of environmental forces on competitors was analysed (Illustration 3.4(b)), it showed that Pharmcare was still outperforming its traditional competitor (Company W), but potentially vulnerable to changing dynamics in the general industry structure courtesy of niche players (X and Y).

There are two main dangers in a SWOT exercise:

● *Listing.* A SWOT exercise can generate very long lists of apparent strengths, weaknesses, opportunities and threats, whereas what matters is to be clear about what is really important and what is less important. So prioritisation of issues matters.

● *A summary, not a substitute.* SWOT analysis is an engaging and fairly simple tool. It is also useful in summarising and consolidating other analysis that has been explained in Chapters 2 and 3. It is not, however, a substitute for that analysis. There are two dangers if it is used on its own. The first is that, in the absence of more thorough analysis, managers rely on preconceived, often inherited and biased views. The second is again the danger of a lack of specificity. Identifying very general strengths, for example, does not explain the underlying reasons for those strengths.

SWOT can also help focus discussion on future choices and the extent to which an organisation is capable of supporting these strategies. A useful way of doing this is to use a TOWS matrix[18] as shown in Figure 3.5. This builds directly on the information in a SWOT exercise. Each box

Figure 3.5 The TOWS matrix

		Internal factors	
		Strengths (S)	**Weaknesses (W)**
External factors	**Opportunities (O)**	**SO Strategic options** Generate options here that use srengths to take advantage of opportunities	**WO Strategic options** Generate options here that take advantage of opportunities by overcoming weaknesses
	Threats (T)	**ST Strategic options** Generate options here that use srengths to avoid threats	**WT Strategic options** Generate options here that minimise weaknesses and avoid threats

ILLUSTRATION 3.4

SWOT analysis of Pharmcare

A SWOT analysis explores the relationship between the environmental influences and the strategic capabilities of an organisation compared with its competitors.

(a) SWOT analysis for Pharmcare

	Environmental change (opportunities and threats)					
	Healthcare rationing	Complex and changing buying structures	Increased integration of healthcare	Informed patients	+	−
Strengths						
Flexible salesforce	+3	+5	+2	+2	12	0
Economies of scale	0	0	+3	+3	+6	0
Strong brand name	+2	+1	0	−1	3	−1
Healthcare education department	+4	+3	+4	+5	+16	0
Weaknesses						
Limited competences in biotechnology and genetics	0	0	−4	−3	0	−7
Ever lower R&D productivity	−3	−2	−1	−2	0	−8
Weak ICT competences	−2	−2	−5	−5	0	−14
Over-reliance on leading product	−1	−1	−3	−1	0	−6
Environmental impact scores	+9	+9	+9	+10		
	−6	−5	−13	−12		

(b) Competitor SWOT analyses

	Environmental change (opportunities and threats)				
	Healthcare rationing	Complex and changing buying structures	Increased integration of healthcare	Informed and passionate patients	Overall impact
Pharmcare *Big global player suffering fall in share price, low research productivity and post-mega-merger bureaucracy*	−3 Struggling to prove cost-effectiveness of new drugs to new regulators of healthcare rationing	+6 Well-known brand, a flexible salesforce combined with a new healthcare education department creates positive synergy	−3 Weak ICT and lack of integration following mergers means sales, research and admin. are all underperforming	−2 Have yet to get into the groove of patient power fuelled by the internet	−2 Declining performance over time worsened after merger
Company W *Big pharma with patchy response to change, losing ground in new areas of competition*	−4 Focus is on old-style promotional selling rather than helping doctors control costs through drugs	−4 Traditional salesforce not helped by marketing which can be unaccommodating of national differences	+0 Alliances with equipment manufacturers, but little work done across alliance to show dual use of drugs and new surgical techniques	+4 New recruits in the ICT department have worked cross-functionally to involve patients like never before	−4 Needs to modernise across the whole company
Organisation X *Partnership between a charity managed by people with venture capital experience and top hospital geneticists*	+3 Potentially able to deliver rapid advances in genetic-based illnesses	+2 Able possibly to bypass these with innovative cost effective drug(s)	+2 Innovative drugs can help integrate health care through enabling patients to stay at home	+3 Patients will fight for advances in treatment areas where little recent progress has been made	+10 Could be the basis of a new business model for drug discovery – but all to prove as yet
Company Y *Only develops drugs for less common diseases*	+3 Partnering with big pharma allows the development of drugs discovered by big pharma but not economical for them to develop	0 Focus on small market segments so not as vulnerable to overall market structure, but innovative approach might be risky	+2 Innovative use of web to show why products still worthwhile developing even for less common illnesses	+1 Toll-free call centres for sufferers of less common illnesses. Company, like patients, is passionate about its mission	+6 Novel approach can be considered either risky or a winner, or both!

Questions

1 What does the SWOT analysis tell us about the competitive position of Pharmcare with the industry as a whole?

2 How readily do you think executives of Pharmcare identify the strengths and weaknesses of competitors?

3 Identify the benefits and dangers (other than those identified in the text) of a SWOT analysis such as that in the illustration.

Prepared by Jill Shepherd, Segal Graduate School of Business, Simon Fraser University, Vancouver, Canada.

of the TOWS matrix can be used to identify options that address a different combination of the internal factors (strengths and weaknesses) and the external factors (opportunities and threats). For example, the top left-hand box prompts a consideration of options that use the strengths of the organisation to take advantage of opportunities in the business environment. An example for Pharmcare might be the re-training of the sales force to deal with changes in pharmaceuticals buying. The bottom right-hand box prompts options that minimise weaknesses and also avoid threats; for Pharmcare this might include the need to develop their ICT systems to service better more informed patients. Quite likely this would also help take advantage of opportunities arising from changes in the buying structure of the industry (top right). The bottom left box suggests the need to use strengths to avoid threats, perhaps by building on the success of their healthcare education department to also better service informed patients.

SUMMARY

- *The competitive advantage* of an organisation is likely to be based on the strategic *capabilities* it has that are valuable to customers and that its rivals do not have or have difficulty in obtaining. Strategic capabilities comprise both *resources* and *competences*.

- The concept of *dynamic capabilities* highlights that strategic capabilities need to change as the market and environmental context of an organisation changes.

- Sustainability of competitive advantage is likely to depend on an organisation's capabilities being of at least *threshold value* in a market but also being *valuable*, relatively *rare*, *inimitable* and *non-substitutable*.

- Ways of *diagnosing organisational capabilities* include:

- Analysing an organisation's *value chain* and *value network* as a basis for understanding how value to a customer is created and can be developed.

  - *Activity mapping* as a means of identifying more detailed activities which underpin strategic capabilities.

  - *SWOT analysis* as a way of drawing together an understanding of the strengths, weaknesses, opportunities and threats an organisation faces.

VIDEO CASE

Visit **MyStrategyLab** and watch the *Maersk* case study.

1 What are the strategic capabilities that Maersk claim provide them with competitive advantage in the global freight market?

2 Drawing on VRIN, suggest on what bases might these be sustainable over time.

RECOMMENDED KEY READINGS

- For an understanding of the resource-based view of the firm, an early and much cited paper is by Jay Barney: 'Firm resources and sustained competitive advantage', *Journal of Management*, vol. 17 (1991), pp. 99–120.

- Michael Porter explains how mapping activity systems can be important in considering competitive strategy in his article 'What is strategy?' (*Harvard Business Review*, November–December 1996, pp. 61–78).

- For a critical discussion of the use and misuse of SWOT analysis see T. Hill and R. Westbrook, 'SWOT analysis: it's time for a product recall', *Long Range Planning*, vol. 30, no. 1 (1997), pp. 46–52.

REFERENCES

1. The concept of resource-based strategies was introduced by B. Wernerfelt, 'A resource-based view of the firm', *Strategic Management Journal*, vol. 5, no. 2 (1984), pp. 171–80. A much cited paper is by Jay Barney: 'Firm resources and sustained competitive advantage', *Journal of Management*, vol. 17, no. 1 (1991), pp. 99–120.

2. For summary papers on dynamic capabilities see C.L. Wang and P.K. Ahmed, 'Dynamic capabilities: a review and research agenda', *International Journal of Management Reviews*, vol. 9, no. 1 (2007), pp. 31–52, and V. Ambrosini and C. Bowman, 'What are dynamic capabilities and are they a useful construct in strategic management?', *International Journal of Management Reviews*, vol. 11, no. 1 (2009), pp. 29–49.

3. David Teece has written about dynamic capabilities; see D. Teece, Explicating dynamic capabilities: the nature and microfoundations of (sustainable) enterprise performance, *Strategic Management Journal*, vol. 28 (2007), pp. 1319–50, pp. 1320–21.

4. D. Leonard-Barton, 'Core capabilities and core rigidities: a paradox in managing new product development', *Strategic Management Journal*, vol. 13 (1992), pp. 111–25.

5. K.M. Eisenhardt and J.A. Martin, 'Dynamic capabilities: what are they?', *Strategic Management Journal*, vol. 21, no. 10/11 (2000), pp. 1105–21.

6. Gary Hamel and C.K. Prahalad were the academics who promoted the idea of core competences. For example, G. Hamel and C.K. Prahalad, 'The core competence of the corporation', *Harvard Business Review*, vol. 68, no. 3 (1990), pp. 79–91.

7. The VRIN criteria were originally introduced by Jay Barney in his 1991 paper (see 1 above).

8. 'Can Apple survive without Steve Jobs', *Sunday Times*, 18 January 2009.

9. This is borne out in a meta-study of research on RBV by S.L. Newbert, 'Empirical, research on the Resource Based View of the firm: an assessment and suggestions for future research, *Strategic Management Journal*, vol. 28, (2007), pp. 121–46.

10. The seminal paper on causal ambiguity is S. Lippman and R. Rumelt, 'Uncertain imitability: an analysis of inter-firm differences in efficiency under competition', *Bell Journal of Economics*, vol. 13 (1982), pp. 418–38.

11. The importance of non-substitutability and ways of identifying possible bases of substitution are discussed in M.A. Peteraf and M.E. Bergen, 'Scanning dynamic competitive landscapes: a market and resource based framework', *Strategic Management Journal*, vol. 24, no. 10 (2003), pp. 1027–42.

12. An extensive discussion of the value chain concept and its application can be found in M.E. Porter, *Competitive Advantage*, Free Press, 1985.

13. For an extended example of value chain analysis see Andrew Shepherd, 'Understanding and using value chain analysis', in V. Ambrosini (ed.), *Exploring Techniques of Analysis and Evaluation in Strategic Management*, Prentice Hall, 1998.

14. See M. Porter, 'What is strategy?', *Harvard Business Review*, November–December 1996, pp. 61–78; and N. Siggelkow, 'Evolution towards fit', *Administrative Science Quarterly*, vol. 47, no. 1 (2002), pp. 125–59.

15. We are grateful for this example based on the doctoral dissertation of Bjorn Haugstad, 'Strategy as the intentional structuration of practice, translation of formal strategies into strategies in practice', submitted to the Saïd Business School, University of Oxford in 2009.

16. 'Disaggregation' is a term used by D. Collis and C. Montgomery, 'Competing on resources', *Harvard Business Review*, July–August 2008, pp. 140–50.

17. The idea of SWOT as a commonsense checklist has been used for many years: for example, S. Tilles, 'Making strategy explicit', in I. Ansoff (ed.), *Business Strategy*, Penguin, 1968. For a critical discussion of the (mis)use of SWOT, see T. Hill and R. Westbrook, 'SWOT analysis: it's time for a product recall', *Long Range Planning*, vol. 30, no. 1 (1997), pp. 46–52.

18. See H. Weihrich, 'The TOWS matrix – a tool for situational analysis', *Long Range Planning*, April 1982, pp. 54–66.

'Inside Dyson': a distinctive company?

Jill Shepherd, Segal Graduate School of Business, Simon Fraser University, Vancouver, Canada

Dyson is a private company, famous for its distinctive vacuum cleaners. It is not listed on a stock market and James Dyson, its founder and master inventor, has accumulated a personal fortune of over £1bn (~€1.1bn; ~$1.5bn). He is the sole owner of the company and is one of the few people to appear on Top Rich lists who has made money from his own inventions.

In 2005 the profit of the company reached £100m despite selling fewer vacuum cleaners than competitor Hoover. In terms of value rather than units sold, Dyson sells more in the US than Hoover, a company it sued for patent infringement winning around $5 (~€3.5) million. It is a global company, distributing its products in 45 countries including competitive markets such as China, the USA and Japan, as well as in its home market of the UK.

The company is built upon innovative products that are marketed as robust, presented well in bright colours and often in advertisements featuring James Dyson himself. From bag-less vacuum cleaners to energy-efficient and time-efficient hand-dryers for public places, to desk fans with no blades; all of the products are distinctive. His latest idea involves space saving kitchen appliances and even whole kitchens. All elements of the kitchens will be cubes with controls sliding into the main body so that the cubes fit and stack together into bigger cubes.

It hasn't all been straightforward success though. Dyson was about to launch a vacuum that could pick up water and dust. Customers were suspicious that such '3 in 1' products would not work and were not at all positive about wetting their carpets no matter how attractive the product design. Similarly a purple and silver washing machine with two rotating drums did not sell well and was also withdrawn.

Sir James Dyson

Dyson promote a story of their own heritage that suggests that the way the company works today is a

Source: Getty Images.

function of the early career development path of its leader. Dyson studied in art schools, rebelling against his family's tradition of reading Classics at Cambridge University. At art school he sought to apply engineering to functional problems in a way that respected design as an art. His first commercially successful vacuum product used cyclone technology. But from the beginning, he had problems convincing manufacturers both that the technology could be transferred to vacuum cleaners and could be patented. His confident answer was to set up his own firm: adopting unconventional routes and taking risks are still embedded within the organisational culture of Dyson.

Though, by 2010, the company was run by CEO Martin McCourt, James Dyson's own image and personal brand remained central to the firm's promotion. Apart from featuring in many of their adverts, he was highly visible beyond corporate boundaries. He appears to enjoy promoting engineering and design. He finances yearly design awards, collaborated with fashion designer Issey Miyake in an engineering themed fashion show and attempted to fund a Dyson School of Design Innovation. This latter endeavour was abandoned when the UK government put too many hurdles in its way thus limiting Dyson's own independence.

Engineering and design

Investment in R&D at Dyson quadrupled between 2004 and 2009. Dyson HQ is in a rural part of the west of England and is home to 350 engineers and scientists as well as the usual company personnel. It is also linked to 20 specialist laboratories all close by. Their large testing facility in Malaysia operates continually with over 120 testing stations. The operation in the UK employs 1200 varied people: some experienced, some freshly qualified, some with 'way out' ideas. James Dyson has said:

> 'We want people who are creative and courageous – unconditioned fresh-thinkers. We don't strap people into a suit and plonk them behind a desk, we like to give people the chance to make a difference.'

Success revolves around engineering ideas that are fine-tuned, not always on computer screens, but in the hands of engineers who make 100s, even 1000s of prototypes. Special computerised technology helps the engineers develop prototypes but they also use plasticine, cardboard or whatever material they wish to make prototypes in an almost child-like fashion. The engineers will tell you that the journey from prototype to prototype is an iterative journey of failures that creates new ideas. In walkabouts and feedbacks, they are encouraged to fiddle, to 'take the road less travelled' and to be 'less than sensible'. The same engineers report that, whilst competitors may have good robust engineering, they are not as inventive in terms of initial ideas and do not have the persistence and patience to make wacky ideas work in robust terms.

There is a clear corporate-level commitment to product development with half of all profit being channelled into the creation of new ideas supported by their mantra of *thinking, testing, breaking, questioning*. It is product engineering that takes centre stage on the company website and generally in all company communications. This company is obvious in its desire to promote the idea that a Dyson product means new, different, a radical change: a Dyson product whether vacuum or washing machine *is* an innovation and the bright colours help these clever products stand out from the crowd. For example, the Dyson air multiplier™ performs the same function as a conventional air fan but in a radically different way. Conventional fans cause buffering of the air as the blades interrupt its flow. The multiplier™ 'amplifies surrounding air, giving an uninterrupted stream of flow of smooth air'. When you look at its sleek design you wonder whether it is a function of the innovation in engineering or design or the blurring of the two. Either way, design is deeply embedded in engineering and of all the capabilities at Dyson engineering is king.

Unlike Apple, another design great, who designs then subcontracts all manufacturing, Dyson believe the combination of design engineering and manufacturing is crucial in developing the most inimitable competences that can be protected through patents. Dyson believes in patents to protect its differentiated products, but this does not mean competitors do not try to imitate. Within Dyson's vacuums there is 'patented Ball technology for improved manoeuvrability'. The Miele equivalent has 'unique swivel head technology'. Hoover USA has Wind Tunnel vacuums available in 'fresh colours'. Dyson's colours are usually bright and it does launch exclusive editions based on novel colours. Dyson's hand-blade hand dryer wipes water off your hands in seconds using less energy rather than evaporating water as in standard hand dryers. The competitor product from US specialists in hand drying, the Xlerator, also claims to dry hands in seconds and with far less energy than standard hand dryers. The Dyson desk fan has 11 patent separate applications and involved every discipline within the company.

Global working

James Dyson was heavily criticised in the UK press for taking the managerial decision to place the manufacturing part of his vacuum value chain in Malaysia and later that of his hand dryers in Nanjing in China. He needed, he said, to follow competitors to lower cost manufacturing as margins were being eaten away. One hundred jobs were lost in the UK in the first move and several hundred in the second. Later, with manufacturing costs down and profits up, more engineers were hired in the UK. James Dyson says the decision to move to Malaysia was not an easy one for him. It was not solely based on cost but also his belief that he needed to have a testing facility nearer to suppliers and those were all in the East. In contrast, Miele and Excel Dryer Corporation keep their manufacturing in their home countries.

Dyson claims to be helping national competitiveness by pulling the UK up the value chain as global competition heats up. China claims contracts like Dyson's help pull China up the manufacturing value chain too towards ever more complex products of the highest quality. Dyson himself appears to view China as a major market. He has made choices to reflect that, such as launching his hand dryers there by offering them free to the Sofitel Hotel in Nanjing. As the costs of making things seem to be an ever decreasing part of the price a consumer pays, perhaps design and development are the future.

Dyson's secrecy of success

Undoubtedly a success story, it is a firm that prefers to keep its secret of success just that – secret. So much is evident, for example in their UK HQ. Access to the building and then subsequent areas is via thumb print and even then some areas are out of bounds. They have even developed their own sound-absorbing panels to ensure that conversations can be kept secret.

Postscript: In March 2010 James Dyson stood down as chairman, although he maintained his role as 'chief inventor'.

Questions

1 Using frameworks from the chapter, analyse the strategic capabilities of Dyson.

2 To what extent do you think any of the capabilities can be imitated by competitors?

3 Which of Dyson's distinctive capabilities may, over time, become threshold capabilities?

4 Bearing in mind your answers to questions 1 and 2, how crucial is Sir James Dyson to the future of of the company? What might be the effect of his completely leaving or selling the company?

Dyson and its competitors

Company	Location of headquarters	Product range	Manufacturing locations	Relative company size (1 largest, 5 smallest) based on approximate global turnover	Distribution	Distinctive capabilities?
Dyson	UK	Vacuums, fan, hand dryers, moving into integrated kitchens and robotic vacuums following the success of iRobots	Asia	4	Own online and through retail outlets	Engineering design
Electrolux	Sweden	Range of vacuums, washing machines, fridges and ovens and a robotic vacuum	Not known	2	Retail outlets	Emphasis on energy-saving products Brand licensing of over 50 brands
Hoover (Techtronic Floor Care Technology Limited)	USA and Hong Kong for (TTI)	Vacuums and for TTI Floor Care power tools, outdoor power equipment, floor care appliances, solar-powered lighting and electronic measuring products In USA Hoover range includes patented and trade-marked 'Wind Tunnel' with no loss of suction	Not known, possibly various around Asia	1	Vacuums sold through retail outlets and own online shop in the USA	Possibly the sheer scale of its global operations rather than any particular capability gives it the edge?
Hoover Limited	UK (Italy)	Vacuums and a wide range of domestic appliances			Hoovers sold in retail outlets and online accessories only	
Miele	Germany	Domestic appliances from microwaves to wine storage	Germany ('90% of value creation within Germany')	3	Only through stores including Miele stores, Miele specialists and Miele studios Online stores also	Engineering that results in highly reliable and robust products
Excel Dryer Corporation	USA	A range of hand dryers	USA (products very much advertised as 'Made in USA')	5	Can be bought direct or through licensed distributors Sees end users (e.g. restaurants), distributors, architects and government as customers	Transformation possibly, given the choice by new owner in 1997 to collaborate with a partner – Invent Resources – that produced the Xlerator product and changed the financial profile of the company

4

STRATEGIC PURPOSE

Learning outcomes

After reading this chapter you should be able to:

- Consider appropriate ways to express the *strategic purpose* of an organisation in terms of *statements of purpose*, *values*, *vision*, *mission* or *objectives*.

- Identify the components of the *governance chain* of an organisation.

- Understand differences in *governance structures* and the advantages and disadvantages of these.

- Identify differences in the *corporate responsibility* stances taken by organisations.

- Undertake *stakeholder analysis* as a means of identifying the influence of different stakeholder groups in terms of their power and interest.

- Understand how *organisational culture* can influence its purpose and strategy.

Key terms

Corporate governance p. 82

Corporate social responsibility p. 87

Cultural web p. 98

Governance chain p. 83

Mission statement p. 79

Objectives p. 80

Organisational culture p. 95

Paradigm p. 96

Stakeholder mapping p. 91

Stakeholders p. 78

Statements of corporate values p. 80

Vision statement p. 80

PEARSON mystrategylab

MyStrategyLab is designed to help you make the most of your studies.

Visit **www.mystrategylab.com** to discover a wide range of resources specific to this chapter, including:

- A personalised **Study plan** that will help you understand core concepts.
- **Audio** and **video clips** that put the spotlight on strategy in the real world.
- **Online glossaries** and **flashcards** that provide helpful reminders when you're looking for some quick revision.

See p. xiv for further details.

(4.1) INTRODUCTION

In September 2008 Lehman Brothers, then the fourth largest investment bank in the United States, collapsed: the biggest banking collapse in history. The view of the financial press was that the failure was avoidable. In their view central to the problem was not only a flawed strategy, but the failure of the Lehman board to be more responsible and proactive in monitoring and constraining CEO Dick Fuld's reckless pursuit of that strategy. It was a failure of both strategy and governance.

The previous two chapters have looked respectively at the influence of the environment and capabilities on an organisation's strategic position. These were important in the downfall of Lehman Brothers, but this case also shows the importance of being clear about what purposes drive the strategy of organisations, who and what influences such purposes and who monitors performance against them. These are the concerns of this chapter. An important concept here is that of **stakeholders, those individuals or groups that depend on an organisation to fulfil their own goals and on whom, in turn, the organisation depends.** An underlying question is whether the strategic purpose of the organisation should be determined in response to the expectations of a particular stakeholder, for example shareholders in the case of a commercial enterprise, or to broader stakeholder interests – at the extreme society and the social good. Figure 4.1 summarises the different influences on strategic purpose discussed in the chapter:

www.mystrategylab.com
KEY CONCEPT
Stakeholders

● Section 4.2 develops the discussion in Chapter 1 about different ways in which organisations express *strategic purpose*, including statements of *values*, *vision*, *mission* and *objectives*.

Figure 4.1 Influences on strategic purpose

- Section 4.3 considers *corporate governance* and the *regulatory framework* within which organisations operate. The concern is with the way in which formally constituted bodies such as investors or boards influence strategic purpose through the formalised processes of supervising executive decisions and actions. In turn this raises issues of *accountability*: who are strategists accountable to?

- Section 4.4 is concerned with issues of *social responsibility*. Here the question is which purposes an organisation *should* fulfil. How should managers respond to the expectations society has of their organisations?

- In all this it is, then, important to understand *different stakeholder expectations* and their relative influence on strategic purpose. This requires an understanding of both the *power* and *interest* of different stakeholder groups. This is addressed through *stakeholder analysis* in section 4.5.

- Finally, section 4.6 considers how *organisational culture* can influence the purpose and the strategy of an organisation. It also provides a framework – the cultural web – by which the culture of an organisation can be understood.

(4.2) ORGANISATIONAL PURPOSE: VALUES, MISSION, VISION AND OBJECTIVES

Harvard University's Cynthia Montgomery[1] argues that defining and expressing a clear and motivating purpose for the organisation is at the core of a strategist's job. In the absence of such clarity, the strategy of an organisation is a mystery to those who work within the organisation and those who observe it from the outside. They end up having to interpret for themselves why the organisation is doing what it is doing. Such a purpose may be expressed in different ways.

4.2.1 Statements of mission, vision and value

Montgomery's view is that the stated purpose of the organisation must address the question: what is the organisation there to do that makes a difference, and to whom? If the stakeholders of an organisation can relate to such a purpose it can be highly motivating. So she suggests that executives need to find ways of expressing strategic purpose in ways that are easy to grasp and that people can relate to. There are three ways in which executives typically attempt to do this:

- A **mission statement** aims **to provide employees and stakeholders with clarity about the overriding purpose of the organisation**, sometimes referred to in terms of the apparently simple but challenging question: 'What business are we in?' A mission statement should make this clear in terms of long-term purpose. The two linked questions managers might ask are 'What would be lost if the organisation did not exist?' and 'How do we make a difference?' Though they do not use the term 'mission statement', Jim Collins and Jerry Porras[2] suggest

KEY CONCEPT

Mission statement

this can be addressed by managers starting with a descriptive statement of what the organisation does, then repeatedly delving deeper into the purpose of what the organisation is there for by asking 'why do we do this?' They use the example of managers in a gravel and asphalt company arriving at the conclusion that its mission is to make people's lives better by improving the quality of built structures.

- A **vision statement is concerned with the desired future state of the organisation**; an aspiration that will enthuse, gain commitment and stretch performance. So here the question is: 'What do we want to achieve?' Porras and Collins suggest managers can identify this by asking: 'If we were sitting here in twenty years what do we want to have created or achieved?'

- **Statements of corporate values communicate the underlying and enduring core 'principles' that guide an organisation's strategy and define the way that the organisation should operate.**[3] So a question to ask is: 'Would these values change with circumstances?' And if the answer is 'yes' then they are not 'core' and not 'enduring'. An example is the importance of leading-edge research in some universities. Whatever the constraints on funding, such universities hold to the enduring centrality of this.

Illustration 4.1 shows examples of mission, vision and value statements. Many critics regard such statements as bland and too wide-ranging.[4] However, they have become widely adopted, arguably because if there is substantial disagreement within the organisation or with stakeholders as to its mission or vision, there can be real problems in resolving the strategic direction of the organisation. So they can be a useful means of focusing debate on the fundamentals of the organisation.

Collins and Porras claim that the long-run success of many US corporates – such as Disney, General Electric or 3M – can be attributed (at least in part) to their clarity on such statements of purpose.[5] There are, however, potential downsides to public statements of corporate purpose and values if an organisation demonstrably fails to live them out in practice. For example, Lehman Brothers' (see Illustration 4.2) 2007 annual report included 12 principles among which were 'doing the right thing', 'demonstrating a commitment to excellence', 'demonstrating smart risk management', 'acting always with ownership mentality' and, of course, 'maximizing shareholder value'.

4.2.2 Objectives

Whether or not organisations use mission, vision or value statements, they use objectives. **Objectives are statements of specific outcomes that are to be achieved** and are often expressed in financial terms. They could be the expression of desired sales or profit levels, rates of growth, dividend levels or share valuation. Organisations may also have market-based objectives, many of which are quantified as targets – such as market share, customer service, repeat business and so on. Increasingly, organisations are also setting objectives referred to as 'the triple bottom line', by which is meant not only economic objectives such as those above, but also environmental and social objectives to do with their corporate responsibility to wider society (see section 4.4 below).

ILLUSTRATION 4.1

Mission, vision and values statements

Can well-crafted statements of mission, vision or values be an important means of motivating an organisation's stakeholders?

Whirlpool

Vision

Every home . . . Everywhere . . . with Pride, Passion and Performance.

Our vision reinforces that every home is our domain, every customer and customer activity our opportunity. This vision fuels the passion that we have for our customers, pushing us to provide innovative solutions to uniquely meet their needs.

Pride . . . in our work and each other.

Passion . . . for creating unmatched customer loyalty for our brands.

Performance . . . that excites and rewards global investors with superior returns.

We bring this vision to life through the power of our unique global enterprise and our outstanding people . . . working together . . . everywhere.

Mission

Everyone, passionately creating loyal customers for life.

Our mission defines our focus and what we do differently to create value. We are a company of people captivated with creating loyal customers. From every job, across every contact, we will build unmatched customer loyalty . . . one customer at a time.

Values

Our values are constant and define the way that all Whirlpool Corporation employees are expected to behave and conduct business everywhere in the world.

Respect – We must trust one another as individuals and value the capabilities and contributions of each person.

Integrity – We must conduct all aspects of business honorably – ever mindful of the longtime Whirlpool Corporation belief that there is no right way to do a wrong thing.

Diversity and inclusion – We must maintain the broad diversity of Whirlpool people and ideas. Diversity honors differences, while inclusion allows everyone to contribute. Together, we create value.

Teamwork – We must recognize that pride results in working together to unleash everyone's potential, achieving exceptional results.

Spirit of winning – We must promote a Whirlpool culture that enables individuals and teams to reach and take pride in extraordinary results and further inspire the 'Spirit of winning' in all of us.

Save the Children

The charity, Save the Children, operates in over 120 countries worldwide.

Vision

Save the Children's vision is a world in which every child attains the right to survival, protection, development and participation.

Mission

Save the Children's mission is to inspire breakthroughs in the way the world treats children, and to achieve immediate and lasting change in their lives.

Values

● **Accountability**: we take personal responsibility for using our resources efficiently, achieving measurable results, and being accountable to supporters, partners and, most of all, children.

● **Ambition**: we are demanding of ourselves and our colleagues, set high goals and are committed to improving the quality of everything we do for children.

● **Collaboration**: we respect and value each other, thrive on our diversity, and work with partners to leverage our global strength in making a difference for children.

● **Creativity**: we are open to new ideas, embrace change, and take disciplined risks to develop sustainable solutions for and with children.

● **Integrity**: we aspire to live to the highest standards of personal honesty and behaviour; we never compromise our reputation and always act in the best interests of children.

Sources: Whirlpool and Save the Children websites 2010.

Questions

1 Which of these statements do you think are likely to motivate which stakeholders? Why?

2 Could any of them have been improved? How?

3 Identify other statements of mission, vision, purpose or values that you think are especially well crafted and explain why.

Managers need to consider two issues in particular with regard to setting objectives.

● *Objectives and measurement.* Some managers argue that objectives are not helpful unless their achievement can be measured. Certainly there are times when specific quantified objectives are required, for example when urgent action is needed and it becomes essential for management to focus attention on a limited number of priority requirements. However, it may be that in other circumstances – for example, in trying to raise the aspirations of people in the organisation – more attention needs to be paid to qualitative statements of purpose such as mission or vision statements than to quantified objectives.

● *Identifying core objectives.*[6] Managers in most companies set objectives which are financial in nature because they recognise that unless adequate profits are made to satisfy shareholders and allow for reinvestment in the business, it will not survive. It may be, however, that there are other aspects of business performance upon which survival and prosperity of the business are based. For example, how the organisation is distinctive from its rivals, or how it is to achieve competitive advantage and sustain it. As Chapter 3 pointed out, this is likely to be on the basis of capabilities that are valued by customers and distinctive from competition. Identifying objectives that capture the bases of such competitive advantage and allow monitoring of performance against it become crucial too. For example, low-cost airlines such as Ryanair set an objective on turnaround time for their aircraft because this is at the core of their distinctive low-cost advantage.

Whatever statements of mission, vision, values are employed, or whatever the objectives that are set, it is important to understand who and what influences what they are. The rest of the chapter examines this.

CORPORATE GOVERNANCE

Corporate governance **is concerned with the structures and systems of control by which managers are held accountable to those who have a legitimate stake in an organisation.**[7] These are the stakeholders that, in ownership and management terms, influence an organisation. Governance has become an increasingly important issue for organisations for three main reasons.

● *The separation of ownership and management control* of organisations (which is now the norm except with very small businesses) means that most organisations operate within a hierarchy, or chain, of governance. This chain represents those groups that influence an organisation through their involvement in either ownership or management of an organisation.

● *Corporate failures and scandals*, such as that of Enron in 2001 and Lehman Brothers and the Royal Bank of Scotland in 2008, have fuelled public debate about how different parties in the governance chain should interact and influence each other. Most notable here is the relationship between shareholders and the boards of businesses, but an equivalent issue in the public sector is the relationship between government or public funding bodies and public-sector organisations.

● *Increased accountability to wider stakeholder interests* has also been increasingly advocated; in particular, the argument that corporations need to be more visibly accountable and/or responsive, not only to 'owners' and 'managers' in the governance chain but to wider social interest.

The **governance chain** shows the roles and relationships of different groups involved in the governance of an organisation. In a small family business, the governance chain is simple: there are family shareholders, a board with some family members and there are managers, some of whom may be family too. In large businesses, however, influence on governance can be complex. Figure 4.2 shows a governance chain for a typical large, publicly quoted organisation. Here the size of the organisation means there are extra layers of management

Governance
chain

Figure 4.2 The chain of corporate governance: typical reporting structures

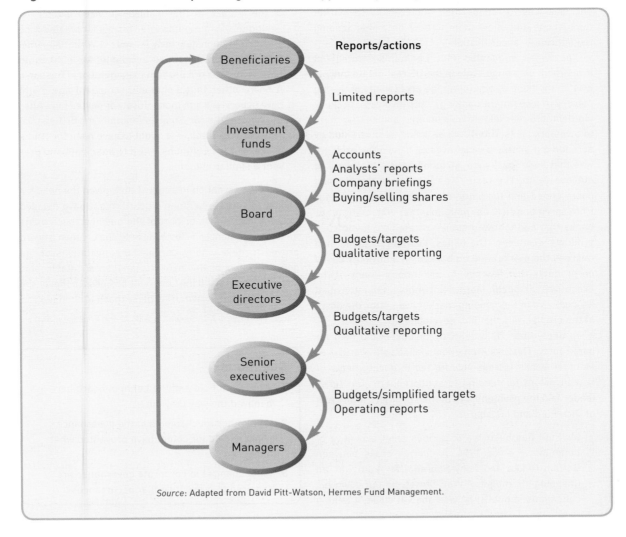

Source: Adapted from David Pitt-Watson, Hermes Fund Management.

ILLUSTRATION 4.2

The collapse of Lehman Brothers

Executive decisions may not always be in the best interest of shareholders; with disastrous results.

In 2008, Lehman Brothers was the fourth largest investment bank in the USA. Founded in the mid-1800s, its chief executive was Dick Fuld. Under his guidance the bank had been pursuing a strategy of rapid growth and, in common with other banks, up to 2008 this included the development of derivative products linked to the housing boom. The idea was to reduce their vulnerability to market fluctuations and allow them to take on higher lending risks through 'securitisation'.

The Times suggested that Lehman's strategy of investment on a huge scale in the US real estate market was 'in the hope of emulating the profitability of the big players in investment banking'. This involved: 'packaging debt into marketable instruments and selling them to investors . . . [so that] . . . risk could be diversified by spreading it across a wide investor base'. The problem was that such 'packages' included assets that were of dubious value. The result was that, when the housing boom ended and the value of housing plummeted, far from spreading risk, Lehman, together with many other banks that had followed similar strategies, found such products worthless. The banks, Lehman included, had misread the market and embarked on a strategy based on products that few people understood (many of the executives included). Moreover Lehman had intensified its exposure in the housing market even after the onset of the credit crisis that had developed.

In September 2008 Lehman collapsed and filed for bankruptcy. The knock-on effect was felt the world over as other banks increasingly turned to governments or new investors for funding to support them. *The Times* leader laid the problems of Lehman Brothers at the feet of Dick Fuld and his board:

Mr Fuld has been the imperious chief executive of Lehmans . . . since 1994. A curious cross between Gordon Gekko and Tony Soprano, Mr Fuld was an unapologetic mogul of Wall Street: he put down his colleagues in public: he was good at straight talking but not so practised at straight-listening and ultimately he deluded himself and those around him that, having seen off a brush with bankruptcy in the late 1990s, he and his bank had taken the precautions necessary to weather any financial storm. At Lehman's annual general meeting last April (2008), he said: 'The worst of the impact on the financial services industry is behind us.' Two months later his bank revealed $2.8 (~€2.0) billion in quarterly losses . . . What happened to Lehman Brothers was avoidable. Mr Fuld could have ensured more prudent management of the bank. A board other than Lehman's compliant one might have supervised him more closely or ousted him. After the failure of Bear Stearns (another major financial services business) . . . it ought to have been the prime concern of the Lehmans board to anticipate and prevent a similar outcome.

The Times went on to suggest that, given the need for capital to survive, Lehman's board might have decided to sell the business or part of the business such as its fund management arm. Instead: 'Fuld and Lehman's board proved to have wholly unrealistic expectations of the genuine value of the bank . . . (and) . . . a catastrophic failure to understand the Lehman's business model or the nature of the financial market place that had changed . . .'

Source: *The Times*, p. 2, 16 September 2008; © The Times/nisyndication.com.

Questions

1 Why might Fuld and the Lehman board have behaved the way they did?

2 What other mechanisms in the governance chain should (or could) have prevented what happened?

3 What changes in corporate governance are required to prevent similar occurrences?

internally, while being publicly quoted introduces more investor layers too. Individual investors (the ultimate beneficiaries) often invest in public companies through investment funds, for example unit trusts or pension funds, which then invest in a range of companies on their behalf. Such funds are typically controlled by trustees, with day-to-day investment activity undertaken by investment managers. So the ultimate beneficiaries may not even know in which companies they have a financial stake and have little power to influence the companies' boards directly.

The relationships in such governance chains can be understood in terms of the *principal–agent model*.[8] 'Principals' pay 'agents' to act on their behalf, just as homeowners employ estate agents to sell their homes. In Figure 4.2, the beneficiaries are the ultimate principals and fund trustees and investment managers are their agents in terms of achieving good returns on their investments. Further down the chain, company boards are principals too, with senior executives their agents in managing the company. There are many layers of agents between ultimate principals and the managers at the bottom, with the reporting mechanisms between each layer liable to be imperfect.

Principal–agent theory assumes that agents will not work diligently for principals unless incentives are carefully and appropriately aligned. However, it can be seen from Figure 4.2 that in large companies board members and other managers driving strategy are likely to be very remote from the ultimate beneficiaries of the company's performance. In such circumstances, the danger is twofold:

- *Self-interest*. Any agent in the chain may act out of self-interest. Managers will be striving for promotion and/or increased earnings, investment managers will be seeking to increase their bonuses, and so on.

- *Misalignment of incentives and control*. As influence passes down the governance chain, the expectations of one group are not passed on to the next appropriately. For example, ultimate beneficiaries may be mainly concerned with the long-term security of their pension fund, but the investment managers or the executives with whom they interact may place a greater emphasis on short-term growth.

The result may be that decisions are taken that are not in the best interests of the final beneficiary. This is just what has happened in the case of many of the corporate scandals of recent years, such as Lehman Brothers (see Illustration 4.2).

In this context, the governance chain helps highlight important issues that affect the management of strategy:

- *Responsibility to whom?* A fundamental question in large corporations is whether executives should regard themselves as *solely* responsible to shareholders, or as acting on behalf of a wider range of stakeholders.

- *Who are the shareholders?* If managers do see themselves as primarily responsible to shareholders, what does this mean in terms of the governance chain? As explained above, the final beneficiaries are far removed from the managers, so for many managers responsibility to them is notional. In practical terms, directors of a firm are likely to engage most frequently with institutional representatives of those shareholders – an investment manager or analyst from a pension fund or insurance company perhaps. Strategists within a firm therefore face a difficult choice, even if they espouse primary responsibility to shareholders. Do they develop strategies they believe to be in the best interest of a highly fragmented group of unknown shareholders; or to meet the needs and aspirations of the investment managers? A similar problem exists for public-sector managers. They may see themselves as developing strategies in the public good, but they may face direct scrutiny from another body such as a government department or an agency appointed by the government. Is the strategy to be designed for the general public good, or to meet the scrutiny of the government department?

- *The role of boards.* Boards of directors typically consist of both executives and non-executive directors. The balance between these varies by type of organisation and by country. However, the principle is that the non-executive directors are there either to represent particular stakeholders, or to take a dispassionate view on the strategy and performance of the firm. The danger is that non-executive directors become too aligned with executives within the company. In the US and UK, critics have pointed out that many non-executive directors are chosen on the basis of their previous association and links with senior executives within a firm, with the danger that this reduces the likelihood of their objectivity in performing their roles. There have been attempts to reduce these dangers with, for example, codes of conduct for the appointment of non-executive directors.

- *Scrutiny and control.* Given the concerns about governance that have grown in the last decade, there have been increasing attempts to build means of scrutinising and controlling the activities of 'agents' in the chain to safeguard the interests of the final beneficiaries. Figure 4.2 shows the information typically available to each 'player' in the chain to judge the performance of others. There are increasing statutory requirements as well as voluntary codes placed upon boards to disclose information publicly and regulate their activities. None the less, managers have a great deal of discretion as to what information to provide to whom and what information to require of those who report to them. For example, how specific should a chief executive be in explaining future strategy to shareholders in public statements such as annual reports? What are the appropriate targets and measures to incentivise and control management within a firm? Are the typical accountancy methods (such as return on capital employed) the most appropriate measures or should measures be specifically designed to fit the needs of particular strategies? How managers answer these questions will depend on what they decide the strategic purpose of the organisation is, which itself will be influenced by their view on to whom they see themselves responsible.

(4.4) CORPORATE SOCIAL RESPONSIBILITY

The sheer size and global reach of many companies means that they are bound to have significant influence on society. Further, the widely publicised corporate scandals and failures of the last two decades have fuelled a concern about the role they play. The regulatory environment and the corporate governance arrangements for an organisation determine its minimum obligations towards its stakeholders. More widely, **corporate social responsibility** (CSR) **is the commitment by organisations to 'behave ethically and contribute to economic development while improving the quality of life of the workforce and their families as well as the local community and society at large'.**[9] CSR is therefore concerned with the ways in which an organisation exceeds its minimum obligations to stakeholders specified through regulation.

Organisations may take different stances on CSR, which are reflected in how they manage such responsibilities. There are four stereotypes that can be used to illustrate these differences. They represent a progressively more inclusive 'list' of stakeholder interests and a greater breadth of criteria against which strategies and performance will be judged.[10]

- *The laissez-faire view* (literally 'let do' in French) represents an extreme stance. Proponents argue that the only responsibility of business is to make a profit and provide for the interests of shareholders.[11] It is for government to prescribe, through legislation and regulation, the constraints which society chooses to impose on businesses in their pursuit of economic efficiency. Organisations should meet these minimum obligations but no more. Expecting companies to exercise social duties beyond this can, in extreme cases, undermine the authority of government.

- *Enlightened self-interest* is tempered with recognition of the long-term financial benefit to the shareholder of well-managed relationships with other stakeholders. The justification for social action is that it makes good business sense. An organisation's reputation is important to its long-term financial success. Given that employees see it as important that their employer acts in a socially responsible manner, a more proactive stance on social issues also helps in recruiting and retaining staff. So, like any other form of investment or promotion expenditure, corporate philanthropy or welfare provision might be regarded as sensible expenditure.[12] The sponsorship of major sporting or arts events by companies is an example. The avoidance of 'shady' marketing practices is also necessary to prevent the need for yet more legislation in that area. Managers here would take the view that organisations not only have responsibility to their shareholders, but also a responsibility for *relationships with* other stakeholders (as against *responsibilities to* other stakeholders). So communication with stakeholder groups is likely to be more interactive than for *laissez-faire*-type organisations.

- A *forum for stakeholder interaction* explicitly incorporates multiple stakeholder interests and expectations rather than just shareholders as influences on organisational purposes and strategies. Here the argument is that the performance of an organisation should be measured in a more pluralistic way than just through the financial bottom line. Companies in this category might retain uneconomic units to preserve jobs, avoid manufacturing or selling 'anti-social' products and be prepared to bear reductions in profitability for the social good. Some financial service organisations have also chosen to offer socially responsible investment 'products' to investors. These include only holdings in organisations that meet high standards of social responsibility in their activities.

- *Shapers of society* regard financial considerations as of secondary importance or a constraint. These are activists, seeking to change society and social norms. The firm may have been founded for this purpose, as in the case of Traidcraft UK, a public limited company established with the specific mission of fighting world poverty. Here the social role is the *raison*

ILLUSTRATION 4.3

The social impact of business strategies

The activities of businesses can have significant impacts on societies. But what motivates such activities?

Social good or spotting the market trend?

In 2009 Pepsi Co launched a range of healthy snacks targeting 8–12-year-old schoolchildren. There were also plans to launch a children's porridge under the Quaker brand and to publish a health audit of its products. This followed Pepsi Co's decision five years earlier to stop promoting full-sugar Pepsi and focus on the diet and non-sugared alternatives, Pepsi Max and Diet Pepsi. The company also claimed to have reduced saturated fat in its Walkers Crisps by 70 per cent by switching from palm oil to sunflower oil. Salman Amin, Pepsi Co's CEO in Britain, explained that, while it would take years: 'I think we will lick obesity as a social issue. . . . I'm a huge optimist.' Commentators also pointed out that Pepsi Co had, in the past, been good at spotting trends in food consumption and capitalising on them.

Cheap medicines for the world's poor or a smart competitive move?

In early 2009 Andrew Witty, the Chief Executive of GlaxoSmithKlein (GSK) announced the decision to cut its prices in the 50 least developed countries in the world to no more than 25 per cent of levels in the UK and the US prices on all medicines produced by GSK, re-invest 20 per cent of any profits it made in the least developed countries into hospitals, clinics and staff and share knowledge about potential drugs currently protected by patents by making them available in a 'patent pool'. This followed repeated criticisms of drug companies for defending their patents, fighting off generic alternatives and refusing to drop prices for HIV drugs despite the HIV/AIDS crisis in Africa and Asia. Witty hoped it might 'stimulate a different behaviour' adding: 'maybe someone has to move before many people move'.

While campaigners widely applauded the decisions, there remained some concerns. Why shouldn't current HIV drugs be included in the patent pool? And might the GSK decision undermine the generics industry already attempting to supply cheap drugs to poor countries? Indeed the *Guardian* (14 February 2009) wrote 'GSK would love to undermine the Indian and Chinese generics companies, which sell copies of their drugs at rock bottom prices in Africa and Asian countries where patents do not apply.'

Powering African homes – or cheap power for Europe?

In 2009 the World Bank announced its $80 (~€56) billion support to build the Grand Inga Dam in the Democratic Republic of Congo. This would feed electricity to South Africa, Egypt, Nigeria and other countries in Africa. At 40,000 MW it would have twice the generation capacity of the Three Gorges Dam in China. However, the feasibility study also examined the possibility of extending supply to southern Europe. Critics argued it was a: 'flight of fancy that would only benefit huge Western multinationals and quite possibly feed African energy into European households' when less than 30 per cent of Africans have access to electricity – in some African countries as low as 10 per cent. Supporters, on the other hand, pointed out that it could bring electricity to 500 million African homes and that diverting power to Europe had the benefit of attracting additional financing, thus potentially aiding the local community.

Sources: (1) The *Observer*, 23 August 2009, p. 3; (2) *Financial Times*, 4 March 2009, p. 4; (3) The *Observer* Media and Business, 23 August 2009, p. 1.

Questions

1 How would you categorise each of the decisions in terms of the stances on social responsibility in section 4.4?

2 To what extent and how should the development of strategic options consider the impact on society?

d'être of the business. Such organisations may see their strategic purpose as 'changing the rules of the game' through which they may benefit, but by which they wish to assure that society benefits. *The extent to which* this is a viable stance depends upon issues of regulation, corporate governance and accountability. For example, it is easier for a privately owned organisation to operate in this way, since it is not accountable to external shareholders.

Illustration 4.3 shows different examples of company activities that have significant social impacts.

Managers' increasing sympathy with CSR is not solely for ethical reasons, but because there is a belief that there are advantages to businesses in so doing and dangers if they do not.[13] Social responsibility is justified in terms of the 'triple bottom line' – social and environmental benefits as well as increased profits. Indeed, it is argued that socially responsible strategies should be followed because they can provide a basis of gaining competitive advantage. The need is to seek 'win–win' situations to optimise the economic return on environmental investments. Fighting the AIDS pandemic in Africa is not just a matter of 'good works' for a pharmaceutical company or an African mining company, it is central to their own interests. Similarly, helping reduce carbon emissions provides a business opportunity for a car manufacturer.[14]

4.5 STAKEHOLDER EXPECTATIONS

It should be clear from the preceding sections that the decisions managers have to make about the purpose and strategy of their organisation are influenced by the expectations of stakeholders. This poses a challenge because there are likely to be many stakeholders, especially for a large organisation (see Figure 4.3), with different, perhaps conflicting, expectations. This means that managers need to take a view on (i) which stakeholders will have the greatest influence, therefore (ii) which expectations they need to pay most attention to and (iii) to what extent the expectations and influence of different stakeholders vary.

4.5.1 Stakeholder groups

External stakeholders can be usefully divided into four types in terms of the nature of their relationship with the organisation and how they might affect the success or failure of a strategy:[15]

- *Economic stakeholders*, including suppliers, competitors, distributors (whose influence can be identified using the five forces framework from Chapter 2 (Figure 2.2) and shareholders (whose influence can be considered in terms of the governance chain discussed in section 4.3).

- *Social/political stakeholders*, such as policy-makers, regulators and government agencies that may directly influence the strategy or the context in which strategy is developed.

- *Technological stakeholders*, such as key adopters, standards agencies and owners of competitive technologies that will influence the diffusion of new technologies and the adoption of industry standards.

Figure 4.3 Stakeholders of a large organisation

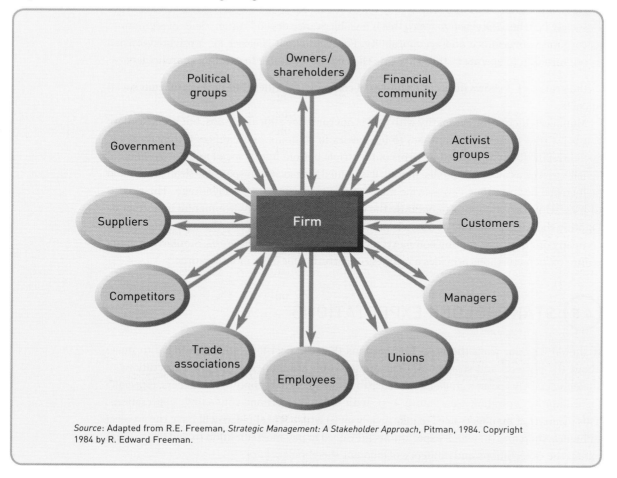

Source: Adapted from R.E. Freeman, *Strategic Management: A Stakeholder Approach*, Pitman, 1984. Copyright 1984 by R. Edward Freeman.

- *Community stakeholders*, who are affected by what an organisation does; for example, those who live close to a factory or, indeed, wider society. These stakeholders have no formal relationship with the organisation but may, of course, take action (e.g. through lobbying or activism) to influence the organisation.

The influence of these different types of stakeholders is likely to vary in different situations. For example, the 'technological group' will be crucial for strategies of new product introduction while the 'social/political' group is usually particularly influential in the public-sector context or for companies operating in different countries with different political and legal systems.

There are also stakeholder groups internal to an organisation, which may be departments, geographical locations or different levels in the hierarchy. Individuals may belong to more than one stakeholder group and such groups may 'line up' differently depending on the issue or strategy in hand. Of course, external stakeholders may seek to influence an organisation's strategy through their links with internal stakeholders. For example, customers may exert pressure on sales managers to represent their interests within the company.

Since the expectations of stakeholder groups will differ, it is normal for conflict to exist regarding the importance or desirability of aspects of strategy. In most situations, a compromise will need to be reached. It may, however, also be possible in developing a strategy to look for compatible stakeholder expectations. For example, managers of the Cornish conservation tourist attraction, the Eden Project, looked for 'synergies around purpose' among different stakeholders to obtain support and funding for it. Both the European Union and the local economic development agency were interested in developing the economy of Cornwall, one of the poorest areas in the UK, and the Millennium Commission, a government-sponsored funding body, was interested in developing local iconic architecture.

The stakeholder concept is, then, valuable when trying to understand the political context within which strategy develops.

4.5.2 Stakeholder mapping[16]

Stakeholder mapping can be used to gain an understanding of stakeholder influence. The approach to **stakeholder mapping** here **identifies stakeholder expectations and power and helps in understanding political priorities.** It underlines the importance of two issues:

- The *interest* each stakeholder has in imposing its expectations on the organisation's purposes and choice of strategies.
- The *power* each stakeholder has to influence strategy.

These two dimensions form the basis of the power/interest matrix shown as Figure 4.4. The matrix classifies stakeholders in relation to the power they hold and the extent to which they

Figure 4.4 Stakeholder mapping: the power/interest matrix

Source: Adapted from A. Mendelow, *Proceedings of the Second International Conference on Information Systems*, Cambridge, MA, 1986.

are likely to show interest in supporting or opposing a particular strategy. The matrix helps in thinking through stakeholder influences on the development of strategy. However, it must be emphasised that how managers handle relationships will depend on the governance structures under which they operate (see section 4.3) and the stance taken on corporate responsibility (section 4.4). For example, in some countries unions may be weak, but in others they may be represented on supervisory boards; banks may take an 'arm's-length' relationship with regard to strategy in some countries, but be part of the governance structures in others. A *laissez-faire* type of business may only pay attention to stakeholders with the most powerful economic

ILLUSTRATION 4.4

Stakeholder mapping at Tallman GmbH

Stakeholder mapping can be a useful tool for determining the political priorities for specific strategic developments or changes.

Tallman GmbH was a German bank providing both retail and corporate banking services throughout Germany, Benelux and France. There were concerns about its loss in market share in the corporate sector which was serviced from two centres – Frankfurt (for Germany and Benelux) and Toulouse (for France). It was considering closing the Toulouse operation and servicing all corporate clients from Frankfurt. This would result in significant job losses in Toulouse, some of which would be replaced in Frankfurt alongside vastly improved IT systems.

Two power/interest maps were drawn up by the company officials to establish likely stakeholder reactions to

the proposed closure of the Toulouse operation. Map A represents the likely situation and map B the preferred situation – where support for the proposal would be sufficient to proceed.

Referring to map A, it can be seen that, with the exception of customer X and IT supplier A, the stakeholders in box B are currently opposed to the closure of the Toulouse operation. If Tallman was to have any chance of convincing these stakeholders to change their stance to a more supportive one, the company must address their questions and, where possible, alleviate their fears. If such fears were overcome, these people might become important

Map A: The likely situation

	Shareholder M (-) Toulouse office (-) Customer X (+) French minister (-) Marketing (-) **B** IT supplier A (+)
A	**B**
Customer Z German minister	Customer Y (+) Frankfurt office (+) Corporate finance (+)
C	**D**

Map B: The preferred situation

French minister	Shareholder M (-) Toulouse office (-) Marketing (-) IT supplier A (+)
A	**B**
Customer Z German minister	Customer X (+) Customer Y (+) Frankfurt office (+) Corporate finance (+)
C	**D**

influence (for example, investors), whereas shapers of society might seek to engage with and influence the expectations and involvement of stakeholders who would not typically see themselves as influential.

In order to show the way in which the matrix may be used, take the example of a business where managers see themselves as formulating strategy by trying to ensure the compliance of stakeholders with their own assessment of strategic imperatives. In this context, the matrix indicates the type of relationship that managers might typically establish with stakeholder groups in the different quadrants. Clearly, the acceptability of strategies to *key players* (segment D)

allies in influencing the more powerful stakeholders in boxes C and D. The supportive attitude of customer X could be usefully harnessed in this quest. Customer X was a multinational with operations throughout Europe. It had shown dissatisfaction with the inconsistent treatment that it received from Frankfurt and Toulouse.

The relationships Tallman had with the stakeholders in box C were the most difficult to manage since, while they were considered to be relatively passive, largely due to their indifference to the proposed strategy, a disastrous situation could arise if their level of interest was underrated. For example, if the German minister were replaced, her successor might be opposed to the strategy and actively seek to stop the changes. In this case they would shift to box D.

The acceptability of the proposed strategy to the current players in box D was a key consideration. Of particular concern was customer Y (a major French manufacturer who operated only in France – accounting for 20 per cent of Toulouse corporate banking income). Customer Y was opposed to the closure of the Toulouse operation and could have the power to prevent it from happening, for example by the withdrawal of its business. The company clearly needed to have open discussions with this stakeholder.

By comparing the position of stakeholders in map A and map B, and identifying any changes and mismatches, Tallman could establish a number of tactics to change the stance of certain stakeholders to a more positive one and to increase the power of certain stakeholders. For example, customer X could be encouraged to champion the proposed strategy and assist Tallman by providing media access, or even convincing customer Y that the change could be beneficial.

Tallman could also seek to dissuade or prevent powerful stakeholders from changing their stance to a negative one: for example, unless direct action were taken, lobbying from her French counterpart may well raise the German minister's level of interest. This would have implications for how the company handled the situation in France. Time could be spent talking the strategy through with the French minister and also customer Y to try to shift them away from opposition at least to neutrality, if not support.

Activity

To ensure that you are clear about how to undertake stakeholder mapping, produce your own complete analysis for Tallman GmbH against a different strategy, that is *to service all corporate clients from Toulouse*. Ensure that you go through the following steps:

1 Plot the most likely situation (map A) – remembering to be careful to *reassess* interest and power for each stakeholder in relation to this *new* strategy.

2 Map the preferred situation (map B).

3 Identify the mismatches – and hence the political priorities. Remember to include the need to *maintain* a stakeholder in its 'opening' position (if relevant).

4 Finish off by listing the actions you would propose to take and give a final view of the degree of political risk in pursuing this new strategy.

is of major importance. It could be that these are major investors or particular individuals or agencies with a lot of power – for example, a major shareholder in a family firm or a government funding agency in a public-sector organisation. Often the most difficult issues relate to stakeholders in segment C. Although these might, in general, be relatively passive, a disastrous situation can arise when their level of interest is underrated and they reposition to segment D and frustrate the adoption of a new strategy. Institutional shareholders such as pension funds or insurance firms can fall into this category. They may show little interest unless share prices start to dip, but may then demand to be heard by senior management. Managers might choose to address the expectations of stakeholders in segment B, for example community groups, through information provision. It may be important not to alienate such stakeholders because they can be crucially important 'allies' in influencing the attitudes of more powerful stakeholders: for example, through lobbying.

Stakeholder mapping can also help in understanding the following issues:

- In *determining purpose and strategy*, which stakeholder expectations need to be most considered?
- Whether the *actual levels of interest and power* of stakeholders properly reflect the corporate governance framework within which the organisation is operating, as in the examples above (institutional investors, community groups).
- Who the key *blockers* and *facilitators* of a strategy are likely to be and the appropriate response.
- Whether *repositioning* of certain stakeholders is desirable and/or feasible: for example, to lessen the influence of a key player or, in certain instances, to ensure that there are more key players who will champion the strategy (this is often critical in the public-sector context).
- *Maintaining* the level of interest or power of some key stakeholders: for example, public 'endorsement' by powerful suppliers or customers may be critical to the success of a strategy. It may also be necessary to discourage some stakeholders from repositioning themselves. This is what is meant by *keep satisfied* in relation to stakeholders in segment C, and to a lesser extent *keep informed* for those in segment B.

All this can raise difficult ethical issues for managers in deciding the role they should play in the political activity surrounding stakeholder management. This takes the debate back to the considerations of governance. For example, are managers really the honest brokers who weigh the conflicting expectations of stakeholder groups? Or should they be answerable to one stakeholder – such as shareholders – and hence is their role to ensure the acceptability of their strategies to other stakeholders? Or are they, as many authors suggest, the real power themselves, constructing strategies to suit their own purposes and managing stakeholder expectations to ensure acceptance of these strategies?

Illustration 4.4 shows some of the practical issues of using stakeholder mapping to understand the political context surrounding a new strategy. The example relates to a German bank considering the centralisation of its corporate banking services in its headquarters in Frankfurt with the implication of the closure of its Toulouse office.

(4.6) CULTURAL INFLUENCES

Organisational culture is the taken-for-granted assumptions and behaviours that make sense of people's organisational context and therefore contributes to how groups of people respond and behave in relation to issues they face. It therefore has important influences on the development and change of organisational strategy. For example, the purpose of the organisation may not always be stated explicitly; none the less there may be a 'taken for granted' purpose embedded in the history and culture of the organisation. Or it could be that, despite an explicit statement of purpose and of the strategy, perhaps the result of strategic planning or the arrival of a new chief executive, the organisation's direction continues to be driven by its culture. Understanding the underlying cultural influences on an organisation is therefore important.

Organisational
culture

Different cultural contexts are likely to influence individuals. The sections that follow will identify the important factors and issues in terms of different cultural frames of reference and then show how culture can be analysed and characterised as a means of understanding its influences on both current and future organisational purposes and strategies.

4.6.1 National cultures

Many writers, perhaps the best-known of whom is Geert Hofstede,[17] have shown how attitudes to work, authority, equality and other important factors differ from one country to another. Organisations that operate internationally need to understand and cope with such differences, which can manifest themselves in terms of different standards, values and expectations in the various countries in which they operate. For example, Euro Disney's attempt to replicate the success of the Disney theme parks in the US was termed 'cultural imperialism' in the French media and has experienced difficulties. Wal-Mart failed to develop its retail presence in Germany because it failed to understand how German shopping behaviour differed from US.

4.6.2 Organisational culture

Edgar Schein[18] suggests that culture can be conceived as consisting of four different layers:

- *Values* may be easy to identify in terms of those formally stated by an organisation since they are often explicit, perhaps written down (see section 4.2). For example, in the last decade, many banks espoused values of shareholder value creation, careful risk management and, of course, high levels of customer service. But they indulged in highly risky lending, resulting in the need for huge government financial support in 2009. Clearly the values that drove the strategies were different. It is therefore important to delve beneath espoused values to uncover underlying, perhaps taken-for-granted, values that can help explain the strategy actually being pursued by an organisation.

- *Beliefs* are more specific. They can typically be discerned in how people talk about issues the organisation faces; for example, a belief that the company should not trade with particular countries or a belief in the importance of high levels of customer service.

With regard to both values and beliefs, it is important to remember that in relation to culture, the concern is with the collective rather than individuals' values and beliefs. Indeed, it may be that individuals in organisations have values and beliefs that at times run counter to their organisation's.

- *Behaviours* are the day-to-day way in which an organisation operates and can be seen by people both inside and often outside the organisation. This includes the work routines, how the organisation is structured and controlled and 'softer' issues around symbolic behaviours (see section 4.6.5 below). These behaviours may become the taken-for-granted 'ways we do things around here' that are potentially the bases for inimitable strategic capabilities (see section 3.3.3), but also significant barriers to achieving strategic change if that becomes necessary (see section 10.5.2).

- *Taken-for-granted assumptions* are the core of an organisation's culture. They are the aspects of organisational life which people find difficult to identify and explain. In this book we refer to them as the 'organisational paradigm'. The **paradigm** **is the set of assumptions held in common and taken for granted in an organisation.** These assumptions represent *collective experience* without which people would have to 'reinvent their world' for different circumstances that they face. The paradigm can underpin successful strategies by providing a basis of common understanding in an organisation, but can also be a major problem, for example when major strategic change is needed, or when organisations try to merge and find they are incompatible. The importance of the paradigm is discussed further in section 4.6.5.

4.6.3 Organisational subcultures

In seeking to understand the relationship between culture and an organisation's strategies, it may be possible to identify some aspects of culture that pervade the whole organisation. However, there may also be important *subcultures*. These may relate directly to the structure of the organisation: for example, the differences between geographical divisions in a multinational company, or between functional groups such as finance, marketing and operations. Differences between divisions may be particularly evident in organisations that have grown through acquisition. Also different divisions may be pursuing different types of strategy that require or foster different cultures. Indeed, aligning strategic positioning and organisational culture is a critical feature of successful organisations. Differences between business functions can also relate to the different nature of work in different functions. For example, in an oil company like Shell or BP differences are likely between those functions engaged in 'upstream' exploration, where time horizons may be in decades, and those concerned with 'downstream' retailing, with much shorter, market-driven time horizons. Arguably, this is one reason why both Shell and BP pay so much attention to trying to forge a corporate culture that crosses such functions.

4.6.4 Culture's influence on strategy

The taken-for-granted nature of culture is what makes it centrally important in relation to strategy and the management of strategy. There are three primary reasons for this.

- *Cultural 'glue'*. There are benefits in the taken-for-granted nature of culture. Josephine Rydberg-Dumont, president of IKEA, argues that, because all employees take as given the way the firm operates, it reduces the need for constant supervision. Moreover, since an aspect of the culture is to constantly question the status quo, it 'fuels' innovation. There are then benefits to the taken-for-granted aspect of culture.

- *Captured by culture*. Organisations can, however, be 'captured' by their culture. Managers, faced with a changing business environment, are more likely to attempt to deal with the situation by searching for what they can understand and cope with in terms of the existing culture. Culture is, in effect, an unintended driver of strategy.

- *Managing culture*. Because it is difficult to observe, identify and control that which is taken for granted, it is also difficult to manage. This is why having a way to analyse culture so as to make it more evident is important – the subject of the next section.

The effect of culture on strategy is shown in Figure 4.5. Faced with a stimulus for action, such as declining performance, managers first try to improve the implementation of existing strategy. This might be through trying to lower costs, improve efficiency, tighten controls or

Figure 4.5 Culture's influence on strategy development

Source: Adapted from P. Gringer and J.-C. Spender, *Turnaround: Managerial Recipes for Strategic Success*, Associated Business Press, 1979, p. 203.

improve accepted way of doing things. If this is not effective, a change of strategy may occur, but a change in line with the existing culture. For example, managers may seek to extend the market for their business, but assume that it will be similar to their existing market, and therefore set about managing the new venture in much the same way as they have been used to. Alternatively, even where managers know intellectually that they need to change strategy, they may find themselves constrained by organisational routines and assumptions or political processes. This often happens, for example, when there are attempts to change highly bureaucratic organisations to be customer-oriented. Even if people who accept the need to change a culture's emphasis on the importance of conforming to established rules, routines and reporting relationships, they do not readily do so. It is a fallacy to assume reasoned argument necessarily changes deeply embedded assumptions rooted in collective experience built up over long periods of time. Readers need only think of their own experience in trying to persuade others to rethink their religious beliefs, or indeed, allegiances to sports teams, to realise this. So it is with groups and organisations: people prefer the familiar and typically minimise uncertainty or ambiguity. They are likely to continue to do so until there is, perhaps, dramatic evidence of the redundancy of the culture such as a financial crisis or major loss of market share.

4.6.5 Analysing culture: the cultural web

In order to understand the existing culture and its effects it is important to be able to analyse an organisation's culture. The cultural web[19] is a means of doing this (see Figure 4.6). The **cultural web shows the behavioural, physical and symbolic manifestations of a culture** that inform and are informed by the taken-for-granted assumptions, or paradigm, of an organisation. The cultural web can be used to understand culture in any of the frames of reference discussed above but is most often used at the organisational and/or functional levels. The elements of the cultural web are as follows:

● The *paradigm* is at the core of the web. As previously defined, it is the set of assumptions held in common and taken for granted in an organisation: in effect it is the *collective experience* applied to a situation to make sense of it and inform a likely course of action. The assumptions of the paradigm are, quite likely, very basic but may or may not align with the logic of a strategy. For example, it may seem self-evident that a newspaper business's core assumptions are about the centrality of news coverage and reporting. However, from a strategic point of view, increasingly newspapers' revenues are reliant on advertising income and the strategy may need to be directed to this. The paradigm of a charity may be about doing good works for the needy, but this cannot be achieved if it is not run effectively for the purpose of raising money. It is quite likely that, even if the rational view is to build a strategy around revenue generation for the newspaper or the charity, people in those organisations may still interpret issues and behave in line with its paradigm. So understanding what the paradigm is and how it informs debate on strategy matters. The problem is that, since it is unlikely to be talked about, or even be something that people are conscious of, trying to identify it can be difficult; especially if you are part of that organisation. Outside observers may find it easier to identify simply by listening to what people say and watching what they do and

Figure 4.6 The cultural web: some useful questions

Stories

- What core beliefs do stories reflect?
- What stories are commonly told e.g. to newcomers
- How do these reflect core assumptions and beliefs?
- What norms do the mavericks deviate from?

Symbols

- What objects, events or people do people in the organisation particularly identify with?
- What are these related to in the history of the organisation?
- What aspects of strategy are highlighted in publicity?

Routines and rituals

- Which routines are emphasised?
- Which are embedded in history?
- What behaviour do routines encourage?
- What are the key rituals?
- What assumptions and core beliefs do they reflect?
- What do training programmes emphasise?
- How easy are rituals/routines to change?

Power structures

- Where does power reside? Indicators include:
  (a) status
  (b) claim on resources
  (c) symbols of power
- Who 'makes things happen'?
- Who stops things happening?

Stories Symbols

Routines and rituals **Paradigm** Power structures

Control systems Organisational structures

Control systems

- What is most closely monitored/controlled?
- Is emphasis on reward or punishment?
- Are controls rooted in history or current strategies?
- Are there many/few controls?

Organisational structures

- What are the formal *and* informal structures?
- How rigid are the structures?
- How hierarchical are the structures?
- Do structures encourage collaboration or competition?
- What types of power structure do they support?

Overall

- What do the answers to these questions suggest are the (few) fundamental assumptions that are the paradigm?
- How would you characterise the dominant culture?
- How easy is this to change?

emphasise. One way of 'insiders' getting to see the assumptions they take for granted is to focus initially on other aspects of the cultural web, because these are to do with more visible manifestations of culture. Moreover, these other aspects are likely to act to reinforce the assumptions within that paradigm.

- *Routines* are 'the way we do things around here' on a day-to-day basis. These may have a long history and may well be common across organisations. At their best, they lubricate the working of the organisation, and may provide a basis for distinctive organisational capabilities. However, they can also represent a taken-for-grantedness about how things should happen which, again, can guide how people respond to issues and be difficult to change.

- The *rituals* of organisational life are particular activities or special events that emphasise, highlight or reinforce what is important in the culture. Examples include training programmes, interview panels, promotion and assessment procedures, sales conferences and so on. An extreme example, of course, is the ritualistic training of military recruits to prepare them for the discipline required in conflict. However, rituals can also be informal activities such as drinks in the pub after work or gossiping around photocopying machines.

- The *stories* told by members of an organisation to each other, to outsiders, to new recruits and so on, may act to embed the present in its organisational history and also flag up important events and personalities. They typically have to do with successes, disasters, heroes, villains and mavericks (who deviate from the norm). They can be a way of letting people know what is conventionally important in an organisation.

- *Symbols*[20] are objects, events, acts or people that convey, maintain or create meaning over and above their functional purpose. For example, offices and office layout, cars and job titles have a functional purpose, but are also typically signals about status and hierarchy. Particular people may come to represent specially important aspects of an organisation or historic turning points. The form of language used in an organisation can also be particularly revealing, especially with regard to customers or clients. For example, the head of a consumer protection agency in Australia described his clients as 'complainers'. In a major teaching hospital in the UK, consultants described patients as 'clinical material'. While such examples might be amusing, they reveal an underlying assumption about customers (or patients) that might play a significant role in influencing the strategy of an organisation. Although symbols are shown separately in the cultural web, it should be remembered that many elements of the web are symbolic. So, routines, control and reward systems and structures are not only functional but also symbolic.

- *Power* is the ability of individuals or groups to persuade, induce or coerce others into following certain courses of action. So *power structures* are distributions of power to groups of people in an organisation. The most powerful individuals or groups are likely to be closely associated with the paradigm. For example, in firms that experience strategic drift, it is not unusual to find powerful executives who have long association with long-established ways of doing things.

- *Organisational structures* are the roles, responsibilities and reporting relationships in organisations. These are likely to reflect power structures and how they manifest themselves emphasises which roles and relationships really matter in an organisation. Formal hierarchical, mechanistic structures may emphasise that strategy is the province of top managers and everyone else is 'working to orders'. Structures with less emphasis on formal reporting relationships might indicate more participative strategy-making. Highly devolved structures may signify that collaboration is less important than competition and so on.

- *Control systems* are the formal and informal ways of monitoring and supporting people within and around an organisation and tend to emphasise what is seen to be important in the organisation. They include measurements and reward systems. For example, public-service organisations have often been accused of being concerned more with stewardship of funds than with quality of service. This is reflected in their control systems, which are more about accounting for spending rather than with quality of service. Individually based bonus schemes related to volume are likely to signal a culture of individuality, internal competition and an emphasis on sales volume rather than teamwork and an emphasis on quality.

Illustration 4.5 shows a cultural web drawn up by the partners of a medium-sized law firm as part of a strategic review. The key point to emerge was that the culture of the firm was dominated by their personalities and personal styles linked to an expectation of collective commitment and the need to 'fit in'. This was an issue for the firm as they faced a strategic choice of whether to try to sell their firm on to a much larger one or attempt to grow the firm with themselves at the helm. The problem for either choice was the dominance of these senior partners in the firm's culture: they were seen as 'the brotherhood; the heart of the firm'. If they were to sell the firm, they each would leave and so take away a significant element of the firm's formula for success. If they were to try to grow the firm, how would they duplicate themselves and develop the leadership potential of others to fill the expanding roles?

In addition to showing the cultural web itself, Figure 4.6 also outlines some of the questions that might help build up an understanding of culture using the web. It is important to emphasise that the need is to surface that which is taken for granted. For example, there is a danger in seeing public statements of an organisation's values, beliefs and purposes – for example, in annual reports, mission or values statements and business plans – as useful descriptions of the organisational culture. This is not to suggest that there is any organised deception. It is simply that the statements of values and beliefs are often carefully considered and carefully crafted statements of the aspirations of a particular stakeholder (such as the CEO) rather than descriptions of the actual culture.

ILLUSTRATION 4.5

The cultural web of a law firm

The cultural web can be used to identify the behaviours and taken-for-granted assumptions of an organisation.

This is an adapted version of a cultural web produced by partners and managers of a law firm.

Heroic commitment to the firm:
if you don't fit, don't share
the right principles,
you exit

Unity, inclusivity and
conformity

Stories
- Heroes
- Epic travel
- Commitment to the firm
- Wrong/bad people being sacked
- The salvation – our big money making deal

Symbols
- No one has offices
- All desks same size
- Being made a partner
- Dispersed share ownership
- Heading up major client accounts

Rituals/routines
- We celebrate long service to the firm
- We have routines that are about 'us leader, you follower'
- We don't really celebrate the success of the firm

Paradigm
- Almost a secret society element to it
- A brotherhood
- Like pioneers of our way of doing business
- Evangelising

Power
- The CEO and like minded senior partners
- Energy, drive, assertiveness
- Egotism
- Male

Controls
- Lots of measurement
- Anxiety about control
- Overly anxious about monitoring

Structure
- Meetings; lots of them
- Absence of guiding principles
- Segmented structure

Rituals are about
being the right kind of
person.
*'We do leaving very well,
"Sinatra tours" for long
service.'*

Power is the property
of individuals, manifest
in their visible energy.
*'Bursting into a room
with an armful of papers
is power, noise is power.'*

We are concerned about control,
but paradoxically we love a crisis
to rush in and solve

Meetings dominate the
structure; everyone
wants 'their say'.

Questions

1 How would you characterise the dominant culture here?

2 How do the various elements of the web interrelate?

3 Draw up a cultural web for an organisation of your choice.

SUMMARY

- An important managerial task is to decide how the organisation should express its strategic purpose through statements of *mission, vision, values* or *objectives*.

- The purpose of an organisation will be influenced by the expectations of its *stakeholders*.

- The influence of some key stakeholders will be represented formally within the *governance structure* of an organisation. This can be represented in terms of a *governance chain*, showing the links between ultimate beneficiaries and the managers of an organisation.

- Organisations adopt different stances on *corporate social responsibility* depending on how they perceive their role in society.

- Different stakeholders exercise different influence on organisational purpose and strategy, dependent on the extent of their power and interest. Managers can assess the influence of different stakeholder groups through *stakeholder analysis*.

- *Organisational culture* may influence purpose and strategy and can be understood by means of the *cultural web*.

VIDEO CASE

Visit **MyStrategyLab** and watch the *Eden* case study.

1 Write a statement of Eden's mission, vision and values.

2 Explain how Eden's management developed its strategy on the basis of aligning stakeholder interests.

RECOMMENDED KEY READINGS

- The case for the importance of clarity of strategic values and vision is especially strongly made by J. Collins and J. Porras, *Built to Last: Successful Habits of Visionary Companies*, Harper Business, 2002 (in particular see chapter 11).

- For a review of different stances on corporate social responsibility see P. Mirvis and B. Googins, 'Stages of corporate citizenship', *California Management Review*, vol. 48, no. 2 (2006), pp. 104–26. Also see A.B. Carroll and K.M. Shabana, 'The business case for Corporate Social Responsibility, *International Journal of Management Reviews*, vol. 12, no. 1 (2010), pp. 85–105.

- For more about the stakeholder concept and analysis see K. Scholes, 'Stakeholder mapping: a practical tool for managers', in V. Ambrosini with G. Johnson and K. Scholes (eds), *Exploring Techniques of Analysis and Evaluation in Strategic Management*, Prentice Hall, 1998.

- For a more thorough explanation of the cultural web and how organisation culture can affect strategy see G. Johnson, 'Managing strategic change – strategy, culture and action', *Long Range Planning*, vol. 25, no. 1 (1992), pp. 28–36.

REFERENCES

1. Cynthia A. Montgomery, 'Putting leadership back into strategy', *Harvard Business Review*, January 2008, pp. 54–60.

2. J. Collins and J. Porras, 'Building your company's vision', *Harvard Business Review*, September–October 1996, pp. 65–77.

3. P. Lencioni, 'Make your values mean something', *Harvard Business Review*, vol. 80, no. 7 (2002), pp. 113–17.

4. For example, see B. Bartkus, M. Glassman and B. McAfee, 'Mission statements: are they smoke and mirrors?', *Business Horizons*, vol. 43, no. 6 (2000), pp. 23–28; and B. Bartkus, M. Glassman and B. McAfee, 'Mission statement quality and financial performance', *European Management Journal*, vol. 24, no. 1 (2006), pp. 86–94.

5. See J. Collins and J. Porras, *Built to Last: Successful Habits of Visionary Companies*, Harper Business, 2002.

6. See Sayan Chatterjee, 'Core objectives: clarity in designing strategy', *California Management Review*, vol. 47, no. 2 (2005), pp. 33–49.

7. This definition is based on, but adapted from, that in S. Jacoby, 'Corporate governance and society', *Challenge*, vol. 48, no. 4 (2005), pp. 69–87.

8. The principal–agent model is part of agency theory which developed within organisational economics but is now widely used in the management field as described here. A useful reference is: K. Eisenhardt, 'Agency theory: an assessment and review', *Academy of Management Review*, vol. 14, no. 1 (1989), pp. 57–74.

9. This definition is based on that by the World Business Council for Sustainable Development.

10. Based on research undertaken at the Center for Corporate Citizenship at the Boston College, reported in P. Mirvis and B. Googins, 'Stages of corporate citizenship', *California Management Review*, vol. 48, no. 2 (2006), pp. 104–26.

11. Often quoted as a summary of Milton Friedman's argument is M. Friedman: 'The social responsibility of business is to increase its profits', *New York Times Magazine*, 13 September 1970.

12. See M. Porter and M. Kramer, 'The competitive advantage of corporate philanthropy', *Harvard Business Review*, vol. 80, no. 12 (2002), pp. 56–68.

13. D. Vogel, 'Is there a market for virtue? The business case for corporate social responsibility', *California Management Review*, vol. 47, no. 4 (2005), pp. 19–45.

14. These examples are given by Porter and Kramer in 'The competitive advantage of corporate philanthropy', *Harvard Business Review*, vol. 80, no. 12 (2002), pp. 56–68.

15. A fuller explanation of how these three groups interact with organisations can be found in J. Cummings and J. Doh, 'Identifying who matters: mapping key players in multiple environments', *California Management Review*, vol. 42, no. 2 (2000), pp. 83–104.

16. This approach to stakeholder mapping has been adapted from A. Mendelow, *Proceedings of the 2nd International Conference on Information Systems*, Cambridge, MA, 1991.

17. See G. Hofstede, *Culture's Consequences*, Sage, 2nd edn. 2001.

18. See E. Schein This definition of culture is taken from E. Schein, *Organisational Culture and Leadership*, 2nd edition, Jossey-Bass, 1997, p. 6.

19. A fuller explanation of the cultural web can be found in G. Johnson, *Strategic Change and the Management Process*, 1987, and G. Johnson, 'Managing strategic change: strategy, culture and action', *Long Range Planning*, vol. 25, no. 1 (1992), pp. 28–36.

20. The significance of organisational symbolism is explained in G. Johnson, 'Managing strategic change: the role of symbolic action', *British Journal of Management*, vol. 1, no. 4 (1990), pp. 183–200.

Cultural turnaround at Club Med

Frédéric Fréry, ESCP Europe

In 2010, the repositioning of Club Med as an 'upscale, friendly and multicultural' tour operator was supposed to be achieved, through the complete renovation of its portfolio of vacation villages. However, the outcome of this strategy, implemented since the early 2000s, when Club Med had faced the loss of impetus of its historical model, was still unclear. Such a repositioning clearly clashed with Club Med's history and culture, generally associated with a relaxed atmosphere, rough and ready amenities and an open-minded lifestyle.

The 2009 results showed that, even if operating profits were finally up after several years of decrease,

Source: Shutterstock.

Figure 1 Club Med revenues (million euros)

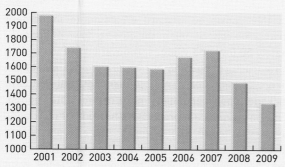

€1m is about $1.4m.

Figure 2 Club Med net profits (million euros)

€1m is about $1.4m.

revenues were still declining. Club Med's Chairman and CEO Henri Giscard d'Estaing explained that the net loss (€58m; ~$81m) resulted from four elements: (1) the overall economic crisis, (2) the H1N1 flu virus and its impact on tourism, (3) the renovation cost of the villages, and (4) a 'limited number of property transactions, due to the mortgage crisis'. He also announced the opening of five new villages in China between 2010 and 2015. His promise was to 'deliver a new profitable Club Med for 2010'.

However, the break with Club Med's history and culture had to succeed: since 2004, this strategic turnaround had cost around €1bn.

Club Med's history: the years of growth

Club Med was founded after the Second World War by Gérard Blitz and Gilbert Trigano.

Coming from a Belgian diamond merchant family, Gérard Blitz was a world-class athlete in swimming and water-polo. In 1950, he spent some days of vacation in a tent village close to Calvi, Corsica. This gave him the idea to create a 'vacation camp' under the sun. He founded the Belgian association 'Club Méditerranée' in April 1950 and opened his first village on a desert beach on the island of Mallorca, Spain.

Blitz bought his tents from a French supplier, Gilbert Trigano. Apart from owning a family tent business, Trigano was a former resistance fighter and a reporter for the French Communist newspaper *L'Humanité*. Attracted by the vacation village concept, fascinated by Blitz's personality, Trigano became the treasurer of the association in 1953, then president in 1963. The same year, Club Méditerranée was incorporated.

In 1955, Club Méditerranée opened a second tent village in Tahiti (Blitz's wife was of Tahitian origin). In 1956, a winter village was opened in Leysin, Switzerland, and in 1965, Club Méditerranée opened its first permanent village in Agadir, Morocco.

In 1966, in order to finance a vast international expansion plan in Northern Africa, Europe, America and Asia, the company was listed at the Paris stock exchange. During the next 20 years, dozens of villages opened, including two giant sailing ships, *Club Med 1* and *Club Med 2*.

First difficulties

In 1991, the year Blitz died, Operation Desert Storm strongly impacted the tourist industry and Club Med suffered heavy losses. In 1993, Gilbert Trigano was replaced as chairman and CEO by his son, Serge. In spite of his turnaround plan, Serge Trigano did not manage to put the situation right. In 1997, upset shareholders replaced him with an external manager, Philippe Bourguignon, the former CEO of EuroDisney.

Bourguignon's ambition was to 'transform a vacation villages company into a service company'. He implemented a growth strategy, both organic (new concepts such as a low-cost village for young people) and external (takeover of another tour operator and of a gym clubs chain). This ambitious expansion strategy came with a severe cost-cutting plan, a shift in human resource management (in the villages, many Club Med employees were replaced with local suppliers) and the implementation of a real IT infrastructure (many processes were still done manually). Club Med became profitable in 1998. In 1999, net profits grew by 48 per cent. In 2000, revenues and profits soared again (+28 per cent and +51 per cent respectively). In three years, Club Med attracted more than 300,000 new customers. In 2001, when Gilbert Trigano died, Club Med had 127 villages, 24,200 employees and 1.8 million customers.

However, the terrorist attacks of 9/11 caused an immediate collapse of the tourist market. Bourguignon's volume strategy was no longer sustainable. Since he was disowned by Club Med's employees – who criticised his autocratic management and were used to Trigano's paternalism – he resigned from the chairmanship in 2002. He was replaced by the CEO he had recruited himself from Danone, Henri Giscard d'Estaing. Giscard d'Estaing was also the elder son of the former President of the French Republic.

The repositioning plan

When Giscard d'Estaing became chairman and CEO, Club Med was facing two external threats:

- The tourist industry was heavily affected by the terrorist threat.
- Thanks to the internet, new low-cost entrants were rapidly expanding, and incumbents were offered vacation villages, similar to the Club Med concept, but at lower prices.

All this convinced Giscard d'Estaing to implement an upscale repositioning: the closing down of approximately 50 low-end villages, renovation of the existing infrastructure, opening of new prestigious establishments, a significant rise in services (all-inclusive package, open-bar policy, more comfortable rooms), but also a significant price rise. The number of villages decreased to 80 and a much more sophisticated advertising campaign was launched. Between 1998 and 2008, the proportion of highend villages went from 18 per cent to 47 per cent, whereas low-end villages were disappearing. The clientele also evolved significantly: households with a high revenue accounted for 63 per cent of customers in 2003, and 82 per cent in 2005.

This repositioning was mainly financed by selling property, which reduced financial costs and amortisation, limited debt, and allowed Club Med to offer an acceptable balance sheet for investors to finance the renovation of its villages. However, two external events weakened this strategy: the market was still in a downturn (on top of terrorist threats, the 2004 tsunami in Asia also had an impact), and from 2007 the mortgage crisis brutally reduced the opportunity for property profits.

In 2010, analysts were still uncertain about the results of this profound strategic reorientation, which was disrupting Club Med's historical culture.

The roots of Club Med's culture

For more than 50 years, Club Med exhibited a distinct culture. Gilbert Trigano used to say that he had created a 'profoundly psychological industry'.

Marked by the Second World War, Blitz had created Club Med because he thought that all Europeans deserved vacations on the seaside and under the sun. He defined his concept as the 'antidote against civilisation'. According to Gilbert Trigano:

'More than Gérard, I tried to reconcile capitalism with utopia. I remember these early mornings when we were boldly building the world with a total madness, but we knew perfectly what we were doing: we knew we wanted to influence people's life and future.'

Blitz was an idealist and Trigano a pragmatist, but they agreed on 'gathering people hurt by modern society in a peaceful and soft place where they could regain their forces, an artificial environment to teach people to smile again'.

To do so, they built up a culture with rich symbols, rituals and myths. Villages were isolated from their local environment in order to break from day-to-day life. Amenities were limited: tents at first, then huts – often without electricity – with shared bathrooms. In this closed world, as of 1951, customers were named GMs (Gracious Members) and coordinators GOs (Gracious Organisers). On arrival, welcomed by GOs, GMs had to ban professional jargon and social origins. At the restaurant, there were only eight-people tables, in order to force GMs to make new acquaintances. As of 1956, Club Med banned money from the villages and implemented a payment system based on plastic pearl necklaces.

GOs were the keystone of the whole system. They were expected to maintain a permanent festive atmosphere through shows, village dances and sport competitions. During the first years, Blitz personally recruited them with his wife, Claudine. Gilbert Trigano insisted:

'Claudine informally played the role of head of personnel, which was a key role because everything relies on GOs. She and Gérard were the tutelary parents of the Club, they choose children in their image and maintain family relations with them.'

From an organisational point of view, the best GOs could become general managers of a village, in charge of all the operational aspects, from animation to hospitality and security. The best general managers – a job it was difficult to cope with after the age of 45, because it required an almost permanent night-and-day presence with GMs – could access administrative positions at Club Med headquarters in Paris, even if these coordinators were not necessarily good executives.

Under the trident logo (a reference to Poseidon and the Mediterranean Sea), Club Med generated a 'sea, sex and sun' alchemy which reached its apogee in the 1970s.

Towards a new culture

In the 1990s, this life in a community was no longer in line with social evolution. Loose morals were unacceptable for families. Villages were more and more considered as ghettos, without any contact with local cultures. Undue familiarity between GOs and GMs repelled some customers and the obligation to participate in all activities was seen as brigading.

As a consequence, as of 2002, after having asked Serge Trigano about Club Med's historical culture, Giscard d'Estaing attempted deep cultural change. An ambiance charter was produced. It highlighted the core values of the company: multicultural, pioneer, kindness, freedom, responsibility. It also spelled out inappropriate behaviours for GOs: cronyism, hasty judgement, individualism. As thick as a phone book, it also explained new procedures and limited 'vulgar' activities such as water games or roles played by a member of the opposite sex. A school village opened in Vittel in France, in order to train 10,000 employees (out of a total of 16,000). The goal was to reconsider relational behaviours, ways of dressing and attitudes. The organisation of the village was also modified. General managers – who used to supervise directly 15 services – were now assisted by two deputies (one in charge of hospitality, the other in charge of leisure).

A transformation in progress

This evolution was still in progress by 2010. Even if customer satisfaction had increased, the occupancy rate had not. Nothing indicated that shareholders would give Giscard d'Estaing enough time to complete Club Med's transformation: the share price plummeted from €54 in August 2007 to €13 in January 2010.

Even if Giscard d'Estaing maintained that his strategy was beginning to bear fruit, in mid-2009 he had had to react to the potential threat of a hostile takeover bid from external investors, who estimated that an upscale repositioning was inconsistent with Club Med's values and business model. An increase in capital dispelled this threat, but analysts were still cautious about the result of such a strategic and cultural turnaround.

Sources: clubmed.net; psychologies.com; *Les Echos*, 10 September 2007, 17 September 2007, 14 December 2009; *Challenges*, 11 December 2009; *Le Monde*, 16 December 2007; ESCP Europe monograph by J. de Florival and C. Hamard, 2007.

Questions

1 Analyse Club Med's culture before 2000.

2 Explain the reasons for Club Med's success between the 1950s and the 1990s.

3 How do you explain Club Med's difficulties in the early 1990s?

4 Why did Bourguignon's plan fail? Do you think that Giscard d'Estaing's plan will be more successful?

5

BUSINESS STRATEGY

Learning outcomes

After reading this chapter you should be able to:

- Identify *strategic business units* (SBUs) in organisations.

- Assess business strategy in terms of the generic strategies of *cost leadership*, *differentiation* and *focus*.

- Assess the benefits of *cooperation* in business strategy.

Key terms

Competitive advantage p. 111
Competitive strategy p. 111
Cost-leadership strategy p. 112
Differentiation p. 116
Focus strategy p. 119
Strategic business unit p. 110

(5.1) INTRODUCTION

www.mystrategylab.com
**KEY
CONCEPT**

Strategic
business unit
(SBU)

This chapter is about strategic choices at the level of strategic business units. A **strategic business unit (SBU) is any business that supplies goods or services to a distinct domain of activity**. Thus a strategic business unit might be an independent restaurant business, which has to decide a range of issues such as menus, décor and prices in the light of competition from other restaurants locally. On the other hand, a strategic business unit might be a subsidiary of a large diversified corporation such as Unilever or Nestlé, where every business unit must decide how it should operate in its own particular market. For example, Unilever's ice-cream business has to decide how it will compete against Nestlé's ice-cream business on a range of dimensions including product features, pricing, branding and distribution channels. These kinds of *business* strategy issues are distinct from the question as to whether Unilever should own an ice-cream business in the first place: this is a matter of *corporate* strategy, the subject of Chapter 6.

Figure 5.1 shows the two main themes that provide the structure for the rest of the chapter: first competitive strategy and then interactive strategy, where the relationship with competitors is particularly important.

- *Generic competitive strategies*, including *cost-leadership*, *differentiation* and *focus*, and considering the *strategy clock*.
- *Interactive strategies*, building on the notion of generic strategies to consider interaction with competitors, especially moves and counter-moves and possible cooperation.

Business strategy is not relevant just to the private business sector. Charities and public sector organisations both cooperate and compete. Thus charities compete between each other for support from donors. Public-sector organisations also need to be 'competitive' against comparable organisations in order to satisfy their stakeholders and secure their funding. Schools compete in terms of examination results, while hospitals compete in terms of waiting

Figure 5.1 Business strategy

times, treatment survival rates and so on. Although some of the detailed implications may vary between sectors, wherever comparison is possible with other similar organisations, basic principles of business strategy are likely to be relevant. Very few organisations can afford to be demonstrably inferior to peers, and almost all have to make choices on key competitive variables such as costs, prices and quality.

 ## 5.2 GENERIC COMPETITIVE STRATEGIES

This section introduces the competitive element of business strategy, with cooperation addressed particularly in section 5.4. **Competitive strategy is concerned with how a strategic business unit achieves competitive advantage in its domain of activity.** In turn, **competitive advantage is about how an SBU creates value for its users both greater than the costs of supplying them and superior to that of rival SBUs.** There are two important features of competitive advantage here. To be *competitive* at all, the SBU must ensure that users (customers or funders) see sufficient value that they are prepared to pay more than the costs of supply. To have an *advantage*, the SBU must be able to create greater value than competitors. In the absence of a competitive advantage, the SBU is always vulnerable to attack by competitors with better products or services or offering lower prices, and could be driven out of business.

Michael Porter[1] argues that there are two fundamental means of achieving competitive advantage. An SBU can have lower costs than its competitors. Or it can have products or services that are so exceptionally valuable to customers that it can charge higher prices than competitors. In defining competitive strategies, Porter adds a further dimension based on the scope of customers that the business chooses to serve. Businesses can choose to focus on narrow customer segments, for example a particular demographic group such as the youth market. Alternatively, they can attempt to target a broad range of customers, across a range of characteristics such as age, wealth or geography.

Porter's distinctions define three 'generic' strategies: in other words, basic types of strategy that hold across many kinds of business situations. These three generic strategies are illustrated in Figure 5.2. In the top left-hand corner is a strategy of *cost-leadership*, as exemplified in the British women's clothing market by retailers such as Matalan. Matalan seeks to use large economies of scale and tight cost discipline to serve a wide range of women with reasonably fashionable clothing at a good price. Monsoon's shops pursues a strategy of *differentiation*, offering arty styles to women across a range of ages at significantly higher prices. The third generic strategy is *focus*, involving a narrow competitive scope. Porter distinguishes between cost focus and differentiation focus, but for him, narrow scope is such a distinctive fundamental principle that these two are merely variations on the same basic theme of narrowness. For example, Evans targets only women needing larger-sized clothing, achieving a higher price for its distinctive products through a *differentiation focus* strategy. On the other hand, the clothing lines of the major supermarkets target shoppers who are simply looking for good-value standard clothing for their families, a *cost focus* strategy. The rest of this section discusses these three generic strategies in more detail.

Figure 5.2 Three generic strategies

5.2.1 Cost-leadership

Cost-leadership strategy involves becoming the lowest-cost organisation in a domain of activity. There are four key *cost drivers* that can help deliver cost leadership, as follows:

● *Input costs* are often very important, for example labour or raw materials. Many companies seek competitive advantage through locating their labour-intensive operations in countries with low labour costs. Examples might be service call-centres in India or manufacturing in China. Location close to raw material sources can also be advantageous, as for example the Brazilian steel producer CSN which benefits from its own local iron-ore facilities.

● *Economies of scale* refer to how increasing scale usually reduces the average costs of operation over a particular time period, perhaps a month or a year. Economies of scale are important wherever there are high fixed costs. Fixed costs are those costs necessary for any level of output: for example, a pharmaceutical manufacturer typically needs to do extensive R&D before it produces a single pill. Economies of scale come from spreading these fixed costs over high levels of output: the average cost due to an expensive R&D project halves when output increases from 1 million to 2 million units. Economies of scale in purchasing can also reduce input costs. The large airlines, for example, are able to negotiate steep discounts from aircraft manufacturers. For the cost-leader, it is important to reach the output level equivalent to the *minimum efficient scale*. Note, though, that *diseconomies of scale* are possible. Large volumes of output that require special overtime payments to workers or involve the neglect of equipment maintenance can soon become very expensive. As in Figure 5.3,

Figure 5.3 Economies of scale and the experience curve

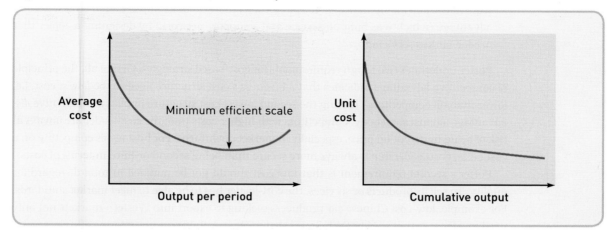

therefore, the economies of scale curve is typically somewhat U-shaped, with the average cost per unit actually increasing beyond a certain point.

- *Experience*[2] can be a key source of cost efficiency. The *experience curve* implies that the cumulative experience gained by an organisation with each unit of output leads to reductions in unit costs (see Figure 5.3). There is no time limit: simply the more experience an organisation has in an activity, the more efficient it gets at doing it. The efficiencies are basically of two sorts. First, there are gains in labour productivity as staff learn to do things more cheaply over time (this is the specific *learning curve* effect). Second, costs are saved through more efficient designs or equipment as experience shows what works best. The experience curve has three important implications for business strategy. First, entry timing into a market is important: early entrants into a market will have experience that late entrants do not yet have and so will gain a cost advantage. Second, it is important to gain and hold market share, as companies with higher market share have more 'cumulative experience' simply because of their greater volumes. Finally, although the gains from experience are typically greatest at the start, as indicated by the steep initial curve in Figure 5.3, improvements normally continue over time. Opportunities for cost reduction are theoretically endless. Figure 5.3 compares the experience curve and economies of scale in order to underline the contrast here. Unlike scale, where diseconomies appear beyond a certain point, the experience curve implies at worst a flattening of the rate of cost reduction. Cost savings due to accumulated experience are continuously available.

- *Product/process design* also influences cost. Efficiency can be 'designed in' at the outset. For example, engineers can choose to build a product from cheap standard components rather than expensive specialised components. Organisations can choose to interact with customers exclusively through cheap web-based methods, rather than via telephone or stores. Organisations can also tailor their offerings in order to meet the most important customer needs, saving money by ignoring others. This, arguably, is the strategy of Barnet, the 'easy-Council' (Illustration 5.1). In designing a product or service, it is important to recognise *whole-life costs*, in other words, the costs to the customer not just of purchase, but of subsequent use and maintenance. In the photocopier market, for example, Canon eroded Xerox's advantage (which was built on service and a support network) by designing a copier that needed far less servicing.

Porter underlines two tough requirements for cost-based strategies. First of all, the principle of competitive advantage indicates that a business's cost structure needs to be *lowest* cost, i.e. lower than all competitors'. Having the second lowest cost structure implies a competitive *dis-* advantage against somebody. Competitors with higher costs than the cost-leader are always at risk of being undercut on price, especially in market downturns. For businesses competing on a cost basis, cost-leadership is always more secure than being second or third in terms of costs.

Porter's second requirement is that low cost should not be pursued in total disregard for quality. To sell its products or services, the cost-leader has to be able to meet market standards. For example, low-cost Chinese car producers seeking to export into Western markets not only need to offer cars that are cheap, but cars that meet acceptable norms in terms of style, service network, reliability, resale value and other important characteristics. Cost-leaders have two options here:

● *Parity* (in other words, equivalence) with competitors in product or service features valued by customers. Parity allows the cost-leader to charge the same prices as the average competitor in the marketplace, while translating its cost advantage wholly into extra profit (as in the second column of Figure 5.4). The Brazilian steel producer CSN, with its cheap iron-ore sources, is able to charge the average price for its steel, and take the cost difference in greater profit.

Figure 5.4 Costs, prices and profits for generic strategies

ILLUSTRATION 5.1

easyCouncils: a strategy for low-cost council services

The London Borough of Barnet has chosen a budget airline model for its services, on the lines of easyJet.

In 2008–09, with pressures on budgets increasing, Conservative Party-controlled councils in the United Kingdom were looking to save costs by adopting the low-cost model pioneered by airlines such as Ryanair and easyJet. Barnet, a borough council in North London with a population of over 300,000, is one of the pioneers.

The Conservative borough council is led by a former PwC management consultant, Mike Freer. In a context of falling central government subsidies, and wanting to save local taxes, the council is looking to cut costs by £15m (~€16.5; ~$22.5) a year. In 2008, the council launched a consultation process on radical reform called 'Future Shape'. In 2009, they declared their intention to adopt a budget airline model, which council officials dubbed 'easyCouncil'.

Mike Freer gave some examples. Just as budget airlines allow passengers to pay extra for priority boarding, in future householders will be able to pay extra to jump the queue in order to get faster responses on planning applications for new buildings or house extensions. Similarly, as airline passengers can choose whether to have a meal or not (and pay accordingly), users of adult social care will be allowed to choose their own options. Freer explained to the *Guardian*:

> 'In the past we would do things for our residents rather than letting them choose for themselves. We would tell them they need one hour help shopping, or one hour cleaning, or meals-on-wheels, and they would get it, like it or not. Instead, we will assess what level of personal care they need, place a value on it and give them the budget. If they say, "Frankly, I'd like a weekend in Eastbourne [a holiday resort]", they can have it.'

Opposition Labour leader Alison Moore warned in the *Guardian*:

> 'There is a real danger of problems in the local community and that vulnerable people will lose out. People who are dependent on care services may find that they aren't there at the same quality as before.'

John Burgess, branch secretary of the main local government services trade union, commented:

> 'Democratically accountable public services are the best way to ensure quality services and value for money. Comparing public services to gimmicks used by a cheap airline company beggars belief.'

Barnet citizens differed on the new approach. 87-year-old Sarah Walker broke a bone in an accident, forcing her to spend three weeks in hospital. When she returned home, she was initially badly disabled and feared being sent to a local authority care home, from which she would never return. The council's new policy of avoiding expensive care homes and instead offering a burst of intensive help to ease the disabled into independence worked for her:

> 'I had three carers a day for the first week. One in the morning, one at lunchtime and one in the evening. They gave me the confidence to get back to doing things for myself. At the end of six weeks, I was managing quite well and I'm independent now. It would be a waste of money if they were sending someone once a week for ever more, so this was the right approach for me.'

On the other hand, 68-year-old Bill Kelly compared the Council's logic to electronic tagging in order to save the costs of prison for criminals: 'I can see Mr Freer giving us all ankle tags so they know where we are.'

Sources: R. Booth, 'Tory-Controlled Borough of Barnet adopts budget airline model', *Guardian*, 27 August 2009; J. Burgess, 'The budget airline model won't work for councils', *Guardian*, 2 September 2009.

Questions

1 What are the advantages and disadvantages of this approach to low-cost council services?

2 In what sense do borough councils 'compete'?

● *Proximity* (closeness) to competitors in terms of features. Where a competitor is sufficiently close to competitors in terms of product or service features, customers may only require small cuts in prices to compensate for the slightly lower quality. As in the third column in Figure 5.4, the proximate cost-leader still earns better profits than the average competitor because its lower price eats up only a part of its cost advantage. This proximate cost-leadership strategy might be the option chosen initially by Chinese car manufacturers in export markets, for example.

5.2.2 Differentiation strategies

For Porter, the principal alternative to cost-leadership is differentiation.[3] **Differentiation involves uniqueness along some dimension that is sufficiently valued by customers to allow a price premium**. Relevant points of differentiation vary between markets. Within each market too, businesses may differentiate along different dimensions. Thus in clothing retail, competitors may differentiate by store size, locations or fashion. In cars, competitors may differentiate by safety, style or fuel efficiency. Where there are many alternative dimensions that are valued by customers, it is possible to have many different types of differentiation strategy in a market. Thus, even at the same top end of the car market, BMW and Mercedes differentiate in different ways, the first typically with a sportier image, the second with more conservative values. The strategy canvas provides one means of mapping these various kinds of differentiation (see section 2.4.3).

Managers can identify potential for differentiation by using perceptual mapping of their products or services against those of competitors. For example, Figure 5.5 maps customer perceptions of American airline companies along two bundles of attributes: flight performance attributes such as delays, and service attributes such as baggage problems or boarding complaints. Most of the larger airlines are quite closely bunched together. For example, US Air and Delta are not significantly differentiated from each other in terms of on-time flights, and they are perceived similarly in terms of service elements such as boarding, ticketing and reservations. One airline that does stand out as a differentiator is Southwest, which does well in terms of both flight delays and service. In the period studied, Southwest was also the most profitable of these airlines. It seems that Southwest was able to differentiate on attributes that were highly valued by its customers.

However, the attributes on which to differentiate need to be chosen carefully. Differentiation strategies require clarity about two key factors:

● *The strategic customer*. It is vital to identify clearly the strategic customer on whose needs the differentiation is based. This is not always straightforward, as discussed in section 2.4.2. For example, for a newspaper business, the strategic customers could be readers (who pay a purchase price), advertisers (who pay for advertising), or both. Finding a distinctive means of prioritising customers can be a valuable source of differentiation.

● *Key competitors*. It is very easy for a differentiator to draw the boundaries for comparison too tightly, concentrating on a particular niche. Thus specialist Italian clothing company Benetton

Figure 5.5 Mapping differentiation in the US airline industry

Service attributes
Strong

Alaska Airlines ○

Southwest ○

US Air ○
Delta ○

Flight performance attributes   Poor ←————— Northwest ○ —————→ Strong

Continental ○

○ American

United ○

Poor

Source: Simplified from Figure 1, in D. Gursoy, M. Chen and H. Kim, 'The US airlines relative positioning', *Tourism Management*, vol. 26, no. 5 (2005), pp. 57–67: p. 62.

originally had a strong position with its specialist knitwear shops. However, it lost ground because it did not recognise early enough that general retailers such as Marks & Spencers could also compete in the same product space of colourful pullovers and similar products.

There is an important condition for a successful differentiation strategy. Differentiation allows higher prices, but usually comes at a cost. To create a point of valuable differentiation typically involves additional investments, for example in R&D, branding or staff quality. The differentiator can expect that its costs will be higher than those of the average competitor. But, as in column 4 in Figure 5.4, the differentiator needs to ensure that the additional costs of differentiation do not exceed the gains in price. It is easy to pile on additional costs in ways that are not valued sufficiently by customers. The failures under British ownership of the luxury car companies Rolls-Royce and Bentley against top-end Mercedes cars are partly attributable to the expensive crafting of wood and leather interiors, the full cost of which even wealthy customers were not prepared to pay for. Just as cost-leaders should not neglect quality, so should differentiators attend closely to costs, especially in areas irrelevant to their sources of differentiation. As in Illustration 5.2, Volvo's differentiation strategy in the Indian bus market seems to have involved keeping an eye on costs as well.

ILLUSTRATION 5.2

Volvo's different Indian buses

Volvo has a strategy to sell buses at nearly four times the prevailing market price.

The Indian bus market has long been dominated by two home-players, subsidiaries of major Indian conglomerates: Tata Motors and Ashok Leyland. The two companies made simple coaches on a design that had hardly changed for decades. On top of a basic truck chassis, the two companies bolted a rudimentary coach body. Engines were a meagre 110–120 horse-power, and roared heartily as they hauled their loads up the steep mountain roads of India. Mounted at the front, the heat from the over-strained engines would pervade the whole bus. Air conditioning was a matter of open windows, through which the dust and noise of the Indian roads would pour. Suspension was old-fashioned, guaranteeing a shaky ride on pot-holed roads. Bags were typically slung on the top of the bus, where they were easily soiled and at high risk of theft. But at least the buses were cheap, selling to local bus companies at around Rs 1.2m (€15,000; $21,000).

In 1997, Swedish bus company Volvo decided to enter the market, with buses prices at Rs 4m, nearly four times as much as local products. Akash Passey, Volvo's first Indian employee, commissioned a consultancy company to evaluate prospects. The consultancy company recommended that Volvo should not even try. Passey told the *Financial Times*: 'My response was simple – I took the report and went to the nearest dustbin and threw it in.' Passey entered the market in 2001 with the high-priced luxury buses.

Passey used the time to develop a distinctive strategy. His basic product had superior features. Volvo's standard engines were 240–250 hp and mounted at the back, ensuring a faster and quieter ride. Air conditioning was standard, of course. The positioning of the engine and the specific bus design of the chassis meant a more roomy interior, plus storage for bags internally. But Passey realised this would not be enough. He commented to the *Financial Times*: 'You had to do a lot of things to break the way business is done normally.'

Volvo offered post-sale maintenance services, increasing life expectancy of buses from three to ten years, and allowing bus operating companies to dispense with their own expensive maintenance workshops. Free training was given to drivers, so they drove more safely and took more care of their buses. The company advertised the benefits of the buses direct to customers in cinemas, rather than simply promoting them to the bus operators. To kick-start the market, Volvo supplied about 20 subsidised trial units to selected operators. Volvo trainees rode these buses, alerting the company immediately when something went wrong so Volvo could immediately send its engineers. Faster, smoother and more reliable travel allowed the bus operators to increase their ticket prices for the luxury Volvo buses by 35 per cent.

Business people and the middle classes were delighted with the new Volvo services. Speedier, more comfortable journeys allowed them to arrive fresh for meetings and potentially to save the costs of overnight stays. Tata and Ashok Leyland both now produce their own luxury buses, with Mercedes and Isuzu following Volvo into the market. None the less, the phrase 'taking a Volvo' has become synonymous with choosing a luxury bus service in India, rather as 'hoover' came to refer to any kind of vacuum cleaner.

In 2008, Volvo opened a new state-of-the-art bus factory in Bangalore. It is Volvo's most efficient bus factory worldwide, producing a fully built bus in 20–25 days. Annual capacity is 1000 buses per year.

Source: J. Leahy, 'Volvo takes a lead in India', *Financial Times*, 31 August 2009.

Questions

1 Rank the elements of Passey's strategy for Volvo in order of importance. Could any have been dispensed with?

2 How sustainable is Volvo's luxury bus strategy?

5.2.3 Focus strategies

Porter distinguishes focus as the third generic strategy, based on competitive scope. A **focus strategy targets a narrow segment of domain of activity and tailors its products or services to the needs of that specific segment to the exclusion of others**. Focus strategies come in two variants, according to the underlying sources of competitive advantage, cost or differentiation. In air travel, Ryanair follows a *cost-focus strategy*, targeting price-conscious holiday travellers with no need for connecting flights. In the domestic detergent market, the Belgian company Ecover follows a *differentiation-focus* strategy, gaining a price premium over rivals on account of its ecological cleaning products.

The focuser achieves competitive advantage by dedicating itself to serving its target segments better than others which are trying to cover a wider range of segments. Serving a broad range of segments can bring disadvantages in terms of coordination, compromise or inflexibility. Focus strategies are able to seek out the weak spots of broad cost-leaders and differentiators:

- *Cost focusers* identify areas where broader cost-based strategies fail because of the added costs of trying to satisfy a wide range of needs. For instance, in the United Kingdom food retail market, Iceland Foods has a cost-focused strategy concentrated on frozen and chilled foods, reducing costs against generalist discount food retailers such as Aldi which have all the complexity of fresh foods and groceries as well as their own frozen and chilled food ranges.

- *Differentiation focusers* look for specific needs that broader differentiators do not serve so well. Focus on one particular need helps to build specialist knowledge and technology, increases commitment to service and can improve brand recognition and customer loyalty. For example, ARM Holdings dominates the world market for mobile phone chips, despite being only a fraction of the size of the leading microprocessor manufacturers, AMD and Intel, which also make chips for a wide range of computers.

Successful focus strategies depend on at least one of three key factors:

- *Distinct segment needs.* Focus strategies depend on the distinctiveness of segment needs. If segment distinctiveness erodes, it becomes harder to defend the segment against broader competitors. For example, now that the boundaries are blurring between smartphones used by general consumers and smartphones used by business people, Research in Motion (RIM) no longer has a clear niche with its BlackBerry business phones.

- *Distinct segment value chains.* Focus strategies are strengthened if they have distinctive value chains that will be difficult or costly for rivals to construct. If the production processes and distribution channels are very similar, it is easy for a broad-based differentiator to push a specialised product through its own standardised value chain at a lower cost than a rival focuser. In detergents, Procter & Gamble cannot easily respond to Ecover because achieving the same ecological friendliness would involve transforming its purchasing and production processes.

- *Viable segment economics.* Segments can easily become too small to serve economically as demand or supply conditions change. For example, changing economies of scale and greater competition have eliminated from many smaller cities the traditional town-centre department stores, with their wider ranges of different kinds of goods from hardware to clothing.

5.2.4 'Stuck in the middle'?

Porter claims that managers face a crucial choice between the generic strategies of cost-leadership, differentiation and focus. According to him, it is unwise to blur this choice. As earlier, the lowest-cost competitor can always undercut the second lowest-cost competitor. For a company seeking advantage through low costs, therefore, it makes no sense to add extra costs by half-hearted efforts at differentiation. For a differentiator, it is self-defeating to make economies that jeopardise the basis for differentiation. For a focuser, it is dangerous to move outside the original specialised segment, because products or services tailored to one set of customers are likely to have inappropriate costs or features for the new target customers. This was a risk for RIM as it moved its BlackBerry business phones into the broader consumer market, for whom its e-mail encryption was not important. Porter's argument is that managers are generally best to choose which generic strategy they are pursuing and then stick to it rigorously. Otherwise there is a danger of being *stuck in the middle*, doing no strategy well.

Porter's warning about the danger of being stuck in the middle provides a useful discipline for managers. It is very easy for them to make incremental decisions that compromise the basic generic strategy. As profits accumulate, the successful cost-leader will be tempted to stop scrimping and saving. In hard times, a differentiator might easily cut back the R&D or advertising investments essential to its long-term differentiation advantage. Consistency with generic strategy provides a valuable check for managerial decision-making.

5.2.5 The Strategy Clock

The **Strategy Clock** provides another way of approaching the generic strategies (see Figure 5.6).[4] The Strategy Clock has two distinctive features. First, it is based on prices, not costs: it is easier to compare competitors on prices in the market than internal costs. Second, the circular design of the clock allows for more continuous choices than Michael Porter's sharp contrast between cost-leadership and differentiation: there is a full range of incremental adjustments that can be made between the 7 o'clock position at the bottom of the low-price strategy and the 2 o'clock position at the bottom of the differentiation strategy. Organisations often travel around the clock, as they adjust their pricing and benefits over time.

The Strategy Clock identifies three zones of feasible strategies, and one zone likely to lead to ultimate failure:

- *The differentiation zone.* This zone contains a range of feasible strategies for building on high perceptions of product or service benefits amongst customers. Close to the 12 o'clock position is a strategy of *differentiation without price premium*. Differentiation without a price premium combines high perceived benefits and moderate prices, typically used to gain market share. If high benefits also entail relatively high costs, this moderate pricing strategy would only be sustainable in the short term. Once increased market share had been achieved, it might be logical to move to *differentiation with price premium* closer to a 1 or 2 o'clock position. Movement all the way towards the 2 o'clock position is likely to involve

Figure 5.6 The Strategy Clock

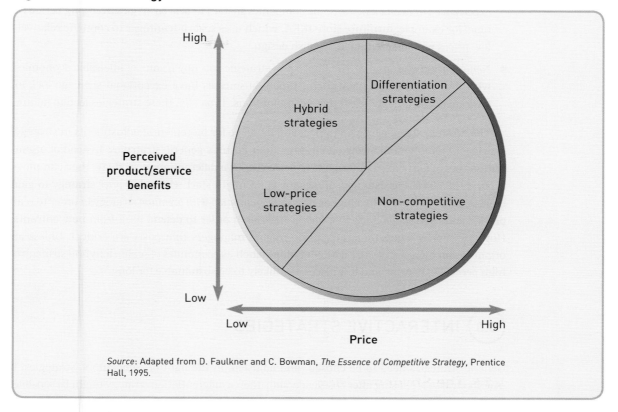

Source: Adapted from D. Faulkner and C. Bowman, *The Essence of Competitive Strategy*, Prentice Hall, 1995.

a focus strategy, in Michael Porter's terms. Such a *focused differentiation* strategy targets a niche where the higher prices and reduced benefits are sustainable, for instance because of a lack of competition in a particular geographical area.

- *The low-price zone.* This zone allows for different combinations of low prices and low perceived value. Close to the 9 o'clock position, a standard *low-price* strategy would gain market share, by combining low prices with reasonable value (at parity with competitors). Again, if reasonable benefits are associated with higher costs, this position is unlikely to be sustainable for long. Either cuts in benefits or increases in prices would be desirable over time. A variation on the standard low-price strategy is the *no frills* strategy, close to the 7 o'clock position. No frills strategies involve both low benefits and low prices, similar to low-cost airlines such as Ryanair (which even proposed to charge for use of its on-board toilets).

- *The hybrid strategy zone.* A distinctive feature of the Strategy Clock is the scope it allows between low-price and differentiation strategies. Hybrid strategies involve both lower prices than differentiation strategies, and higher benefits than low-price strategies. Hybrid strategies are often used to make aggressive bids for increased market-share. They can also be an effective way of entering a new market, for instance overseas. Even in the case of innovations with high benefits, it can make sense to price low initially in order to gain experience curve efficiencies. Some companies sustain hybrid strategies over long periods of time: for example, furniture store IKEA, which uses scale advantages to combine relatively low prices with differentiated Swedish design.

● *Non-competitive strategies.* The final set of strategies occupy a zone of infeasible economics, with low benefits and high prices. Unless businesses have exceptional strategic lock-in, customers will quickly reject these combinations. Typically, these strategies lead to failure.

The Strategy Clock's focus on price, and its scope for incremental adjustments in strategy, provide a more dynamic view on strategy than Porter's generic strategies. Instead of organisations being fairly fixed in terms of either a cost or a differentiation strategy, they can move around the clock. For example, an organisation might start with a *low-price* strategy to gain market-share, later shift to a higher-priced *differentiation with premium* strategy in order to reap profits, and then move back to a *hybrid strategy* in order to defend itself from new entrants. However, Porter's generic strategies do remind managers that costs are critical. Unless an organisation has some secure cost advantage (such as economies of scale), a hybrid strategy of high perceived benefits and low prices is unlikely to be sustainable for long.

⑤.③ INTERACTIVE STRATEGIES

Generic strategies need to be chosen, and adjusted, in the light of competitors' strategies. If everybody else is chasing after cost-leadership, then a differentiation strategy might be sensible. Thus business strategy choices *interact* with those of competitors. This section starts by considering business strategy in the light of competitor moves, especially in hypercompetition. It then addresses the option of cooperation and closes with game theory, which helps managers choose between competition and more cooperative strategies.

5.3.1 Interactive price and quality strategies

Richard D'Aveni depicts competitor interactions in terms of movements against the variables of price (the vertical axis) and perceived quality (the horizontal axis), similar to the Strategy Clock: see Figure 5.6.[5] Although D'Aveni applies his analysis to the very fast-moving environments he terms 'hypercompetitive' (for instance, high-technology), similar reasoning applies wherever competitors' moves are interdependent. Strategy is a matter of interactive moves and counter-moves.

Figure 5.7 shows different organisations competing by emphasising either low prices or high quality or some mixture of the two. Graph i. starts with a 'first value line', describing various trade-offs in terms of price and perceived quality that are acceptable to customers. The cost-leading firm (here L) offers relatively poor perceived quality, but customers accept this because of the lower price. While the relative positions on the graph should not be taken exactly literally, in the car market this cost-leading position might describe some of

Figure 5.7 Interactive price and quality strategies

(i) Differentiator (D) improves quality

(ii) Mid-point business (M) counter-attacks on price

NB axes are not necessarily to linear scales.

Source: Adapted from *Hypercompetition: Managing the Dynamics of Strategic Manoeuvring*, The Free Press (D'Aveni, R. 1984) p. 50, with the permission of The Free Press, a Division of Simon & Schuster, Inc. Copyright ©1994 by Richard D'Aveni. All rights reserved.

Hyundai's products. The differentiator (D) has a higher price, but much better quality. This might be Mercedes. In between, there are a range of perfectly acceptable combinations, with the mid-point firm (M) offering a combination of reasonable prices and reasonable quality. This might be Ford. M's strategy is on the first value line and therefore entirely viable at this stage. On the other hand, firm U is uncompetitive, falling behind the value line. Its price is higher than M's, and its quality is worse. U's predicament is typical of the business that is 'stuck in the middle', in Porter's terms. U no longer offers acceptable value and must quickly move back onto the value line or fail.

In any market, competitors and their moves or counter-moves can be plotted against these two axes of price and perceived value. For example, in graph i of Figure 5.7, the differentiator (D) makes an aggressive move by substantially improving its perceived quality while holding its prices. This improvement in quality shifts customer expectations of quality right across the market. These changed expectations are reflected by the new, second value line (in green). With the second value line, even the cost-leader (L) may have to make some improvement to quality, or accept a small price cut. But the greatest threat is for the mid-point competitor, M. To catch up with the second value line, M must respond either by making a substantial improvement in quality while holding prices, or by slashing prices, or by some combination of the two.

However, mid-point competitor M also has the option of an aggressive counter-attack. Given the necessary capabilities, M might choose to push the value line still further outwards, wrong-footing differentiator D by creating a third value line that is even more demanding in

ILLUSTRATION 5.3

McCafés challenge Starbucks

Starbucks coffee chain is having to change its strategy in response to McDonald's.

In 2009, Starbucks was in trouble. With 16,000 outlets and operating in 49 countries, Starbucks was the world's largest coffee chain. But economic recession was taking its toll, with 2009 sales 5 per cent down on the previous year's. And fast-food chain McDonald's was pushing hard its cheap coffee concept, McCafés.

The McCafé concept had emerged in Australia in the 1990s. McCafés typically operate within or next to regular McDonald's outlets. They use high-quality coffee machines and sell different blends of coffee according to the tastes of local markets. The coffee is priced substantially lower than Starbucks' traditional prices. By 2009, nearly half of Germany's 1200 McDonald's restaurants operated a McCafé, and McCafés were spreading rapidly across Europe. The target was 1200 McCafés in Europe by the end of 2009, against Starbucks' 1300.

Starbucks' response to recession and competition was vigorous. Company founder and CEO Howard Schultz proclaimed:

> 'We are laser-focused on delivering the finest quality coffee and getting the customer experience right every time. We have . . . been putting our feet into the shoes of our customers and are responding directly to their needs. Our customers are telling us they want value and quality and we will deliver that in a way that is meaningful to them and authentic to Starbucks.'

The company announced a €500m ($700m) cost reduction programme, with investments in operational efficiencies and new technologies. Starbucks also entered the $17bn instant coffee market, launching its Starbucks Via™ Ready Brew coffee head-to-head against brands such as Nestlé and Maxwell House. In particular, it began to transform the format of its stores.

Traditionally, all Starbucks stores have been designed on the basis of a standard palette of colours and furniture, worldwide. Now, in Seattle – the very city where Starbucks had originally started – the company opened a new store without any of the usual branding. Named '15th Ave. Coffee and Tea', the new store was based on close study of local independent coffee stores. One local store-owner complained about Starbucks' researchers: 'They spent the last 12 months in our store up on 15th [Avenue] with these obnoxious folders that said "Observation".' The 15th Ave. Coffee and Tea store is a radical departure. Starbucks' logo is completely absent, and wine and beer are available. Table tops come from a landscaper's stone yard and the shop uses discarded theatre seats. Evenings offer live music and poetry readings.

In the United Kingdom, Starbucks' largest European market, the same thinking is being applied. Facing competition from companies like Costa Coffee, McDonald's and Wetherspoons, Darcy Willson-Rymer, Starbucks' local managing director, commented to the *Independent*: 'What we did was set the standard, then we allowed people to catch us up.' The UK's Starbucks chain is abandoning the old identikit format. Local artefacts, bolder colours, bigger community noticeboards and even second-hand furniture will all be used to create more individual stores. Carrot sticks and porridge are joining the usual high-calorie cakes and paninis. Willson-Rymer explained: 'In every store, there will be something that is locally relevant. The thing that needs to be the same in every store is the latte, the cappuccino, the product and the culture of coffee tastings and the knowledge.' He commented on past mistakes thus: 'The business is run 80 per cent heart and 20 per cent head, and we tried to flip it on its head. I don't know what the right proportion is, but I believe that the heart is back in the company.'

Sources: 'Starbucks tests new names for stores', *Seattle Times*, 16 July 2009; 'Starbuck chief admits: our shops are all wrong', *Independent*, 18 September 2009; 'McDonald's set to mug Starbucks in Europe', *Financial Times*, 26 May 2009.

Questions

1 Plot the moves of McDonald's and Starbucks on the axes of price and perceived quality, as in Figure 5.7.

2 What should be the response of a company with a similar original position as Starbucks (for example, Costa Coffee in the UK)?

terms of the price-perceived quality trade-off. The starting point in graph ii. of Figure 5.7 is all three competitors L, M and D successfully reaching the second value line (uncompetitive U has disappeared). However, M's next move is to go beyond the second value line by making radical cuts in price while sustaining its new level of perceived quality. Again, customer expectations are changed and a third value line (in red) is established. Now it is differentiator D that is at most risk of being left behind, and it faces hard choices about how to respond in terms of price and quality.

Plotting moves and counter-moves in these terms underlines the dynamic and interactive nature of business strategy. Economically viable positions along the value line are always in danger of being superseded as competitors move either downwards in terms of price or outwards in terms of perceived quality. The generic strategies of cost-leadership and differentiation should not be seen as static positions, but as dynamic trajectories along the axes of price and quality. The movement towards more 'local' Starbucks stores demonstrates the need to be continually moving along the trajectory of differentiation (see Illustration 5.3).

5.3.2 Cooperative strategy

So far the emphasis has been on competition and competitive advantage. However, the competitive moves and counter-moves in section 5.4.1 make it clear that sometimes competition can escalate in a way that is dangerous to all competitors. It can be in the self-interest of organisations to restrain competition. Moreover, advantage may not always be achieved just by competing. Collaboration between some organisations in a market may give them advantage over other competitors in the same market, or potential new entrants. Collaboration can be explicit in terms of formal agreements to cooperate, or tacit in terms of informal mutual understandings between organisations. In short, business strategy has to include cooperative options as well as competitive ones.[6]

Figure 5.8 illustrates various kinds of benefits from cooperation between firms in terms of Michael Porter's five forces of buyers, suppliers, rivals, entrants and substitutes (section 2.3.1). Key benefits of cooperation are as follows:

- *Suppliers*. In Figure 5.8, cooperation between rivals A and B in an industry will increase their purchasing power against suppliers. Moreover, cooperation between rivals A and B may enable them to standardise requirements, enabling suppliers to make cost reductions to all parties' benefit. For example, two car manufacturers might agree on common component specifications, allowing their supplier to gain economies through production of the standardised part on a greater scale.

- *Buyers*. Conversely, cooperation between rivals A and B will increase their power as suppliers vis-à-vis buyers. It will be harder for buyers to shop around. Such *collusion* between rivals can help maintain or raise prices, as for example in the South African airline industry (see Illustration 5.4). On the other hand, buyers may benefit if their inputs are standardised, again enabling reductions in costs that all can share. For example, if food manufacturers supplying a retailer agree on common pallet sizes for deliveries, the retailer can manage its warehouses much more efficiently.

Figure 5.8 Cooperating with rivals

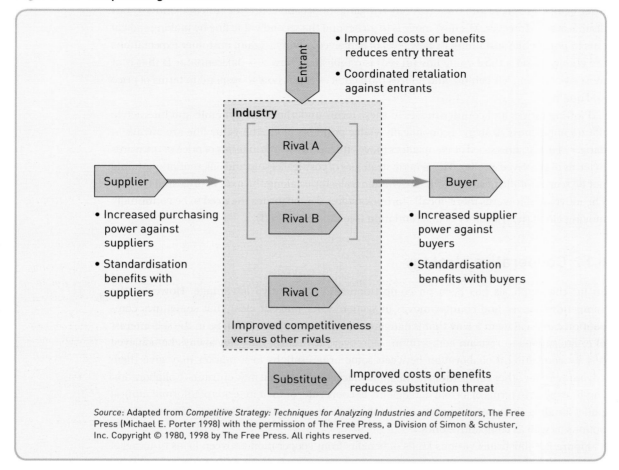

- *Rivals.* If cooperative rivals A and B are getting benefits with regard to both buyers and suppliers, other competitors without such agreements – in Figure 5.8, rival C – will be at a competitive disadvantage. Rival C will be in danger of being squeezed out of the industry.

- *Entrants.* Similarly, potential entrants will likely lack the advantages of the combined rivals A and B. Moreover, A and B can coordinate their retaliation strategies against any new entrant, for example by cutting prices by the same proportions in order to protect their own relative positions while undermining the competitiveness of the new entrant.

- *Substitutes.* Finally, the improved costs or efficiencies that come from cooperation between rivals A and B reduces the incentives for buyers to look to substitutes. Steel companies have cooperated on research to reduce the weight of steel used in cars, in order to discourage car manufacturers from switching to lighter substitutes such as aluminium or plastics.

Further kinds of cooperation will be considered under alliance strategy in section 9.4.

ILLUSTRATION 5.4

Cup-winners: competition and collusion in South Africa

Were South Africa's airlines cooperating to take advantage of the 2010 World Cup?

The 2010 Football World Cup was a great opportunity to put South Africa on the world tourism map. Up to 3 million international visitors were expected to visit the country during the month of June, many of whom might be encouraged to come back in the future. It was, of course, also a great opportunity for South African business. But in February 2010, the major domestic airlines were accused of exploiting the surge of demand by trying to fix prices together.

Domestic airline travel between matches would be important, as the World Cup involves 10 stadiums scattered around a large country. From Cape Town to Johannesburg is 880 miles, or 17 hours of hard driving. There are 2000 domestic flights a day.

The dominant player in both the domestic and international market is South African Airways (SAA), the national flag-carrier. Another major domestic player is Comair, which is part-owned by British Airways, operator of many services between South Africa and Europe. However, many new airlines have entered the market in recent years. Significant low-cost airlines in South Africa are SA Express (founded 1994), SA Airlink (founded 1996), Kulula (founded 2001 by Comair), 1Time (founded 2004) and Mango (founded 2006). SA Airlink, SA Express and SAA had been part of a strategic alliance until 2006. Competition is a challenge for airlines: a half-full flight costs nearly as much as a full one, but of course earns half the money. It is not surprising then that SAA has made persistent losses in recent years.

The accusation of price-fixing had come in December 2009 from SAA itself, when the company offered cooperation with the competition authority in return for leniency. The accusation centred on a November e-mail sent by Comair's chief executive Erik Venter to SAA, 1Time, SA Airlink, Mango and SA Express regarding pricing strategy during the World Cup. The e-mail said: 'airlines have the option to either not provide any inventory [seats] for sale until such time [as they knew where matches would be played and when] or price all inventory at peak-time rates until such time as they have greater certainty'.

The *Sunday Times* reported the head of the competition authority as saying of Comair: 'they have set out a methodology to influence the pricing outcome'. CEO Venter riposted that the e-mail

> 'reflected textbook airline pricing principles that any commercial airline would implement, based on supply and demand and cost recovery . . . The email clearly states that Comair expects airline prices to fall once the airlines have implemented their extra capacity for the World Cup, and that the pricing is anticipated to average out at the level experienced over a typical South African peak holiday season.'

SAA and the other airlines had some history with regard to price-fixing. For example, in 2006, SAA, Kulula, SA Express and SA Airlink had been fined for agreeing a simultaneous standard increase in fuel surcharges. SAA had also been accused of offering travel agents inducements to recommend its flights to customers even when they knew cheaper flights were available. One low-cost competitor, Nationwide, had allegedly been driven out of business by this practice. The *Guardian* reported the England Football Supporters' Federation as warning:

> 'England's regular travellers are having to take a long and sober look at the costs involved in following the team. It would be a mistake for South Africa to regard the World Cup as a four-week opportunity to rip off fans.'

Sources: 'Airlines investigated for price-fixing during World Cup', *Guardian*, 30 January 2010; 'Probes into airlines to proceed', *Sunday Times*, 31 January 2010; 'South African body probes claims of over-pricing', *BBC*, 15 February 2010.

Questions

1 What would be the advantages *and* the disadvantages of raising prices artificially during the World Cup?

2 Suggest three reasons why it may make sense that SAA raised the price-fixing accusation, rather than any other airline.

SUMMARY

- Business strategy is concerned with seeking competitive advantage in markets at the *business* rather than *corporate* level.

- Business strategy needs to be considered and defined in terms of *strategic business units* (SBUs).

- Different *generic strategies* can be defined in terms of cost-leadership, differentiation and focus.

- *Cooperative strategies* may offer alternatives to competitive strategies or may run in parallel.

VIDEO CASE

Visit **MyStrategyLab** and watch the *Land Rover* case study.

1 Identify Land Rover's generic strategy, in terms of Porter's generic strategies or the Strategy Clock, or both.

2 Given its competition, how sustainable is Land Rover's strategy?

RECOMMENDED KEY READINGS

- The foundations of the discussions of generic competitive strategies are to be found in the writings of Michael Porter, which include *Competitive Strategy* (1980) and *Competitive Advantage* (1985), both published by Free Press. Both are recommended for readers who wish to understand the background to discussions in section 5.3 on competitive strategy and competitive advantage.

REFERENCES

1. This section draws heavily on M. Porter, *Competitive Advantage*, Free Press, 1985. For a more recent discussion of the generic strategies concept, see J. Parnell, 'Generic strategies after two decades: a reconceptualisation of competitive strategy', *Management Decision*, vol. 48, no. 8 (2006), pp. 1139–54.

2. See A.C. Hax and N.S. Majluf, in R.G. Dyson (ed.), *Strategic Planning: Models and Analytical Techniques*, Wiley, 1990.

3. B. Sharp and J. Dawes, 'What is differentiation and how does it work?', *Journal of Marketing Management*, vol. 17, nos 7/8 (2001), pp. 739–59, reviews the relationship between differentiation and profitability.

4. See D. Faulkner and C. Bowman, *The Essence of Competitive Strategy*, Prentice Hall, 1995.

5. R. D'Aveni, *Hypercompetition: the Dynamics of Strategic Maneuvering*, Free Press, New York, 1995.

6. Useful books on collaborative strategies are Y. Doz and G. Hamel, *Alliance Advantage: The Art of Creating Value through Partnering*, Harvard Business School Press, 1998; and D. Faulkner, *Strategic Alliances: Cooperating to Compete*, McGraw-Hill, 1995.

Madonna: the reigning queen of pop?

Phyl Johnson, Strategy Explorers

She's the highest-ever paid female singer, in 2009 had the highest-earning tour of any artist and is second only to the Beatles in her haul of 11 UK number one albums. But the music industry has always been the backdrop for one-hit wonders and brief careers. Pop-stars who have remained at the top for decades are very few. Madonna is one such phenomenon; the question is, after almost 30 years at the top, how much longer can it last?

Described by *Billboard Magazine* as the smartest business woman in show business, Madonna Louise Ciccone began her music career in 1983 with the hit single 'Holiday' and in 2008, enjoyed success with the album *Hard Candy* featuring the hit single '4 Minutes' with Justin Timberlake. In the meantime, she had con-sistent chart success with many singles and 18 albums, multiple sell-out world tours, major roles in six films, picked up numerous music awards, was inducted into the Rock and Roll Hall of Fame and has been the style icon behind a range of products (Pepsi, Max Factor, Gap, H&M and Louis Vuitton), and become a worldwide bestselling children's author.

The foundation of Madonna's business success has been her ability to sustain her reign as the 'queen of pop'. Phil Quattro, the President of Warner Brothers, said 'she always manages to land on the cusp of what we call contemporary music. Every established artist faces the dilemma of maintaining their importance and relevance, Madonna never fails to be relevant.' Madonna's chameleon-like ability to change persona, change her music genre with it and yet still achieve major record sales has been the hallmark of her success and is seemingly not replicable by other male and female artists.

Madonna's early poppy style was targeted at young 'wannabe' girls. The image that she portrayed through hits such as 'Holiday' and 'Lucky Star' in 1983 was picked up by Macy's, the US-based department store. They produced a range of Madonna lookalike clothes that mothers were happy to purchase for their daughters. One year later in 1984, Madonna underwent

Source: Lehtikuva OY/Rex Features.

her first image change and in doing so offered the first hint of the smart cookie behind the media image. In the video for her hit *Material Girl*, she deliberately mirrored the glamour-based, sexual pussycat image of Marilyn Monroe whilst simultaneously mocking both the growing materialism of the late eighties and the men fawning after her. Media analysts Sam and Diana Kirschner commented that with this kind of packaging, Madonna allowed the record companies to keep hold of a saleable 'Marilyn image' for a new cohort of fans, but also allowed her original fan base of now growing up wannabe girls to take the more critical message from the music. The theme of courting controversy but staying marketable enough has been recurrent throughout her career.

Table 1

Releases	Year	Image	Target audience
Lucky Star	1982	Trashy pop	Young wannabe girls, dovetailing from fading disco to emerging 'club scene'
Like a Virgin *Like a Prayer*	1984	Originally a Marilyn glamour image, then became a Saint & Sinner	More grown-up, rebellious-fan base, more critical female audience and male worshippers
Vogue *Erotica* *Bedtime Stories*	1990 1992 1994	Erotic porn star, sadomasochistic, sexual control, more Minelli in *Cabaret* than Monroe	Peculiar mix of target audiences: gay club scene, 90s women taking control of their own lives, also pure male titillation
Something to Remember *Evita*	1995	Softer image, ballads preparing for glamour image of Evita film role	Broadest audience target, picking up potential film audiences as well as regular fan base. Most conventional image. Max Factor later used this mixture of Marilyn and Eva Peron to market their glamour image.
Ray of Light	1998	Earth mother, eastern mysticism, dance music fusion	Clubbing generation of the 90s, new cohort of fans plus original fan base of now 30-somethings desperately staying trendy
Music	2000	Acid rock, tongue-in-cheek Miss USA/cowgirl, cool Britannia	Managing to hit the changing club scene and 30-something Brits
American Life	2003	Militaristic image Che Guevara Anti-consumerism of American dream	Unclear audience reliant on existing base
Confessions on a Dance Floor	2005	Retro-80s disco imagery, high motion dance-pop sound	Strong gay-icon audience, pop-disco audience, danced-based audience
Hard Candy	2008	Pop, dance, electro-pop urban	Deliberate move toward a more urban R&B direction with collaborations with Justine Timberlake and Kayne West pulling in a new young audience
Celebration	2009	Queen of pop	Compilation of hits from her entire career targeted at enduring/touring fan base

Madonna's subsequent image changes were more dramatic. First, she took on the Catholic Church in her 1989 video *Like a Prayer* where, as a red-dressed 'sinner', she kissed a black saint easily interpreted as a Jesus figure. Her image had become increasingly sexual while also holding on to a critical social theme: e.g. her pointed illustration of white-only imagery in the Catholic Church. At this point in her career, Madonna took full control of her image in the $60 (~€42) million deal with Time-Warner that created her record company Maverick. In 1991, she published a coffee-table soft porn book entitled *Sex* that exclusively featured pictures of herself in erotic poses. Her image and music also reflected this erotic theme. In her 'Girlie' tour, her singles 'Erotica' and 'Justify my Love' and her fly-on-the wall movie *In Bed with Madonna* she played out scenes of sadomasochistic and lesbian fantasies. Although allegedly a period of her career she would rather forget, Madonna more than survived it. In fact, she gained a whole new demographic of fans who not only respected her artistic courage but also did not miss the fact that Madonna was consistent in her message: her sexuality was her own and not in need of a male gaze.

Changing gear in 1996, Madonna finally took centre stage in the lead role in the film *Evita* which she had chased for over five years. She achieved the image transition from erotica to saint-like persona of Eva Peron and won critical acclaim to boot. Another vote of confidence from the 'establishment' came from Max Factor, who in 1999 signed her up to front their relaunch campaign which was crafted around a glamour theme. Procter & Gamble (owners of the Max Factor make-up range) argued that they saw Madonna as 'the closest thing the 90s has to an old-style Hollywood star . . . she is a real woman'.

Madonna's album *Ray of Light* was released in 1998. Radio stations world-wide were desperate to get hold of the album which was billed as her most successful musical voyage to date. In a smart move, Madonna had teamed up with techno pioneer William Orbit to write and produce the album. It was a huge success, taking Madonna into the super-trendy techno sphere, not the natural environment for a pop-star from the early eighties. Madonna took up an 'earth mother / spiritual' image and spawned a trend for all things eastern in fashion and music. This phase may have produced more than just an image as it is the time in Madonna's life that locates the beginning of her continued faith in the Kabbalah tradition of eastern spiritual worship.

By 2001, her next persona was unveiled with the release of her album *Music*. Here her style had moved on again to 'acid rock'. With her marriage to her second husband, British movie director Guy Ritchie, the ultimate 'American Pie' had become a fully-fledged Brit babe earning the endearing nickname of 'Madge' in the British press.

By 2003 some commentators were suggesting that an interesting turn of events hinted that perhaps 'the cutting edge' Madonna, 'the fearless', was starting to think about being part of, rather than beating, the establishment. When she launched her new Che Guevara-inspired image, instead of maximising the potential of this image in terms of its political and social symbolism during the second Gulf War, in April 2003 she withdrew her militaristic image and video for the album *American Life*. That action, timed with the publication of her children's book *The English Roses* based on the themes of compassion and friendship, sparked questions in the press around the theme 'has Madonna gone soft?'

By late 2003 she negotiated a glitzy, high-profile ad campaign for the Gap clothing retailer in which she danced around accompanied by rapper Missy Elliot to a retrospective re-mix of her eighties track 'Get into the Groove'. Here Madonna was keeping the 'thirty-somethings', who remembered the track from first time around, happy. They could purchase jeans for themselves and their newly teenage daughters while also purchasing the re-released CD (on sale in-store).

Late 2005 saw the release of the world record breaking, Grammy and Brit Award winning *Confessions on a Dance Floor* album which was marketed as her comeback album after her lowest selling *American Life*. Here Madonna focused on the high selling principle of re-mix, choosing samples of the gay-iconic disco favourites of Abba and Giorgio Moroder to be at the heart of her symbolic reinvention of herself from artist to DJ. The 'Confessions' world tour achieved the highest-selling peak of her career with the album breaking the world record for solo female artists when it debuted at number one in over 40 countries.

Throughout 2008 Madonna lived through a mixed period in her personal and professional lives. In the wake of her divorce from her second husband, she attracted large amounts of negative publicity for the adoption of her youngest children from Malawi. There was also mixed media reaction to the publicity shots for her *Hard Candy* album as Madonna was back to her erotic best: wearing thigh-high boots and little else but with her highly toned body used to full effect. At 51 years of age some commentators questioned: is this sexy or smutty; does Madonna need dignity? Either way, her image, undeniably sultry and alluring, was still hitting the high notes.

Crucially, in 2009, as the music world moved into a phase where its highest earners were not those with the most record sales but those with the best-selling tours, Madonna reigned supreme. Her world record breaking 'Sticky and Sweet' world tour topped *Billboard*'s money-makers chart with a reported $242 million in revenue. This level of revenue was $100 million ahead of her nearest competitor Bon Jovi and showed her razor-sharp appreciation that her records were simply advertisements for her tours. Madonna, along with all artists, had seen record sales falling, and with online music sales still relatively small, had realised that live music, endorsements and merchandising were her best revenue-generating avenues going forward. She signed a new ten-year record deal with Live Nation, the largest concert promotion company in the world, ensuring that she retains 90 per cent of gross touring revenues as well as 50 per cent of endorsements.

Sell-out tours crucially rely on a return and return again fan base. Madonna used the 2009 release of *Celebration* (her definitive collection of hit singles) to keep her fan base warm until her next world trek. But at 50 plus, how long can Madonna keep it up? In 2008, Lady Gaga was emerging onto the scene: another singer with a taste for outrage, she was half Madonna's age. Still, The Eagles, Neil Diamond, The Police and Billy Joel all appeared in the tour-earning top 20 of 2008. But these veterans are all male and selling nostalgia rather than their own sexually charged image. As an ageing female star, Madonna is moving into new territory yet again.

Sources: 'Bennett takes the reins at Maverick', *Billboard Magazine*, 7 August 1999; 'Warner Bros expects Madonna to light up international markets', *Billboard Magazine*, 21 February 1998; 'Maverick builds on early success', *Billboard Magazine*, 12 November 1994; Jardine, A. 'Max Factor strikes gold with Madonna', *Marketing*, vol. 29 (1999), pp. 14–15; Kirschner, S. and Kirschner, D. (1997) 'MTV, adolescence and Madonna: a discourse analysis', in *Perspectives on Psychology and the Media*, American Psychological Association, Washington, DC; 'Warner to buy out maverick co-founder', *Los Angeles Times*, 2 March 1999; 'Why Madonna is back in Vogue', *New Statesman*, 18 September 2000; 'Madonna and Microsoft', *Financial Times*, 28 November 2000; 'Power of goodbye: Madonna's split may herald record industry's death', *Times Online*, 12 October 2007.

Questions

1 Describe and explain the strategy being followed by Madonna in terms of the explanation of competitive strategy given in Chapter 5.

2 Why has she experienced sustained success over three decades?

3 Can Madonna sustain her success?

6

CORPORATE STRATEGY AND DIVERSIFICATION

Learning objectives

After reading this chapter, you should be able to:

- Identify alternative strategy options, including *market penetration*, *product development*, *market development* and *diversification*.

- Distinguish between different diversification strategies (*related* and *conglomerate diversification*) and evaluate *diversification drivers*.

- Assess the relative benefits of *vertical integration* and *outsourcing*.

- Analyse the ways in which a *corporate parent* can add or destroy value for its portfolio of business units.

- Analyse a *portfolio* of business units and judge which to invest in and which to divest.

Key terms

Backward integration p. 142

BCG matrix p. 150

Conglomerate (unrelated) diversification p. 136

Diversification p. 135

Dominant logic p. 140

Economies of scope p. 139

Forward integration p. 142

Market development p. 138

Market penetration p. 136

Outsourcing p. 144

Parental developer p. 150

Portfolio manager p. 148

Product development p. 137

Related diversification p. 135

Scope p. 134

Synergy p. 140

Synergy manager p. 148

Vertical integration p. 141

PEARSON mystrategylab

MyStrategyLab is designed to help you make the most of your studies. Visit **www.mystrategylab.com** to discover a wide range of resources specific to this chapter, including:

- A personalised **Study plan** that will help you understand core concepts.
- **Audio** and **video clips** that put the spotlight on strategy in the real world.
- **Online glossaries** and **flashcards** that provide helpful reminders when you're looking for some quick revision.

See p. xiv for further details.

(6.1) INTRODUCTION

Chapter 5 was concerned with choices at the level of single business or organisational units. This chapter is about choices of *products* and *markets* for an organisation to enter or exit. Organisations often choose to enter many new product and market areas. For example, the Virgin Group started out in the music business, but is now highly diverse, operating in the holiday, cinema, retail, air-travel and rail markets. Sony began by making small radios, but now produces games, music and movies, as well as a host of electronic products. As organisations add new units, their strategies are no longer concerned just with the business-level, but with the *corporate-level* choices involved in having many different businesses or markets.

Figure 6.1 indicates the basic themes of this chapter. First of all, there are questions to do with the *scope*, or breadth, of the corporate whole. **Scope is concerned with how far an organisation should be diversified in terms of products and markets**. One way of thinking about this is in terms of different diversification strategies according to novelty of products or markets. Another way of increasing the scope of an organisation is through *vertical integration*, where the organisation acts as an internal supplier or a customer to itself (as for example an oil company supplies its petrol to its own petrol stations). Here we also consider the possibility of *outsourcing*, where an organisation 'dis-integrates' by subcontracting an internal activity to an external supplier.

Scope raises the two other key themes of the chapter. First, given that an organisation has decided to operate in different areas of activity, what should be the role of the 'corporate-level' (head-office) executives who act as 'parents' to the individual business units that make up their organisation's portfolio? How do corporate-level activities, decisions and resources add value to the actual businesses? The second theme is, within an overall diversification strategy, which specific business units should be included in the corporate *portfolio*, and how should

Figure 6.1 Strategic directions and corporate-level strategy they be managed financially? Here, portfolio matrices help structure corporate-level choices about which businesses to invest in and which to divest.

This chapter is not just about large commercial businesses. Even small businesses may consist of a number of business units. For example, a local builder may be undertaking contract work for local government, work for industrial buyers and work for local homeowners. Not only are these different market segments, but the capabilities required for competitive success are also likely to be different. Moreover, the owner of that business has to take decisions about the extent of investment and activity in each segment. Public-sector organisations such as local government or health services also provide different services, which correspond to business units in commercial organisations.

(6.2) STRATEGY DIRECTIONS

KEY CONCEPT

Strategy directions

The Ansoff product/market-growth matrix[1] provides a simple way of generating four basic directions for corporate strategy: see Figure 6.2 for an adapted version. An organisation typically starts in the zone around point A, the top left-hand corner of Figure 6.2. According to Ansoff, the organisation has a choice between *penetrating* still further within its existing sphere (staying in zone A) or increasing its diversity along the two axes of increasing novelty of markets or increasing novelty of products. **Diversification involves increasing the range of products or markets served by an organisation. Related diversification involves diversifying**

Figure 6.2 Corporate strategy directions

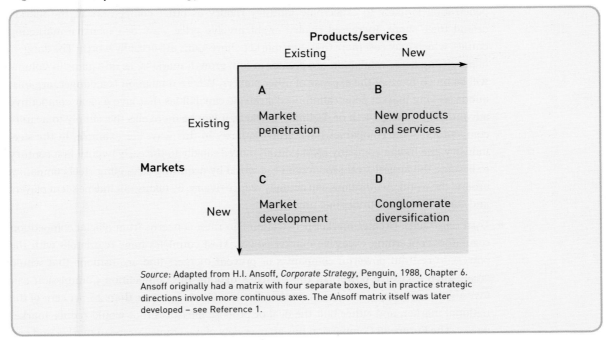

Source: Adapted from H.I. Ansoff, *Corporate Strategy*, Penguin, 1988, Chapter 6. Ansoff originally had a matrix with four separate boxes, but in practice strategic directions involve more continuous axes. The Ansoff matrix itself was later developed – see Reference 1.

into products or services with relationships to the existing business. Thus on Ansoff's axes the organisation has two related diversification strategies available: moving rightwards by *developing new products* for its existing markets (zone B) or moving downwards by bringing its existing products into *new markets* (zone C). In each case, the further along the two axes, the more diversified is the strategy. Alternatively, the organisation can move in both directions at once, following a *conglomerate diversification* strategy with altogether new markets and new products (zone D). Thus **conglomerate (unrelated) diversification involves diversifying into products or services with no relationships to the existing businesses**.

Ansoff's axes can be used effectively in brainstorming strategic options, checking that options in all four zones have been properly considered. This section will consider each of Ansoff's four main directions. Section 6.4 will then examine the additional option of *vertical integration*.

6.2.1 Market penetration

For a simple, undiversified business, the most obvious strategic option is often increased penetration of its existing market, with its existing products. **Market penetration implies increasing share of current markets with the current product range**. This strategy builds on established strategic capabilities and does not require the organisation to venture into uncharted territory. The organisation's scope is exactly the same. Moreover, greater market share implies increased power vis-à-vis buyers and suppliers (in terms of Porter's five forces), greater economies of scale and experience curve benefits.

However, organisations seeking greater market penetration may face three constraints:

● *Retaliation from competitors.* In terms of the five forces (section 2.3.1), increasing market penetration is likely to exacerbate industry rivalry as other competitors in the market defend their share. Increased rivalry might involve price wars or expensive marketing battles, which may cost more than any market-share gains are actually worth. The dangers of provoking fierce retaliation are greater in low-growth markets, as any gains in volume will be much more at the expense of other players. Where retaliation is a danger, organisations seeking market penetration need strategic capabilities that give a clear competitive advantage. In low-growth or declining markets, it can be more effective simply to acquire competitors. Some companies have grown quickly in this way. For example, in the steel industry, the Indian company LNM (Mittal) moved rapidly in the early twenty-first century to become the largest steel producer in the world by acquiring struggling steel companies around the world. Acquisitions can actually reduce rivalry, by taking out independent players and controlling them under one umbrella.

● *Legal constraints.* Greater market penetration can raise concerns from official competition regulators concerning excessive market power. Most countries have regulators with the powers to restrain powerful companies or prevent mergers and acquisitions that would create such excessive power. In the United Kingdom, the Competition Commission can investigate any merger or acquisition that would account for more than 25 per cent of the national market, and either halt the deal or propose measures that would reduce market power. The European Commission has an overview of the whole European market and can similarly intervene. For example, when the German T-Mobile and French Orange companies proposed to merge their UK mobile phone operations in 2010, the European Commission insisted that the merged companies should divest a quarter of their combined share of the key mobile phone 1800 MHz spectrum.[2]

- *Economic constraints.* Market penetration may also not be an option where economic constraints are severe, for instance during a market downturn or public-sector funding crisis. Here organisations need to consider the strategic option of *retrenchment*, withdrawal from marginal activities in order to concentrate on the most valuable segments and products within their existing business. However, where growth is still sought after, the Ansoff axes suggest further directions, as follows.

6.2.2 Product development

Product development is where organisations deliver modified or new products (or services) to existing markets. This can involve varying degrees of diversification along the rightward axis of Figure 6.2. For Sony, developing its Walkman products from the original tape-based product, through CDs and recently to MP3s involved little diversification: although the technologies differed, Sony was targeting the same customers and using very similar production processes and distribution channels. A more radical form of product development would be Axel Springer's move into the online media businesses: effectively the same consumer markets are involved as for its existing newspaper and magazine businesses, but the production technologies and distribution channels are radically different (see Illustration 6.1). This form of product diversification would typically be described as *related diversification*, as Axel Springer's online business would be related through similar customers to its existing newspaper and magazine customers.

Despite the potential for relatedness, product development can be an expensive and high-risk activity for at least two reasons:

- *New strategic capabilities.* Product development strategies typically involve mastering new processes or technologies that are unfamiliar to the organisation. For example, many banks entered online banking at the beginning of this century, but suffered many setbacks with technologies so radically different from their traditional high-street branch means of delivering banking services. Success frequently depended on a willingness to acquire new technological and marketing capabilities, often with the help of specialised information technology and e-commerce consultancy firms. Thus product development typically involves heavy investments and high risk of project failures.

- *Project management risk.* Even within fairly familiar domains, product development projects are typically subject to the risk of delays and increased costs due to project complexity and changing project specifications over time. An extreme example is Boeing's Dreamliner 787 plane: making innovative use of carbon-fibre composites, the Dreamliner had incurred two and a half years of delay by launch in 2010, and required $2.5bn (~€1.75bn) write-offs due to cancelled orders.

Strategies for product development are considered further in Chapter 8.

ILLUSTRATION 6.1

Corporate strategy choices for Axel Springer

This German publishing company has many opportunities, and the money to pursue them.

In 2007, Mathias Döpfner, chairman and chief executive of Axel Springer publishers, had about €2bn ($2.8bn) to invest in new opportunities. The previous year, the competition authorities had prohibited his take-over of Germany's largest television broadcaster, ProSiebenSat.1 . . . Now Döpfner was looking for alternative directions.

Founded in 1946 by Axel Springer himself, by 2007 the company was already Germany's largest publisher of newspapers and magazines, with more than 10,000 employees and over 150 titles. Famous print titles included *Die Welt*, the *Berliner Morgenpost, Bild* and *Hörzu*. Outside Germany, Axel Springer was strongest in eastern Europe. The company also had a scattering of mostly small investments in German radio and television companies. Axel Springer described its strategic objectives as market leadership in the German language core business, internationalisation and digitalisation of the core business.

Döpfner had opportunities for further penetration with his existing markets and products. Increased digitalisation of the core newspapers and magazines business was clearly important and would require substantial funding. There were also opportunities for the launch of new print magazine titles in the German market.

However, Döpfner was considering expanding also into new markets and new products. Such moves would likely involve acquisitions: 'It goes without saying', he told

the *Financial Times*, 'that whenever a large international media company comes on to the market (i.e. is up for sale), we will examine it very closely – whether in print, TV or the online sector'. Döpfner mentioned several specific kinds of acquisition opportunity. For example, he was still interested in buying a large European television broadcaster, even if it would probably have to be outside Germany. He was also attracted by the possibility of buying undervalued assets in the old media (i.e. print), and turning them around in the style of a private-equity investor: 'I would love to buy businesses in need of restructuring, where we can add value by introducing our management and sector expertise.' However, Döpfner reassured his shareholders by affirming that he felt no need 'to do a big thing in order to do a big thing'.

Main source: Financial Times Deutschland, 2 April 2007.

Questions

1 Referring to Figure 6.2, classify the various strategic directions Mattias Döpfner is considering for Axel Springer.

2 Using the Ansoff axes, what other options could Döpfner pursue?

6.2.3 Market development

If product development is risky and expensive, an alternative strategy is market development. **Market development involves offering existing products to new markets**. Again, the degree of diversification varies along Figure 6.2's downward axis. Typically, of course, market development entails some product development as well, if only in terms of packaging or service. None the less, market development remains a form of related diversification given its origins in similar products. Market development takes two basic forms:

- *New users.* Here an example would be aluminium, whose original users, packaging and cutlery manufacturers, are now supplemented by users in aerospace and automobiles.

- *New geographies.* The prime example of this is internationalisation, but the spread of a small retailer into new towns would also be a case.

In all cases, it is essential that market development strategies be based on products or services that meet the *critical success factors* of the new market (see section 2.4.3). Strategies based on simply off-loading traditional products or services in new markets are likely to fail. Moreover, market development faces similar problems to product development. In terms of strategic capabilities, market developers often lack the right marketing skills and brands to make progress in a market with unfamiliar customers. On the management side, the challenge is coordinating between different users and geographies, which might all have different needs. *International* market development strategy is considered in Chapter 7.

6.2.4 Conglomerate diversification

Conglomerate (or unrelated) diversification takes the organisation beyond both its existing markets and its existing products (i.e. zone D in Figure 6.2). In this sense, it radically increases the organisation's scope. Conglomerate diversification strategies are not trusted by many observers, because there are no obvious ways in which the businesses are better off for being together, while there is a clear cost in the managers at headquarters who control them. For this reason, conglomerate companies' share prices often suffer from what is called the 'conglomerate discount' – in other words, a lower valuation than the individual constituent businesses would have if stand-alone. In 2009, the French conglomerate Vivendi, with wide interests in mobile telephony and media, was trading at an estimated discount of 24 per cent on the value of its constituent assets. Naturally, shareholders were pressurising management to sell off its more highly valued parts on the open market.

However, it is important to recognise that the distinction between related and unrelated conglomerate diversification is often a matter of degree. Also relationships might turn out not to be as valuable as expected. Thus the large accounting firms have often struggled in translating their skills and client contacts developed in auditing into effective consulting practices. Similarly, relationships may change in importance over time, as the nature of technologies or customers change.

(6.3) DIVERSIFICATION DRIVERS

Diversification might be chosen for a variety of reasons, some more value-creating than others.[3] Growth in organisational size is rarely a good enough reason for diversification on its own: growth must be profitable. Indeed, growth can often be merely a form of 'empire building', especially in the public sector. Diversification decisions need to be approached sceptically.

Four potentially value-creating drivers for diversification are as follows.

- *Exploiting economies of scope.* **Economies of scope refers to efficiency gains through applying the organisation's existing resources or competences to new markets or services.**[4] If an organisation has under-utilised resources or competences that it cannot effectively close or sell to other potential users, it is efficient to use these resources or competences by diversification into a new activity. In other words, there are economies to be gained by extending the scope of the organisation's activities. For example, many universities have large resources in terms of halls of residence, which they must have for their students but which are under-utilised out of term-time. These halls of residence are more efficiently used if the universities expand the scope of their activities into conferencing and tourism during vacation periods. Economies of scope may apply to both *tangible* resources, such as halls of residence, and *intangible* resources and competences, such as brands or staff skills.

- *Stretching corporate management competences ('dominant logics').* This is a special case of economies of scope, and refers to the potential for applying the skills of talented corporate-level managers (referred to as 'corporate parenting skills' in section 6.5) to new businesses. The **dominant logic** **is the set of corporate-level managerial competences applied across the portfolio of businesses.**[5] Corporate-level managers may have competences that can be applied even to businesses which do not share resources at the operating-unit level. Thus the French luxury-goods conglomerate LVMH includes a wide range of businesses – from champagne, through fashion and perfumes, to financial media – that share very few operational resources or business-level competences. However, LVMH creates value for these specialised companies by applying corporate-level competences in developing classic brands and nurturing highly creative people that are relevant to all its individual businesses. See also the discussion of dominant logic at Berkshire Hathaway in Illustration 6.3 later.

- *Exploiting superior internal processes.* Internal processes within a diversified corporation can often be more efficient than external processes in the open market. This is especially the case where external capital and labour markets do not yet work well, as in many developing economies. In these circumstances, well-managed conglomerates can make sense, even if their constituent businesses do not have operating relationships with each other. For example, China has many conglomerates because they are able to mobilise investment, develop managers and exploit networks in a way that stand-alone Chinese companies, relying on imperfect markets, cannot. China's largest privately owned conglomerate, the Fosun Group, owns steel mills, pharmaceutical companies and China's largest retailer, Yuyuan Tourist Mart.[6]

- *Increasing market power.*[7] Being diversified in many businesses can increase power vis-à-vis competitors in at least two ways. First, having the same wide portfolio of products as a competitor increases the potential for *mutual forbearance*. The ability to retaliate across the whole range of the portfolio acts to discourage the competitor from making any aggressive moves at all. Two similarly diversified competitors are thus likely to forbear from competing aggressively with each other. Second, having a diversified range of businesses increases the power to *cross-subsidise* one business from the profits of the others. On the one hand, the ability to cross-subsidise can support aggressive bids to drive competitors out of a particular market. On the other hand, knowing this power to cross-subsidise a particular business, competitors without equivalent power will be reluctant to attack that business.

Where diversification creates value, it is described as 'synergistic'.[8] **Synergy** **refers to the benefits gained where activities or assets complement each other so that their combined effect is greater than the sum of the parts** (the famous 2 + 2 = 5 equation). Thus a film company and a music publisher would be synergistic if they were worth more together than separately. However, synergies are often harder to identify and more costly to extract in practice than managers like to admit.[9]

Indeed, some drivers for diversification involve negative synergies, in other words value destruction. Three potentially value-destroying diversification drivers are:

- *Responding to market decline* is one common but doubtful driver for diversification. Rather than let the managers of a declining business invest spare funds in a new business, conventional finance theory suggests it is usually best to let shareholders find new growth investment opportunities for themselves. For example, it is arguable that Microsoft's diversification into electronic games such as the Xbox – whose launch cost $500m (~€350m) in marketing alone – is a response to declining prospects in its core Windows operating systems business. But if future profits in the core business are likely to be low, shareholders might prefer Microsoft simply to hand back the surplus directly to them, rather than spending it on attacking strong companies such as Sony and Nintendo. If shareholders had wanted to invest in the games business, they could have invested in the original dominant companies themselves.

- *Spreading risk* across a range of markets is another common justification for diversification. Again, conventional finance theory is very sceptical about risk-spreading by diversification. Shareholders can easily spread their risk by taking small stakes in dozens of very different companies themselves. Diversification strategies, on the other hand, are likely to involve a limited range of fairly related markets. While managers might like the security of having more than one market, shareholders typically do not need each of the companies they invest in to be diversified as well – they would prefer managers to concentrate on managing their core business as well as they can. However, conventional finance theory does not apply to private businesses, where the owners have a large proportion of their assets tied up in their company: here, it can make sense to diversify risk across a number of distinct activities, so that if one part is in trouble, the whole business is not pulled down.

- *Managerial ambition* can sometimes drive inappropriate diversification. It is argued that the managers of British banks such as Royal Bank of Scotland (at one point the fifth largest bank in the world) and HBOS (Britain's largest housing-lender) promoted strategies of excessive growth and diversification into new markets during the first decade of the twenty-first century. Such growth and diversification gave the managers short-term benefits in terms of managerial bonuses and prestige. But going beyond their areas of true expertise soon brought financial disaster, leading to the nationalisation of RBS and the takeover of HBOS by rival Lloyds bank.

(6.4) VERTICAL INTEGRATION

As well as diversification, another direction for corporate strategy can be vertical integration. Vertical integration describes entering activities where the organisation is its own supplier or customer. Thus it involves operating at another stage of the value network (see section 3.4.1). This section considers both vertical integration and vertical dis-integration, particularly in the form of outsourcing.

6.4.1 Forward and backward integration

Vertical integration can go in either of two directions:

- **Backward integration refers to development into activities concerned with the inputs into the company's current business** (i.e. they are further back in the value network). For example, the acquisition by a car manufacturer of a component supplier would be a backward integration move.

- **Forward integration refers to development into activities concerned with the outputs of a company's current business** (i.e. are further forward in the value network). For a car manufacturer, forward integration would be into car retail, repairs and servicing.

Thus vertical integration is like diversification in increasing corporate scope. The difference is that it brings together activities up and down the same value network, while diversifcation typically involves more or less different value networks. However, because realising synergies involves bringing together different value networks, diversification (especially related diversification) is sometimes also described as *horizontal integration*. For example, a company diversified in cars, trucks and buses could find benefits in integrating aspects of the various design or component-sourcing processes. The relationship between horizontal integration and vertical integration is depicted in Figure 6.3.

Vertical integration is often favoured because it seems to 'capture' more of the profits in a value network. The car manufacturer gains the retailer's profits as well. However, it is important to be aware of two dangers. First, vertical integration involves investment. Expensive

Figure 6.3 Diversification and integration options: car manufacturer example

ILLUSTRATION 6.2

Deadly outsourcing? The Ministry of Defence under pressure

The UK's Ministry of Defence faces a dilemma over whether to outsource more of its support services, possibly at the expense of the safety of its own personnel.

Under pressure from budget cuts, and still committed to an expensive war in Afghanistan, in November 2009 the United Kingdom's Ministry of Defence (MoD) was planning to outsource more of its logistics and equipment support. This announcement came just one month after the publication of the official report on the 2006 Nimrod military aircraft crash, in which 14 personnel had died. The chairman of the inquiry, Charles Haddon-Cave, had castigated the MoD for 'lamentable' safety procedures. But he had also criticised two private-sector contractors, BAE Systems and Qinetiq, who had been involved in the safety checks for the doomed Nimrod aircraft. Haddon-Smith complained: 'there has been a shift in culture and priorities at the MoD towards business and financial targets at the expense of. . . . safety and airworthiness'.

But now the Ministry of Defence was launching its Defence Support Review (DSR), where it announced: 'past efficiencies have . . . been delivered from a range of increasingly innovative arrangements with industry. . . . The cost base has, and will continue to, migrate to industry.' The Defence Support Review claimed its recommendations could save £474m (~€521m; ~$711m) in the first four years of its plan, and up to £2.4bn over the subsequent six years. The BAE Systems contract for the support of Tornado fighter aircraft had already delivered savings of £1.3bn. The main MoD civil service union replied that it was '. . . concerned that the DSR is premature and will damage the MoD's ability to support the front-line'.

The Royal Air Force is the most committed of the three armed services to outsourcing support work to contractors. Minor repairs on aircraft are done in-theatre by RAF mechanics. However, more substantial maintenance is done by contractors such as BAE Systems, Rolls-Royce and Qinetiq at main operating bases distributed around the world. Contracts typically guarantee that aircraft will be available to fly a certain number of hours over an agreed period.

The Royal Navy relies on BAE Systems and Babcock for support of its submarine and surface fleets. It leases fishery protection vessels from BAE Systems as well. Availability contracts work less well for ships than for aircraft because there are fewer of them, making it harder to keep a contracted number of ships in service over an agreed period. The Army is the most reluctant to outsource repair and maintenance work, relying more on the in-house Defence Support Group. However, in 2008, it signed a contract with BAE Systems to sustain about 400 Panther command and liaison vehicles.

BAE Systems is the second largest defence contractor in the world, behind the American Lockheed-Martin. It makes and supports aircraft, missiles, ships, submarines and armoured vehicles. In 2009, BAE Systems employed over 30,000 people in the UK, about 10 per cent of all UK defence industry jobs. The 2006 Parliamentary Select Committee on Defence had established that about 5 per cent of all MoD defence contracts by value go to BAE Systems each year, while BAE Systems derived 28 per cent of their sales from the MoD. BAE Systems was effectively a monopoly supplier in the UK of air systems and aircraft support.

Sources: House of Commons Defence Committee, 7th Report, 2006; J. Lerner, 'MoD considers call for rise of outsourcing', Financial Times, 17 November 2009; 'Learning from the Nimrod Disaster', Financial Times, 30 October 2009.

Questions

1 Compare the arguments for defence outsourcing from strategic capabilities and transaction costs points of view.

2 If you were outsourcing aircraft maintenance, what might you be concerned about and how might you design the contract and the tendering process to reduce those concerns?

investments in activities that are less profitable than the original core business will be unattractive to shareholders because they are reducing their *average* or overall rate of return on investment. Second, even if there is a degree of relatedness through the value network, vertical integration is likely to involve quite different strategic capabilities. Thus car manufacturers who integrate forward into car service and repair have found that managing networks of small service outlets is very different from managing large manufacturing plants. Growing appreciation of both the risks of diluting overall returns on investment and the distinct capabilities involved at different stages of the value network has led many companies in recent years to vertically *dis*-integrate.

6.4.2 To integrate or to outsource?

As above, it is often proposed to replace vertically integrated operations by outsourcing or subcontracting. **Outsourcing is the process by which activities previously carried out internally are subcontracted to external suppliers.** Outsourcing can refer to the subcontracting of components in manufacturing, but is now particularly common for services such as information technology, customer call centres and human resource management. The argument for outsourcing to specialist suppliers is often based on strategic capabilities. Specialists in a particular activity are likely to have superior capabilities than an organisation for which that particular activity is not a central part of their business. A specialist IT contractor is usually better at IT than the IT department of a steel company.

However, Nobel prize-winning economist Oliver Williamson has argued that the decision to integrate or outsource involves more than just relative capabilities.[10] In assessing whether to integrate or outsource an activity, he warns against underestimating the long-term costs of *opportunism* by external subcontractors (or, indeed, any other organisation in a market relationship). Subcontractors are liable over time to take advantage of their position, either to reduce their standards or to extract higher prices. Market relationships tend to fail in controlling subcontractor opportunism where:

- there are *few alternatives* to the subcontractor and it is hard to shop around;
- the product or service is *complex and changing*, and therefore impossible to specify fully in a legally binding contract;
- investments have been made in *specific assets*, which the subcontractor knows will have little value if they withhold their product or service.

Both capabilities and transaction cost reasoning have influenced the outsourcing decisions of the Ministry of Defence, see Illustration 6.2.

In sum, the decision to integrate or subcontract rests on the balance between two distinct factors:

- *Relative strategic capabilities.* Does the subcontractor have the potential to do the work significantly better?
- *Risk of opportunism.* Is the subcontractor likely to take advantage of the relationship over time?

6.5 VALUE CREATION AND THE CORPORATE PARENT

Given the doubt over diversification and integration strategies, it is clear that sometimes corporate parents are not adding value to their constituent businesses. Where there is no added value, it is usually best to divest the relevant businesses from the corporate portfolio. Thus when Carphone Warehouse recognised that its businesses would be more valuable separate rather than together, it decided in 2010 to break itself up entirely, creating a specialised retail business (including Best Buy, Europe's largest phone retailer) on the one hand, and a specialised home broadband service (TalkTalk) on the other. In the public sector too, units such as schools or hospitals are increasingly being given freedom from parenting authorities, because independence is seen as more effective. This section examines how corporate parents can both add and destroy value, and considers three different parenting approaches that can be effective.

6.5.1 Value-adding and value-destroying activities of corporate parents

Any corporate parent needs to demonstrate that they create more value than they cost. This applies to both commercial and public-sector organisations. For public-sector organisations, privatisation or outsourcing is likely to be the consequence of failure to demonstrate value. Companies whose shares are traded freely on the stock markets face a further challenge. They must demonstrate they create more value than any other rival corporate parent could create. Failure to do so is likely to lead to a hostile takeover or break-up. Rival companies that think they can create more value out of the business units can bid for the company's shares, on the expectation of either running the businesses better or selling them off to other potential parents. If the rival's bid is more attractive and credible than what the current parent can promise, shareholders will back them at the expense of incumbent management.

In this sense, competition takes place between different corporate parents for the right to own and control businesses. In the competitive market for the control of businesses, corporate parents must show that they have *parenting advantage*, on the same principle that business units must demonstrate competitive advantage. Parents therefore must have a very clear approach to how they create value. In practice, however, many of their activities can be value-destroying as well as value-creating.

Value-adding activities[11]

There are four main types of activity by which a corporate parent can add value.

- *Envisioning*. The corporate parent can provide a clear overall vision or *strategic intent* for its business units. This vision should guide and motivate the business unit managers in order to maximise corporation-wide performance through commitment to a common purpose. The vision should also provide stakeholders with a *clear external image* about what the organisation as a whole is about: this can reassure shareholders about the rationale for having a diversified strategy in the first place. Finally, a clear vision may provide a *discipline* on the corporate parent to stop it wandering into inappropriate activities or taking on unnecessary costs.

● *Coaching and facilitating.* The corporate parent can help business unit managers *develop strategic capabilities*, by coaching them to improve their skills and confidence. They can also facilitate cooperation and sharing across the business units, so improving the *synergies* from being within the same corporate organisation.

● *Providing central services and resources.* The centre is obviously a provider of capital for *investment*. The centre can also provide central services such as treasury, tax and human resource advice, which if centralised can have *sufficient scale* to be efficient and to build up *relevant expertise*. Centralised services often have greater *leverage*: for example, combining the purchases of separate business units increases their bargaining power for shared inputs such as energy. This leverage can be helpful in *brokering* with external bodies, such as government regulators, or other companies in negotiating alliances. Finally, the centre can have an important role in managing expertise within the corporate whole, for instance by *transferring managers* across the business units or by creating shared *knowledge management* systems via corporate intranets.

● *Intervening.* The corporate parent can also intervene within its business units in order to ensure appropriate performance. It can closely *monitor* business unit performance and *improve performance* either by replacing weak managers or by assisting them in turning around their businesses. The parent can also *challenge and develop* the strategic ambitions of business units, so that satisfactorily performing businesses are encouraged to perform even better.

Value-destroying activities

There are, however, three broad ways in which the corporate parent may destroy value:

● *Adding management costs.* Most basically, the staff and facilities of the corporate centre can be expensive. The corporate centre typically has the best-paid managers and the most luxurious offices. It is the actual businesses that have to generate the revenues that pay for them. If their costs are greater than the value they create, then the corporate centre's managers are net value-destroying.

● *Adding bureaucratic complexity.* As well as these direct financial costs, there is the 'bureaucratic fog' created by an additional layer of management and the need to coordinate with sister businesses. These typically slow down managers' responses to issues and lead to compromises between the interests of individual businesses.

● *Obscuring financial performance.* One danger in a large diversified company is that the underperformance of weak businesses can be obscured. Weak businesses might be cross-subsidised by the stronger ones. Internally, the possibility of hiding weak performance diminishes the incentives for business unit managers to strive as hard as they can for their businesses: they have a parental safety-net. Externally, shareholders and financial analysts cannot easily judge the performance of individual units within the corporate whole. Diversified companies' share prices are often marked down, because shareholders prefer the 'pure plays' of stand-alone units, where weak performance cannot be hidden.[12]

These dangers suggest clear paths for corporate parents that wish to avoid value destruction. They should keep a close eye on centre costs, both financial and bureaucratic, ensuring that they are no more than required by their corporate strategy. They should also do all they can to promote financial transparency, so that business units remain under pressure to perform and shareholders are confident that there are no hidden disasters.

Overall, there are many ways in which corporate parents can add value. It is, of course, difficult to pursue them all and some are hard to mix with others. For example, a corporate parent that does a great deal of top-down intervening is less likely to be seen by its managers as a helpful coach and facilitator. Business unit managers will concentrate on maximising their own individual performance rather than looking out for ways to cooperate with other business unit managers for the greater good of the whole.

6.5.2 Corporate parenting types

Corporate parenting roles tend to fall into three main types, each coherent within itself but distinct from the others.[13] These three types of corporate parenting role are summarised in Figure 6.4.

Figure 6.4 Portfolio managers, synergy managers and parental developers

Source: Adapted from M. Goold, A. Campbell and M. Alexander, *Corporate Level Strategy*, Wiley, 1994.

The portfolio manager

The **portfolio manager operates as an active investor in a way that shareholders in the stock market are either too dispersed or too inexpert to be able to do.** In effect, the portfolio manager acts as an agent on behalf of financial markets and shareholders with a view to extracting more value from the various businesses than the shareholders could achieve themselves. Their role is to identify and acquire under-valued assets or businesses and improve them. The portfolio manager might do this, for example, by acquiring another corporation, divesting low-performing businesses within it and intervening to improve the performance of those with potential. Such corporations may not be much concerned about the relatedness (see section 6.2) of the business units in their portfolio, typically adopting a conglomerate strategy. Their role is not to get closely involved in the routine management of the businesses, only to act over short periods of time to improve performance. In terms of the value-creating activities identified earlier, the portfolio manager concentrates on intervening and the provision (or withdrawal) of investment.

Portfolio managers seek to keep the cost of the centre low, for example by having a small corporate staff with few central services, leaving the business units alone so that their chief executives have a high degree of autonomy. They set clear financial targets for those chief executives, offering high rewards if they achieve them and likely loss of position if they do not. Such corporate parents can, of course, manage quite a large number of such businesses because they are not directly managing the everyday strategies of those businesses. Rather they are acting from above, setting financial targets, making central evaluations about the well-being and future prospects of such businesses, and investing, intervening or divesting accordingly.

Illustration 6.3 includes a description of the portfolio parenting approach of Warren Buffett at Berkshire Hathaway.

The synergy manager

Obtaining synergy is often seen as the prime rationale for the corporate parent.[14] The **synergy manager is a corporate parent seeking to enhance value for business units by managing synergies across business units.** Synergies are likely to be particularly rich in the case of related diversification. In terms of value-creating activities, the focus is threefold: envisioning to build a common purpose; facilitating cooperation across businesses; and providing central services and resources. For example, at Apple, Steve Jobs's vision of his personal computers being the digital hub of the new digital lifestyle guides managers across the iMac computer, iPod, iPhone and iPad businesses to ensure seamless connections between the fast-developing offerings. The result is enhanced value through better customer experience. A metals company diversified into both steel and aluminium might centralise its energy procurement, gaining synergy benefits through increased bargaining power over suppliers.

However, achieving such synergistic benefits involves at least three challenges:

- *Excessive costs.* The benefits in sharing and cooperation need to outweigh the costs of undertaking such integration, both direct financial costs and opportunity costs. Managing synergistic relationships tends to involve expensive investments in management time.

ILLUSTRATION 6.3

Eating its own cooking: Berkshire Hathaway's parenting

A portfolio manager may seek to manage a highly diverse set of business units on behalf of its shareholders.

Berkshire Hathaway's chairman and CEO is Warren Buffett, one of the world's richest men – and also one of the most plain-spoken about how to run a business. With annual sales now over $100bn (€70bn), Buffett founded this conglomerate with a small textile business in the early 1960s. Berkshire Hathaway's businesses are now highly diverse. They include large insurance businesses (GEICO, General Re, NRG), manufacturers of carpets, building products, clothing and footwear, retail companies and NetJets, the private jet service. The company also has significant long-term minority stakes in businesses such as Coca-Cola and General Electric. Aged 79, Buffett remains highly active: in 2008, he took a 10 per cent stake in Goldman Sachs, the world's leading investment bank, and in 2009 he completed the purchase of BNSF, the second largest railway company in the United States. Since the mid-1960s, Berkshire has averaged a growth in book value of 20.3 per cent each year.

The 2009 Berkshire Hathaway annual report explains how Buffett and his deputy chairman, Charlie Munger, run the business. With regard to shareholders, Buffett writes:

Charlie Munger and I think of our shareholders as owner-partners, and of ourselves as managing partners. (Because of the size of our shareholdings we are also, for better or worse, controlling partners.) We do not view the company itself as the ultimate owner of our business assets, but instead view the company as a conduit through which our shareholders own the assets. . . . In line with Berkshire's owner-orientation, most of our directors have a major portion of their net worth invested in the company. We eat our own cooking.

Berkshire has a clear 'dominant logic':

Charlie and I avoid businesses whose futures we can't evaluate, no matter how exciting their products may be. In the past, it required no brilliance for people to foresee the fabulous growth that awaited such industries as autos (in 1910), aircraft (in 1930) and television sets (in 1950). But the future then also included competitive dynamics that would decimate almost all of the companies entering those industries. Even the

survivors tended to come away bleeding. Just because Charlie and I can clearly see dramatic growth ahead for an industry does not mean we can judge what its profit margins and returns on capital will be as a host of competitors battle for supremacy. At Berkshire we will stick with businesses whose profit picture for decades to come seems reasonably predictable. Even then, we will make plenty of mistakes.

Buffett also explains how they manage their subsidiary businesses:

Charlie and I are the managing partners of Berkshire. But we subcontract all of the heavy lifting in this business to the managers of our subsidiaries. In fact, we delegate almost to the point of abdication: Though Berkshire has about 257,000 employees, only 21 of these are at headquarters. Charlie and I mainly attend to capital allocation and the care and feeding of our key managers. Most of these managers are happiest when they are left alone to run their businesses, and that is customarily just how we leave them. That puts them in charge of all operating decisions and of dispatching the excess cash they generate to head-quarters. By sending it to us, they don't get diverted by the various enticements that would come their way were they responsible for deploying the cash their businesses throw off. Furthermore, Charlie and I are exposed to a much wider range of possibilities for investing these funds than any of our managers could find in his or her own industry.

Questions

1 In what ways does Berkshire Hathaway conform (and not conform) to the archetypal portfolio manager described in section 6.5.2?

2 Suggest some industries and businesses, or types of industries and businesses that Warren Buffett is likely never to invest in.

- *Overcoming self-interest.* Managers in business units need to cooperate. Especially where managers are rewarded largely according to the performance of their own particular business unit, they may, however, be unwilling to sacrifice their time and resources for the common good.

- *Illusory synergies.* Claimed synergies often prove illusory when managers actually have to put them into practice.

The parental developer

The **parental developer** **seeks to employ its own central capabilities to add value to its businesses.** This is not so much about how the parent can develop benefits *across* business units or transfer capabilities between business units, as in the case of managing synergy. Rather parental developers focus on the resources or capabilities they have as parents which they can transfer *downwards* to enhance the potential of business units. For example, a parent could have a valuable brand or specialist skills in financial management or product development. If such parenting capabilities exist, corporate managers then need to identify a '*parenting opportunity*': a business which is not fulfilling its potential, but which could be improved by applying the parenting capability, such as branding or product development. Such parenting opportunities are therefore more common in the case of related rather than unrelated diversified strategies and are likely to involve exchanges of managers and other resources across the businesses. Key value-creating activities for the parent will be the provision of central services and resources. For example, a consumer products company might offer substantial guidance on branding and distribution from the centre; a technology company might run a large central R&D laboratory.

6.6 THE BCG (OR GROWTH/SHARE) MATRIX

This section explains a model commonly used by managers to consider financial investment and divestment within their portfolios of business, as ITC would need to do (see Illustration 6.4). It is primarily concerned with:

- the *balance* of the portfolio, e.g. in relation to its markets and the needs of the corporation;

- the *attractiveness* of the business units in terms of how strong they are individually and how profitable their markets or industries are likely to be.

The **Boston Consulting Group (BCG) matrix** or growth/share matrix uses market share and market growth criteria for determining the attractiveness and balance of a business portfolio (see Figure 6.5).[15] High market share and high growth are, of course, attractive. However, the BCG matrix also warns that high growth demands heavy investment, for instance to expand capacity or develop brands. There needs to be a balance within the portfolio, so that there are some low-growth businesses that are making sufficient surplus to fund the investment needs of higher-growth businesses.

The growth/share axes of the BCG matrix define four sorts of business:

- A *star* is a business unit within a portfolio which has a high market share in a growing market. The business unit may be spending heavily to keep up with growth, but high market

Figure 6.5 The growth/share (or BCG) matrix

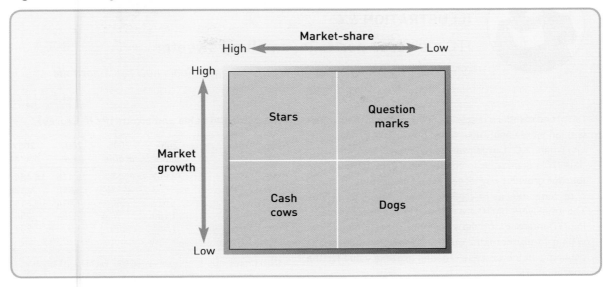

share should yield sufficient profits to make it more or less self-sufficient in terms of investment needs.

- A *question mark (or problem child)* is a business unit within a portfolio that is in a growing market, but does not yet have high market share. Developing question marks into stars, with high market share, takes heavy investment. Many question marks fail to develop, so the BCG advises corporate parents to nurture several at a time. It is important to make sure that some question marks develop into stars, as existing stars eventually become cash cows and cash cows may decline into dogs.

- A *cash cow* is a business unit within a portfolio that has a high market share in a mature market. However, because growth is low, investments needs are less, while high market share means that the business unit should be profitable. The cash cow should then be a cash provider, helping to fund investments in question marks.

- *Dogs* are business units within a portfolio that have low share in static or declining markets and are thus the worst of all combinations. They may be a cash drain and use up a disproportionate amount of managerial time and company resources. The BCG usually recommends divestment or closure.

The BCG matrix has several advantages. It provides a good way of visualising the different needs and potential of all the diverse businesses within the corporate portfolio. It warns corporate parents of the financial demands of what might otherwise look like a desirable portfolio of high-growth businesses. It also reminds corporate parents that stars are likely eventually to wane. Finally, it provides a useful discipline to business unit managers, underlining the fact that the corporate parent ultimately owns the surplus resources they generate and can allocate them according to what is best for the corporate whole. Cash cows should not hoard their profits.

ILLUSTRATION 6.4

ITC's diverse portfolio: smelling sweeter

What was once the Imperial Tobacco Company of India now has a portfolio stretching from cigarettes to fragrances.

ITC is one of India's largest consumer goods companies, with an increasingly diversified portfolio of products. Its chairman, Y.C. Deveshwar describes its strategy thus: 'It is ITC's endeavour to continuously explore opportunities for growth by synergising and blending its multiple core competences to create new epicentres of growth. The employees of ITC are inspired by the vision of growing ITC into one of India's premier institutions and are willing to go the extra mile to generate value for the economy, in the process creating growing value for the shareholders.'

ITC was founded in 1910 as the Imperial Tobacco Company of India, with brands such as Wills, Gold Cut and John Players. ITC now holds about two-thirds of the market for cigarettes in India, with Philip Morris and BAT affiliated companies distant seconds with about 13 per cent each. However, cigarettes in India are highly discouraged by the Indian government, and increasingly heavily taxed.

ITC has a long diversification history. The company's original activities in the growth of leaf tobacco developed into a range of agricultural businesses within India, including edible oils, fruit pulp, spices and frozen foods. ITC had set up a packaging and printing business in the 1920s, originally to supply its cigarette business. By 2009, this was India's largest packaging solutions provider. In 1975, ITC had entered the hotel business, becoming the country's second largest operator with over 100 hotels by 2009, ranging from de luxe to economy. In 1979, the company also entered the paperboard industry, and three decades later was the country's largest producer, accounting for 29 per cent of the market by value.

The early twenty-first century had seen many new diversification initiatives, especially in the booming Fast Moving Consumer Goods (FMCG) sector. Initially it started in the food business, with Kitchens-of-India ready-to-eat gourmet foods, the *Aashirvaad* wheat-flour

ITC segmental sales and profits (Rs in Crores)

Segment	2005 sales	2005 profits	2009 sales	2009 profits
Cigarettes	10,002	2,288	15,115	4,184
Other FMCG	563	(195)	3,010	(483)
Hotels	577	141	1,014	316
Agribusiness	1,780	96.4	2,284	256
Paperboard, paper and packaging	1,565	280	1,719	509

5 Rs in Crores ~ US $1,000,000 ~€700,000. Profits are before interest and tax. Figures in brackets are losses.

business, Sunfeast biscuits and Bingo snacks. ITC's own agri-businesses were an important source of supply for these initiatives. *Aashirvaad* reached over 50 per cent Indian market share, while Sunfeast gained 12 per cent market share and Bingo 11 per cent by 2008. At the same time, ITC took advantage of the strong brand values of its Wills cigarettes to launch Wills Lifestyle, a range of upmarket clothing stores, with its own designs. In 2009, Wills Lifestyle was recognised as India's 'Most Admired Fashion Brand of the Year'. In 2005, ITC launched its personal care business, again using its cigarette brand-names: for example, 'Essenza Di Wills' (fragrances) and 'Fiama Di Wills' (hair and skin care).

Sources: ITC annual reports; M. Balaji, 2006, *ITC: Adding Shareholder Value through Diversifications*, IBSCDC; B. Gopal and S. Kora, 2009, *Indian Conglomerate ITC*, IBS Research Center.

Questions

1 How well does ITC's portfolio fit in terms of the BCG matrix?

2 Identify and evaluate the various synergies in ITC's business.

However, there are at least three potential problems with the BCG matrix:

- *Definitional vagueness.* It can be hard to decide what high and low growth or share mean in particular situations. Managers are often keen to define themselves as 'high-share' by defining their market in a particularly narrow way (for example, ignoring relevant international markets).

- *Capital market assumptions.* The notion that a corporate parent needs a balanced portfolio to finance investment from internal sources (cash cows) assumes that capital cannot be raised in external markets, for instance by issuing shares or raising loans. The notion of a balanced portfolio may be more relevant in countries where capital markets are under-developed or in private companies that wish to minimise dependence on external shareholders or banks.

- *Unkind to animals.* Both cash cows and dogs receive ungenerous treatment, the first being simply milked, the second terminated or cast out of the corporate home. This treatment can cause *motivation problems*, as managers in these units see little point in working hard for the sake of other businesses. There is also the danger of the *self-fulfilling prophecy*. Cash cows will become dogs even more quickly than the model expects if they are simply milked and denied adequate investment. Finally, the notion that a dog can be simply sold or closed down also assumes that there are *no ties to other business units* in the portfolio, whose performance might depend in part on keeping the dog alive. This portfolio approach to dogs works better for conglomerate strategies, where divestments or closures are unlikely to have knock-on effects on other parts of the portfolio.

SUMMARY

- Many corporations comprise several, sometimes many, business units. Decisions and activities above the level of business units are the concern of what in this chapter is called the *corporate parent*.
- Organisational *scope* is often considered in terms of *related* and *unrelated* diversification.
- *Divestment* and *outsourcing* should be considered as well as diversification, particularly in the light of relative strategic capabilities and the transaction costs of *opportunism*.
- Corporate parents may seek to add value by adopting different parenting roles: the *portfolio manager*, the *synergy manager* or the *parental developer*.
- The *BCG (or growth/share) matrix* helps corporate parents manage their portfolios of businesses.

VIDEO CASE

Visit **MyStrategyLab** and watch the *Friday's* case study.

1 What are the benefits and disadvantages of Friday's relationship with supermarkets? Relatively, how strong is Friday's compared with competitors in this relationship?

2 Explain Friday's diversification strategy in terms of the Ansoff axes and strategic relatedness.

RECOMMENDED KEY READINGS

- An accessible discussion of corporate strategy is provided by A. Campbell and R. Park, *The Growth Gamble: When Leaders Should Bet on Big New Businesses*, Nicholas Brealey, 2005.

- M. Goold and K. Luchs, 'Why diversify: four decades of management thinking' in D. Faulkner and A. Campbell (eds), *The Oxford Handbook of Strategy*, vol. 2, Oxford University Press, pp. 18–42, provides an authoritative overview of the diversification option over time.

REFERENCES

1. This figure is an extension of the product/market matrix: see I. Ansoff, *Corporate Strategy*, 1988, Chapter 6. The Ansoff matrix was later developed into the one shown below.

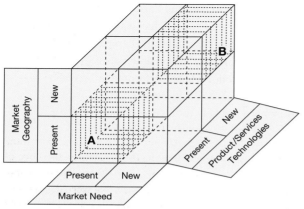

Source: H. Ansoff, *The New Corporate Strategy*, Wiley, 1988.

2. For the European Commission competition authority, http://ec.europa.eu/comm/competition; for the UK Competition Commission, see http://www.competition-commission.org.uk/.

3. For discussions of the challenge of sustained growth and diversification, see A. Campbell and R. Parks, *The Growth Gamble*, Nicholas Brearly (2005) and D. Laurie, Y. Doz and C. Sheer, 'Creating new growth platforms', *Harvard Business Review*, vol. 84, no. 5, (2006), 80–90.

4. On economies of scope, see D.J. Teece, 'Towards an economic theory of the multi-product firm', *Journal of Economic Behavior and Organization*, vol. 3 (1982), pp. 39–63.

5. See C.K. Prahalad and R. Bettis, 'The dominant logic: a new link between diversity and performance', *Strategic Management Journal*, vol. 6, no. 1 (1986), pp. 485–501; R. Bettis and C.K. Prahalad, 'The dominant logic: retrospective and extension', *Strategic Management Journal*, vol. 16, no. 1 (1995), pp. 5–15.

6. See C. Markides, 'Corporate strategy: the role of the centre' in A. Pettigrew, H. Thomas and R. Whittington (eds), *Handbook of Strategy and Management*, Sage, 2002. For a discussion of recent Chinese diversification patterns, see

A. Delios, N. Zhou and W.W. Xu, 'Ownership structure and the diversification and performance of publicly-listed companies in China', *Business Horizons*, vol. 51, no. 6 (2008), pp. 802–21.

7. These benefits are often discussed in terms of 'multimarket' or 'multipoint' competition: see J. Anand, L. Mesquita and R. Vassolo, 'The dynamics of multimarket competition in exploration and exploitation activities', *Academy of Management Journal*, vol. 52, no. 4 (2009), pp. 802–21.

8. M. Goold and A. Campbell, 'Desperately seeking synergy', *Harvard Business Review*, vol. 76, no. 2 (1998), pp. 131–45.

9. A. Pehrson, 'Business relatedness and performance: a study of managerial perceptions', *Strategic Management Journal*, vol. 27, no. 3 (2006), pp. 265–82.

10. For a discussion and cases on the relative guidance of transaction cost and capabilities thinking, see R. McIvor, 'How the transaction cost and resource-based theories of the firm inform outsourcing evaluation', *Journal of Operations Management*, vol. 27, no. 1 (2009), pp. 45–63. See also T. Holcomb and M. Hitt, 'Toward a model of strategic outsourcing', *Journal of Operations Management*, vol. 25, no. 2 (2007), pp. 464–81.

11. M. Goold, A. Campbell and M. Alexander, *Corporate Level Strategy*, Wiley, 1994, is concerned with both the value-adding and value-destroying capacity of corporate parents.

12. E. Zuckerman, 'Focusing the corporate product: securities analysts and de-diversification', *Administrative Science Quarterly*, vol. 45, no. 3 (2000), pp. 591–619.

13. The first two rationales discussed here are based on M. Porter, 'From competitive advantage to corporate strategy', *Harvard Business Review*, vol. 65, no. 3 (1987), pp. 43–59.

14. See A. Campbell and K. Luchs, *Strategic Synergy*, Butterworth/Heinemann, 1992.

15. For a more extensive discussion of the use of the growth share matrix see A.C. Hax and N.S. Majluf in R.G. Dyson (ed.), *Strategic Planning: Models and Analytical Techniques*, Wiley, 1990; and D. Faulkner, 'Portfolio matrices', in V. Ambrosini (ed.), *Exploring Techniques of Analysis and Evaluation in Strategic Management*, Prentice Hall, 1998.

CASE EXAMPLE

Virgin: the global entrepreneur

John Treciokas

Introduction

Richard Branson founded Virgin in 1970 and has effectively used his personality to bring the Virgin brand to the attention of the consumer. Virgin's businesses are portrayed in an exciting light with a personal touch and this gives the Virgin brand a softer feel than other large multinational companies. The Virgin Group has grown over the last 40 years to become one of the largest private companies in the UK. Virgin currently has more than 200 branded companies worldwide, employing in the region of 50,000 employees in 29 countries with revenues in excess of £11 billion (approx. €12bn; $16 bn) in 2008.

The largest and most celebrated business, Virgin Atlantic, celebrated 25 years of flying people across the Atlantic in 2009 with a striking advertising campaign which portrayed the excitement and fun of flying with, or working at, Virgin. Branson believes in the value of careful brand enhancement and the benefits of transferring this brand image across a diverse portfolio. Research has shown that the Virgin name is associated with words such as: 'fun', 'innovative', 'daring' and 'successful'.

However, does such a portfolio of businesses make strategic sense and will Virgin's conglomerate group of diverse companies survive after Richard Branson departs? These were the key questions facing the company in 2010, the start of a new decade.

Growth and strategy

Virgin began selling music records in 1970 when Branson was just 20 years old and its rapid growth led to an Oxford Street shop a year later. Further expansion into the music industry followed with the Virgin record label in 1973. From an early stage in the business, Virgin courted controversy by signing the Sex Pistols, a 'punk rock group' whose rude and anti-establishment behaviour quickly brought them and Virgin high public exposure. Risk-taking and courting publicity epitomised

Source: Steve Bell/Rex Features.

Branson's philosophy from the outset.

Virgin Atlantic was founded in 1984 and a year after Virgin Holidays began. These became the core of the Virgin group. In 1987 Virgin Records America was established: Branson commented, 'we were flying there a lot so it made sense to expand there too'. In 1988 Virgin Megastores (retail outlets with a huge selection of recorded music and related products) were opened in Glasgow and Paris, followed by numerous other British, European, American, Japanese and Pacific Basin cities. Virgin was becoming an international company.

Virgin, at this stage of its existence, was involved largely in two industries: travel/holidays and music. From the 1990s onwards there followed numerous acquisitions, divestments and joint ventures that resulted in a highly diversified group. Chief among these were:

- In 1992 the sale of Virgin Records to EMI for £510m, mainly to raise funds for Branson to invest further in his favourite business (Virgin Atlantic).
- The acquisition of the Our Price chain of shops in 1994, making Virgin Retail the UK's largest music retailer.
- The launch of a low-cost airline, Virgin Express in 1996.
- The acquisition in 1997 of the ailing West Coast rail franchise in the UK. Virgin Trains set about trying to

improve its services and five years later introduced the tilting Pendolino trains, allowing faster services.

- The start of Branson's interest in the media business with the launch of Virgin One, a tabloid TV channel, in 1997.
- In 1999 the launch of Virgin Mobile, using other providers' networks via a joint venture with what is now T-mobile.
- The launch of a network of health clubs in 1999 and, in 2006, the acquisition of the Holmes Place health chain to give it a significant market share in the UK.
- The sale in 2000 by Virgin of 49 per cent of Virgin Atlantic to Singapore Airlines – perhaps accepting that this was a risky and expensive business. Branson insisted, however, that Virgin would not lose its majority control in this core business.
- In 2008 Virgin Mobile in India was launched, in partnership with the Tata group. Tata Teleservices provided the network service, though it is marketed under the Virgin brand. The offering included music, entertainment and news on India's film industry, sports and stock market. The target market was the younger population – some 51 per cent of the 1.1 billion people in India are under 25 and two-thirds are under 35.
- In 2007, Virgin had tried a major move into the financial industry, with the attempted takeover of Northern Rock, a troubled British mortgage bank. The move was resisted by the press and some politicians – Branson has never quite been accepted by the establishment. However, at the beginning of 2010, Virgin continued this strategy with the purchase of a little-known private bank (Church House Trust) which enabled it to apply for a full banking licence and to offer its own mortgages and current accounts. Will this be the next major plank in the Virgin empire?

A move to merge several of its offerings occurred in 2006, when four Virgin companies combined to become one media company providing television, broadband, telephone and mobile phone services in partnership with NTL-Telewest. This company, trading as Virgin Media, had a total of 9 million subscribers, giving it a strong position to compete with, and aggressively challenge, its major rival BSkyB. Virgin began to offer

Table 1 Other strategic developments: 1990–2010

1993	Virgin Radio commences broadcasting.
1994	Launch of Virgin Vodka and Virgin Cola.
1995	Launch of Virgin Direct, an investment product.
1996	Launch of Virgin Net, an internet service provider.
1997	Virgin Trains is founded to run a rail franchise in the UK.
1997	Virgin Cosmetics launches with four flagship stores.
1997	Virgin One commences operations in tabloid TV.
2000	Nine new companies are launched, including a new low-cost airline and mobile phone service, both in Australia.
2006	Virgin Express airline merged with SN Brussels Airline.
2006	Launch of airline in Nigeria.

complete packages for the family, including a broad range of television packages, broadband at home and away, home telephone services and mobile phone services. This package often included free hardware to lock customers in for up to two years on a contract.

Since 2000 Virgin has also set up a rather futuristic attempt to launch a passenger service into suborbital space (Virgin Galactic) as well as more down-to-earth businesses like Virgin Comics and Virgin Healthcare. The table also shows other strategic developments during this time.

Branson has also become increasingly interested in environmental issues, with the launch of the Virgin Earth Challenge. In 2007, he announced this challenge to produce practical designs that can remove large amounts of carbon dioxide from the atmosphere and offered a \$25m (about €17.5m) prize. This initiative was part of a number of initiatives brought together by Branson under the banner of 'World Citizen'. These included 'People & Planet', with the aim of ensuring that Virgin companies contribute to a sustainable society; Virgin Unite, a not-for-profit entrepreneurial foundation, with the aim of partnering to develop new ways to improve social and environmental issues; and the Virgin Green Fund to invest in companies in renewable energy and resource efficiency sectors in Europe and the US. Richard Branson also joined 'The Elders' – a group of leaders brought together by Nelson Mandela to promote peace and tackle humanitarian problems. It seems that Branson, like Microsoft's Bill Gates, was turning his attention to non-profit and CSR issues.

Corporate rationale

Branson's 2008 book, *Business Stripped Bare*, had the subtitle: 'the adventures of a global entrepreneur'. Virgin states on its own website that it is a 'leading branded venture capital organisation' and companies are part of a family rather than a hierarchy. It has minimal layers of management, no bureaucracy and a small global HQ.

Branson sees Virgin as adding value in three main ways in addition to the brand. These are: its public relations and marketing skills; its experience with 'green-field' start-ups; and its understanding of the opportunities presented by 'institutionalised' markets – by this he means those dominated by a few competitors who are not giving good value to customers because they have become inefficient, complacent or preoccupied with rivals.

The key criterion for whether Virgin backs a new venture is 'does an opportunity exist for restructuring a market and creating competitive advantage?' Each business is 'ring-fenced', so that lenders to one company have no rights over the assets of another and financial results are not consolidated. Virgin has a mix of privately owned and public-listed companies, as well as a mix of start-up small businesses and very large corporate ventures. Each may have very different strategic reasoning: some may be an attempt to keep Virgin in the public consciousness or possibly a method of training and developing managers. Some larger start-ups are serious strategic moves into new industries.

Increasingly large financial pockets and a proven track record in highly competitive industries have also enabled Virgin to enter into business opportunities with joint venture partners.

The future

Not all of Virgin's companies are successful and not all meet the standards of customer service that Virgin would like to see – both Virgin Media and Virgin Rail have had many customer complaints. None the less, Branson has created an image with the British public of a 'cheeky entrepreneur' who has battled the mighty 'monopoly' of British Airways and whose Virgin brand has grown into a business empire. The other lesser-known image – according to Branson-watcher and journalist Tom Bower – is one of a ruthless, crafty businessman always trying to get one over on his rivals.

It is difficult to discover the overall financial position of Virgin as it is made up of so many individual companies (many private) and there are no consolidated accounts. However, Bower states (2008) that the financial accounts show that the Virgin holding company lost £3.9m, even as its mainstay air-travel subsidiary made a profit of £123m. Sir Richard has argued that he pursues growth, not profits, and builds companies for the long term. With the aviation industry in crisis in 2009/10 and Virgin's dependence on airlines, this must raise concerns for the future of the organisation.

Richard Branson does not mention his departure in interviews but states that the company has been carefully groomed to continue without him, and that the brand is now globally well known, thus implying that his publicity stunts are no longer required. However, can Virgin survive as an entity without Branson?

References and sources:

www.Virgin.com; Tom Bower, *Branson*, Harper Perennial, 2008; www.businessweek.com/November 2007; www.reuters.com, 16 December 2009; *The Economist*, 'Virgin rebirth', 12 September 2008; *The Economist*, 'Toyota slips up', 12 December 2009; Sharlene Goff, *Financial Times*, 8 January 2010.

Questions

1 Describe Virgin's various diversification moves in terms of Ansoff's axes (Figure 6.2).

2 How does Virgin add value as a corporate parent? Is there anything more it should do to add value?

3 Assess whether moving further into the banking industry is the right strategic option for Virgin. Does the continued pursuit of this industry suggest a more careful hidden strategic plan that is not revealed to outsiders?

4 What would be the challenges faced by a successor to Richard Branson, and what might they do?

7

INTERNATIONAL STRATEGY

Learning outcomes

After reading this chapter, you should be able to:

- Assess the *internationalisation potential* of different markets.

- Identify sources of competitive advantage in international strategy, through both *global sourcing* and exploitation of *local factors*.

- Distinguish between the four *generic international strategies*.

- *Rank markets* for entry or expansion, taking into account attractiveness, cultural and other forms of distance and competitor retaliation threats.

- Assess the relative merits of different *market entry modes*, including joint ventures, licensing and foreign direct investment.

Key terms

CAGE framework p. 173

Global–local dilemma p. 169

Global sourcing p. 167

Global strategy p. 161

International strategy p. 161

Porter's Diamond p. 165

Staged international expansion model p. 178

Yip's globalisation framework p. 161

(7.1) INTRODUCTION

The last chapter introduced market development as a strategy, in relation to the Ansoff axes. This chapter focuses on a specific but important kind of market development, operating in different geographical markets. This is a challenge for all kinds of organisations nowadays. There are of course the large traditional multinationals such as Nestlé, Toyota and McDonald's. But recent years have seen the rise of emerging-country multinationals from Brazil, Russia, India and China. New firms are increasingly 'born global' too, building international relationships right from the start. Facebook, first launched in 2004, entered the United Kingdom just two years later and reached Japan in 2008.

Figure 7.1 identifies five main themes of this chapter, with international strategy as the core. The themes are as follows:

- *Internationalisation drivers.* Drivers include market demand, the potential for cost advantages, government pressures and inducements and the need to respond to competitor moves. Given the risks and costs of international strategy, managers need to know that the drivers are strong to justify adopting an international strategy in the first place.

- *Geographical advantage.* In international competition, advantages might come from both geographic location of the original business and from the international configuration of their value network. Managers need to appraise these potential sources of competitive advantage carefully: if there are no competitive advantages, international strategy is liable to fail.

- *International strategy.* If drivers and advantages are sufficiently strong to merit an international strategy, then a range of generic international strategies are opened up, from the simplest export strategies to the most complex global strategies.

Figure 7.1 International strategy framework

- *Market selection*. Having adopted the broad approach to international strategy, the question next is which country markets to prioritise and which to steer clear of. The issues here range from the economic to the cultural and political.

- *Entry mode*. Finally, once target countries are selected, managers have to determine how they should enter each particular market. Again, export is a simple place to start, but there are licensing, franchising, joint-venture and wholly owned subsidiary alternatives to consider as well.

The chapter distinguishes between international strategy and global strategy. **International strategy refers to a range of strategic options for operating outside an organisation's country of origin.** Global strategy is only one kind of strategic option. **Global strategy involves high coordination of extensive activities dispersed geographically in many countries around the world.** This chapter keeps open alternative options to full global strategy.

(7.2) INTERNATIONALISATION DRIVERS

There are many general pressures increasing internationalisation. Barriers to international trade, investment and migration are all now much lower than they were a couple of decades ago. Better international legal frameworks means that it is less risky to deal with unfamiliar partners. Improvements in communications – from cheaper air travel to the internet – make movement and the spread of ideas much easier around the world. Not least, the success of new economic powerhouses such as the so-called BRICs – Brazil, Russia, India and China – is generating new opportunities and challenges for business internationally.[1]

However, not all these internationalisation trends are one-way. Nor do they hold for all industries. For example, migration is now becoming more difficult between some countries. Trade barriers still exist for some products, especially those relating to defence technologies. Many countries protect their leading companies from takeover by overseas rivals. Markets vary widely in the extent to which consumer needs are standardising – compare computer search engines to the highly variable national tastes in chocolate. Some so-called multinationals are in fact concentrated in very particular markets, for example North America and Western Europe, or have a quite limited set of international links, for example supply or outsourcing arrangements with just one or two countries overseas. In short, managers need to beware 'global baloney', by which economic integration into a single homogenised and competitive world is wildly exaggerated. As in the Chinese retail market (Illustration 7.1), international drivers are usually a lot more complicated than that: Chinese markets are not only very different from Western ones, but vary widely within China itself.

Given internationalisation's complexity, international strategy should be underpinned by a careful assessment of trends in each particular market. Erasmus University's George Yip provides a framework for analysing 'drivers of globalisation'. In the terms of this chapter, these globalisation drivers can be thought of as 'internationalisation drivers' more generally. In this book, therefore, **Yip's globalisation framework sees international strategy potential as determined by market drivers, cost drivers, government drivers and competitive drivers** (see Figure 7.2).[2]

KEY CONCEPT

Yip's globalisation framework

ILLUSTRATION 7.1

Chinese retail: global or local?

Internationalisation is not a simple process, as supermarket chains Carrefour and Wal-Mart have found in China.

China is a magnet for ambitious Western supermarket chains. With an annual growth rate of 13 per cent a year, the Chinese market is predicted by Business Monitor International to grow in value by $1.2 (~€0.84) trn. between 2009 and 2014. 520 million people are expected to join the Chinese upper middle class by 2025.

Two leading Western companies in the Chinese retail market are French supermarket chain Carrefour and the world's largest retailer, the American Wal-Mart. The two companies have had very different strategies. French supermarket chain Carrefour was the first to enter the Chinese market in a substantial fashion, entering in 1995, after six years' experience in neighbouring Taiwan. Carrefour is following a decentralised strategy: except in Shanghai, where it has several stores, Carrefour allows its local store managers, scattered across the many different regions of China, to make their own purchasing and supply decisions. By 2009, Carrefour was the fifth largest retailer in China, though this meant only 0.6 per cent overall market share. Wal-Mart was close behind with 0.5 per cent share. Wal-Mart's initial approach had been based on its standard centralised purchasing and distribution strategy, supplying as much as it can from its new, state-of-the-art distribution centre in Shenzen. In 2009, however, Wal-Mart experimented with a smaller-scale local store format, which it intends to roll-out nationally. It is also integrating the Chinese operations of a budget Taiwanese retailer.

One early discovery for Wal-Mart was that Chinese consumers prefer frequent shopping trips, buying small quantities each time. While Wal-Mart assumed that Chinese consumers would drive to out-of-town stores and fill their cars with large frozen multi-packs on a once-a-week shop like Americans, in fact Chinese customers would break open the multi-packs to take just the smaller quantities they required. Now Wal-Mart supplies more of its frozen foods loose, offering customers a scoop so they can take exactly the amount they want. Wal-Mart also now allows trade unions into its stores, in marked contrast to its policy in the rest of the world.

Another discovery for Western retailers is the amount of regional variation in this vast and multi-ethnic country. In the north of China, soya sauces are important; in central China, chilli pepper sauces are required; in the south, it is oyster sauces that matter. For fruit, northerners must have dates; southerners want lychees. In the north, the cold means more demand for red meat and, because customers are wearing layers of clothing, wider store aisles. Northerners don't have much access to hot water, so they wash their hair less frequently, meaning that small sachets of shampoo sell better than large bottles. And, unlike other Chinese, apparently the citizens of Zhejiang province like their toilet paper as 'rough as sandpaper'.

The growth of companies such as Carrefour and Wal-Mart demonstrates that there is a substantial market for the Western retail model. Carrefour, for example, was a pioneer of 'private label' goods in China, while Wal-Mart brings logistical expertise. But progress has been slow and Chinese companies such as market-leader GOME have imitated. Wal-Mart has yet to make a profit in China; Carrefour finally is, but its 2–3 per cent margins are significantly below the nearly 5 per cent margins it enjoys in France. In 2008, Carrefour suffered from a Chinese boycott after a Parisian protest over Tibet associated with the Beijing Olympics and in 2009 Carrefour was obliged to deny that it was considering leaving China.

Sources: Financial Times, Wall Street Journal and Euromonitor (various).

Questions

1 What are the pros and cons of the different China strategies pursued by Carrefour and Wal-Mart?

2 What might be the dangers for a large Western retailer in staying out of the Chinese market?

Figure 7.2 Drivers of internationalisation

Source: Adapted from G. Yip, *Total Global Strategy II*, Financial Times Prentice Hall, 2003, Chapter 2.

In more detail, the four drivers are as follows:

- *Market drivers*. A critical facilitator of internationalisation is standardisation of market characteristics. There are three components underlying this driver. First, the presence of *similar customer needs and tastes*: for example, the fact that in most societies consumers have similar needs for easy credit has promoted the worldwide spread of a handful of credit card companies such as Visa. Second is the presence of *global customers*: for example, car component companies have become more international as their customers, such as Toyota or Ford, have internationalised, and required standardised components for all their factories around the world. Finally, *transferable marketing* promotes market globalisation: brands such as Coca-Cola are still successfully marketed in very similar ways across the world.

- *Cost drivers*. Costs can be reduced by operating internationally. Again, there are three main elements to cost drivers. First, increasing volume beyond what a national market might support can give *scale economies*, both on the production side and in purchasing of supplies. Companies from smaller countries such as the Netherlands and Switzerland tend therefore to become proportionately much more international than companies from the United States, which have a vast market at home. Scale economies are particularly important in industries with high product-development costs, as in the aircraft industry, where initial costs need to be spread over the large volumes of international markets. Second, internationalisation is promoted where it is possible to take advantage of variations in *country-specific differences*. Thus it makes sense to locate the manufacture of clothing in China or Africa, where labour is still considerably cheaper, but to keep design activities in cities such as New York, Paris, Milan or London, where fashion expertise is concentrated. The third element is *favourable logistics*, or the costs of moving products or services across borders relative to their final value. From this point of view, computer microchips are easy to source internationally, while bulky materials such as assembled furniture are harder.

● *Government drivers*. These can both facilitate and inhibit internationalisation. The relevant elements of policy are numerous, including tariff barriers, technical standards, subsidies to local firms, ownership restrictions, local content requirements, controls over technology transfer, intellectual property (patenting) regimes and currency and capital flow controls. No government allows complete economic openness and openness typically varies widely from industry to industry, with agriculture and high-tech industries related to defence likely to be particularly sensitive. Nevertheless, the World Trade Organization continues to push for greater openness and the European Union and the North American Free Trade Agreement have reduced trade barriers significantly in their specific regions.[3]

● *Competitive drivers*. These relate specifically to globalisation as an integrated world-wide strategy rather than simpler international strategies. These have two elements. First, *interdependence* between country operations increases the pressure for global coordination. For example, a business with a plant in Mexico serving both the US and the Chinese markets has to coordinate carefully between the three locations: surging sales in one country, or a collapse in another, will have significant knock-on effects on the other countries. The second element relates directly to competitor strategy. The presence of *globalised competitors* increases the pressure to adopt a global strategy in response because competitors may use one country's profits to cross-subsidise their operations in another. A company with a loosely coordinated international strategy is vulnerable to globalised competitors, because it is unable to support country subsidiaries under attack from targeted, subsidised competition. The danger is of piecemeal withdrawal from countries under attack, and the gradual undermining of any overall economies of scale that the international player may have started with.[4]

The key insight from Yip's drivers framework is that the internationalisation potential of industries is variable. There are many different factors that can support or inhibit it, and an important step in determining an internationalisation strategy is a realistic assessment of the true scope for internationalisation in the particular industry. In the Chinese retail case (Illustration 7.1), it may be that the drivers for Western entry are as much competitive as market.

(7.3) NATIONAL AND INTERNATIONAL SOURCES OF ADVANTAGE

As is clear from the earlier discussion of cost drivers in international strategy, the geographical location of activities is a crucial source of potential advantage and one of the distinguishing features of international strategy relative to other diversification strategies. As INSEAD's Bruce Kogut has explained, an organisation can improve the configuration of its *value chain and network*[5] by taking advantage of country-specific differences (see section 3.4.1). There are two principal opportunities available: the exploitation of particular *locational advantages*, often in the company's home country, and sourcing advantages overseas via an *international value network*.

7.3.1 Locational advantage: Porter's Diamond[6]

As for any strategy, internationalisation needs to be based on strategic capabilities providing a sustainable competitive advantage. This competitive advantage has usually to be substantial. After all, a competitor entering a market from overseas typically starts with considerable *dis*advantages relative to existing home competitors, who will usually have superior market knowledge, established relationships with local customers, strong supply chains and the like. A foreign entrant must have significant competitive advantages to overcome such disadvantages. The example of the American giant retailer Wal-Mart provides an illustration: Wal-Mart has been successful in many Asian markets with relatively under-developed retail markets, but in 2006 was forced to withdraw from Germany's more mature market after nearly a decade of failure. In Germany, unlike in most Asian markets, Wal-Mart had no significant competitive advantage over domestic retailers.

The sources of sustainable competitive advantage in general are considered in Chapters 3 and 6. However, the international context specifically raises the potential of locational sources of advantage. Countries, and regions within them, often become associated with specific types of enduring competitive advantage: for example, the Swiss in private banking, the northern Italians in leather and fur fashion goods, and the Taiwanese in laptop computers. Michael Porter has proposed a four-pointed 'diamond' to explain why some locations tend to produce firms with sustained competitive advantages in some industries more than others (see Figure 7.3). Specifically, **Porter's Diamond suggests that locational advantages may stem from local factor conditions; local demand conditions; local related and supporting industries; and from local firm strategy structure and rivalry**. These four interacting determinants of locational advantage work as follows:

KEY CONCEPT

Porter's Diamond

- *Factor conditions.* These refer to the 'factors of production' that go into making a product or service (i.e. raw materials, land and labour). Factor condition advantages at a national level can translate into general competitive advantages for national firms in international markets. For example, the linguistic ability of the Swiss has provided a significant advantage to their banking industry. Cheap energy has traditionally provided an advantage for the North American aluminium industry.

Figure 7.3 Porter's Diamond – the determinants of national advantages

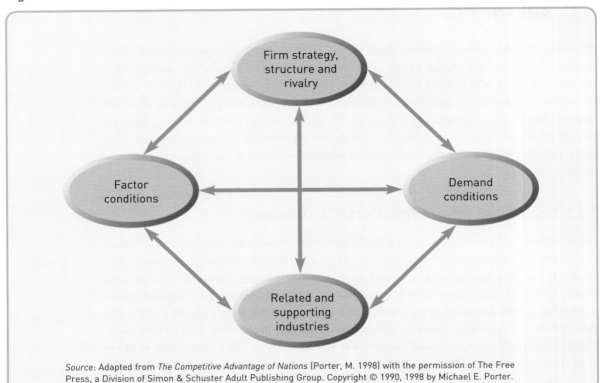

Source: Adapted from *The Competitive Advantage of Nations* (Porter, M. 1998) with the permission of The Free Press, a Division of Simon & Schuster Adult Publishing Group. Copyright © 1990, 1998 by Michael E. Porter. All rights reserved.

- *Home demand conditions.* The nature of the domestic customers can become a source of competitive advantage. Dealing with sophisticated and demanding customers at home helps train a company to be effective overseas. For example, Japanese customers' high expectations of electrical and electronic equipment provided an impetus for those industries in Japan, leading to global dominance of those sectors. Sophisticated local customers in France and Italy have helped keep their local fashion industries at the leading edge for many decades.

- *Related and supporting industries.* Local 'clusters' of related and mutually supporting industries can be an important source of competitive advantage. These are often regionally based, making personal interaction easier. In northern Italy, for example, the leather footwear industry, the leatherworking machinery industry and the design services which underpin them group together in the same regional cluster to each other's mutual benefit. California's Silicon Valley forms a cluster of hardware, software, research and venture-capital organisations which together create a virtuous circle of high-technology enterprise.

- *Firm strategy, industry structure and rivalry.* The characteristic strategies, industry structures and rivalries in different countries can also be bases of advantage. German companies' strategy of investing in technical excellence gives them a characteristic advantage in engineering industries and creates large pools of expertise. A competitive local industry structure is also helpful: if too dominant in their home territory, local organisations can become complacent and lose advantage overseas. Some domestic rivalry can actually be an advantage, therefore. For example, the long-run success of the Japanese car companies is partly based on government policy sustaining several national players (unlike in the United Kingdom, where they were all merged into one) and the Swiss pharmaceuticals industry became strong in part because each company had to compete with several strong local rivals.

Porter's Diamond has been used by governments aiming to increase the competitive advantage of their local industries. The argument that rivalry can be positive has led to a major policy shift in many countries towards encouraging local competition rather than protecting home-based industries. Governments can also foster local industries by raising safety or environmental standards (i.e. creating sophisticated demand conditions) or encouraging cooperation between suppliers and buyers on a domestic level (i.e. building clusters of related and supporting industries in particular regions).

For individual organisations, however, the value of Porter's Diamond is to identify the extent to which they can build on home-based advantages to create competitive advantage in relation to others on a global front. For example, Dutch brewing companies – such as Heineken – had an advantage in early internationalisation due to the combination of sophisticated consumers and limited room to grow at home. Benetton, the Italian clothing company, has achieved global success by using its experience of working through a network of largely independent, often family-owned manufacturers to build its network of franchised retailers. Before embarking on an internationalisation strategy, managers should seek out sources of general locational advantage to underpin their company's individual sources of advantage.

7.3.2 The international value network

However, the sources of advantage need not be purely domestic. For international companies, advantage can be drawn from the international configuration of their *value network* (see section 3.4.1). Here the different skills, resources and costs of countries around the world can be systematically exploited in order to locate each element of the value chain in that country or region where it can be conducted most effectively and efficiently. This may be achieved both through foreign direct investments and joint ventures, but also through **global sourcing, i.e. purchasing services and components from the most appropriate suppliers around the world, regardless of their location.** For example, in the UK, the National Health Service has been sourcing medical personnel from overseas to offset a shortfall in domestic skills and capacity.

Different locational advantages can be identified:

● *Cost advantages* include labour costs, transportation and communications costs and taxation and investment incentives. Labour costs are important. American and European firms, for example, are increasingly moving software programming tasks to India where a computer programmer costs an American firm about one-quarter of what it would pay for a worker with comparable skills in the USA. As wages in India have risen, Indian IT

ILLUSTRATION 7.2

Boeing's global nightmare

Boeing's decision to outsource production of its new Dreamliner aircraft turns into a logistical nightmare.

Work on Boeing's 787 Dreamliner aircraft began in 2003. Test flights did not begin until 2009, two years late. Airlines had cancelled orders and the company had had to pay compensation to customers for delivery delays. The company's CEO, Jim McNerney, admitted in 2009: 'We wouldn't do it exactly the same way. There's plenty of blame to go round. It's not just our suppliers' fault. It's equally our fault in many cases.'

Modern aircraft are tricky to develop. Boeing had experienced delays on its earlier 737 and 747 programmes, and more recently Airbus, the market leader, had significant problems with its giant A380 aircraft. But for Boeing the 787 was crucial to recapturing the lead from Airbus. Boeing was taking a radically different route to its European rival, going for a long-range, 250–300-seat jet, by contrast to Airbus's flagship A380 with its potential 853 seats. The project was due to cost Boeing $10bn (~€7bn) in development and involve radically new technologies that would provide 20 per cent gains in fuel efficiency. Most radical of all, however, was the decision to subcontract 70 per cent of production to suppliers around the world.

The roll-call of 50 subcontractors was impressive. For example, in Japan, Mitsubishi would make the wings, Kawasaki would do the forward fuselage, while Fuji would take responsibility for the centre wing box. Sweden's Saab would make the cargo doors, while Italy's Alenia would produce the horizontal stabiliser and central fuselage. More suppliers came from France, Germany, South Korea and the United Kingdom. Back in the United States there were more than ten subcontractors, including such respected names as General Electric and Moog. Three 747 cargo planes, named 'Dreamlifters', were dedicated to transporting the various components from around the world to Boeing's assembly plant in the United States.

There were several potential advantages to this outsourcing. Boeing would get access to the technological expertise of specialists around the world. These specialist subcontractors would supply some of the development funding. The fact that parts of the plane would be made in different countries was likely to help in the sale of aircraft to the respective national airlines. Costs of labour were likely to be lower outside the US and Boeing would have a smaller workforce of its own to manage during the inevitable downturns of the boom-and-bust aircraft industry.

But there were some unanticipated problems. Alenia found itself obliged to replant a 300-year-old olive grove before it could build its factory in southern Italy. Vought, an American supplier, in turn subcontracted some work to an Israeli company, who neglected to supply assembly instructions in English. Boeing had to send its engineers around the world to smooth out technical problems. Back in the United States, Boeing's own workers were unhappy to see so much work go overseas and imposed a 58-day strike during 2008.

Despite all these problems, the Dreamliner looks set for commercial success. Even after cancellations, its launch order book was for a record-breaking 892 aircraft, at $145m a piece. CEO Jim McNerney reflected none the less: 'we have learned a lot and have the scars to prove it'. He promised that Boeing would build later variants of the 787 more in-house.

Source: Flight International, 12 September 2008; Financial Times, 14 July 2008; Reuters, 22 September 2009.

Questions

1 What are the pros and cons of specifically *international* outsourcing?

2 Boeing will still subcontract some production work for later variants of the 787. What criteria should guide its choice of subcontractors?

firms have already begun moving work to even more low-cost locations such as China, with some predicting that subsidiaries of Indian firms will come to control as much as 40 per cent of China's IT service exports.

- *Unique local capabilities* may allow an organisation to enhance its competitive advantage. For example, leading European pharmaceuticals company GSK has R&D laboratories in Boston and the Research Triangle in North Carolina in order to establish research collaborations with the leading universities and hospitals in those areas. Internationalisation, therefore, is increasingly not only about exploiting an organisation's existing capabilities in new national markets, but about developing strategic capabilities by drawing on capabilities found elsewhere in the world.

- *National market characteristics* can enable organisations to develop differentiated product offerings aimed at different market segments. American guitar-maker Gibson, for example, complements its US-made products with often similar, lower-cost alternatives produced in South Korea under the Epiphone brand. However, because of the American music tradition, Gibson's high-end guitars benefit from the reputation of still being 'made in the USA'.

Of course, one of the consequences of organisations trying to exploit the locational advantages available in different countries' organisations can be that they create complex networks of intra- and inter-organisational relationships. Boeing, for example, has developed a global web of R&D activities through its subsidiaries and partnerships with collaborating organisations (see Illustration 7.2).

7.4 INTERNATIONAL STRATEGIES

Given the ability to obtain sources of international competitive advantage through home-based factors or international value networks, organisations still face difficult questions about what kinds of strategies to pursue in their markets. Here the key problem is typically the so-called global–local dilemma. **The global–local dilemma relates to the extent to which products and services may be standardised across national boundaries or need to be adapted to meet the requirements of specific national markets.** For some products and services – such as televisions – markets appear similar across the world, offering huge potential scale economies if design, production and delivery can be centralised. For other products and services – such as television programming – tastes still seem highly national-specific, drawing companies to decentralise operations and control as near as possible to the local market. This global–local dilemma can evoke a number of responses from companies pursuing international strategies, ranging from decentralisation to centralisation, with positions in between.

This section introduces four generic types of international strategy, based on choices about the international *configuration* of the various activities an organisation has to carry out and the degree to which these activities are then *coordinated* internationally (see Figure 7.4). More precisely, configuration refers to the geographical dispersion or concentration of activities such as manufacturing and R&D, while coordination refers to the extent to which operations

KEY CONCEPT

Four international strategies

Figure 7.4 Four international strategies

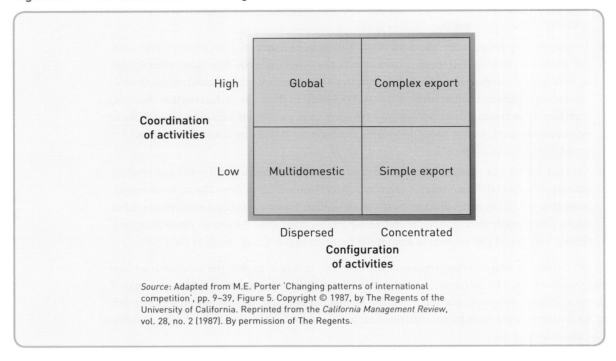

Source: Adapted from M.E. Porter 'Changing patterns of international competition', pp. 9–39, Figure 5. Copyright © 1987, by The Regents of the University of California. Reprinted from the *California Management Review*, vol. 28, no. 2 (1987). By permission of The Regents.

in different countries are managed in a decentralised way or a centrally coordinated way. The four basic international strategies are:[7]

- *Simple export*. This strategy involves a concentration of activities (particularly manufacturing) in one country, typically the country of the organisation's origin. At the same time, marketing of the exported product is very loosely coordinated overseas, perhaps handled by independent sales agents in different markets. Pricing, packaging, distribution and even branding policies may be determined locally. This strategy is typically chosen by organisations with a strong locational advantage – as determined by the Porter Diamond, for example – but where the organisation either has insufficient managerial capabilities to coordinate marketing internationally or where coordinated marketing would add little value, for example in agricultural or raw material commodities.

- *Multidomestic*. This strategy is similarly loosely coordinated internationally, but involves a dispersion overseas of various activities, including manufacturing and sometimes product development. Instead of export, therefore, goods and services are produced locally in each national market. Each market is treated independently, with the needs of each local domestic market given priority – hence 'multidomestic'. Local adaptations can make the overall corporate portfolio increasingly diversified. This strategy is appropriate where there are few economies of scale and strong benefits to adapting to local needs. This multidomestic strategy is particularly attractive in professional services, where local relationships are critical, but it carries risks towards brand and reputation if national practices become too diverse.

- *Complex export*. This strategy still involves location of most activities in a single country, but builds on more coordinated marketing. Economies of scale can still be reaped in manufacturing and R&D, but branding and pricing opportunities are more systematically managed. The coordination demands are, of course, considerably more complex than in the simple export strategy. This is a common stage for companies from emerging economies, as they retain some locational advantages from their home country, but seek to build a stronger brand and network overseas with growing organisational maturity.

- *Global strategy*. This strategy describes the most mature international strategy, with highly coordinated activities dispersed geographically around the world. Using international value networks to the full, geographical location is chosen according to the specific locational advantage for each activity, so that product development, manufacturing, marketing and headquarters functions might all be located in different countries. For example, Detroit-based General Motors designed its Pontiac Le Mans at the firm's German subsidiary, Opel, with its high engineering skills; developed its advertising via a British agency with the creativity strengths of London; produced many of its more complex components in Japan, exploiting the sophisticated manufacturing and technological capabilities; and assembled the car in South Korea, a location where a lower-cost, yet skilled, labour force was available. All this, of course, required high investments and skill in coordination.

In practice, these four international strategies are not absolutely distinct. Managerial coordination and geographical concentration are matters of degree rather than sharp distinctions. Companies may often oscillate within and between the four strategies. Their choices, moreover, will be influenced by changes in the internationalisation drivers introduced earlier. Where, for example, tastes are highly standardised, companies will tend to favour complex export or global strategies. Where economies of scale are few, the logic is more in favour of multidomestic strategies.

(7.5) MARKET SELECTION AND ENTRY

Having decided on an international strategy built on significant sources of competitive advantage and supported by strong internationalisation drivers, managers need next to decide which countries to enter. Not all countries are equally attractive. To an extent, however, countries can initially be compared using standard environmental analysis techniques, for example along the dimensions identified in the PESTEL framework (see section 2.2.1) or according to the industry five forces (section 2.3.1). However, there are specific determinants of market attractiveness that need to be considered in internationalisation strategy, and they can be analysed under two main headings: the intrinsic characteristics of the market and the nature of the competition. A key point here is how initial estimates of country attractiveness can be modified by various measures of *distance* and the likelihood of competitor *retaliation*. The section concludes by considering different *entry modes* into national markets.

7.5.1 Market characteristics

At least four elements of the PESTEL framework are particularly important in comparing countries for entry:

- *Political.* Political environments vary widely between countries and can alter rapidly. Russia since the fall of Communism has seen frequent swings for and against private foreign enterprise. Governments can, of course, create significant opportunities for organisations. For example, the British government has traditionally promoted the financial services industry in the City of London by offering tax advantages to high-earning financiers from abroad and providing a 'light-touch' regulatory environment. It is important, however, to determine the level of *political risk* before entering a country. Carrefour, for example, found itself the subject of an unexpected consumer boycott in China because of political tensions surrounding Tibet (see Illustration 7.1).

- *Economic.* Key comparators in deciding entry are levels of Gross Domestic Product and disposable income which help in estimating the potential size of the market. Fast-growth economies obviously provide opportunities, and in developing economies such as China and India growth is translating into an even faster creation of a high-consumption middle class. However, companies must also be aware of the stability of a country's currency, which may affect its income stream. There can be considerable *currency risk*: thus British companies that relied on international subcontractors faced increased costs as the value of the Pound Sterling fell during the economic crisis of 2009–10.

- *Social.* Social factors will clearly be important, for example the availability of a well-trained workforce or the size of demographic market segments – old or young – relevant to the strategy. Cultural variations need to be considered, for instance in defining tastes in the marketplace.

- *Legal.* Countries vary widely in their legal regime, determining the extent to which businesses can enforce contracts, protect intellectual property or avoid corruption. Similarly, policing will be important for the security of employees, a factor that in the past has deterred business in some South American countries.

A common procedure is to rank country markets against each other on criteria such as these and then to choose the countries for entry that offer the highest relative scores. However, Pankaj Ghemawat from Spain's IESE business school has pointed out that what matters is not just the attractiveness of different countries relative to each other, but also the compatibility of the countries with the internationalising firm itself.[8]

Thus Ghemawat underlines the importance of *match* between country and firm. For firms coming from any particular country, some countries are more 'distant' – or mismatched – than others. For example, a Spanish company might be 'closer' to a South American market than an East Asian market and might therefore prefer that market, even if it ranked lower on standard criteria of attractiveness. As well as a relative ranking of countries, therefore, each company has to add its assessment of countries in terms of closeness of match.

Ghemawat's 'CAGE framework' measures the match between countries and companies according to four dimensions of distance, reflected by the letters of the acronym. Thus the

Figure 7.5 International cross-cultural comparison

Note: Based on a survey of managers on standard dimensions (selection presented here).

Source: M. Javidan, P. Dorman, M. de Luque and R. House, 'In the eye of the beholder: cross-cultural lessons in leadership from Project GLOBE', *Academy of Management Perspectives*, February 2006, pp. 67–90 (Figure 4: USA vs China, p. 82). (GLOBE stands for 'Global Leadership and Organizational Behavior Effectiveness'.)

CAGE framework emphasises the importance of cultural, administrative, geographical and economic distance, as follows:

● *Cultural distance*. The distance dimension here relates to differences in language, ethnicity, religion and social norms. Cultural distance is not just a matter of similarity in consumer tastes, but extends to important compatibilities in terms of managerial behaviours. Here, for example, US firms might be closer to Canada than to Mexico, which Spanish firms might find relatively compatible. Figure 7.5 draws on the GLOBE survey of 17,000 managers from 62 different societal cultures around the world to contrast specifically the orientations of American and Chinese managers on some key cultural dimensions. According to this GLOBE survey, American managers appear to be typically more risk-taking, while Chinese managers are more autonomous.

● *Administrative and political distance.* Here, distance is in terms of incompatible administrative, political or legal traditions. Colonial ties can diminish difference, so that the shared heritage of France and its former West African colonies creates certain understandings that go beyond linguistic advantages. See also, for example, the experience of the Brazilian Vale company in Mozambique, where shared Portuguese heritage made a difference (Illustration 7.3). Institutional weaknesses – for example slow or corrupt administration – can open up distance between countries. So too can political differences: Chinese companies are increasingly able to operate in parts of the world that American companies are finding harder, for example parts of the Middle East and Africa.

● *Geographical distance.* This is not just a matter of the kilometres separating one country from another, but involves other geographical characteristics of the country such as size, sea-access and the quality of communications infrastructure. For example, Wal-Mart's difficulties in Europe relate to the fact that its logistics systems were developed in the geographically enormous space of North America, and proved much less suitable for the smaller and denser countries of Europe. Transport infrastructure can shrink or exaggerate physical distance. France is much closer to large parts of Continental Europe than to the United Kingdom, because of the barrier presented by the English Channel and Britain's relatively poor road and rail infrastructure.

● *Economic.* The final element of the CAGE framework refers particularly to wealth distances. There are of course huge disparities in wealth internationally: around the world, there are 4–5 billion people in 2010 beneath the poverty threshold of income less than $2 a day.[9] Multinationals from rich countries are typically weak at serving such very poor consumers. However, these rich-country multinationals are losing out on large markets if they only concentrate on the wealthy elites overseas. University of Michigan academic C.K. Prahalad has pointed out that the aggregated wealth of those at the 'base of the pyramid' in terms of income distribution is very substantial: simple mathematics means that those 4–5 billion below the poverty threshold represent a market of more than $2000bn per year. If rich-country multinationals can develop new capabilities to serve these numerically huge markets, they can bridge the economic distance, and thereby both significantly extend their presence in booming economies such as China and India and bring to these poor consumers the benefits that are claimed for Western goods. See Illustration 7.4 for examples of innovative base-of-the-pyramid strategies in India.

7.5.2 Competitive characteristics

Assessing the relative attractiveness of markets by PESTEL and CAGE analyses is only the first step. The second element relates to competition. Here, of course, Michael Porter's five forces framework can help (see section 2.3.1). For example, country markets with many existing competitors, powerful buyers (perhaps large retail chains such as in much of North America and Northern Europe) and low barriers to further new entrants from overseas would typically be unattractive. However, an additional consideration is the likelihood of retaliation from other competitors.

ILLUSTRATION 7.3

Vale – a Brazilian giant in different cultures

Rapid overseas expansion brings this Brazilian multinational some contrasting experiences.

Until the late 1990s, Brazil's Vale mining company was a state-owned sleeping giant. 2001 brought the appointment as CEO of 42-year-old former investment banker Roger Agnelli, since when the company has transfomed itself into a dynamic conglomerate. Agnelli commented in 2010: 'Vale used to be fundamentally an iron-ore company. We used to operate essentially in Brazil. Now we are in 36 countries.' Vale is the world's largest producer of iron ore, the second largest producer of nickel and has a declared ambition of being one of the world's largest fertiliser producers. It has copper operations in South Africa, steel in California and coal in Australia.

Nevertheless, iron ore remains the driver of the business. The booming Chinese market has been a gift. Between 2001 and 2009, Vale's iron ore production increased from 122m tonnes to 300m tonnes, with China alone accounting for approaching half of all sales. In the recession year of 2009, iron ore was still profitable, while its non-ferrous and coal activities were by and large unprofitable. However, the nickel business in Canada and the coal business in Mozambique offer very contrasting insights into the challenges of Vale's new international businesses.

Vale's $17.6bn (~€12.3bn) takeover in 2006 of Inco, the world's largest nickel producer, was its first major overseas acquisition. Canada's largest national newspaper, the *Globe and Mail*, described Vale's arrival as 'The great Canadian mining disaster'. Many Canadians resented this takeover by what they regarded as a business from a developing country. The first top manager sent over by Vale spoke poor English. Of 29 senior Canadian managers in early 2007, three years later 23 had departed, mostly voluntarily. The Canadians regarded nickel, which requires underground mining and goes into many high-tech businesses, as technically much more complex than iron ore, a surface-mined basic commodity. According to the *Financial Times*, one Canadian manager said that iron ore was a high school diploma business, nickel

was a PhD business. At one tense meeting a Brazilian manager riposted: 'How come, if you're so smart, you didn't take *us* over?'. In July 2009, Inco's Canadian workers went on strike, remaining so into 2010.

A contrast so far has been Vale's experience in Mozambique. Like many Brazilian companies, Vale has been attracted to the two African countries of Angola and Mozambique because of the shared cultural and linguistic heritage of Portuguese colonialism. About half the 3 million black African slaves sent to Brazil between 1700 and 1850 came from Angola and in the 1820s, settlers in Angola and Mozambique applied to join the newly independent Brazil in a federation. Mozambique has some of the largest coal reserves in the world, but rudimentary infrastructure. Vale is working with Odebrecht, a Brazilian construction company, to develop not only the coal reserves, but to build a power station and the rail and port infrastructure necessary to get the coal to international markets. So vast is the task that Odebrecht has become Mozambique's largest single employer. Vale is planning £830m (€950m) of investment in Mozambique over the next couple of years. Agnelli is enthusiastic about long-term African prospects: 'The thing about Africa is that sooner or later it will become a reality . . . Africa is the future of the world's natural resources – along with South America.'

Sources: 'Vale's transformation', *Financial Times*, 25 February 2010; 'Brazil accelerates investment in Africa', *Financial Times*, 9 February 2010; 'Heading in opposite directions', *Financial Times*, 11 February 2010.

Questions

1 Is there any downside to Vale's ties to the Chinese market, and what should Vale do to mitigate this?

2 Suggest three reasons for Vale's different reception in Canada and Mozambique.

Retaliation relates to rivalry in the five forces framework. It is important not only to assess the attractiveness of the market in terms of size and growth, but also in terms of how rivals are likely to react and how powerful their retaliation might be. As in Figure 7.6, therefore, country markets can be assessed according to three criteria:

- *Market attractiveness* to the new entrant, based on PESTEL and CAGE analyses, for example. In Figure 7.6, countries A and B are the most attractive to the entrant.

- *Defender's reactiveness*, likely to be influenced by the market's attractiveness to the defender but also by the extent to which the defender is working with a globally integrated, rather than multidomestic, strategy. A defender will be more reactive if the markets are important to it and it has the managerial capabilities to coordinate its response. Here, the defender is highly reactive in countries A and D.

- *Defender's clout*, i.e. the power that the defender is able to muster in order to fight back. Clout is typically a function of share in the particular market, but might be influenced by connections to other powerful local players, such as retailers or government. In Figure 7.6, clout is represented by the size of the bubbles, with the defender having most clout in countries A, C, D and F.

Figure 7.6 International competitor retaliation

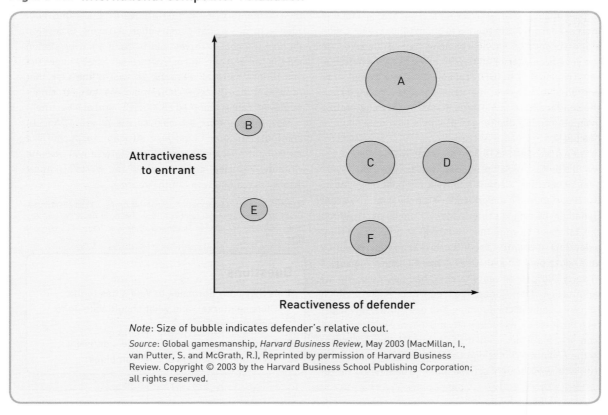

Note: Size of bubble indicates defender's relative clout.

ILLUSTRATION 7.4

Base of the Pyramid strategies

In India, Base of the Pyramid strategy means more than just low prices. Base of the Pyramid involves reshaping distribution channels, designing new products and forming partnerships.

Distribution channels

Procter & Gamble, the global consumer goods company, generates $20bn (~€14bn) worth of sales from developing markets. To reach poorer communities, however, it has to rely on tiny, crowded and often chaotic retail stores. Its strong brands and expensive packaging were often hidden from view underneath a ramshackle counter. Procter & Gamble has therefore hired a team of local sales agents in order to build ties with store owners, to educate them in the importance of display and to negotiate better shelf space for its products.

Product design

Nokia, the world's largest mobile phone company, has three R&D facilities in India. In order to serve markets where electricity is hard to find, they have produced a mobile phone that can operate for more than two weeks on a single charge – and which comes with a flashlight. Recognising that phones are often too costly on an individual basis, Nokia's phone allows friends and families to share a device by maintaining as many as five separate phone books and providing controls on how much any individual user can talk or spend.

Partnerships

Coca-Cola has developed an orange-flavoured fortified beverage called Vitingo, which will sell in 18 gram packets at Rs 2.50 (€0.04) each. The beverage has added nutrients (iron, vitamin C, folic acid and so on) to compensate for deficiencies in many poor people's diet, a problem called 'Hidden hunger'. After a successful pilot project, during 2009 Coca-Cola is entering 30 Orissa districts in partnership with the local non-governmental organisation and micro-finance insitution BISWA.

Sources: *The Economic Times*, 11 January 2010; *People and Strategy*, 1 April 2009.

Questions

1 Can you imagine any risks or dangers that Western companies might face in pursuing Base of the Pyramid strategies?

2 Is there anything that Western companies might learn from Base of the Pyramid strategies in emerging markets that might be valuable in their home markets?

Choice of country to enter can be significantly modified by adding reactiveness and clout to calculations of attractiveness. Relying only on attractiveness, the top-ranked country to enter in Figure 7.6 is country A. Unfortunately, it is also one in which the defender is highly reactive, and the one in which it has most clout. Country B becomes a better international move than A. In turn, country C is a better prospect than country D, because, even though they are equally attractive, the defender is less reactive. One surprising result of taking defender reactiveness and clout into account is the re-evaluation of country E: although ranked fifth on simple attractiveness, it might rank overall second if competitor retaliation is allowed for.

This sort of analysis is particularly fruitful for considering the international moves of two interdependent competitors, such as Unilever and Procter & Gamble or British Airways and

Singapore Airlines. In these cases, the analysis is relevant to any aggressive strategic move, for instance the expansion of existing operations in a country as well as initial entry. Especially in the case of globally integrated competitors, moreover, the overall clout of the defender must be taken into account. The defender may choose to retaliate in other markets than the targeted one, counter-attacking wherever it has the clout to do damage to the aggressor. Naturally, too, this kind of analysis can be applied to interactions between diversified competitors as well as international ones: each bubble could represent different products or services.

7.5.3 Entry modes

Once a particular national market has been selected for entry, an organisation needs to choose how to enter that market. Entry modes differ in the degree of resource commitment to a particular market and the extent to which an organisation is operationally involved in a particular location. In order of increasing resource commitment, the four key entry mode types are: *exporting*; contractual arrangement through *licensing and franchising* to local partners, as McDonald's does to restaurant operators; *joint ventures*, in other words the establishment of jointly owned businesses; and *wholly owned subsidiaries*, either through the acquisition of established companies or 'greenfield' investments, the development of facilities from scratch.

The *staged international expansion* model emphasises the role of experience in determining entry mode. Internationalisation typically brings organisations into unfamiliar territory, requiring managers to learn new ways of doing business.[10] The **staged international expansion model** proposes a sequential process whereby companies gradually increase their commitment to newly entered markets, as they build market knowledge and capabilities. Thus firms might enter initially by licensing or exporting, thereby acquiring some local knowledge while minimising local investments. As they gain knowledge and confidence, firms can then increase their exposure, perhaps first by a joint venture and finally by creating a wholly owned subsidiary. An example is the entry of automobile manufacturer BMW into the American market. After a lengthy period of exporting from Germany to the USA, BMW set up a manufacturing plant in Spartanburg, South Carolina in order to strengthen its competitive position in the strategically important American market.

However, the gradualism of staged international expansion is now challenged by two phenomena:

- '*Born-global firms*', in other words new small firms that internationalise rapidly at early stages in their development.[11] New technologies now help small firms link up to international sources of expertise, supply and customers world-wide. For such firms, waiting till they have enough international experience is not an option: international strategy is a condition of existence. Facebook's rapid international expansion was driven by the company's fear that once national social networks had taken root, it would be very difficult to dislodge them: in the German-speaking world, StudiVZ pre-empted Facebook's entry by setting up in 2005, and it still had 15 million members in 2010.

- *Emerging-country multinationals* also often move quickly through entry modes. Prominent examples are the Chinese white-goods multinational Haier, the Indian pharmaceuticals company Ranbaxy Laboratories and Mexico's Cemex cement company.[12] Such companies typically develop *unique capabilities* in their home market that then need to be rolled out quickly worldwide before competitors catch up. For example, Haier became skilled at very efficient production of simple white goods, providing a cost advantage that is transferable outside its Chinese manufacturing base. Haier now has factories in Italy and the United States, as well as the Philippines, Malaysia, Indonesia, Egypt, Nigeria and elsewhere round the world.

Where the demands and pace of international competition rule out more gradualist staged expansion, two fundamental principles can help guide choice of market entry mode:

- *The breadth of competitive advantage* in the target market. This determines whether entry into the market can be done relying upon the company's own capabilities, or whether it must draw on the capabilities of local partners, for instance to access distribution channels or to manufacture locally.

- *Tradability*, in other words the ability to rely on trading relationships, rather than the firm's own local presence. Tradability is determined by two factors: ease of transport from home country to target country, and the quality of legal protection in the target country. Legal protection refers for example to the ability to enforce contracts, to safeguard performance standards or to protect intellectual property such as patented technologies. Tradability is low where it is unsafe to trade through market-based contracts with local partners or where distances make transport too difficult.

Other case-specific factors are liable to enter the calculation of appropriate entry mode as well, not least the availability of suitable local partners. None the less, the two principles of competitive advantage and tradability do suggest the following broad guidelines for entry mode (Figure 7.7):

Figure 7.7 Modes of international market entry

- *Export* is the baseline option, and is suitable where the product or services are easily transported from country to country and where the home-based competitive advantages are sufficiently broad to minimise reliance on local companies.

- *License or franchise* the product or service where competitive advantages are too narrow to go it alone, but the legal environment is such that local licensees and franchisees can be relied on not to abuse their contracts, under-perform on standards or steal the intellectual property.

- *Joint ventures* work where competitive advantages are narrow, but local licensees or franchisees cannot be trusted with intellectual property or long-term performance. A joint venture involving shared ownership gives the foreign company more direct control and ensures that the local partner has an interest in maximising the value of the common enterprise rather than solely their own stand-alone interests.

- *Wholly owned subsidiary* is an attractive route where competitive advantages are sufficiently broad not to depend on local partners, but where none the less transport difficulties rule out simple export. Such wholly owned subsidiaries can be via new 'greenfield' investments (as for example many Japanese car companies have entered European markets) or via acquisition, where the integration of a local firm completes the breadth of competitive advantage required.

SUMMARY

- Internationalisation potential in any particular market is determined by *Yip's four drivers*: market, cost, government and competitors' strategies.

- Sources of advantage in international strategy can be drawn from both global sourcing through the *international value network* and national sources of advantage, as captured in *Porter's Diamond*.

- There are four main types of international strategy, varying according to extent of coordination and geographical configuration: *simple export, complex export, multidomestic* and *global*.

- Market selection for international entry or expansion should be based on *attractiveness*, multidimensional measures of *distance* and expectations of competitor retaliation.

- Modes of entry into new markets include *export, licensing and franchising, joint ventures* and *overseas subsidiaries*.

VIDEO CASE

Visit *MyStrategyLab* and watch the *Electrolux* case study.

1 Describe Electrolux's changing international strategy in terms of the four strategies of Figure 7.4. Why is it changing in this way?

2 What career options might a manager in a large subsidiary such as the Italian Zanussi see within the Electrolux international portfolio?

RECOMMENDED KEY READINGS

- An invigorating perspective on international strategy is provided by G. Yip, *Total Global Strategy II*, Prentice Hall, 2003. A comprehensive general textbook is S. Segal-Horn and D. Faulkner, *Understanding Global Strategy*, Southwestern, 2010.

REFERENCES

1. T. Friedman, *The World Is Flat: the Globalized World in the Twenty-First Century*, Penguin, 2006.
2. G. Yip, *Total Global Strategy II*, Prentice Hall, 2003.
3. Useful industry-specific data on trends in openness to trade and investment can be found at the World Trade Organization's site, www.wto.org.
4. G. Hamel and C.K. Prahalad, 'Do you really have a global strategy?', *Harvard Business Review*, vol. 63, no. 4 (1985), pp. 139–48.
5. B. Kogut, 'Designing global strategies: comparative and competitive value added changes', *Sloan Management Review*, vol. 27 (1985), pp. 15–28.
6. M. Porter, *The Competitive Advantage of Nations*, Macmillan, 1990.
7. This typology builds on the basic framework of M. Porter, 'Changing patterns of international competition', *California Management Review*, vol. 28, no. 2 (1987), pp. 9–39, but adapts its terms for the four strategies into more readily understandable terms.
8. P. Ghemawat, 'Distance still matters', *Harvard Business Review*, September (2001), pp. 137–47.
9. C.K. Prahalad and A. Hammond, 'Serving the world's poor, profitably', *Harvard Business Review*, September (2002), 48–55.
10. For detailed discussions about the role of learning and experience in market entry see: M.F. Guillén, 'Experience, imitation, and the sequence of foreign entry: wholly owned and joint-venture manufacturing by South Korean firms and business groups in China, 1987–1995', *Journal of International Business Studies*, vol. 83 (2003), pp. 185–98.
11. G. Knights and T. Cavusil, 'A taxonomy of born-global firms', *Management International Review*, vol. 45, no. 3 (2005), pp. 15–35.
12. For analyses of emerging-country multinationals, see the special issue on 'The internationalization of Chinese and Indian firms – trends, motivations and strategy', *Industrial and Corporate Change*, vol. 18, no. 2 (2009).

Lenovo computers: East meets West

Introduction

In May 2005, the world's thirteenth largest personal computer company, Lenovo, took over the world's third largest personal computer business, IBM's PC division. Lenovo, at that time based wholly in China, was paying $1.75bn (~€1.23bn) to control a business that operated all over the world and had effectively invented the personal computer industry back in 1981. Michael Dell, the creator of the world's largest PC company, commented simply: 'it won't work'.

Lenovo had been founded back in 1984 by Liu Chuanzhi, a 40-year-old researcher working for the Computer Institute of the Chinese Academy of Sciences. His early career had included disassembling captured American radar systems during the Vietnam War and planting rice during the Chinese Cultural Revolution. Liu Chuanzhi had started with $25,000 capital from the Computer Institute and promised his boss that he would build a business with revenues of $250,000. Working in the Computer Institute's old guardhouse, and borrowing its office facilities, one of Liu's first initiatives was reselling colour televisions. But real success started to come in 1987, when Lenovo was one of the first to package Chinese-character software with imported PCs.

Lenovo began to take off, with Liu using the support of his father, well placed in the Chinese government, to help import PCs cheaply through Hong Kong. During 1988, Lenovo placed its first job advertisement, and recruited 58 young people to join the company. While the founding generation of Lenovo staff were in their forties, the new recruits were all in their twenties, as the Cultural Revolution had prevented any university graduation for a period of 10 years in China. Among the new recruits was Yang Yuanqing, who would be running Lenovo's PC business before he was 30, and later become Chairman of the new Lenovo–IBM venture at the age of 41. It was this new team which helped launch the production of the first Lenovo PC in 1990, and drove the company to a 30 per cent market

Lenovo's Chairman, Yang Yuanqing
Source: Press Association Images/Kin Cheung/AP.

share within China by 2005. The company had partially floated on the Hong Kong Stock Exchange in 1994.

The deal

Work on the IBM PC deal had begun in 2004, with Lenovo assisted by management consultancy McKinsey & Co. and investment banker Goldman Sachs. IBM wanted to dispose of its PC business, which had only 4 per cent market share in the USA and suffered low margins in a competitive market dominated by Dell and Hewlett Packard. Higher-margin services and mainframe computers would be IBM's future. As well as Lenovo, IBM had private equity firm Texas Pacific Group in the bidding. Lenovo offered the better price, but Texas Pacific was persuaded enough to take a stake in the new group, while IBM took 13 per cent ownership. The government-owned Chinese Academy of Sciences still owned 27 per cent of the stock, the largest single shareholder.

The new Chairman, Yang Yuanqing, had a clear vision of what the company was to achieve, while recognising some of the challenges:

'In five years, I want this (Lenovo) to be a very famous PC brand, with maybe double the growth of the industry. I want to have a very healthy profit margin, and maybe some other businesses beyond PCs, worldwide. We are at the beginnings of this new company, so we can define some fundamentals about the culture. The three words I use to describe this are "trust, respect, compromise".'

He continued:

'As a global company maybe we have to sacrifice some speed, especially during our first phase. We need more communication. We need to take time to understand each other. But speed was in the genes of the old Lenovo. I hope it will be in the genes of the new Lenovo.'

IBM was not leaving its old business to sink or swim entirely on its own. Lenovo had the right to use the IBM brand for PCs for five years, including the valuable ThinkPad name. IBM's salesforce would be offered incentives to sell Lenovo PCs, just as they had had with IBM's own-brand machines. IBM Global Services was contracted to provide maintenance and support. IBM would have two non-voting observers on the Lenovo board. Moreover, Stephen Ward, the 51-year-old former head of IBM's PC division, was to become Lenovo's Chief Executive Officer.

Managing the new giant

Having an IBM CEO was not entirely a surprise. After all, the $13bn business was nearly 80 per cent ex-IBM and customers and employees had to be reassured of continuity. But there were some significant challenges for the new company to manage none the less.

Things had not started well. When the Chinese team first flew to New York to meet the IBM team, they had not been met at the airport as they had expected and was normal polite practice in China. Yang and Ward had disagreed about the location of the new headquarters, Yang wishing it to be shared between Beijing and near New York. Ward had prevailed, and Yang moved his family to the USA. The new organisation structure kept the old IBM business and the original Lenovo business as separate divisions. But still the new company needed considerable liaison with China, a 13-hour flight away, across 12 time zones. Teleconferencing between the East Coast and China became a way of life, with the Americans calling typically at either 6.00 in the morning or 11.00 at night to catch their Chinese colleagues. Calls were always in English, with many Chinese less than fluent and body language impossible to observe.

The Chinese nature of the company was an issue for some constituencies. IBM had had a lot of government business, and populist members of the US Congress whipped up a scare campaign about Chinese computers entering sensitive domains. In Germany, labour laws allowed a voluntary transition of IBM employees to Lenovo, and many German workers chose not to transfer, leaving the company short-staffed. There was some discomfort among former IBM employees in Japan about Chinese ownership. Between the two dominant cultures, American and Chinese, there were considerable differences. Qiao Jian, Vice President for Human Resources, commented:

'Americans like to talk; Chinese people like to listen. At first we wondered why they kept talking when they had nothing to say. But we have learnt to be more direct when we have a problem, and the Americans are learning to listen.'

Cultural differences were not just national. Lenovo was a new and relatively simple company – basically one country, one product. Multinational giant IBM Corporation, founded in 1924, was far more complex. The Lenovo management team, mostly in their thirties, were much younger than IBM's, and the average age of the company as a whole was just 28. IBM was famous for its management processes and routines. Qiao Jian commented: 'IBM people set a time for a conference call and stick to it every week. But why have the call if there is nothing to report?' On the other hand, IBM people had a tendency for being late for meetings, something that was strictly discouraged within Lenovo.

Some results

At first, the response to the new Lenovo was positive. IBM customers stayed loyal and the stock price began to climb (see Figure 1). Remaining IBM executives recognised that at least they were part of a business committed to PCs, rather than the Cinderella in a much larger IBM empire. The fact that a Lenovo PC manufactured in China had a labour cost of just $3.00 offered a lot of opportunity.

Figure 1 Lenovo Group's stock price, 2001–06, compared with NASDAQ index

Source: http://finance.yahoo.com/echarts.

However, market leader Dell responded to the new company with heavy price cuts, offering $100 savings on the average machine. With market share in the crucial American market beginning to slip, ex-IBM CEO Stephen Ward was replaced in December 2005 by William Amelio. This was a coup for Lenovo, as Amelio had been running Dell's Asia–Pacific region. As well as knowing Lenovo's competitor from the inside, Amelio, based for several years in Singapore, had a good understanding of Asian business:

> 'In the five years I have been in Asia, one thing I have learned . . . is to have a lot more patience. I have to be someone who has a high sense of urgency and drive, but I have also learned how to temper that in the various cultures that I have dealt with in order to be more effective.'

Amelio started by addressing costs, removing 1,000 positions, or 10 per cent, from Lenovo's non-China workforce. He integrated the IBM business and the old Lenovo business into a single structure. The company launched a new range of Lenovo-branded PCs for small and medium-sized American businesses, a market traditionally ignored by IBM. To improve its reach in this segment, Lenovo expanded sales to big American retailers such as Office Depot. US market share began to recover, pushing beyond 4 per cent again. Lenovo began to consider entry into the Indian market.

Amelio's actions seemed to pay off. After a precipitous slide during the first half of 2006, the stock price turned up. But there was no disguising that the stock price in the autumn of 2006 was still below where it was five years earlier, and that it continued to trail the hi-tech American NASDAQ index.

Sources: L. Zhijun, *The Lenovo Affair*, Wiley, Singapore, 2006; *Business Week*, 7 August (2006), 20 April (2006), 22 December (2005) and 9 May (2005); *Financial Times*, 8 November (2005), 9 November (2005) and 10 November (2005).

Questions

1 What national sources of competitive advantage might Lenovo draw from its Chinese base? What disadvantages derive from its Chinese base?

2 In the light of the CAGE framework and the MacMillan *et al.* competitor retaliation framework (Figure 7.6), comment on Lenovo's entry into the American market.

3 Now that Lenovo is international, what type of generic international strategy should it pursue – simple export, multidomestic, complex export or global?

8

INNOVATION STRATEGIES

Learning outcomes

After reading this chapter you should understand how to:

- Identify and respond to key *innovation dilemmas*, such as the relative emphases to place on technologies or markets, product or process innovations, open or closed innovation and the underlying business model.

- Anticipate and to some extent influence the *diffusion* (or spread) of innovations.

- Decide when being a *first-mover* or a *follower* is most appropriate in innovation.

- Calculate how an *incumbent* organisation should respond to innovative challengers.

Key terms

Business model p. 192

Diffusion p. 194

Disruptive innovation p. 200

First-mover advantage p. 198

Innovation p. 187

Open innovation p. 191

Platform leadership p. 191

S-curve p. 195

Tipping point p. 195

(8.1) INTRODUCTION

This chapter is about taking new products and services into the market. Such innovations are fundamental to competing in today's economy. They can be an important source of differentiation in the marketplace, as for Apple and its range of innovative products. They can also be a source of cost-advantage, as Amazon's internet-retailing allowed it to undercut traditional retailers in many markets. But innovations also pose hard choices. For example, should a company look always to be a pioneer in new technologies, or rather be a fast follower, as Samsung has been in tablet computing? How should a company react to radical innovations that threaten to destroy their existing revenues, as the Kodak film business had to with the rise of electronic cameras?

As Figure 8.1 shows, this chapter examines innovation under three main themes: dilemmas, diffusion and leadership or followship. In more detail:

● Section 8.2 starts with four fundamental *innovation dilemmas*: technology push as against market pull; product innovation rather than process innovation; open versus closed innovation; and, finally, technological as opposed to broader business model innovation. None of these are absolute 'either-or' dilemmas, but managers and entrepreneurs must choose where to concentrate their limited resources.

● Section 8.3 considers issues surrounding the *diffusion*, or spread, of innovations in the marketplace. Diffusion processes often follow *S-curve patterns*, raising further typical issues for decision, particularly with regard to tipping points and tripping points.

Figure 8.1 Innovation themes

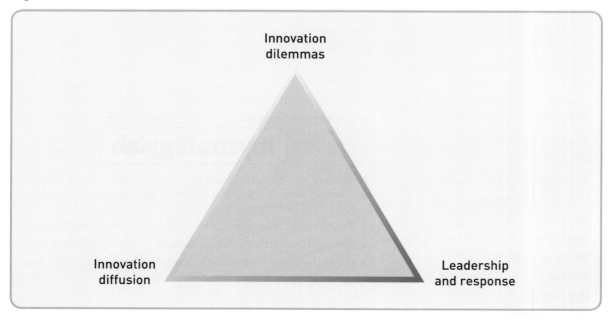

● Section 8.4 completes the discussion of innovation by considering strategic choices. This includes *first-mover* advantages and disadvantages, the advantages of being '*fast second*' into a market, and the issue of how established *incumbents* should respond to innovative challengers.

INNOVATION DILEMMAS

Innovation raises fundamental strategic dilemmas for strategists. Innovation is more complex than just invention. *Invention* involves the conversion of new knowledge into a new product, process or service. **Innovation involves the conversion of new knowledge into a new product, process or service *and* the putting of this new product, process or service into actual use.**[1] The strategic dilemmas stem from this more extended process. Strategists have to make choices with regard to four fundamental issues: how far to follow technological opportunity as against market demand; how much to invest in product innovation rather than process innovation; how far to open up innovation activities to outside contributions; and finally, whether to focus on technological innovation rather than extending innovation to their whole business model.[2]

8.2.1 Technology push or market pull

People often see innovation as driven by technology. In the pure version of this *technology push* view, it is the new knowledge created by technologists or scientists that pushes the innovation process. Research and development laboratories produce new products, processes or services and then hand them over to the rest of the organisation to manufacture, market and distribute. According to this push perspective, managers should listen primarily to their scientists and technologists, let them follow their hunches and support them with ample resources. Generous R&D budgets are crucial to making innovation happen.

An alternative approach to innovation is *market pull*. Market pull reflects a view of innovation that goes beyond invention and sees the importance of actual use. The role of market pull has been promoted since MIT professor Eric von Hippel's discovery that in many sectors users, not producers, are common sources of important innovations.[3] In designing their innovation strategies, therefore, organisations should listen in the first place to users rather than their own scientists and technologists. Von Hippel refines this focus on users to point out that in many markets it is not ordinary users that are the source of innovation, but *lead-users*. In medical surgery, top surgeons often adapt existing surgical instruments in order to carry out new types of operation. In extreme sports such as snowboarding or windsurfing, it is leading sportspeople who make the improvements necessary for greater performance. In this view, then, it is the pull of users in the market that is responsible for innovation. Managers need to build close relationships with lead-users such as the best surgeons or sporting champions. Marketing and sales functions identify the lead-users of a field and then scientists and technologists translate their inventive ideas into commercial products, processes or services that the wider market can use.

There are merits to both the technology push and market pull views. Relying heavily on existing users can make companies too conservative, and vulnerable to disruptive technologies that uncover needs unforeseen by existing markets (see section 8.4.3). On the other hand, history is littered with examples of companies that have blindly pursued technological excellence without regard to real market needs. Technology push and market pull are best seen as extreme views, therefore, helping to focus attention on a fundamental choice: relatively how much to rely on science and technology as sources of innovation, rather than what people are actually doing in the marketplace. In practice, most organisations find a compromise between the two views, with the balance varying both between industries and over time. At the skateboarding company Sole Technology, users were key at start-up, but internally led innovation became more important as the company's resources grew (see Illustration 8.1).

The key issue for managers is to be aware of the dilemma and to review their organisation's balance between the two extremes consciously rather than relying on habit or prejudice. Two broad guidelines can assist:

● *radical innovation* is often facilitated by technology push, rather than by insights from existing consumers

● *high-risk innovation* is more associated with technology push than market pull.

8.2.2 Product or process innovation

Just as managers must find a balance between technological push and market pull, so must they determine the relative emphasis to place on product or process innovation. *Product innovation* relates to the final product (or service) to be sold, especially with regard to its features; *process innovation* relates to the way in which this product is produced and distributed, especially with regard to improvements in cost or reliability. Some firms specialise more in product innovation, others more in process innovation. For example, in computers, Apple has generally concentrated its efforts on designing attractive product features (for instance the iPad tablet computer), while Dell has innovated in terms of efficient processes, for instance direct sales, modularity and build-to-order.

The relative importance of product innovation and process innovation typically changes as industries evolve over time. Usually, the first stages of an industry are dominated by product innovation based on new features. Thus the early history of the automobile was dominated by competition as to whether cars should be fuelled by steam, electricity or petrol, have their engines at the front or at the rear, and have three wheels or four.[4] Industries eventually coalesce around a *dominant design*, the standard configuration of basic features: after Henry Ford's 1908 Model T, cars generally became petrol-driven, with their engines at the front and four wheels. Once such a dominant design is established, innovation switches to process innovation, as competition shifts to producing the dominant design as efficiently as possible. Henry Ford's great process innovation was the moving assembly line, introduced in 1913. Finally, the cycle is liable to start again, as some significant innovation challenges the dominant design: in the case of cars recently, the emergence of electric power.

ILLUSTRATION 8.1

Shoes for skateboarders

Innovation at Sole Technologies is driven by both users and technology.

After taking a degree in industrial software, Pierre André Senizergues started his career as a professional skateboarder in France. In less than 20 years, he created an action shoe and apparel business with $200m (~€140m) sales, and seven brands, including Etnies with its famous distinctive 'E' and the big snowboarding boot brand ThirtyTwo. He also created the first skateboard shoe research laboratory in the world.

Things had not started out so promisingly for Senizergues. In 1988 he signed to ride for the skateboard brand of a new French venture. The very next year he was forced to retire from professional skateboarding with back problems. Although he spoke poor English and had little business experience, he persuaded his employers to grant him the licence to sell its Etnies shoes in the United States. The first five years were very hard, but Senizergues introduced his own designs and from the mid-1990s Etnies began to take off. In 1996, Senizergues bought the Etnies brand from the French venture and incorporated it and other brands – including éS, Emerica and ThirtyTwo – under the Sole Technology umbrella. Growth over the next ten years ran at double digits per annum.

From the first, Senizergues had been able to use his expertise as a professional skateboarder in his designs. He told the *Financial Times*: 'In this market, you have to be authentic, you have to come from skateboarding.' For example, in the 1990s he had noticed that skateboarders were buying unsuitable low-top shoes for their looks, rather than high-top shoes with the proper performance characteristics. Senizergues responded by designing low-top shoes

that had the necessary durability. His company has stayed close to its sports, sponsoring more than 100 athletes around the world. It listens closely to customers. The company's website has a design-your-own-shoe facility and it often releases potential specifications for its new products through blogs, in order to solicit feedback and ideas. The average age of Sole Technology's 400 employees is 28, with many still involved in action sports.

However, Senizergues has also built the world's first skateboarding research facility, the Sole Technology Institute. With 10,000 square feet, it reproduces typical skateboarding obstacles such as rails, stairs and ledges. Senizergues believes that it is time for skateboarding to do its own biomechanical research, instead of borrowing technologies developed in other sports. One of the outputs of the Sole Technology Institute has been the G202 gel-and-air technology. As the trend for girls' shoes moved towards slim silhouettes during 2006, this gel-and-air technology has allowed Sole Technology to keep right abreast of fashion.

Sources: *Financial Times*, 23 August 2006; *Footwear News*, 20 February 2006; www.soletechnology.com.

Questions

1 For what reasons is it important to be 'authentic' in the skateboarding shoe market?

2 If a big company like Nike or Adidas was looking to grow in this market, what would you advise them to do?

Figure 8.2 Product and process innovation

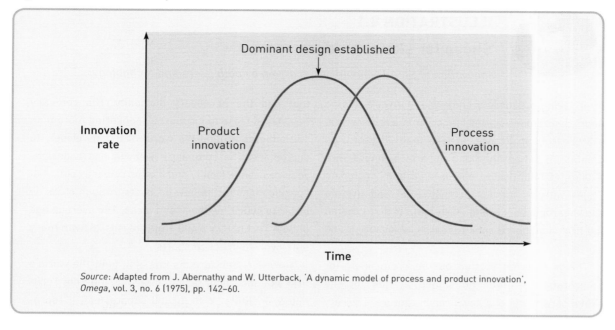

Source: Adapted from J. Abernathy and W. Utterback, 'A dynamic model of process and product innovation', *Omega*, vol. 3, no. 6 (1975), pp. 142–60.

Figure 8.2 provides a general model of the relationship between product and process innovation over time. The model has several strategic implications:

- *New developing industries* typically favour product innovation, as competition is still around defining the basic features of the product or service.

- *Maturing industries* typically favour process innovation, as competition shifts towards efficient production of a dominant design of product or service.

- *Small new entrants* typically have the greatest opportunity when dominant designs are either not yet established or beginning to collapse. Thus, in the early stages of the automobile industry, before Ford's Model T, there were more than 100 mostly small competitors, each with their own combination of product features. The recent challenge to the petrol-based dominant design has provided opportunities to small automobile companies such as the Californian start-up Tesla Motors, which had produced more than 1000 electric Roadsters by the beginning of 2010.

- *Large incumbent firms* typically have the advantage during periods of dominant design stability, when scale economies and the ability to roll out process innovations matter most. With the success of the Model T and the assembly line, by the 1930s there were just four large American automobile manufacturers, Ford, General Motors, Chrysler and American Motors, all producing very similar kinds of cars.

This sequence of product to process innovation is not always a neat one. In practice, product and process innovation are often pursued in tandem.[5] For example, each new generation of microprocessor also requires simultaneous process innovation in order to manufacture the new microprocessor with increasing precision. However, the model does help managers confront the issue of where to focus, whether more on product features or more on process efficiency. It also points to whether competitive advantage is likely to be with small new entrants or large incumbent firms. Other things being equal, small start-ups should time their entry for periods of instability in dominant design and focus on product rather than process innovation.

8.2.3 Open or closed innovation

The traditional approach to innovation has been to rely on the organisation's own internal resources – its laboratories and marketing departments. Innovation in this approach is secretive, anxious to protect intellectual property and avoid competitors free-riding on ideas. This 'closed' model of innovation contrasts with the newer 'open model' of innovation.[6] **Open innovation involves the deliberate import and export of knowledge by an organisation in order to accelerate and enhance its innovation.** The motivating idea of open innovation is that exchanging ideas openly is likely to produce better products more quickly than the internal, closed approach. Speedier and superior products are what are needed to keep ahead of the competition, not obsessive secrecy.

Open innovation is being widely adopted. For example, technology giant IBM has established a network of ten 'collaboratories' with other companies and universities, in countries ranging from Switzerland to Saudi Arabia. Last.fm, the online music service, hosts special 'hack days', where it invites its users for a day of free food, drink and work on developing new applications together. The American InnoCentive company has a network of 64 knowledge 'seekers', including giants Procter & Gamble, Eli Lilly and Dow Chemical, which set 'challenges' for which prizes of up to $1m are given for solutions: so far, more than 348 challenges have been solved with the participation of over 165,000 'solvers'.

Open innovation typically requires careful support of collaborators. In particular, dominant firms may need to exercise platform leadership. **Platform leadership refers to how large firms consciously nurture independent companies through successive waves of innovation around their basic technological 'platform'.**[7] Video games console companies such as Microsoft and Sony have to manage relationships with a host of large and small video games publishers in order to ensure that their consoles are supported by an attractive set of games, making full use of the latest technological possibilities. Similarly, mobile phone companies such as Google and Apple have to encourage and support the thousands of independent producers of 'apps' for their phones.

The balance between open and closed innovation depends on three key factors:

- *Competitive rivalry.* In highly rivalrous industries, partners are liable to behave opportunistically and steal advantages. Closed innovation is better where such rivalrous behaviours can be anticipated.
- *One-shot innovation.* Opportunistic behaviour is more likely where innovation involves a major shift in technology, likely to put winners substantially ahead and losers permanently behind. Open innovation works best where innovation is more continuous, so encouraging more reciprocal behaviour over time.

● *Tight-linked innovation.* Where technologies are complex and tightly interlinked, open innovation risks introducing damagingly inconsistent elements, with knock-on effects throughout the product range. Apple, with its smoothly integrated range of products from computers to phones, has therefore tended to prefer closed innovation in order to protect the quality of the user experience.

8.2.4 Technological or business-model innovation

Many successful innovations do not rely simply upon new science or technology, but involve reorganising into new combinations all the elements of a business. Here innovators are creating whole new *business models*, bringing customers, producers and suppliers together in new ways, with or without new technologies.[8] A **business model describes how an organisation manages incomes and costs through the structural arrangement of its activities.** For Ryanair, business-model innovation involved the generation of revenues via direct sales through the internet, thereby cutting out intermediary travel agents, while also using cheap secondary airports. Internet sales and cheaper airports were much more important than technological innovation. The internet technology itself was not Ryanair's creation and it had the same aeroplanes as most of its competitors. Thus it can be as effective to innovate in terms of business model as in technology.

Opportunities for business-model innovation can be analysed in terms of the value chain, value net or activity systems frameworks introduced in sections 3.4.1 and 3.4.2.[9] These frameworks point managers and entrepreneurs to two basic areas for potential innovation:

● *The product.* A new business model may redefine what the product or service is and how it is produced. In terms of the value chain specifically, this concerns technology development, procurement, inbound logistics, operations and procurement. For example, when Nucor pioneered electric-arc mini-mill technology in the steel industry, it was able to use scrap metal as its raw material rather than pure iron, employ non-unionised labour and outsource a lot of its product development to its equipment supplier Voest Alpine.

● *The selling.* A new business model may change the way in which the organisation generates its revenues, with implications for selling and distribution. In terms of the value chain, this concerns outbound logistics, marketing, sales and service. Nucor, for example, sold its cheap but low-quality steel at standard prices on the internet, by contrast to the traditional steel producers' reliance on elaborate negotiations with individual customers on prices and specifications.

The business model concept emphasises the fundamental features of how business activities are organised. In terms of business models, mature industries therefore often have a lot of standardisation. For example, most accounting firms are organised in similar ways, earning the majority of their income from audit and relying on a high ratio of junior staff to partners. Business strategy within an industry characterised by standardised business models is mostly about differentiation. Thus accounting firms might differentiate themselves within the same model by emphasising particular kinds of sectoral expertise or international networks.

ILLUSTRATION 8.2
Blockbuster's busted business model

Blockbuster's store rental model is challenged by new business models for movie and game distribution.

There are a lot of ways for people to see a movie nowadays. They can go to the cinema. They can buy a DVD from specialist retailers such as HMV or large supermarkets such as Tesco or Lidl. They can order a DVD online and receive it through the post. They can download movies via the internet. They can rent via a kiosk or vending machine. Or they can do it the old-fashioned way and rent it from a video store.

Blockbuster, of course, is famous for its stores: in 2010 it had 7000 stores in 18 countries around the world. The first Blockbuster store opened in 1985 in Texas. Soon Blockbuster was the world's largest movie rental company, and in 1994 was bought by media conglomerate Viacom for $7.6bn (~€5.3bn). Ten years later, as Blockbuster's growth stalled, Viacom spun it off as an independent company again, now valued at $7.5bn.

Blockbuster's business model had been an attractive one at first. Two decades ago, in a period of limited television channels, movie rental had given customers unheard-of choice of viewing. Blockbuster used its huge buying power to obtain the latest releases from the film studios at little cost. Blockbuster would give 40 per cent of the rental income to the studios and supply them with information on usage for market research purposes. Studios typically would hold back from releasing the movie to other rental companies or to retailers for an initial period, making Blockbuster the essential outlet for the latest hits. Blockbuster was able to leverage this business model into rapid growth, using a mixture of its own stores, franchising and acquisitions. It also extended the model to the rental of video games.

However, the market is now much more complex. For a start, television channels began to proliferate. In the United States, Netflix emerged in 1997, originally using a rental-by-mail model. By 2009, Netflix had mailed its two-billionth DVD. In the United Kingdom,

DVD mail-rental company Lovefilm was founded in 2002, and by 2010 had 50 per cent of the national market, as well as a strong position in Scandinavia. The mail-rental model offers customers a far greater choice (Lovefilm has 70,000 titles, against the few hundred in a typical Blockbuster store) and needs only a few centralised distribution centres, as against a labour-intensive network of retail stores. Moreover, as internet capacity has improved, both Netflix and Lovefilm have also begun to stream movies straight to customers' computers. Another rental model was pioneered by 2003 start-up Redbox, which had established a network of 22,000 DVD vending machines across the United States by the end of 2009.

Blockbuster responded in several ways. In 2004, it launched its own on-line rental service, with customers able to return their DVDs simply through a local store. In 2009, Blockbuster launched its own vending machines in the United States. The company closed more than 1800 stores. It withdrew from some national markets altogether, for example Spain, Portugal, Ecuador and Peru. But still 2009 was a year of heavy financial losses. The Blockbuster shareprice, which had peaked at over $30 in 2002, had fallen to 41 cents in 2010.

Sources: Financial Times, 24 February 2010; The Times, 28 December 2009; Express on Sunday, 28 February 2010.

Questions

1 Compare the pros and cons of the various business models for movie consumption.

2 What potential competitive advantages did Blockbuster have as a company as the new business models emerged in the last decade or so?

However, the fundamental nature of business models means that business-model innovation tends to imply radical change. Business-model innovation is not just a matter of technology, but involves a wide range of the firm's activities. Thus the business model concept helps managers and entrepreneurs consider science and technology as just one part of the whole package that contributes to innovation. Innovation can be drawn from all parts of the value chain, not just technology development. Indeed, radical technological innovation often requires business-model innovation too. For example, in order to promote adoption of its innovative electric cars in France, Toyota has formed a partnership with electricity supplier EDF and local authorities to create networks of subsidised public charging points. Illustration 8.2 describes the radical repercussions of business-model innovation in the movie rental business.

(8.3) INNOVATION DIFFUSION

So far, this chapter has been concerned with sources and types of innovation, for example technology push or market pull. This section moves to the diffusion of innovations after they have been introduced.[10] **Diffusion is the process by which innovations spread among users**. Since innovation is typically expensive, its commercial attractiveness can hinge on the pace – extent and speed – at which the market adopts new products and services. This pace of diffusion is something managers can influence from both the supply and demand sides, and which they can also model using the S-curve.

8.3.1 The pace of diffusion

The pace of diffusion can vary widely according to the nature of the products concerned. It took 38 years for the television to reach 150 million units sold; it took just seven years for Apple's iPod to reach the same number. The pace of diffusion is influenced by a combination of supply-side and demand-side factors, over which managers have considerable control. On the *supply side*, pace is determined by product features such as:

- *Degree of improvement* in performance above current products (from a customer's perspective) that provides incentive to change. For example, 3G mobile phones did not provide sufficient performance improvement to prompt rapid switch in many markets. Managers need to make sure innovation benefits sufficiently exceed costs.

- *Compatibility* with other factors, e.g. digital TV becomes more attractive as the broadcasting networks change more of their programmes to that format. Managers and entrepreneurs therefore need to ensure appropriate complementary products and services are in place.

- *Complexity*, either in the product itself or in the marketing methods being used to commercialise the product. Unduly complex pricing structures, as with many financial service products such as pensions, discourage consumer adoption. Simple pricing structures typically accelerate adoptions.

- *Experimentation* – the ability to test products before commitment to a final decision – either directly or through the availability of information about the experience of other customers. Free initial trial periods are often used to encourage diffusion.

● *Relationship management*, in other words how easy it is to get information, place orders and receive support. Google's 2010 launch of its first phone, the Android Nexus One, was hampered because the company was not used to providing the access to help staff that mobile phone customers generally expect. Managers and entrepreneurs need to put in place an appropriate relationship management processes to assist new users.

On the *demand side*, three key factors tend to drive the pace of diffusion:

● *Market awareness*. Many potentially successful products have failed through lack of consumer awareness – particularly when the promotional effort of the innovator has been confined to 'push' promotion to its intermediaries (e.g. distributors).

● *Network effects* refer to the way that demand growth for some products accelerates as more people adopt the product or service. Once a critical mass of users have adopted, it becomes of much greater benefit, or even necessary, for others to adopt it too. Facebook enjoyed network effects as its usage raced to 150 million in just four years. Likewise, people use Microsoft PowerPoint because almost all their collaborators are likely to use it too.

● *Customer innovativeness*. The distribution of potential customers from early-adopter groups (keen to adopt first) through to laggards (typically indifferent to innovations). Innovations are often targeted initially at early-adopter groups – typically the young and the wealthy – in order to build the critical mass that will encourage more laggardly groups – the poorer and older – to join the bandwagon. Clothing fashion trends typically start with the wealthy and then are diffused to the wider population. Managers and entrepreneurs therefore need to target innovations initially at likely early-adopters.

8.3.2 The diffusion S-curve

The pace of diffusion is typically not steady. Successful innovations often diffuse according to a broad *S-curve* pattern.[11] The shape of the **S-curve** **reflects a process of initial slow adoption of innovation, followed by a rapid acceleration in diffusion, leading to a plateau representing the limit to demand** (Figure 8.3). The height of the S-curve shows the extent of diffusion; the shape of the S-curve shows the speed.

Diffusion rarely follows exactly this pattern, but none the less the S-curve can help managers and entrepreneurs anticipate upcoming issues. In particular, the S-curve points to four likely decision points:

● *Timing of the 'tipping point'*. Demand for a new product or service may initially be slow but then reaches a tipping point when it explodes onto a rapid upwards path of growth.[12] A **tipping point is where demand for a product or service suddenly takes off, with explosive growth**. Tipping points are particularly explosive where there are strong *network effects*: in other words, where the value of a product or service is increased the more people in a network use them. Being aware of a possible tipping point ahead can help managers plan investment in capacity and distribution. Companies can easily underestimate demand. In the mid-1980s, American companies predicted that by 2000 there would be 900,000 mobile phones world-wide. That year came, and 900,000 phones were sold every 19 hours.

Figure 8.3 **The diffusion S-curve**

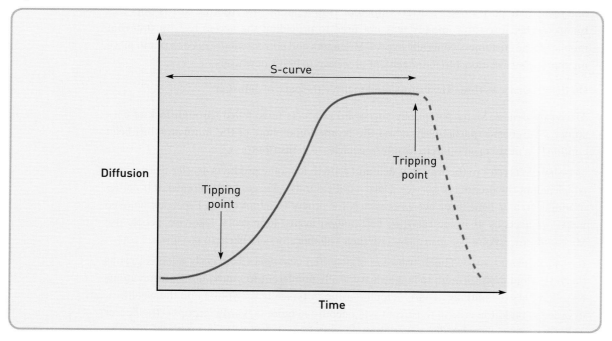

The Finnish company Nokia was able to seize world-wide leadership. Failing to anticipate a tipping point leads to missed sales and easy opportunities for competitors.

- *Timing of the plateau.* The S-curve also alerts managers to a likely eventual slowdown in demand growth. Again, it is tempting to extrapolate existing growth rates forwards, especially when they are highly satisfactory. But heavy investment immediately before growth turns down is likely to leave firms with over-capacity and carrying extra costs in a period of industry shake-out.

- *Extent of diffusion.* The S-curve does not necessarily lead to 100 per cent diffusion among potential users. Most innovations fail to displace previous-generation products and services altogether. For example, in music, traditional turntables and LP discs are still preferred over CD and MP3 players by many disc jockeys and music connoisseurs. A critical issue for managers then is to estimate the final ceiling on diffusion, being careful not to assume that tipping point growth will necessarily take over the whole market.

- *Timing of the 'tripping point'.* The tripping point is the opposite of the tipping point, referring to when demand suddenly collapses.[13] Of course, decline is usually more gradual. However, the presence of network effects can lead to relatively few customer defections setting off a market landslide. Such landslides are very hard to reverse. This is what happened to social networking sites Friendster and MySpace, as American and European users defected to Facebook. The tripping point concept warns managers all the time that a small dip in quarterly sales could presage a rapid collapse.

ILLUSTRATION 8.3

Twitter flies high

How long can the explosive growth of the microblogger Twitter continue? And what is its business model?

Alexa.com estimation of numbers using Twitter

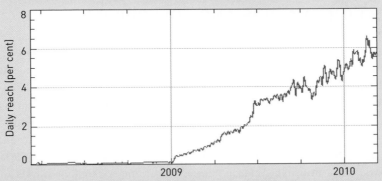

The traffic data are based on the set of Alexa toolbar users, which may not be a representative sample of the global Internet population.

Source: Alexa Internet, www.alexa.com.

Twitter was founded in 2006 by Jack Dorsey, Biz Stone and Evan Williams, all in their early thirties. The original idea for Twitter was conceived during a brainstorming day, and implemented in just two weeks. Biz Stone recalls a dialogue with Evan Williams: 'Early on someone said: "Twitter is fun, but it isn't useful". Ev said: "Neither is icecream".'

A lot of people soon began to think Twitter fun. A key moment was the Spring 2007 South by Southwest film and music festival in Austin, Texas. Twitter hired two large plasma screens streaming Twitter messages from festival-goers. During the event, Twitter usage went from 20,000 'tweets' (messages) per day to 60,000 per day. Then Barack Obama used Twitter publicly during the 2008 US presidential elections. By early 2010, Alexa.com was estimating that more than 6 per cent of global internet users were visiting twitter.com per day ('daily reach').

Twitter usage is free, so a persistent question as Twitter grows is about its business model – how it would earn revenues. Twitter raised $135m (~€94.5m) in venture capital during 2009, but was cautious about how to make the venture pay. Ev Williams said: 'We think Twitter will make money. I just think it will take some time to figure it out.' The founders rejected the use of advertising. However, they were considering how they could get companies to pay for referrals from Twitter to their own websites. At the start of 2010, Biz Stone told the *Financial Times*: 'We need to build a business out of Twitter – that needs to start happening in 2010.'

Meanwhile, social networking site Facebook was developing Twitter-like features and new imitators were springing up. In Japan, for instance, start-up Ameba Now was gaining users by signing up Japanese celebrities, offering Japanese characters and supporting 'smiley' icons, something that Twitter lacks. Within three months of its December 2009 launch, Ameba Now had 1 million users, against Twitter's 4.7 million in Japan. Twitter also has a high wastage rate – only 40 per cent of those who sign on are retained as regular users.

Sources: *New York Times*, 25 March 2009; www.eweek.com, 20 October 2009; *Financial Times*, 1 January 2010 and 12 March 2010.

Questions

1 How should investors in Twitter interpret Alexa.com's daily reach data?

2 Propose three ways that Twitter could make money and consider their respective pros and cons.

To summarise, the S-curve is a useful concept to help managers and entrepreneurs avoid simply extrapolating next year's sales from last year's sales. However, the tripping point also underlines the fact that innovations do not follow an inevitable process, and their diffusion patterns can be interrupted or reversed at any point. Most innovations, of course, do not even reach a tipping point, let alone a tripping point. The Segway Human Transporter, launched in 2001 as the environmentally friendly technology that would replace the car, sold 6,000 units in its first two years, despite launch production capacity of nearly 500,000 a year.

8.4 INNOVATORS AND FOLLOWERS

A key choice for managers is whether to lead or to follow in innovation. The S-curve concept seems to promote leadership in innovation. First-movers get the easy sales of early fast growth and can establish a dominant position. There are plenty of examples of first-movers who have built enduring positions on the basis of innovation leadership: Coca-Cola in drinks and Hoover in vacuum cleaners are powerful century-old examples. On the other hand, many first-movers fail. Even Apple failed with its pioneering Personal Digital Assistant, the Newton, launched in 1993. Hewlett-Packard and Palm captured the PDA market nearly a decade later. This late-entry success is not unusual. Amazon entered the online bookselling market in 1995, four years after the real online pioneer, the Computer Literacy bookstore of Silicon Valley, California.

8.4.1 First-mover advantages and disadvantages

KEY CONCEPT

First-mover advantage

A **first-mover advantage exists where an organisation is better off than its competitors as a result of being first to market with a new product, process or service.** Fundamentally, the first-mover is a monopolist, theoretically able to charge customers high prices without fear of immediate undercutting by competitors. In practice, however, innovators often prefer to sacrifice profit margins for sales growth and, besides, monopoly is usually temporary. There are five potentially more robust first-mover advantages:[14]

- *Experience curve benefits* accrue to first-movers, as their rapid accumulation of experience with the innovation gives them greater expertise than late entrants still relatively unfamiliar with the new product, process or service (see section 5.2.1).

- *Scale benefits* are typically enjoyed by first-movers, as they establish earlier than competitors the volumes necessary for mass production and bulk purchasing, for example.

- *Pre-emption of scarce resources* is an opportunity for first-movers, as late movers will not have the same access to key raw materials, skilled labour or components, and will have to pay dearly for them.

- *Reputation* can be enhanced by being first, especially since consumers have little 'mind-space' to recognise new brands once a dominant brand has been established in the market.

- *Buyer switching costs* can be exploited by first-movers, by locking in their customers with privileged or sticky relationships that later challengers can only break with difficulty. Switching costs can be increased by establishing and exploiting a *technological standard*.

Experience curve benefits, economies of scale and the pre-emption of scarce resources all confer cost advantages on first-movers. It is possible for them to retaliate against challengers with a price war. Superior reputation and customer lock-in provide a marketing advantage, allowing first-movers to charge high prices, which can then be reinvested in order to consolidate their position against late-entry competitors.

But the experience of Apple with its Newton shows that first-mover advantages are not necessarily overwhelming. Late movers have two principal potential advantages:[15]

- *Free-riding*. Late movers can imitate technological and other innovation at less expense than originally incurred by the pioneers. Research suggests that the costs of imitation are only 65 per cent of the cost of innovation.

- *Learning*. Late movers can observe what worked well and what did not work well for innovators. They may not make so many mistakes and be able to get it right first time.

8.4.2 First or second?

Given the potential advantages of late movers, managers and entrepreneurs face a hard choice between striving to be first or coming in later. London Business School's Costas Markides and Paul Geroski argue that the most appropriate response to innovation, especially radical innovation, is often not to be a first-mover, but to be a '*fast second*'.[16] A fast second strategy involves being one of the first to imitate the original innovator. Thus fast second companies may not literally be the second company into the market, but they dominate the second generation of competitors. For example, the French Bookeen company pioneered the e-book market in the early 2000s, but was followed by Sony's eReader in 2006 and Amazon's Kindle in 2007.

There are three contextual factors to consider in choosing between innovating and imitating:

- *Capacity for profit capture*. David Teece emphasises the importance of innovators being able to capture for themselves the profits of their innovations.[17] This depends on the ease with which followers can imitate. The likelihood of imitation depends on two primary factors. First, imitation is likely if the innovation is in itself *easy to replicate*: for example, if there is little tacit knowledge involved or if it is embedded in a product that is sold in the external marketplace (unlike many process technologies) and is therefore easy to 'reverse-engineer' (see section 3.3). Second, imitation is facilitated if *intellectual property rights* are weak, for example where patents are hard to define or impractical to defend. It is unwise for companies to invest in first-moves if imitators are likely to be able quickly to seize their share of innovation profits.

- *Complementary assets*. Possession of the assets or resources necessary to scale up the production and marketing of the innovation is often critical. Many small European biotech start-up companies face this constraint in the pharmaceuticals industry, where marketing and distribution channels in the United States, the world's largest market, are essential complementary assets, but are dominated by the big, established pharmaceutical companies. Small European start-ups can find themselves obliged either to sell out to a larger company with the complementary marketing and distribution assets, or to license their innovation to them on disadvantageous terms. For organisations wishing to remain independent and to exploit their innovations themselves, there is little point in investing heavily to be first-mover in the absence of the necessary complementary assets.

● *Fast-moving arenas.* Where markets or technologies are moving very fast, and especially where both are highly dynamic, first-movers are unlikely to establish a durable advantage. The American electronics company Magnavox was the first to launch an electronic video game console in 1972, the Odyssey. But both the market and the technologies were evolving quickly. Magnavox only survived into the second generation of video game consoles, finally exiting in 1984. The seventh generation is now firmly dominated by Microsoft (entered in 2001), Sony (entered in 1994) and Nintendo (entered in 1983). In slower-moving markets and technologies, such as Coca-Cola's drinks arena, durable first-mover advantages are more probable. Managers and entrepreneurs need, therefore, to assess future market and technological dynamism in calculating the likely value of first-mover advantage.

8.4.3 The incumbent's response

For established companies in a market, innovation is often not so much an opportunity as a threat. Kodak's dominance of the photographic film market was made nearly worthless by the sudden rise of digital photography. Likewise, Blockbuster's network of video stores became redundant with the rise of internet film downloads (see Illustration 8.2).

As Harvard Business School's Clay Christensen has shown, the problem for incumbents can be twofold.[18] First, managers can become too attached to existing assets and skills. After all, these are what their careers have been built on. Second, relationships between incumbent organisations and their customers can become too close. Existing customers typically prefer incremental improvements to current technologies, and are unable to imagine completely new technologies. Incumbents are reluctant to 'cannibalise' their existing business by introducing something radically different. After all, as in Figure 8.4, incumbents usually have some scope for improving their existing technology, along the steady upwards trajectory described as Technology 1. Innovations on this trajectory are termed 'sustaining innovations', because they at least allow the existing technology to meet existing customer expectations.

The challenge for incumbents, however, is disruptive innovation. A **disruptive innovation creates substantial growth by offering a new performance trajectory that, even if initially inferior to the performance of existing technologies, has the potential to become markedly superior**. This superior performance can produce spectacular growth, either by creating new sets of customers or by undercutting the cost base of rival existing business models. Such disruptive innovation involves the shift from Technology 1 in Figure 8.4 to Technology 2. Disruptive innovations are hard for incumbents to adopt because their initial poor performance is likely to upset existing customer relationships and because they typically involve changing their whole business model. Thus, in the music industry, the major record companies were long content to keep on selling traditional CDs through retailers, marketing them through promotions and radio-plugging. They responded to MP3 online music simply by prosecuting operators such as Napster for breach of copyright and highlighting the relatively poor sound quality of peer-to-peer file sharing. However, the British band Arctic Monkeys, and its small independent record company Domino, radically disrupted the majors' marketing model by giving away MP3 tracks free over the internet in order to create an independent fan-base. In 2006,

Figure 8.4 Disruptive innovation

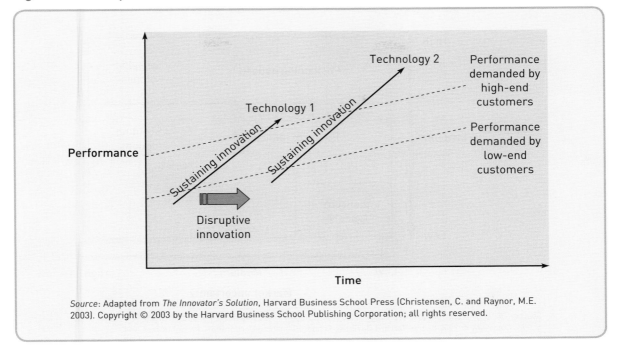

the Arctic Monkeys' debut CD ended up selling nearly 400,000 copies in its first week, a record for the top 20 United Kingdom album chart.

Incumbents can follow two policies to help keep them responsive to potentially disruptive innovations:

● *Develop a portfolio of real options*. Companies that are most challenged by disruptive innovations tend to be those built upon a single business model and with one main product or service. Columbia's Rita McGrath and Wharton's Ian MacMillan recommend that companies build portfolios of *real options* in order to maintain organisational dynamism.[19] Real options are limited investments that keep opportunities open for the future. Establishing an R&D team in a speculative new technology or acquiring a small start-up in a nascent market would both be examples of real options, each giving the potential to scale-up fast should the opportunity turn out to be substantial. McGrath and MacMillan's portfolio identifies three different kinds of options (Figure 8.5). Options where the market is broadly known, but the technologies are still uncertain, are *positioning options*: a company might want several of these, to ensure some position in an important market, by one technology or another. On the other hand, a company might have a strong technology, but be very uncertain about appropriate markets, in which case it would want to bet on several *scouting options* to explore which markets are actually best. Finally, a company would want some *stepping stone* options, very unlikely in themselves to work, but possibly leading to something more promising in the future. Even if they do not turn a profit, stepping stones should provide valuable learning opportunities. An important principle for options is: 'Fail fast, fail cheap, try again'.

Figure 8.5 Portfolio of innovation options

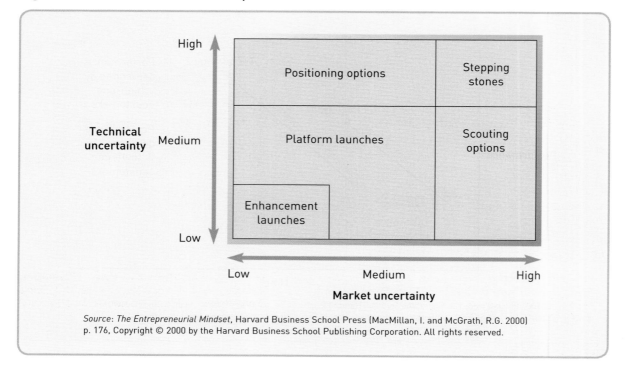

● *Develop new venture units.* New ventures, especially when undertaken from a real options perspective, may need protection from the usual systems and disciplines of a core business. It would make no sense to hold the managers of a real option strictly accountable for sales growth and profit margin: their primary objective is preparation and learning. For this reason, large incumbent organisations often set up innovative businesses as relatively autonomous 'new venture units', sometimes called new venture divisions, typically with managers hired specially from outside. For example, in 2003 Delta Airlines, the American international airline dating from the 1920s, responded to the threat of low-cost airlines in its domestic markets by establishing Song Airlines as a stand-alone competitor. Song adopted the low-cost airline business model, but also innovated with free personal entertainment systems at every seat, including audio MP3 selections, trivia games that could be played against other passengers and satellite television. In-flight safety instructions would be sung in different musical styles, by request. The risks of such autonomous venture units are twofold. First, the new units may be denied resources that the core business could easily supply, such as branding or management information systems. Second, innovation becomes isolated from the core business: for the core organisation, innovation is something that somebody else does. Delta responded to the second risk threat by reabsorbing Song into its main operations, at the same time incorporating several of Song's innovations such as satellite television.

SUMMARY

- Strategists face four fundamental dilemmas in innovation: the relative emphasis to put on *technology push* or *market pull*; whether to focus on *product or process* innovation; *open* versus *closed* innovation; and how far to concentrate on technological innovation as opposed to broader *business-model innovation*.

- Innovations often diffuse into the marketplace according to an *S-curve model* in which slow start-up is followed by accelerating growth (the tipping point) and finally a flattening of demand. Managers should watch out for 'tripping points'.

- Managers have a choice between being first into the marketplace and entering later. Innovators can capture *first-mover advantages*. However, '*fast second*' strategies are often more attractive.

- Established incumbents' businesses should beware *disruptive innovations*. Incumbents can stave off inertia by developing portfolios of *real options* and by organising autonomous *new venture units*.

RECOMMENDED KEY READINGS

- P. Trott, *Innovation Management and New Product Development*, 4th edition, Financial Times Prentice Hall, 2008, provides a comprehensive overview of innovation strategy issues. A lively and accessible survey of many innovation issues, together with a wealth of examples, is C. Markides and P. Geroski, *Fast Second: How Smart Companies Bypass Radical Innovation to Enter and Dominate New Markets*, Jossey-Bass, 2005.

REFERENCES

1. In order to include the public sector, this definition adapts the definition in P. Trott, *Innovation Management and New Product Development*, 3rd edition, Financial Times Prentice Hall, 2005.
2. A good discussion of these dilemmas is in R. Rothwell, 'Successful industrial innovation: critical factors for the 1990s', *R&D Management*, vol. 22, no. 3 (1992), pp. 221–39.
3. J. Abernathy and W. Utterback, 'A dynamic model of process and product innovation', *Omega*, vol. 3, no. 6 (1975), pp. 142–60.
4. P. Anderson and M.L. Tushman, 'Technological discontinuities and dominant designs: a cyclical model of technological change', *Administrative Science Quarterly*, vol. 35 (1990), pp. 604–33.
5. J. Tang, 'Competition and innovation behaviour', *Research Policy*, vol. 35 (2006), pp. 68–82.
6. H. Chesbrough and M. Appleyard, 'Open innovation and strategy', *California Management Review*, vol. 50, no. 1 (2007), pp. 57–73
7. A. Gawer and M. Cusumano, *Platform Leadership: how Intel, Microsoft and Cisco drive industry innovation*, Harvard Business School Press (2002).
8. See the special issue on business models in *Long Range Planning*, 2010, especially D.J. Teece, 'Business models, business strategy and innovation', *Long Range Planning*, vol. 43, nos 3/4 (2010).
9. J. Magretta 'Why business models matter', *Harvard Business Review*, vol. 80, no. 5 (2002), pp. 86–92.

10. Innovation diffusion is discussed in C. Kim and R. Maubourgne, 'Knowing a winning idea when you see one', *Harvard Business Review*, vol. 78, no. 5 (2000), pp. 129–38.
11. J. Nichols and S. Roslow, 'The S-curve: an aid to strategic marketing', *Journal of Consumer Marketing*, vol. 3, no. 2 (1986), pp. 53–64.
12. M. Gladwell, *The Tipping Point*, Abacus, 2000.
13. S. Brown, 'The tripping point', *Marketing Research*, vol. 17, no. 1 (2005), pp. 8–13.
14. C. Markides and P. Geroski, *Fast Second: How Smart Companies Bypass Radical Innovation to Enter and Dominate New Markets*, Jossey-Bass, 2005.
15. F. Suarez and G. Lanzolla, 'The half-truth of first-mover advantage', *Harvard Business Review*, vol. 83, no. 4 (2005), pp. 121–27.
16. C. Markides and P. Geroski, *Fast Second: How Smart Companies Bypass Radical Innovation to Enter and Dominate New Markets*, Jossey-Bass, 2005.
17. D. Teece, *Managing Intellectual Capital*, Oxford University Press, 2000.
18. See J. Bower and C. Christensen, 'Disruptive technologies: catching the wave', *Harvard Business Review*, vol. 73, no. 1 (1995), pp. 43–53.
19. R.G. McGrath and I. MacMillan, *The Entrepreneurial Mindset*, Harvard Business School Press, 2000.

CASE EXAMPLE

Skype: innovators and entrepreneurs

Introduction

Niklas Zennström and Janus Friis have been a golden pair in the internet business. For a period during the early 2000s, their Kazaa peer-to-peer file sharing business was the world's largest music sharing site. After selling that business to Sharman Networks, they moved quickly to establish Skype in 2003, which quickly became the dominant player in the world's VoIP (Voice over Internet Protocol) telephone market. Skype's free Internet-based VoIP service was an attractive alternative to the expensive traditional landline and mobile telephone services, gaining 60 million users by 2005. That same year, they sold Skype to eBay for $2.6bn (~€1.8bn) – an impressive figure for a business whose total revenues were just $60m and had still not turned a profit. The eBay deal, however, turned out not to be an unblemished success.

Two entrepreneurs

Zennström is the older of the two, aged 40 at the sale to eBay. He took a first degree in business and then an MSc in engineering and computer science from Uppsala University in Sweden. He then entered the telecommunications industry, spending nine years in Tele2, a fast-expanding European telecoms group. He met Friis in 1997, hiring him to manage a help-desk. Friis, a Dane, is 11 years younger and failed even to graduate from high school. But from the late 1990s the two worked closely together on a series of new ventures: as well as Kazaa and Skype, these included Altnet, claimed to be the world's first secure peer-to-peer wholesale network, Joltid, a company in traffic optimisation technologies, and the portal everyday.com.

The pair were committed to disruptive innovation. Zennström told the *Financial Times*: 'It's everyone's obligation to fight against monopolies and also companies that provide bad services.' Of the traditional landline and mobile telephone companies, he declares: 'They deserve to be challenged. They provide bad and expensive service.'

Co-founders of Skype – Niklas Zennström (left) and Janus Friis (right)
Source: Steve Forrest/Rex Features.

The Skype business model

Skype's software allows people to use the internet to make free calls to other Skype users all over the world. Given the cost of traditional international calls, this was an exciting idea. Initial funding, however, was not easy to find as the music industry was still pursuing a lawsuit against the two founders regarding the illegal filesharing their earlier Kazaa venture appeared to facilitate. For fear of legal action, Zennström and Friis dared not even enter the USA. Most traditional venture capitalists gave the new venture a wide berth. Moreover, it was not easy to see how to make money out of free calls.

The business model is more complicated than that, of course. Most users have free calls, certainly. However, Skype has very low costs, as customers download the software off the internet and it is the customers' computers and internet connections that make the network. It costs nothing to keep connections open continuously. Marketing is cheap, because customers naturally invite others to join. Skype has no telephone help-desk, citing the overwhelming number of customers and the effectiveness of its standard internet queries services. Skype makes its money from its ancillary services, such as SkypeOut, which allows customers to call traditional landline or mobile numbers for a fee, often very small.

Zennström explains the model: 'We want to make as little money as possible per user. We don't have any cost per user, but we want a lot of them.'

This overturns the traditional landline and mobile phone business model. Traditional telephone companies of both types face high costs of both marketing and capacity building. Customers are typically charged according to distance and by the minute. The traditional principle is to maximise revenues per customer, completely the opposite to Skype. Zennström summarised to *Business Week*:

'When you're a phone company, you have marketing and customer-acquisition costs. When you have a customer, you have an operational cost of running the network. Then you have a cost for billing systems. That's an operator business model.

The business model of Skype is completely different. Skype has a software business model. We don't have any distribution or marketing costs for each user – our software is spread virally. And when we have a new user, we have zero cost for serving that user because they're using P2P (peer-to-peer) software and their own bandwidth. So we have zero costs of getting new users and zero costs of running traffic. Our costs are only business development and software development.'

Comparing the positions of the two types of companies, he added: 'Something that is a great business model for us is probably a terrible model for them.'

As shown in the figure, Skype's service has been attracting snowballing usage. The tipping point came towards the end of 2004, and by March 2010 Skype was achieving more than 23 million users in a single day. Of course, this success raised an awkward paradox. If Skype became near universal, who would be left for people to call using the paid service of SkypeOut to access traditional phones?

eBay's move

Skype was always likely to be for sale. Zennström and Friis had sold Kazaa quickly and their initial funders would want a profitable early exit too. It was not surprising that rumours started during 2005 of possible acquisition from technology giants such as Google, Microsoft and Yahoo!. In the end, however, it was online

Skype Dialtone – Peak number of accounts logged in one day

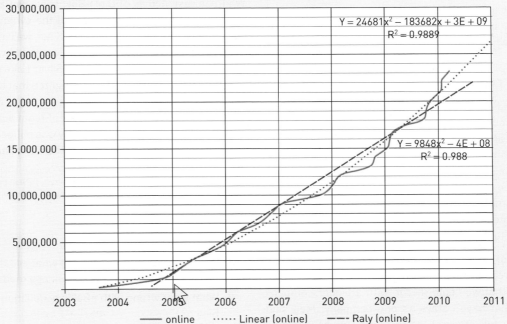

$Y = 24681x^2 - 183682x + 3E + 09$
$R^2 = 0.9889$

$Y = 9848x^2 - 4E + 08$
$R^2 = 0.988$

— online ⋯⋯ Linear (online) – – – Raly (online)

Source: Phil Wolff, *Skype Journal*, 8 March 2010; reproduced with permission.

auctioneer eBay who did the deal, slightly surprisingly as it was not seen as a communications company.

There are similarities in the underlying business models of the two companies. Both benefit from 'network effects', where value rises disproportionately fast with increasing members of the network. One more precise rationale from eBay's point of view was that Skype connections could be placed directly on the eBay site, allowing customers potentially to phone sellers with a single click of the button. Also, sellers could place voice links directly on their eBay sites, so that customers could click directly to a message, paying eBay a fee every time they did. On the other hand, Skype would strengthen its links with eBay's subsidiary PayPal, which Skype already used for managing payments for its SkypeOut service.

For Zennström, however, one major attraction of eBay was that it looked likely to leave Skype more alone. Companies like Yahoo! and Microsoft tend to integrate their acquisitions closely into their existing operations, extinguishing autonomy. Zennström and Friis might be working with eBay for some time. The deal included an 'earn-out' arrangement which would push Skype's final sale price to over $4bn if they managed to meet revenue and profit targets over the coming years. Anyway, the two had an exciting vision for the future: to become the world's biggest and best platform for all communication – text, voice or video – from any internet-connected device, whether a computer or a mobile phone.

eBay's role

eBay had a lot to offer an ambitious company like Skype. Founded only in 1995, it had reached revenues of $4.55bn and 11,600 employees in the space of 10 years. Zennström commented of Meg Whitman, eBay's Chief Executive since 1998: 'I think I can learn a lot of things from Meg. We want to see things through, but we also have some other ideas.' Skype would still have its own strategy, budgets, culture and brands. Zennström insisted to the *Financial Times*:

'One of the important things for us, but also one of the great things with eBay, is that we wanted to make sure that we could merge with a bigger company, but that Skype stays as one company. Meg said: "Take advantage of the resources we have, but we are not going to tell you what to do because you're the best in the world to run your own business."'

The managerial demands of rapid growth were considerable. Staff quadrupled to 300 between 2005 and 2006, and included 30 nationalities scattered all over the world. eBay introduced five of its own senior managers to help, including a new president responsible for day-to-day operations, a chief financial officer and a new human resource director. But Skype was keen to preserve its own culture. According to Zennström, still the CEO, Skype's passionate, pioneering culture had to be both protected and nurtured: 'It's how you operate, how you behave. It starts when we are hiring people. They need to be really thrilled about Skype as a movement, rather than a place to work.'

eBay's exit

While Skype protected its culture, synergies were hard to find. Skype's sales in 2007 had reached $383m, but eBay users were not making the hoped-for use of Skype connections. Targets were missed. In October 2007, Zennström was obliged to step down as CEO and eBay wrote down the value of its investment by $1.4bn. In March 2008, after a 30 per cent slide in share price, Meg Whitman resigned as CEO of eBay. The new CEO, John Donahue, commented on Skype: 'If the synergies are strong, we'll keep it in our portfolio. If not, we'll reassess it.' In September 2009, eBay announced that it was selling 65 per cent of its interest to the Silver Lake group of investors for $2bn. However, it transpired that eBay had neglected to acquire the source-code for Skype software back in 2005. To buy off the threat of legal action and close the deal with Silver Lake, eBay was obliged to give Zennström and Friis 14 per cent of their company back.

Sources: 'Phone service the "zero cost" way', *Business Week online*, 7 January 2004; www.wikipedia.org; *The Economist*, 15 September 2005; *Financial Times*, 17 and 19 April 2006; *Financial Times*, 17 September 2009.

Questions

1 What are the advantages, and what are the possible limits, of Skype's business model?

2 What went wrong with eBay's acquisition of Skype?

9

MERGERS, ACQUISITIONS AND ALLIANCES

Learning outcomes

After reading this chapter you should be able to:

- Establish the potential role of *organic* (stand-alone) strategies.

- Identify key issues in the successful management of *mergers and acquisitions*.

- Identify the key issues in the successful management of *strategic alliances*.

Key terms

Acquisition p. 210

Collective strategy p. 218

Corporate entrepreneurship p. 209

Merger p. 210

Organic development p. 209

Strategic alliance p. 218

(9.1) INTRODUCTION

Mergers, acquisitions and alliances are often in the news. For example, Italian carmaker Fiat has an alliance with the American Chrysler as part of its internationalisation strategy. The American foods conglomerate Kraft acquired the British Cadbury confectionery company in pursuit of its diversification strategy. Acquisition by one company of another, complete merger between two companies, and strategic alliance between different companies are all very common methods for carrying out strategies.

This chapter therefore addresses mergers, acquisitions and alliances as key methods for pursuing strategic options. It will consider them alongside the principal alternative of 'organic' development, in other words the pursuit of a strategy relying on the company's own resources. Figure 9.1 shows how the main strategic options considered in the previous three chapters – diversification, internationalisation and innovation – can all be achieved through mergers and acquisitions, alliances and organic development. Of course, these three methods can also be used for many other strategies, for example consolidating markets or building scale advantages.

The chapter starts with organic development. Organic development is the default option: relying on the organisation's internal resources is the natural first option to consider. The chapter then introduces the two principal external options: first mergers and acquisitions (often abbreviated as M&A) and then strategic alliances.

Figure 9.1 Three strategy methods

(9.2) ORGANIC DEVELOPMENT

The default method for pursuing a strategy is to 'do it yourself', relying on internal capabilities. Thus **organic development is where a strategy is pursued by building on and developing an organisation's own capabilities**. For example, Amazon's entry into the e-books market with its Kindle product was principally organic, relying on its own subsidiary Lab126 and drawing on its expertise in book retailing, internet retail and software. For Amazon, this do-it-yourself (DIY) diversification method was preferable to allying with an existing e-book producer such as Sony or buying a relevant hi-tech start-up such as the French pioneer Bookeen.

There are four principal advantages to relying on organic development:

- *Knowledge and learning.* Using the organisation's existing capabilities to pursue a new strategy can enhance organisational knowledge and learning. Direct involvement in a new market or technology is likely to promote the acquisition and internalisation of deeper knowledge than a hands-off strategic alliance, for example.

- *Spreading investment over time.* Acquisitions typically require an immediate upfront payment for the target company. Organic development allows the spreading of investment over the whole time span of the strategy's development. This reduction of upfront commitment may make it easier to reverse or adjust a strategy if conditions change.

- *No availability constraints.* Organic development has the advantage of not being dependent on the availability of suitable acquisition targets or potential alliance partners. There are few acquisition opportunities for foreign companies wanting to enter the Japanese market, for example. Organic developers also do not have to wait until the perfectly matched acquisition target comes on to the market.

- *Strategic independence.* The independence provided by organic development means that the organisation does not need to make the same compromises as might be necessary if it made an alliance with a partner organisation. For example, partnership with a foreign collaborator is likely to involve constraints on marketing activity in their home market.

The reliance of organic development on internal capabilities can be limiting. It is not easy to use existing capabilities as the platform for major leaps in terms of innovation, diversification or internationalisation, for example. However, as in the example of Amazon's Kindle, organic development can sometimes be sufficiently radical to merit the term 'corporate entrepreneurship'. **Corporate entrepreneurship refers to radical change in the organisation's business, driven principally by the organisation's own capabilities.**[1] Bringing together the words 'entrepreneurship' and 'corporate' underlines the potential for significant change or novelty not only by external entrepreneurship, but also by reliance on internal capabilities from within the corporate organisation. Thus for Amazon, the Kindle was a radical entrepreneurial step, taking it from retailing into the design of innovative consumer electronic products.

The concept of corporate entrepreneurship is valuable because it encourages an entrepreneurial attitude inside the firm. There are many examples of corporate entrepreneurship, such as the creation of low-cost airline Ryanair from inside the aircraft leasing company Guinness Peat. Often, however, organisations have to go beyond their own internal capabilities and look externally for methods to pursue their strategies. The main themes of this chapter, therefore, are first mergers and acquisitions and second strategic alliances.

9.3 MERGERS AND ACQUISITIONS

Mergers and acquisitions (M&A) frequently grab the headlines, as they involve large sums of money and very public competitions for shareholder support. They can also provide a speedy means of achieving major strategic objectives. However, they can also lead to spectacular failures. A famous case is that of the Royal Bank of Scotland, whose 2007 takeover of the Dutch ABN AMRO ended in commercial disaster and the bank's nationalisation by the British government.

9.3.1 Types of mergers and acquisitions

An acquisition involves one firm taking over the ownership ('equity') of another, hence the alternative term 'takeover'. Most acquisitions are ultimately *friendly*, where the acquirer and the target firm agree the terms together, and the target's management recommends acceptance to its shareholders. Sometimes acquisitions are *hostile*: here the would-be acquirer offers a price for the target firm's shares without the agreement of the target's management and the outcome is decided by which side wins the support of shareholders. Thus Cadbury's management initially rejected the hostile bid by Kraft, seeking more friendly alternative partners such as Hershey. On the other hand, **a merger is the combination of two previously separate organisations, typically as more or less equal partners.** For example, in 2009, the French Banque Populaire and Caisse d'Epargne merged to form a new bank called Groupe BPCE, which became the second largest in France. In practice, the terms 'merger' and 'acquisition' are often used interchangeably, hence the common shorthand M&A or just acquisitions.

9.3.2 Motives for mergers and acquisitions

There are three broad types of motive for M&A: strategic, financial and managerial.[2]

Strategic motives for M&A

Strategic motives for M&A involve improving the actual business of the organisation in some way. These motives are often related to the reasons for diversification in general (see section 6.3). Strategic motives can be categorised in three main ways:[3]

● *Extension.* Mergers and acquisitions can be used to extend the reach of a firm in terms of geography, products or markets. Acquisitions can be speedy ways of extending international reach. Thus in 2010 the Chinese Geely car company bought the Swedish Volvo car company in order to build its global presence. Acquisitions can also be an effective way of extending into new markets, as in diversification (see Chapter 6).

● *Consolidation.* Mergers and acquisitions can be used to consolidate the competitors in an industry. Bringing together two competitors can have at least three beneficial effects. In the first place, it increases market power by reducing competition: this might enable the newly consolidated company to raise prices for customers. Second, the combination of two competitors can increase efficiency through reducing surplus capacity or sharing resources, for instance head-office facilities or distribution channels. Finally, the greater scale of the combined operations may increase production efficiency or increase bargaining power with suppliers, forcing them to reduce their prices.

● *Capabilities.* The third broad strategic motive for mergers and acquisitions is to increase a company's capabilities. High-tech companies such as Cisco and Microsoft regard acquisitions of entrepreneurial technology companies as a part of their R&D effort. Instead of researching a new technology from scratch, they allow entrepreneurial start-ups to prove the idea; they then take over these companies in order to incorporate the technological capability within their own portfolio. Capabilities-driven acquisitions are often useful where industries are converging (see section 2.3.1). Thus the telephone company AT&T bought computer company NCR as it perceived industry convergence between telephony and computing.

Financial motives for M&A

Financial motives concern the optimal use of financial resources, rather than directly improving the actual businesses. There are three main financial motives:

● *Financial efficiency.* It is often efficient to bring together a company with a strong balance sheet (i.e. it has plenty of cash) with another company that has a weak balance sheet (i.e. it has high debt). The company with a weak balance sheet can save on interest payments by using the stronger company's assets to pay off its debt, and it can also get investment funds from the stronger company that it could not have accessed otherwise. The company with the strong balance sheet may be able to drive a good bargain in acquiring the weaker company. Also, a company with a booming share price can purchase other companies very efficiently by offering to pay the target company's shareholders with its own shares (equity), rather than paying with cash up front.

● *Tax efficiency.* Sometimes there may be tax advantages from bringing together different companies. For example, one company may be operating in a low-taxation country, and profits from the other company in a higher-tax area can be transferred to be taxed there. Or a company that is making high profits may buy a company that has accumulated losses in order to reduce its own tax liability. Naturally, there are legal restrictions on this strategy.

● *Asset stripping or unbundling.* Some companies are effective at spotting other companies whose underlying assets are worth more than the price of the company as a whole. This makes it possible to buy such companies and then rapidly sell off ('unbundle') different business units to various buyers for a total price substantially in excess of what was originally paid for the whole. Although this is often dismissed as merely opportunistic profiteering ('asset stripping'), if the business units find better corporate parents through this unbundling process, there can be a real gain in economic effectiveness.

Managerial motives for M&A

Acquisitions may sometimes serve managers' interests better than shareholders' interests. 'Managerial' motives are so called, therefore, because they are self-serving rather than efficiency-driven. M&A may serve managerial self-interest for two types of reason:

- *Personal ambition.* There are three ways that acquisitions can satisfy the personal ambition of senior managers, regardless of the real value being created. First, senior managers' personal financial incentives may be tied to short-term growth targets or share-price targets that are more easily achieved by large and spectacular acquisitions than the more gradualist and lower-profile alternative of organic growth. Second, large acquisitions attract media attention, with opportunities to boost personal reputations through flattering media interviews and appearances. Here there is the so-called 'managerial hubris' (vanity) effect: managers who have been successful in earlier acquisitions become over-confident and embark on more and more acquisitions, each riskier and more expensive than the one before.[4] Finally, acquisitions provide opportunities to give friends and colleagues greater responsibility, helping to cement personal loyalty by developing individuals' careers.

- *Bandwagon effects.* Acquisitions are highly cyclical, with booms in M&A activity followed by slumps. In an upswing, there are three kinds of pressure on senior managers to join the acquisition bandwagon. First, when many other firms are making acquisitions, financial analysts and the business media may criticise more cautious managers for undue conservatism. Second, shareholders will fear that their company is being left behind, as they see opportunities for their business being snatched by rivals. Lastly, employees will worry that if their company is not acquiring, it will become the target of a hostile bid itself. For managers wanting a quiet life during a 'merger boom', the easiest strategy may be simply to join in, but the danger is of paying too much for an acquisition that the company does not really need in the first place.

In sum, there are bad as well as good reasons for acquisitions and mergers. The average performance of acquisitions is unimpressive, with some suggesting that half of acquisitions fail.[5] It is therefore well worth asking sceptical questions of any M&A strategy. The converse can be true of course: there can be bad reasons for resisting a hostile takeover. Senior managers may resist being acquired because they fear losing their jobs, even if the price offered represents a good deal for their shareholders.

9.3.3 M&A processes

Acquisitions take time. First, there is the search to identify an acquisition target with the best possible fit. Then there is the process of negotiating the right price. Finally, managers will have to integrate the new and old businesses together, in order to realise the full value of their purchase. In other words, acquisition should be seen as a process over time. Each step in this process imposes different tasks on managers. This section will consider three key steps: target choice, valuation and integration.

Target choice in M&A

Here there are two main criteria to apply: strategic fit and organisation fit.[6]

- *Strategic fit* refers to the extent to which the target firm strengthens or complements the acquiring firm's strategy. Strategic fit will relate to the original strategic motives for the acquisition: extension, consolidation and capabilities. Managers need to assess strategic fit very carefully. The danger is that potential synergies (see section 6.3) in M&A are often exaggerated in order to justify high acquisition prices. Also, negative synergies ('contagion') between the companies involved are easily neglected.[7] An example of negative synergy was when the Bank of America bought the aggressive investment bank Merrill Lynch for $47bn (~£33bn) in 2008. Under its new owner, Merrill Lynch lost business because it was no longer allowed to advise on deals targeting the extensive list of corporations that were already lending clients of Bank of America. Consequently, Merrill Lynch was a less valuable business with its new parent than when free to chase any deal it wanted.

- *Organisational fit* refers to the match between the management practices, cultural practices and staff characteristics between the target and the acquiring firms. Large mismatches between the two are likely to cause significant integration problems. The acquisition of Californian genetic engineering company Genentech by Swiss pharmaceutical company Roche raises many questions of organisational fit (see Illustration 9.1). International acquisitions are particularly liable to organisational misfits, because of cultural and language differences between countries.[8] A comparison of the two companies' cultural webs (section 4.6.5) might be helpful here.

Together, strategic and organisational fit determine the potential for the acquirer to add value, the parenting issue raised in section 6.5. Where there is a bad organisational fit, the acquirer is likely to destroy value through its corporate parenting regardless of how well the target fits strategically.

The two criteria of strategic fit and organisational fit can be used to create a screen according to which potential acquisition targets can be ruled in or ruled out. Note that, because the set of firms that meet the criteria *and* that are actually available for purchase is likely to be small, it is very tempting for managers to relax the criteria too far in order to build a large enough pool of possible acquisitions. Strict strategic and organisational fit criteria are particularly liable to be forgotten after the failure of an initial acquisition bid. Once having committed publicly to an acquisition strategy, senior managers are susceptible to making ill-considered bids for other targets 'on the rebound'.

Valuation in M&A

Negotiating the right price for an acquisition target is absolutely critical. Offer the target too little, and the bid will be unsuccessful: senior managers will lose credibility and the company will have wasted a lot of management time. Pay too much, though, and the acquisition is unlikely ever to make a profit net of the original acquisition price.

Valuation methods include financial analysis techniques such as payback period, discounted cash flow and shareholder value analysis.[9] For acquisition of publicly quoted companies, there

ILLUSTRATION 9.1

Swiss in the Valley

Swiss pharmaceutical giant Roche faced strong resistance to its takeover of Californian biotech company Genentech.

Founded in 1896, by 2009 Swiss pharmaceutical company Roche had 80,000 employees worldwide, sales of $33.6bn (~€23.5bn) and a 56 per cent stake in the San Francisco biotechnology company Genentech. Genentech, however, was jealous of its autonomy, and regarded data on its experiments and trials as not Roche's property. Taking advantage of Genentech's fall in relative value because of a weak dollar, the Swiss company launched a bid for full control, at $89 a share, valuing the company at $44bn. Genentech's management refused the offer.

Genentech had been founded in 1976 by a young venture capitalist and an assistant professor at the San Francisco campus of the University of California. In 1977, the Silicon Valley start-up was the first in the world to express a human gene in bacteria, and in the following year it was the first to produce synthetic human insulin. Roche had bought its stake in the successful young company in 1990, but taken a hands-off approach. By 2009, Genentech was the second largest biotechnology company in the United States, with 11,000 employees. Many of these employees were top scientists, lured to the company by a combination of good salaries, stock options and a large amount of academic freedom. Genentech allowed its scientists to pursue their own research projects one day a week, and to publish articles in scientific journals. In 2008, Genentech had been awarded more patents in molecular biology than the US government and the ten campuses of the University of California combined. *Science* magazine named Genentech as the best employer for scientists seven years in a row. In 2008, former biotech researcher Dr Art Levinson, Genentech's CEO since 1995 and a supporter of the company's traditional Friday 'beer fests', had been voted by another magazine as America's 'nicest' CEO.

Roche was obliged to raise its bid, to $94 per share. Genentech's management reluctantly accepted. They had originally hoped for $112 per share, but the economic crisis of the time made that unrealistic. As shareholders themselves, however, Roche's bid had made the top management and many of Genentech's scientists very wealthy people.

Although now in full control of Genentech, the management challenges for Roche were substantial. Laurence Lasky, a Silicon Valley venture capitalist and former scientist at Genentech, commented of Roche: 'They're Swiss, and Genentech is a bunch of California cowboys'. Roche indeed had a different culture. Based in the staid town of Basel, it was still half-owned by descendants of the founding families. Its products are typically based upon chemical compounds, very different from Genentech's genetic engineering. Like many other 'big pharma' companies, moreover, the stream of new products from its research laboratories was drying up. Roche hoped to replenish its product portfolio by getting full access to Genentech's research, while also saving costs by merging its US headquarters with that of Genentech in California.

Roche chairman Franz Humer, a Swiss lawyer, was none the less very positive, telling the *Wall Street Journal*: 'I am delighted that the intensive negotiations have led to a successful conclusion . . . I have spoken with Art (Levinson) and he's extremely committed to make a success of the new company.' However, a close observer of Genentech remarked: 'the assets of Genentech walk out in tennis shoes every night, and you hope they walk back in next morning'.

Sources: San Francisco Chronicle, 13 March 2009, 17 August 2008; International Herald Tribune, 13 March 2009; Wall Street Journal, 17 March 2009.

Questions

1   Assess the strategic and organisational fits of Roche and Genentech

2   What must Roche do to ensure the success of this takeover?

is the additional guide of the market value of the target company's shares. However, acquirers typically do not simply pay the current market value of the target, but have to pay a so-called *premium for control*. This premium is the additional amount that the acquirer has to pay to win total control compared to the ordinary valuation of the target's shares as an independent company. Depending on the state of the financial markets, this premium might involve paying at least 30 per cent more for the shares than normal. Especially where the target resists the initial bid, or other potential acquirers join in with their own bids, it is very easy for bid prices to escalate beyond the true economic value of the target.

It is, therefore, very important for the acquirer to be strictly disciplined with regard to the price that it will pay. Acquisitions are liable to the *winner's curse* – in order to win acceptance of the bid, the acquirer may pay so much that the original cost can never be earned back.[10] This winner's curse effect operated when the Royal Bank of Scotland's consortium competed with Barclays Bank to acquire the Dutch bank ABN AMRO: the Royal Bank of Scotland won, but the excessive price of £70bn (~$98bn) soon drove the victor into financial collapse and government ownership. The negative effects of paying too much can be worsened if the acquirer tries to justify the price by cutting back essential investments in order to improve immediate profits. In what is called the *vicious circle of overvaluation*, over-paying firms can easily undermine the original rationale of the acquisition by imposing savings on exactly the assets (e.g. brand-marketing, product R&D or key staff) that made up the strategic value of the target company in the first place.

Integration in M&A

The ability to extract value from an acquisition will depend critically on the approach to integrating the new business with the old. Integration is frequently challenging because of problems of organisational fit. For example, there might be strong cultural differences between the two organisations (see section 4.6) or they might have incompatible financial or information technology systems (see section 10.3). Illustration 9.2 describes some integration issues for British car company Jaguar-Land Rover after acquisition by Indian conglomerate Tata. Poor integration can cause acquisitions to fail. It is crucial to choose the correct approach to integration of merged or acquired companies.

INSEAD's Philippe Haspeslagh and David Jemison[11] argue that the most suitable approach to integration depends on two key criteria:

- *The extent of strategic interdependence.* Where there is high interdependence, the presumption is in favour of tight integration. If the acquisition is driven by the need to transfer capabilities (for example, technology) or to share resources (for example, distribution channels), the value can only be extracted through integrating the businesses thoroughly. Of course, some acquisitions take the form of unrelated or conglomerate diversification (see section 6.2). In unrelated acquisitions, the lack of strategic interdependence means there is little need for integration beyond financial systems.

- *The need for organisational autonomy.* The nature of the organisations involved might modify the logic of strategic interdependence, however. An acquired firm that has a very distinct culture, or is geographically distant, or is dominated by prima donna professionals

ILLUSTRATION 9.2

From Nano to Jaguar

In 2008, the Indian Tata group, makers of the ultra-cheap Nano car, bought two iconic British car brands, Jaguar and Land Rover. It had to integrate these in the most demanding times.

The Tata Group is the largest privately owned company in India, with interests spanning from steel to hotels. Its chairman, Ratan Tata, has embarked on an internationalisation strategy that included the takeover of the Anglo-Dutch Corus steel company in 2007. In January 2008, Tata Motors, already producing a range of cars and SUVs, launched the revolutionary Nano, the world's cheapest car, selling for less than $2000 (~€1400). Two months later, Tata Motors acquired its first prestige marques, Jaguar and Land Rover, from the struggling Ford Motors, for $2.3bn.

With 16,000 employees in the UK, based at three manufacturing sites and two design and engineering centres, the takeover caused alarm. Would Tata save money by closing sites? Might it transfer production to its low-cost base in India? Ratan Tata was quick to reassure. On a personal visit to the company, he recalled that his father had bought a classic Jaguar more than half a century ago. He talked about reviving the revered British Daimler brand and returning Jaguar to racing. Jaguar-Land Rover then announced its intention to hire 600 more skilled staff to support a £700m project to develop environmentally friendly cars; and Tata was well-placed to sell Jaguars and Land Rovers in the booming Indian market.

Jaguar-Land Rover still faced challenges. As a subsidiary of Ford, Jaguar-Land Rover had relied on Ford Credit to finance its operations and sales. Now Jaguar-Land Rover needed its own relationships with the banks. All its information technology was based on Ford systems. Jaguar-Land Rover CEO David Smith commented: 'We're pulling companies that were embedded in Ford back out again and switching our financing to other providers. And the IT is an absolute hydra. It's going to be the most difficult part.'

However, Tata did not insist on tight integration into the Indian parent. Oversight is provided by a three-man strategy board, meeting every two months and comprising Ratan Tata, the head of Tata Automotive and David Smith himself. Smith commented: 'Tata wants us to be autonomous – I've got all the executive authority I need. . . . We can make decisions quickly – that's what will be most different from life at Ford.' The Jaguar-Land Rover executive committee, directly responsible for the company's operations, had no Tata representatives. Nevertheless, Jaguar-Land Rover would be making use of Tata Motors' expertise in cost control and the Tata Consultancy Division's skills in information technology.

A year after the takeover, David Smith commented again: 'We are still learning how the relationship with Tata will work. It's clearly more personal and based on individual relationships.' Of Ratan Tata, who had been a passionately involved champion of the Nano and had trained as an architect and engineer, David Smith remarked: '[He] is very interested in the business. The designers love him, because he's an architect and is not only quite capable of telling them what he thinks, he can say it in the right language too.'

By Spring 2009, relationships were being tested by the economic crisis. Jaguar-Land Rover's sales had fallen by more than 30 per cent and the company had plunged into losses. The British government was refusing a financial bail-out. What would Tata do now?

Sources: Management Today, 1 May 2009; Financial Times, 4 August 2008.

Questions

1 In the light of Haspeslagh and Jemison's matrix, assess Tata's initial approach to the integration of Jaguar-Land Rover

2 How might Tata's approach change in the economic crisis?

Figure 9.2 Acquisition integration matrix

Source: P. Haspeslagh and D. Jemison, *Managing Acquisitions*, Free Press, 1991.

or star performers might be better left only loosely or gradually integrated. Sometimes an acquisition can be made precisely because the distinctiveness of the acquired organisation is valuable to the acquirer:[12] in this case, of course, it is best to learn gradually from the distinct culture, rather than risk spoiling it by clumsy integration.

As in Figure 9.2, therefore, these two criteria drive three main approaches to integration, plus a fourth residual approach:

- *Absorption* is preferred where there is strong strategic interdependence and little need for organisational autonomy. Absorption implies rapid adjustment of the acquired company's old strategies to the needs of the new owner, and corresponding changes to the company's culture and systems.

- *Preservation* is appropriate where there is little interdependence and a high need for autonomy – as in a conglomerate, perhaps. Preservation allows old strategies, cultures and systems to continue much as before, with changes confined to the essential minimum such as the financial reporting procedures needed for control.

- *Symbiosis* is indicated where there is strong strategic interdependence, but a high need for autonomy – perhaps in a professional services organisation dependent on the creativity of its staff. Symbiosis implies that both acquired firm and acquiring firm learn the best qualities from the other. Symbiosis takes time and is the most complex of the integration approaches.

- *Holding* is the residual category where there is very little to gain by integration and it is envisaged that the acquisition will be 'held' temporarily before being sold to another company. It is best, in these cases, simply to leave the acquired unit largely alone.

(9.4) STRATEGIC ALLIANCES

KEY CONCEPT

Strategic alliances

Mergers and acquisitions bring together companies through complete changes in ownership. However, companies also often work together in strategic alliances that involve only partial changes in ownership, or no ownership changes at all. The companies remain distinct. Thus **a strategic alliance is where two or more organisations share resources and activities to pursue a strategy**. This is a common method in strategy: Andersen Consulting has estimated that the average large corporation is managing around 30 alliances.[13]

Alliance strategy challenges the traditional organisation-centred approach to strategy. Increasingly, organisations are members of networks of alliances or less formal relationships (long-term supplier or licensing relationships, for example). Here managers need to think about strategy in terms of the collective success of their networks as well as their individual organisations' self-interest.[14] **Collective strategy is about how the whole network of relationships of which an organisation is a member competes against rival networks of relationships.** Thus for Microsoft, competitive success for its Xbox games console relies heavily on the collective strength of its network of independent games developers such as Bungie Studios (makers of Halo), Bizarre Creations (Project Gotham Racing) and Team Ninja (Dead or Alive). Part of Microsoft's strategy must include having a stronger network (or '*ecosystem*') of games developers than its rivals such as Sony and Nintendo. Collective strategy also challenges the individualistic approach to strategy by highlighting the importance of effective collaboration. Thus success involves collaborating as well as competing. Illustration 9.3 describes Apple's approach to collective strategy and collaboration for the iPod.

9.4.1 Types of strategic alliance

In terms of ownership, there are two main kinds of strategic alliance:

- *Equity alliances* involve the creation of a new entity that is owned separately by the partners involved. The most common form of equity alliance is the *joint venture*, where two organisations remain independent, but set up a new organisation jointly owned by the parents. For example, General Motors and Toyota have operated the NUMMI joint venture since 1984, producing cars from both companies in the same plant in California. A *consortium alliance* involves several partners setting up a venture together. For example, IBM, Hewlett-Packard, Toshiba and Samsung are partners in the Sematech research consortium, working together on the latest semiconductor technologies.

- *Non-equity alliances* are typically looser, without the commitment implied by ownership. Non-equity alliances are often based on contracts. One common form of contractual alliance is *franchising*, where one organisation (the franchisor) gives another organisation (the franchisee) the right to sell the franchisor's products or services in a particular location in return for a fee or royalty. Kall-Kwik printing, 7-Eleven convenience stores and McDonald's restaurants are examples of franchising. *Licensing* is a similar kind of contractual alliance, allowing partners to use intellectual property such as patents or brands in return for a fee. *Long-term subcontracting* agreements are another form of loose non-equity alliance,

ILLUSTRATION 9.3

Apple's iPod network

Does Apple manage its network of collaborators well?

By 2009, Apple had sold 200 million iPods. But this success was not Apple's alone. And Apple's relationship with its network of subcontractors and licensees was controversial.

When Apple had first launched the iPod in 2001, it needed help. The iPod combines different kinds of technologies in a uniquely small format. Apple relied substantially on external component suppliers. For example, the fifth-generation iPod hard-drive – accounting for about half the total components costs – was sourced from Toshiba in Japan. The multimedia processor came from American Broadcom. The mobile memory came from the Korean Samsung. The lithium battery was Sony's. Assembly was carried out in Taiwan. The success of the iPod attracted a swarm of companies into the iPod accessory market, with companies such as Griffin from the United States and Logitech from Switzerland supplying attractive add-ons such as docking stations, cases and speakers.

Apple is at the heart, therefore, of a network spanning many companies across the world. However, the company has always been protective of its intellectual property. During the 1980s, Apple had tightly controlled the licensing of its Macintosh computer operating system, restricting independent companies from creating compatible software applications for the mass market. Meanwhile, Microsoft had opened up its operating systems, allowing a flood of independent applications that had helped give it dominance of the market.

Apple somewhat modified its strategy for the iPod. Initially the iPod was a completely closed system that worked only with the Macintosh and iTunes music warehouse. Gradually it allowed other audio file formats to be played on the system, but by 2009 Apple was still resisting Microsoft's WMA format. The company licensed none of its hardware, ensuring control of its production and maintenance of its premium pricing policy. It was impossible for any independent company to manufacture cheap iPods, in the way for instance Taiwanese manufacturers had produced cheap IBM/Microsoft-compatible personal computers during the 1980s. However, the company did license to accessory-producers the technology needed to access iPod ports. Apple benefited from royalties from its licensees, as well as the development of attractive complementary products. But the relationship with accessory-producers was arm's-length, with no information about new iPod products released ahead. A spokesman at accessory-producer Griffin commented: 'It's very much a hands-off relationship. We do not know what [new product] is coming down the pipe ahead of time.'

Apple's strategy seems to be paying off. Microsoft's rival music-player, the Zune, has been a comparative failure. However, Apple's position at the heart of a network can be seen another way: it is also surrounded by some powerful players. For example, Sony is a supplier of lithium batteries. Sony builds iPod accessories such as car adaptors and boomboxes. Sony Music supplies its artists, such as Leona Lewis and Michael Jackson, via the iTunes site. And finally, of course, Sony has its own MP3 music-player, the Walkman, plus its own media download site, mystore.

Sources: M. Cusumano, 'The Puzzle of Apple', *Communications of the ACM*, vol. 51, no. 9 (2008), pp. 22–24; G. Linden, K. Kraemer, and J. Dedrick, 'Who captures value in a global innovation network? Apple's iPod', *Communications of the ACM*, vol. 52, no. 3 (2009), pp. 140–45; P. Taylor, 'iPod ecosystem offers rich pickings', *Financial Times*, 25 January 2006, p. 15.

Questions

1 What are pros and cons of Apple's tight control of licensing?

2 What are the pros and cons of maintaining a 'hands-off' relationship with accessory-producers such as Griffin?

common in automobile supply. For example, the Canadian subcontractor Magna has long-term contracts to assemble the bodies and frames for car companies such as Ford, Honda and Mercedes.

The public and voluntary sectors often get involved in both equity and non-equity strategic alliances. Governments have increasingly encouraged the public sector to contract out the building and maintenance of capital projects such as hospitals and schools under long-term contracts. Individual public organisations often band together to form purchasing consortia as well. A good example of this is university libraries, which typically negotiate collectively for the purchase of journals and books from publishers. Voluntary organisations pool their resources in alliance too. For example, relief organisations in areas suffering from natural or man-made disasters typically have to cooperate in order to deliver the full range of services in difficult circumstances. Although public- and voluntary-sector organisations might often be seen as more naturally cooperative than private-sector organisations, many of the issues that follow apply to all three kinds of organisation.

9.4.2 Motives for alliances

The definition of strategic alliances puts the stress on sharing, of resources or activities. Although sharing is the key motivator for most alliances, there may be less obvious reasons as well. Four broad rationales for alliances can be identified, as summarised in Figure 9.3:

● *Scale alliances*. Here organisations combine in order to achieve necessary scale. The capabilities of each partner may be quite similar (as indicated by the similarity of the A and B organisations in Figure 9.3), but together they can achieve advantages that they

Figure 9.3 Strategic alliance motives

could not easily manage on their own. Thus combining together can provide economies of scale in the production of *outputs* (products or services). Combining might also provide economies of scale in terms of *inputs*, for example by reducing purchasing costs of raw materials or services. Thus health management organisations often combine together to negotiate better prices with pharmaceutical companies. Finally, combining allows the partners to *share risk* as well. Instead of organisations stretching themselves to find enough resources on their own, partnering can help each partner avoid committing so many resources of its own that failure would jeopardise the existence of the whole organisation.

- *Access alliances.* Organisations frequently ally in order to access the capabilities of another organisation that are required in order to produce or sell its products and services. For example, in countries such as China and India, a Western company (in Figure 9.3, organisation A) might need to partner with a local distributor (organisation B) in order to access effectively the national market for its products and services. Here organisation B is critical to organisation A's ability to sell. Access alliances can work in the opposite direction. Thus organisation B might seek a licensing alliance in order to access inputs from organisation A, for example technologies or brands. Here organisation A is critical to organisation B's ability to produce or market its products and services. Access can be about not only tangible resources such as distribution channels or products, but also about intangible resources such as knowledge.

- *Complementary alliances.* These can be seen as a form of access alliance, but involve organisations at similar points in the value network combining their distinctive resources so that they bolster each partner's particular gaps or weaknesses. Figure 9.3 shows an alliance where the strengths of organisation A (indicated by the darker shading) match the weaknesses of organisation B (indicated by the lighter shading); conversely, the strengths of organisation B match the weaknesses of organisation A. By partnering, the two organisations can bring together complementary strengths in order to overcome their individual weaknesses. An example of this is the General Motors–Toyota NUMMI alliance: here the complementarity lies in General Motors getting access to the Japanese car company's manufacturing expertise, while Toyota obtains the American car company's local marketing knowledge.

- *Collusive alliances.* Occasionally, organisations secretly collude together in order to increase their market power. By combining together into cartels, they reduce competition in the marketplace, enabling them to extract higher prices from their customers or lower prices from suppliers. Such collusive cartels are generally illegal, so there is no public agreement (hence the absence of brackets joining the two collusive organisations in Figure 9.3). Mobile phone operators are often accused of collusive behaviour and in 2005 France Telecom and two other French operators were fined over £500m ($700m) for illegal market-sharing.

It can be seen that strategic alliances, like mergers and acquisitions, have mixed motives. Cooperation is often a good thing, but it is important to be aware of collusive motivations. These are likely to work against the interests of other competitors, customers and suppliers.

9.4.3 Strategic alliance processes

Like mergers and acquisitions, strategic alliances need to be understood as processes unfolding over time. Alliances often last for very long periods. For example, the American General Electric and French SNECMA have been partners since 1974 in a continuous alliance for the development and production of small aero-engines. The needs and capabilities of the partners in a long-standing alliance such as this are bound to change over time. However, the absence of full ownership means that emerging differences cannot simply be reconciled by managerial authority; they have to be negotiated between independent partners. This lack of control by one side or the other means that the managerial processes in alliances are particularly demanding. The management challenges, moreover, will change over time.

The fact that neither partner is in control, while alliances must typically be managed over time, highlights the importance of two themes in the various stages of the alliance process:

● *Co-evolution*. Rather than thinking of strategic alliances as fixed at a particular point of time, they are better seen as co-evolutionary processes.[15] The concept of co-evolution underlines the way in which partners, strategies, capabilities and environments are constantly changing. As they change, they need realignment so that they can evolve in harmony. A co-evolutionary perspective on alliances therefore places the emphasis on flexibility and change. At completion, an alliance is unlikely to be the same as envisaged at the start.

● *Trust*. Given the probable co-evolutionary nature of alliances, and the lack of control of one partner over the other, trust becomes highly important to the success of alliances over time.[16] All future possibilities cannot be specified in the initial alliance contract. Each partner will have made investments that are vulnerable to the selfish behaviour of the other. This implies the need for partners to behave in a trustworthy fashion through the whole lifetime of the alliance. Trust in a relationship is something that has to be continuously earned. Trust is often particularly fragile in alliances between the public and private sectors, where the profit motive is suspect on one side, and sudden shifts in political agendas are feared on the other.

The themes of trust and co-evolution surface in various ways at different stages in the lifespan of a strategic alliance. Figure 9.4 provides a simple stage model of strategic alliance evolution. The amount of committed resources changes at each stage, but issues of trust and co-evolution recur throughout:

● *Courtship*. First there is the initial process of courting potential partners, where the main resource commitment is managerial time. This courtship process should not be rushed, as the willingness of both partners is required. Similar criteria apply to alliances at this stage as to acquisitions. Each partner has to see a strategic fit, according to the rationales in section 9.3.2. Equally, each partner has to see an organisational fit. Organisational fit can be considered as for acquisitions (section 9.3.3). However, because alliances do not entail the same degree of control as acquisitions, mutual trust between partners will need to be particularly strong right from the outset.

● *Negotiation*. Partners need of course to negotiate carefully their mutual roles at the outset. In equity alliances, the partners also have to negotiate the proportion of ownership each

Figure 9.4 Alliance evolution

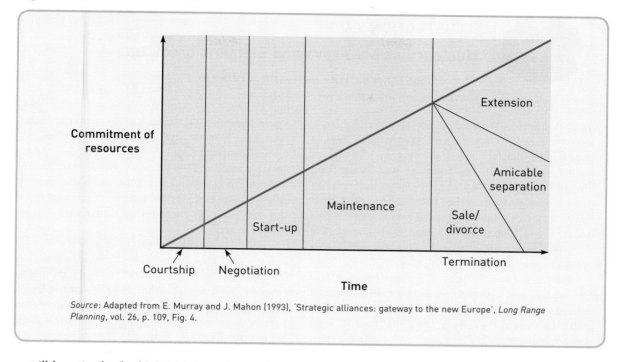

Source: Adapted from E. Murray and J. Mahon (1993), 'Strategic alliances: gateway to the new Europe', *Long Range Planning*, vol. 26, p. 109, Fig. 4.

will have in the final joint venture. Again, there is likely to be a significant commitment of managerial time at this stage, as it is important to get initial contracts clear and correct. In the case of the Areva–Siemens joint venture (Illustration 9.5), Siemens regretted the low share that it originally agreed. Although the negotiation of ownership proportions in a joint venture is similar to the valuation process in acquisitions, strategic alliance contracts generally involve a great deal more. Key behaviours required of each partner need to be specified upfront. However, a ruthless negotiation style can also damage trust going forward. Moreover, co-evolution implies the need to anticipate change. In an acquired unit, it is possible to make adjustments simply by managerial authority. In alliances, initial contracts may be considered binding even when starting conditions have changed. It is wise to include an option for renegotiating initial terms right at the outset.

- *Start-up.* Start-up is the next stage, with considerable investment of material and human resources normally involved. Trust is very important at this stage. First, the initial operation of the alliance puts the original alliance agreements to the test. Informal adjustments to working realities are likely to be required. Also, people from outside the original negotiation team are typically now obliged to work together on a day-to-day basis. They may not have the same understanding of the alliance as those who initiated it. Without the mutual trust to make adjustments and smooth misunderstandings, the alliance is liable to break up. This early period in an alliance's evolution is the one with the highest rate of failure.

- *Maintenance.* This refers to the ongoing operation of the strategic alliance, with increasing resources likely to be committed. The lesson of co-evolution is that alliance maintenance is

ILLUSTRATION 9.4

Nuclear fission: Areva and Siemens break up

Co-evolution is not easy, as two leading French and German companies discover.

In 2001, Siemens, the German industrial conglomerate, and Areva, the French nuclear industry giant, merged their nuclear reactor businesses into a new joint venture called Areva NP. The joint venture was 34 per cent owned by Siemens, 66 per cent owned by Areva. As the German government had promised to exit nuclear power altogether for environmental reasons, Siemens no longer saw nuclear power as central to its strategy. The joint venture agreement gave the French a right-to-buy option for the Siemens minority stake.

In 2009, the new Siemens CEO, Peter Löscher, sent Areva's CEO Ann Lauvergeon a short e-mail announcing that the Germans would be exercising their right to sell their stake to the French. The e-mail took Madame Lauvergeon completely by surprise: 'It made me think of those men who abandon their wives by leaving a note on the kitchen table.' What had gone wrong in the eight years? Areva NP had been a success. It was the global leader in a market for nuclear reactors that was booming again. Rising oil prices and alarm over global warming made nuclear power increasingly attractive. By 2009, after many years of minimal construction, 51 plants were being built around the world, with 171 more planned. Areva NP was active not only in Europe but in the United States and China.

The recovery of the nuclear industry was, in fact, one source of the problem: with a new CEO, Siemens wanted back in. Siemens was frustrated by its lack of control as a minority shareholder, and by the slow decision-making in Areva NP generally. Moreover, it wanted to get a larger slice of the business than just the nuclear reactors – the big profits were elsewhere in the value chain, in fuel and recycling. Areva, the French parent company, already had a significant presence through the whole value chain.

During 2007, Siemens looked either to increase its stake in Areva NP to 50:50 or to take a direct stake in the French parent, Areva. But, more than 80 per cent owned by the French government, Areva was not easily for sale. Moreover, Nicolas Sarkozy, then a senior French government minister and soon French President, told German Chancellor Angela Merkel that France could not tolerate a role for Siemens while the German government refused to back nuclear power in its own country. Siemens had to enrol Merkel's support to prevent Areva from exercising its right-to-buy option and forcing Siemens to sell.

In late 2008, Siemens began talks with the Russian nuclear power giant Rosatom. Rosatom had a presence through the whole value chain, including the highly profitable fuel business. With memories of the Soviet nuclear disaster at Chernobyl still live, Rosatom needed Siemens' high reputation for quality. In March 2009, Siemens and Rosatom announced a joint venture with the ambition of displacing Areva NP as world leader.

Ending the Areva NP joint venture was not simple, however. Siemens' strength was in hardware, but Areva owned the software that made it work. Areva was obliged to buy Siemens' stake (~€4bn; ~$5.6bn), but lacked the funds to do so. Also, the original joint venture agreement had included a non-compete clause in case of break-down. So far as Areva was concerned, Siemens' new joint venture put it in breach of the contract, and so not entitled to the full value of its stake. And the two companies were still working together on various nuclear power stations. Indeed, Areva and Siemens were being jointly sued for €2bn for cost and time over-runs on a project in Finland. It was going to be a messy divorce.

Sources: *L'Expansion*, 1 April 2009; *Financial Times*, 28 April 2009.

Question

In what respects did co-evolution break down in the Areva NP joint venture?

not a simple matter of stability. Alliances have to be actively managed to allow for changing external circumstances. The internal dynamics of the partnership are likely to evolve as well as the partners build experience. Here again trust is extremely important. Gary Hamel has warned that alliances often become *competitions for competence*.[17] Because partners are interacting closely, they can begin to learn each other's particular competences. This learning can develop into a competition for competence, with the partner that learns the fastest becoming the more powerful. The more powerful partner may consequently be able to renegotiate the terms in its favour or even break up the alliance and go it alone. If, on the other hand, the partners wish to maintain their strategic alliance, trustworthy behaviour that does not threaten the other partner's competence is essential to maintaining the cooperative relationships necessary for the day-to-day working of the alliance.

- *Termination.* Eventually, there will be some kind of *termination* of the alliance. Often an alliance will have had an agreed time span or purpose right from the start, so termination is a matter of completion rather than failure. Here separation is amicable. Sometimes, the alliance has been so successful that the partners will wish to extend the alliance by agreeing a new alliance between themselves, committing still more resources. Sometimes too, the alliance will have been a success in another sense, with one partner wishing to buy the other's share in order to commit fully to a particular market, while the other partner is happy to sell. The sale of one half of a joint venture need not be a sign of failure. However, occasionally alliances end in bitter divorces, as when Areva threatened to take Siemens to court (see Illustration 9.4). Termination needs to be managed carefully, therefore. Co-evolution implies that mutual trust is likely to be valuable after the completion of any particular partnership. Partners may be engaged in several different joint projects at the same time. For example, Cisco and IBM are partners on multiple simultaneous projects in wireless communications, IT security, data centres and data storage. The partners may need to come together again for new projects in the future. Thus Nokia, Ericsson and Siemens have had mobile telephone technology joint projects since the mid-1990s. Maintaining mutual trust in the termination stage is vital if partners are to co-evolve through generations of multiple projects.

SUMMARY

- There are three broad *methods* for pursuing strategy: *mergers and acquisitions*, *strategic alliances* and *organic development*. Organic development can be either continuous or radical. Radical organic development is termed *corporate entrepreneurship*.

- Acquisitions can be *hostile* or *friendly*. Motives for mergers and acquisitions can be *strategic*, *financial* or *managerial*. The acquisition process includes *target choice*, *valuation* and *integration*.

- Strategic alliances can be *equity* or *non-equity*. Key motives for strategic alliances include *scale*, *access*, *complementarity* and *collusion*.

- The strategic alliance process relies on *co-evolution* and *trust*.

VIDEO CASE

Visit *MyStrategyLab* and watch the *Prêt-à-Manger* case study.

1 Assess the motives for McDonald's acquisition of a stake in Prêt-à-Manger (section 9.3.3) and assess the strategic and organisational fit (section 9.3.4).

2 In terms of the Haspeslagh and Jemison integration model (section 9.3.4), how *did* McDonald's approach integration and how *should* it have approached integration?

RECOMMENDED KEY READINGS

- A comprehensive book on mergers and acquisitions is: P. Gaughan, *Mergers, Acquisitions and Corporate Restructurings*, 4th edition, Wiley, 2007. For some alternative perspectives, see the collection by D. Angwin (ed.), *Mergers and Acquisitions*, Blackwell, 2007.

- A useful book on strategic alliances is J. Child, D. Faulkner and S. Tallman, *Cooperative Strategy: Managing Alliances, Networks and Joint Ventures*, Oxford University Press, 2005.

REFERENCES

1. D. Garvin and L. Levesque, 'Meeting the challenge of corporate entrepreneurship', *Harvard Business Review*, October 2006, pp. 102–12.
2. R. Schoenberg, 'Mergers and acquisitions', in D.O. Faulkner and A. Campbell (eds), *The Oxford Handbook of Strategy: Vol. II*, Oxford University Press, 2005.
3. This adapts J. Bower, 'Not all M&As are alike – and that matters', *Harvard Business Review*, March 2001, pp. 93–101.
4. M. Hayward and D. Hambrick, 'Explaining the premiums paid for large acquisitions: evidence of CEO hubris', *Administrative Science Quarterly*, vol. 42 (1997), pp. 103–27.
5. R. Schoenberg, 'Mergers and acquisitions', in D.O. Faulkner and A. Campbell (eds), *The Oxford Handbook of Strategy: Vol. II*, Oxford University Press, 2005.
6. This builds on D. Jemison and S. Sitkin, 'Corporate acquisitions: a process perspective', *Academy of Management Review*, vol. 11, no. 1 (1986), pp. 145–63.
7. J.M. Shaver, 'A paradox of synergy: contagion and capacity effects in mergers and acquisitions', *Academy of Management Review*, vol. 31, no. 4 (2006), pp. 962–78.
8. See J. Child, D. Faulkner and R. Pitkethly, *The Management of International Acquisitions*, Oxford University Press, 2001.
9. A useful discussion of valuation methods in acquisitions is in Chapter 9 of D. Sadlter, D. Smith and A. Campbell, *Smarter Acquisitions*, Prentice Hall, 2008.
10. N. Varaiya and K. Ferris, 'Overpaying in corporate takeovers: the winner's curse', *Financial Analysts Journal*, vol. 43, no. 3 (1987), pp. 64–70.
11. P. Haspeslagh and D. Jemison, *Managing Acquisitions: Creating Value through Corporate Renewal*, Free Press, 1991.
12. G. Stahl and A. Voigt, 'Do cultural differences matter in mergers and acquisitions? A tentative model and examination', *Organization Science*, vol. 19, no. 1 (2008), pp. 160–78.
13. Andersen Consulting, *Dispelling the Myths of Strategic Alliances*, 1999.
14. R. Bresser, 'Matching collective and competitive strategies', *Strategic Management Journal*, vol. 9, no. 4 (1988), pp. 375–85.
15. A. Inkpen and S. Curral, 'The coevolution of trust, control, and learning in joint ventures', *Organization Science*, vol. 15, no. 5 (2004), pp. 586–99.
16. A. Arino and J. de la Torre, 'Relational quality: managing trust in corporate alliances', *California Management Review*, vol. 44, no. 1 (2001), pp. 109–31.
17. G. Hamel, *Alliance Advantage: the Art of Creating Value through Partnering*, Harvard Business School Press, 1998.

Final Fantasy captures Lara Croft: acquisitions and alliances in electronic games

During 2009, Japanese games maker Square Enix launched a series of radical strategic initiatives. Famous for its role-playing games such as the *Final Fantasy* series, Square Enix established strategic alliances with the strategy games developers Double Helix and Gas Powered Games in the United States and Wargaming. net in the United Kingdom. Most radically, it also acquired the British Eidos Group, famous for the Lara Croft games. Square Enix President Yōichi Wada commented: 'Our goal is to become one of the top ten players in the world's media and entertainment industry. Since the games market is global, both our contact with our customers and our game development must become global too.'

Source: iStockphoto.

The Japanese games industry

Square Enix's strategic moves came at a challenging time for the Japanese games industry. The Japanese had enjoyed two decades of domination built on the worldwide success of Japanese consoles such as the Sony PlayStation. But the growing success of Microsoft's Xbox gave an opportunity to American games developers to return to the console market. Indeed, American games developers found that their development skills were more transferable in the new cross-over markets, where games needed to be developed for PCs, consoles and mobile phones alike. Moreover, the Americans had the advantage of proximity to Hollywood, bringing in new creative talent and offering opportunities for film tie-ins. At the same time, Japan's ageing population was shrinking the market for traditional electronic games.

Square Enix's Yōichi Wada recognised the predicament of the Japanese industry vis-à-vis the Americans:

In the last five to ten years, the Japanese games industry has become a closed environment, with no new people coming in, no new ideas, almost xenophobic . . . The lag with the US is very clear. The US games industry was not good in the past but it has now attracted people from the computer

industry and from Hollywood, which has led to strong growth.[1]

At the same time, the basic economics of the games industry are changing, with rising costs due to growing technological sophistication. A typical modern game can cost from $3m (about £2m) to over $20m to develop.[2] Games generally take from one to three years to develop. Yet only one in twenty games is estimated ever to make a profit. In other words, the risks are very high and the necessary scale to compete is rising.

Square Enix's strategy

Square Enix itself is the creation of a merger. Square had been founded in 1983, and in 1987 launched the first of its famous *Final Fantasy* role-playing game series. Enix had been founded in 1975, and launched its role-playing *Dragon Quest* series in 1986. The two companies merged in 2003, after the financial failure of Square's film-venture, *Final Fantasy: the Spirit Within*. Yōichi Wada, President of Square, became the president of the new merged company.

Square Enix's strategy is based on the idea of 'polymorphic content'. Its various franchises (*Final Fantasy*, *Dragon Quest* and so on) are developed for all possible hardware or media rather than any single gaming platform. Square Enix games can be played on consoles, PCs, mobile phones or online, and spin-offs include TV series, films, comics and novels. In 2005, Square Enix bought the Japanese arcade-game company Taito Corporation, famous for its *Space Invaders* game. *Space Invaders* versions have appeared on PlayStation, Xbox and Wii consoles, as well as PCs.

By 2008, Yōichi Wada was presiding over a company that was increasingly diversified, with sales of ¥136bn (about €1 bn) and just over 3,000 employees. However, it was still overwhelmingly Japanese (85 per cent of sales at home) and lacked scale by comparison with competitors such as Electronic Arts and Activision, respectively four and three times as large. On the plus side, Square Enix was reportedly cash rich, with a 'war-chest' available for acquisitions of about ¥40bn (about €300m).[3] During the summer of 2008, Square Enix made a friendly bid for the Japanese game developer Tecmo, whose fighting games *Ninja Garden* and *Dead or Alive* were popular in North America and Europe. Tecmo rejected the bid. Wada began to look overseas.

Lara Croft falls

Eidos is a British games company best-known for the action-adventure games series, *Tomb Raider*, starring the extraordinary Lara Croft. However, during 2008, disappointing sales for *Tomb Raider: Underworld* drove its share-price down from £5 (~€5.5; ~$7.5) to around 30 pence. Eidos' founder and chief executive, Jane Cavanagh, was forced to resign. The company declared losses of £136m (about €149m), on sales of £119m (down from £179m two years earlier). In April 2009, Square Enix bought the company for £84m (about €92.4m), a premium of 129 per cent over Eidos' current market value. Given the declining success of the *Tomb Raider* franchise, many speculated that Square Enix had over-paid for its first overseas acquisition.

The acquisition of Eidos did offer Square Enix global reach, however. About one-third of Eidos' sales were in the United States and 40 per cent in Europe, excluding the United Kingdom. Eidos also brought Square Enix its first studios outside Japan, with studios in the United Kingdom, Denmark, Hungary, the United States, Canada and China. Yōichi Wada commented: 'It is significant that we have opened a window for creative talents worldwide.'

Wada chose to keep Phil Rogers, the new Eidos chief executive, in place, along with the rest of his management team. Wada described a new Group structure, in which Square Enix, the arcade business Taito and Eidos would each be stand-alone divisions: 'Our aim is to implement a hybrid management structure which avoids the extremes of being either too global or too local.'[4] He continued: 'The Group's management and administration departments will be integrated, while our product and service delivery will be established locally in each territory to maximise our business opportunities through better understanding of local customers' tastes and commercial practices.' Wada also recognised the new strength that Eidos brought in action-adventure games, by contrast with Square Enix's traditional core of role-playing games. He declared his commitment both to sharing technologies across the businesses and to sustaining particular strengths: 'While promoting shared technology and expertise amongst our studios, we will also develop products which reflect the unique identity of each studio, regardless of locality.' Wada also commented on the nature of the skilled games developers he was acquiring: 'It is always difficult to manage creatives anywhere in the world. We want to cherish the Eidos studio culture but change it where it is necessary.'[5]

One thing that Square Enix was quick to do was to end the Eidos distribution agreement with Warner Bros for its products in the United States. Square Enix regarded itself as strong enough to do that itself.

Strategic alliances

At the same time as acquiring Eidos, Square Enix cemented three significant strategic alliances. In the United Kingdom, Square Enix tied up with the strategy game developer Wargaming.net (famous for the *Massive Assault* series) in order to produce the World War II game *Order of War*. This would enter the market at the end of 2009 as Square Enix's first global product release. In the United States, Square Enix formed partnerships with Gas Powered Games (producer of the *Supreme Commander* strategy game) and with Double Helix (producer of the *Front Mission* strategy series). Together with the Eidos acquisition, these partnerships significantly extended Square Enix's range beyond its traditional core in role-playing games. They also extended the company's geographical reach. Yōichi Wada commented:

> 'We see great opportunities in North American and European markets, both of which are expected to be maintaining sustainable growth over these coming years. Therefore it is crucial that we create alliances with proven developers such as Gas Powered Games in order to serve these significant markets better by providing products and services in tune with customer tastes.'[6]

All three of these new partners were relatively small (around 100 employees each), privately owned and had their origins as start-ups during the 1990s. To take one example, Gas Powered Games had been founded in 1998 by Chris Taylor and colleagues from the games developer Cavedog Entertainment. Chris Taylor had spent his whole career in games, with his first game *Hardball II* released in 1989. In an interview, Chris Taylor explained his motivation for setting up his own company, Gas Powered Games:

> 'I had that dream really from the day I first walked into my first full time job as a games programmer. I wanted to be the guy running the company. . . . We've created our own original IPs (intellectual properties) consistently. Some are great, some are not so great, but the fact is you have to keep throwing darts at the board. You have to keep trying to make great stuff, and you can't do that if you're inside of a large megalithic corporation to the same degree'.[7]

Chris Taylor described how Square Enix, traditionally a role-playing company, and Gas Powered Games, more a strategy game developer, were working together on their first venture, *Supreme Commander 2*:

> 'One of the things that we took as a cue from Square Enix was the way they embrace character and story. We were all into that, so that was easy. When we asked them, "How should we develop our game to work with their philosophy?", they said, "Don't do that because we want you to do what you do. You make games for the Western market, and we're interested in making games for the Western market." So if we changed, we would be missing the point. Which was terrific, because that meant we could do what we loved to do, make great RTS (real-time strategy) games . . . and if we tried to change them in any way, we'd be moving away from the goal.'[8]

A games enthusiast's view

In the space of a few months, Square Enix had transformed its profile. From its base in Japanese-style role-playing games, it was developing a significant presence in strategy and action adventure. It had studios across the world. Its various games titles were big across Asia, Europe and America. Games enthusiast Randy commented on a gamers' website:

> Square Enix publishing a western-developed game? Is the far-reaching JRPG (Japanese role-playing game) developer dumping the androgynous boy-heroes and shovel-wide swords for WWII fatigues and M1 Carbines? No, not entirely. But they *are* bringing Wargaming.net into the fold to do it for them. First, Square Enix buys out the house that Lara Croft built, and now they're into real-time strategy war games. *Nothing in this life makes sense anymore.*[9]

References:
1. M. Palmer, 'Square Enix views Eidos as a jump to next level', *Financial Times*, 28 April 2009.
2. 'Cost of making games set to soar', www.bbcnews.co.uk, 17 November 2005.
3. 'Square Enix needs to show growth scenario to market', *Nikkei*, 9 October 2007.
4. Joint interview with Yoichi Wada and Phil Rogers, www.square-enix.com, 26 May 2009.
5. M. Palmer, 'Square Enix views Eidos as a jump to next level', *Financial Times*, 28 April 2009.
6. 'Square Enix and Gas Powered Games announce strategic partnership', *Newswire Association*, 12 November 2008.
7. P. Elliott, 'Foot on the gas', gamesindustry.biz, 19 August 2008.
8. X. de Matos, 'Interview: Chris Taylor on Supreme Commander 2', joystiq.com, 9 June 2009.
9. Randy, 'Square Enix tries hand at WWII RTS with Order of War', *Gaming Nexus*, 17 April 2009. Italics in original.

Questions

1 Explain why Square Enix chose alliances in some cases and acquisitions in others.

2 How should Square Enix manage its Eidos acquisition in order to maximise value creation, and how might that management approach change over time?

3 What are the strengths and weaknesses of the alliance strategy, and what problems might Square Enix anticipate over time?

10

STRATEGY IN ACTION

Learning outcomes

After reading this chapter you should be able to:

- Analyse main *structural types* of organisations in terms of their strengths and weaknesses.

- Recognise key issues in designing organisational *control systems* (such as planning, performance targeting and cultural systems).

- Recognise how the three strands of strategy, structure and systems should reinforce each other as *organisational configurations*.

- Identify different types of *strategic change programmes*.

- Assess the value of different *leadership styles* in managing strategic change.

PEARSON mystrategylab

MyStrategyLab is designed to help you make the most of your studies. Visit **www.mystrategylab.com** to discover a wide range of resources specific to this chapter, including:

- A personalised **Study plan** that will help you understand core concepts.
- **Audio** and **video clips** that put the spotlight on strategy in the real world.
- **Online glossaries** and **flashcards** that provide helpful reminders when you're looking for some quick revision.

See p. xiv for further details.

(10.1) INTRODUCTION

Chapter 1 explained that strategic management can be thought of as having three main elements: understanding *the strategic position* of an organisation, making *strategic choices* for the future and managing *strategy in action*. As this book is about the fundamentals of strategy, it mainly concentrates on the first two elements, position and choice. But even the most shrewdly chosen strategy is valueless unless it can be turned into action and that is the theme of this chapter. Moreover in deciding what strategy an organisation might follow, managers need to think through whether it is feasible (see the Appendix) and therefore take account of the issues raised here.

This chapter focuses on three issues fundamental to achieving strategy in action (see Figure 10.1):

- The types of *organisational structure* that suit the strategies of the organisation. For example, whether people should be managed in business functions (finance, human resources, etc.) or in product or market divisions (such as geographical regions).

- The *organisational systems* needed to deliver the chosen strategy within any structure. For example, planning processes, performance targets and cultural systems.

- *Leading strategic change*, in particular the characteristics of different programmes of strategic change and the styles of leadership employed in these.

Figure 10.1 Strategy in action

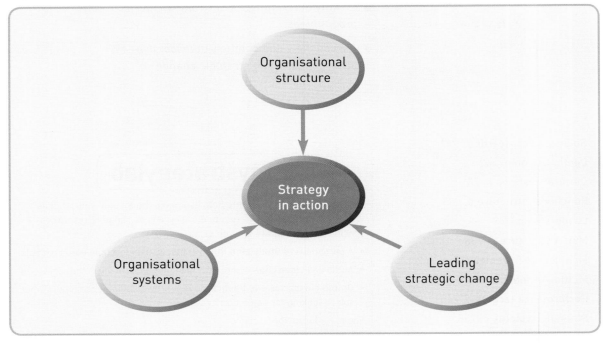

(10.2) STRUCTURAL TYPES

Managers often describe their organisation by drawing an organisation chart, mapping out its formal structure. These charts are important to managers because they identify the 'levels' and roles in an organisation and who is responsible for what. Also because structural reporting lines shape patterns of communication and knowledge exchange: in many organisations people tend not to talk much to people much higher or lower in the hierarchy, or in different parts of the organisation. Structures can therefore be hotly debated (see Illustration 10.1).

This section reviews three basic structural types: functional, multidivisional and matrix.[1] Broadly, the first two of these tend to emphasise one structural dimension over another, either functional specialisms or business units. The matrix structure mixes structural dimensions more evenly, for instance trying to give product and geographical units equal weight. The most appropriate structure depends on the characteristics (sometimes called 'contingencies') of an organisation including organisational size, extent of diversification and type of technology.[2]

10.2.1 The functional structure

Even a small entrepreneurial start-up, once it involves more than one person, needs to divide up responsibilities between different people. The **functional structure** divides responsibilities **according to the organisation's primary specialist roles such as production, research and sales**. Figure 10.2 represents a typical organisation chart for such a functional organisation. This kind of structure is particularly relevant to small or start-up organisations, or larger organisations that have retained narrow, rather than diverse, product ranges. Functional

Figure 10.2 A functional structure

ILLUSTRATION 10.1

Volkswagen: a case of disputed centralisation

A new chief executive introduces a more centralised structure over this multi-brand giant.

Figure 1 Volkswagen, November 2006 (simplified)

VW
Skoda
Bentley
Bugatti

Audi
SEAT
Lamborghini

Figure 2 Volkswagen, January 2007 (simplified)

VW
Skoda
SEAT

Audi
Bentley
Bugatti
Lamborghini

In 2007, following the Porsche car company's building up of a controlling stake and the installation of a new chief executive, German car manufacturer Volkswagen announced a major reorganisation. For the previous few years, Volkswagen had been organised as two groups of brands under the main Volkswagen and Audi labels (see Fig. 1), with technical and marketing expertise clustered around particular brands within these. Now the company was to be reorganised into two main groups, a mass-market group (VW, Skoda, SEAT) and a more luxury market group (Audi, Bentley, Bugatti and Lamborghini). Volkswagen also had a large stake in truck company Scania. The company would be more centralised, with new corporate responsibilities for production, sales, distribution and R&D (see Fig. 2). The new CEO, Martin Winterkorn, would also act as head of R&D and be directly responsible for the VW group of brands.

The stated aim of this more centralised structure was to increase synergies between the various brands. More centralised R&D would help ensure the sharing of engines and components, and centralisation of production would assist the optimisation of factory usage across the company. The departing head of the Volkswagen group took another view. He asserted that, in order to ensure cross-functional integration and motivation, expertise needed to identify closely with particular brands. According to him, the new structure mimicked the centralised Porsche structure, but Porsche was a much smaller company with just one main brand. Porsche's spokespersons responded by recalling that Porsche was the most profitable car company in the world, while Volkswagen was one of the least.

Questions

1 Which type of structure did the old decentralised structure resemble most and which type of structure is Volkswagen moving closer to?

2 What pros and cons can you see in the new Volkswagen structure?

structures may also be used within a multidivisional structure (see below), where the divisions themselves may split themselves up according to functional departments.

Figure 10.2 also summarises the potential advantages and disadvantages of a functional structure. There are advantages in that it gives senior managers direct hands-on involvement in operations and allows greater operational control from the top. It also provides a clear definition of roles and tasks, increasing accountability. Functional departments also provide concentrations of expertise, thus fostering knowledge development in areas of functional specialism.

However, there are disadvantages, particularly as organisations become larger or more diverse. Perhaps the major concern in a fast-moving world is that senior managers focus too much on their functional responsibilities, becoming overburdened with routine operations and too concerned with narrow functional interests. As a result, they find it hard either to take a strategic view of the organisation as a whole or to coordinate separate functions quickly. Thus functional organisations can be inflexible and poor at adapting to change. Separate functional departments tend also to be inward-looking – so-called 'functional silos' – making it difficult to integrate the knowledge of different functional specialists. Finally, because they are centralised around particular functions, functional structures are not good at coping with product or geographical diversity. For example, a central marketing department may try to impose a uniform approach to advertising regardless of the diverse needs of the organisation's various business units around the world.

10.2.2 The multidivisional structure

A **multidivisional structure is built up of separate divisions on the basis of products, services or geographical areas** (see Figure 10.3). Divisionalisation often comes about as an attempt to overcome the problems that functional structures have in dealing with the diversity mentioned above.[3] Each division can respond to the specific requirements of its product/market strategy, using its own set of functional departments. A similar situation exists in many public services, where the organisation is structured around *service departments* such as recreation, social services and education.

There are several potential advantages to divisional structures. As self-standing business units, it is possible to control divisions from a distance by monitoring business performance. Having divisions also provides flexibility because organisations can add, close or merge divisions as circumstances change. Divisional managers have greater personal ownership for their own divisional strategies. Geographical divisions – for example, a European division or a North American division – offer a means of managing internationally. There can be benefits of specialisation within a division, allowing competences to develop with a clearer focus on a particular product group, technology or customer group. Management responsibility for a whole divisional business is good training in taking a strategic view for managers expecting to go on to a main board position.

Divisional structures can, however, also have disadvantages of three main types. First, divisions can become so self-sufficient that they are *de facto* independent businesses, but duplicating the functions and costs of the corporate centre of the company. In such cases, it

Figure 10.3 A multidivisional structure

Head office

Central services
(e.g. finance)

Division A   Division B   Division C   Division D   Division E

Functions   Functions   Functions   Functions   Functions

Advantages
- Flexible (add or divest divisions)
- Control by performance
- Ownership of strategy
- Specialisation of competences
- Training in strategic view

Disadvantages
- Duplication of central and divisional functions
- Fragmentation and non-cooperation
- Danger of loss of central control

may make more sense to split the company into independent businesses and de-mergers of this type have become common. Second, divisionalisation tends to get in the way of cooperation and knowledge-sharing between business units. Expertise is fragmented and divisional performance targets provide poor incentives to collaborate with other divisions. Finally, divisions may become too autonomous, especially where joint ventures and partnership dilute ownership. Here, divisions pursue their own strategies almost regardless of the needs of the corporate parent. In these cases, multidivisionals become *holding companies*, where the corporate centre effectively 'holds' the various businesses in a largely financial sense, exercising little control and adding little value. Figure 10.3 summarises these potential advantages and disadvantages of a multidivisional structure.

10.2.3 The matrix structure

A **matrix structure combines different structural dimensions simultaneously, for example product divisions and geographical territories or product divisions and functional specialisms.**[4] In matrix structures, middle managers typically report to two or three senior managers each.

Matrix structures have several advantages. They promote *knowledge-sharing* because they allow separate areas of knowledge to be integrated across organisational boundaries. Particularly in professional service organisations, matrix organisation can be helpful in

Figure 10.4 Two examples of matrix structures

	Head of languages	Head of science	Head of social studies	etc.
Head of lower school				
Head of upper school				
Head of sixth form				

Head teacher
Subject leadership

Pupil groups

Advantages
- Integrate knowledge
- Flexible
- Allow dual dimensions

Disadvantages
- Length of time to take decisions
- Unclear job and task responsibilities
- Unclear cost and profit responsibilities
- High degrees of conflict

applying particular knowledge specialisms to different market or geographical segments. For example, to serve a particular client, a consulting firm may draw on people from groups with particular knowledge specialisms (e.g. strategy or organisation design) and others grouped according to particular markets (industry sectors or geographical regions). Figure 10.4 shows how a school might combine the separate knowledge of subject specialists to create programmes of study tailored differently to various age groups. Matrix organisations are *flexible*, because they allow different dimensions of the organisation to be mixed together. They are particularly attractive to organisations operating globally, because of the possible mix between local and global dimensions. For example, a global company may prefer geographically defined divisions as the operating units for local marketing (because of their specialist local knowledge of customers). But at the same time it may still want global product units responsible for the world-wide coordination of product development and manufacturing, taking advantage of economies of scale and specialisation.

However, because a matrix structure replaces single lines of authority with multiple cross-matrix relationships, this often brings problems. In particular, it will typically take *longer to reach decisions* because of bargaining between the managers of different dimensions. There may also be *conflict* because staff find themselves responsible to managers from two structural dimensions. In short, matrix organisations are hard to control.

As with any structure, but particularly with the matrix structure, the critical issue in practice is the way it actually works (i.e. behaviours and relationships). The key ingredient in a successful matrix structure can be senior managers good at sustaining collaborative relationships (across the matrix) and coping with the messiness and ambiguity which that can bring.

(10.3) ORGANISATIONAL SYSTEMS

Structure is a key ingredient of organising for success. But structures can only work if they are supported by formal and informal organisational systems. If structures are like the bones in a body, systems are the muscles that control how things move. Illustration 10.2 on the changing structures and systems of the World Health Organization demonstrates the linkages between structures and systems.

10.3.1 Planning systems

All organisations, but especially large organisations, are faced with the challenge of deciding how to support a strategy with appropriate resources; for example, in terms of funding and people and their skills. **Planning systems plan and control the allocation of resources and monitor their utilisation.** An important context in which this occurs is in the oversight exercised by the corporate centre of an organisation, with regard to, for example, its different divisions.

- Michael Goold and Andrew Campbell's[5] typology of three *strategy styles* shows the different ways in which a corporate centre may seek to allocate resources and monitor their utilisation and their advantages and disadvantages. The *strategic planning* style is the archetypal planning system, hence its name. In the Goold and Campbell sense, the strategic planning style combines both a strong planning influence on strategic direction from the corporate centre with relatively relaxed performance accountability for the business units. The logic is that if the centre sets the strategic direction, business unit managers should not be held strictly accountable for disappointing results that might be due to an inappropriate plan in the first place. In the strategic planning style, the centre focuses on inputs in terms of allocating resources necessary to achieve the strategic plan, while exercising a high degree of direct control over how the plan is executed by the businesses. The strategic planning style (not the practice of strategic planning in general) has become less common in the private sector in recent years. The style is seen as too rigid to adapt to changing circumstances and too top-down to reflect real business circumstances on the ground.

- The *financial control* style involves very little central planning. The business units each set their own strategic plans, probably after some negotiation with the corporate centre, and are then held strictly accountable for the results against these plans. This style differs from the strategic planning style in that control is against financial outputs, similar to a performance targeting system. If the businesses devised the plans, then they should take full responsibility for success or failure. Business unit managers in the financial control style have a lot of autonomy and typically receive high bonus payments for success. But failure may easily lead to dismissal.

- The *strategic control* style is in the middle, with a more consensual development of the strategic plan between the corporate centre and the business units and moderate levels of business unit accountability. Under the strategic control style, the centre will typically act as coach to its business unit managers, helping them to see and seize opportunities in a supportive manner. This style often relies on strong cultural systems to foster trust and mutual

ILLUSTRATION 10.2

The World Health Organization's structure comes under pressure

New strategic challenges are shifting the organisation towards centralisation.

2009 was a testing year for the World Health Organization (WHO). The swine flu virus (H1N1), orginating in Mexico in April, swept quickly around the world. In June, the WHO Director-General Dr Margaret Chan declared: 'The world is moving into the early days of its first influenza pandemic of the 21st Century.' It looked like the worst pandemic since the 1968 Hong Kong flu killed an estimated 1 million people worldwide. Hundreds of millions of people rushed to be vaccinated.

As the coordinator of health policy for the United Nations, the WHO has a staff of 8000 health and other experts. About 1800 work at headquarters in Geneva. The remainder are spread around six regional offices (Africa, Europe, South-East Asia, Americas, East Mediterranean and West Pacific) and 147 country offices. WHO projects range from children's medicine, through leprosy eradication to dealing with HIV/AIDS.

Traditionally, the WHO has been decentralised. Regional offices, typically with around 100 professional staff plus support staff, would lead in dealing with the characteristic health problems of their region. They also managed administrative, personnnel, medical supply and field security services within their regions. However, criticisms of inefficiency from member states and the apparent rising threat of pandemics (worldwide disease outbreaks) were creating pressures for change. While there had been famous pandemics in history (for example, the Black Death), since the Hong Kong flu of 1968 there had been the emergence of HIV/AIDs in the 1980s, the SARS scare of 2003, the Avian flu scare of 2004–07 and then the H1N1 crisis of 2009.

Dr Margaret Chan had been director of health in Hong Kong since the 1990s, dealing with SARS and early outbreaks of Avian flu. In 2004, she had become an Assistant Director-General of the WHO. One of her first acts on arriving in Geneva was to set up a Strategic Health Operations Centre, a nerve centre for monitoring disease outbreaks across the world. In 2006, Chan became Director-General of the whole of WHO. She launched a further set of managerial reforms.

Principal among these reforms was the creation in 2008 of a global service centre, based in Kuala-Lumpur. This global service centre provides administrative services and support to all staff in WHO offices worldwide in respect of human resources, payroll, procurement and accounts payable. Most of the previous posts carrying out these functions were in Geneva, the regional offices and country offices were suppressed. A second important reform was the creation of a global management system, launched in 2009. This is based on an Enterprise Resource Management system produced by the American company Oracle, and brings together all existing WHO systems in the areas of finance, human resources, travel, programme planning and procurement.

By December, 2009, the H1N1 pandemic had claimed 10,000 lives across 208 countries. This was less than feared, and some accused the WHO of exaggerating the original threat. Margaret Chan told the *Canadian Press* in an interview:

'I can understand all these suspicions and conspiracy thinking, but I must emphasise that there is no basis for that. . . . All the measures that I put in place in Hong Kong in 1997 (an early outbreak of avian flu) became the gold standard. The aggressive approach by WHO . . . to put SARS back in the box is paying dividends. . . . I think we must remain prudent and observe the evolution of the (H1N1) pandemic in the course of the next 6–12 months before crying victory.'

Sources: www.who.int; *The Canadian Press*, 28 December, 2009; 'A World Health Organization Primer' (www.medscape.com).

Questions

1 How is the strategy of the WHO changing and with what consequences for its structure and systems?

2 What barriers and threats can be envisaged to the direction of the WHO's structural and strategic reforms?

understanding. Thus *the three strategy* styles vary with regard to their reliance on, and application of, planning systems. The direct control of inputs characteristic of the strategic planning style is only appropriate in certain circumstances. In particular, it makes sense where there are large, risky and long-range investments to be allocated: for example, an oil company typically has to take the decision to invest in the ten-year development of an oilfield at the corporate centre, rather than risk delegating it to business units whose resources and time-horizons may be limited. On the other hand, the financial control style is suitable where investments are small, relatively frequent and well understood, as typically in a mature, non-capital-intensive business. The strategic control style is suitable where there are opportunities for collaborating across businesses and there is a need to nurture new ones.

10.3.2 Performance targeting systems

Performance targets focus on the *outputs* of an organisation (or part of an organisation), **such as product quality, revenues or profits.** These targets are often known as key performance indicators (KPIs). The performance of an organisation is judged, either internally or externally, on its ability to meet these targets. However, within specified boundaries, the organisation remains free on how targets should be achieved. This approach can be particularly appropriate in certain situations:

- *Within large businesses* corporate centres may choose performance targets to control their business units without getting involved in the details of how they achieve them. These targets are often cascaded down the organisation as specific targets for sub-units, functions and even individuals.

- In *regulated markets* such as privatised utilities, government-appointed regulators increasingly exercise control through agreed *performance indicators* (PIs), such as service or quality levels, as a means of ensuring 'competitive' performance.

- In *the public services*, where control of resource inputs was the dominant approach historically, governments are attempting to move control processes towards outputs (such as quality of service) and, more importantly, towards outcomes (for example, patient mortality rates in health care).

There are at least three potential problems with targets:[6]

- *Inappropriate measures* of performance are quite common. For example, managers often prefer indicators that are easily measured or choose measures based on inadequate understanding of real needs on the ground. The result is a focus on the required measures rather than the factors that might be essential to long-term success. In the private sector, focus on short-term profit measures is common, at the expense of investment in the long-run prosperity of the business.

- *Inappropriate target levels* are a common problem. Managers are liable to give their superiors pessimistic forecasts so that targets are set at undemanding levels, which can then be easily met. On the other hand, superiors may over-compensate for their managers' pessimism, and end up setting excessively demanding targets. Unrealistically ambitious targets can either demotivate employees who see no hope of achieving them regardless of their effort, or encourage risky or dishonest behaviours in order to achieve the otherwise impossible.

● *Excessive internal competition* can be a result of targets focused on individual or sub-unit performance. Although an organisation by definition should be more than the sum of its parts, if individuals or sub-units are being rewarded on their performance in isolation, they will have little incentive to collaborate with the other parts of the organisation. The struggle to meet individualistic targets will reduce the exchange of information and the sharing of resources.

These acknowledged difficulties with targets have led to the development of techniques designed to encourage a more balanced approach to target-setting. The most fundamental has been the development of the balanced scorecard approach.[7] **Balanced scorecards set performance targets according to a range of perspectives, not only financial**. Thus balanced scorecards typically combine four specific perspectives: the *financial perspective*, which might include profit margins or cash flow; the *customer perspective*, which sets targets important to customers, such as delivery times or service levels; the *internal perspective*, with targets relating to operational effectiveness such as the development of IT systems or reductions in waste levels; and finally the future-oriented *innovation and learning perspective*, which targets activities that will be important to the long-run performance of the organisation, for example investment in training or research. Attending to targets relevant to all four perspectives seeks to ensure that managers do not focus on one set of targets (e.g. financial) at the expense of others, while also keeping an eye to the future through innovation and learning.

KEY CONCEPT
www.mystrategylab.com

Balanced scorecards

10.3.3 Cultural systems

Organisations typically have distinctive cultures which express basic assumptions and beliefs held by organisation members and define taken-for-granted ways of doing things (see Chapter 4). Despite their taken-for-granted nature, organisational cultures can seem a tempting means of managerial control. Managers may therefore try to influence organisational culture through various deliberate mechanisms in order to achieve the kinds of employee behaviour required by their strategy. **Such cultural systems aim to standardise norms of behaviour within an organisation in line with particular objectives**. Cultural systems exercise an *indirect* form of control, because of not requiring direct supervision: it becomes a matter of willing conformity or *self*-control by employees. Control is exerted on the *input* of employees, as the culture defines the norms of appropriate effort and initiative that employees will put into their jobs.

Three key cultural systems are:

● *Recruitment*. Here cultural conformity may be attempted by the selection of appropriate staff in the first place. Employers look to find people who will 'fit'. Thus some employers may favour recruiting people who have already shown themselves to be 'team-players' through sport or other activities.

● *Socialisation*. Here employee behaviours are shaped by social processes once they are at work. It often starts with the integration of new staff through training, induction and mentoring programmes. It typically continues with further training throughout a career. Symbols can also play a role in socialisation, for example the symbolic example of leaders' behaviours or the influence of office décor, dress codes or language.

- *Reward.* Appropriate behaviour can be encouraged through pay, promotion or symbolic processes (for example, public praise). The desire to achieve the same rewards as successful people in the organisation will typically encourage imitative behaviour.

As section 4.6 explained, it is important to recognise that organisations' cultures are not fully under formal management control. Sometimes aspects of organisational culture may persistently contradict managerial intentions, as with peer-group pressure not to respond to organisational strategies. On the other hand, some cultures can bring about desired results, even without deliberate management intervention. For example, workers may form informal 'communities of practice', in which expert practitioners inside or even outside the organisation share their knowledge to generate innovative solutions to problems on their own initiative.[8] Examples of these informal communities of practice range from the Xerox photocopying engineers who would exchange information about problems and solutions over breakfast gatherings at the start of the day, to the programmer networks which support the development of Linux 'freeware' internationally over the internet.

ORGANISATIONAL CONFIGURATION: THE MCKINSEY 7-S FRAMEWORK

It is important that there is compatibility between the structures and systems of organisations. One way of thinking about this is in terms of the concept of organisational configuration. A **configuration** is **the set of organisational design elements that interlink in order to support the intended strategy**. A well known means of considering this is **the McKinsey 7-S framework which highlights the importance of fit between strategy, structure, systems, staff, style, skills and superordinate goals**.[9] Together these seven elements can serve as a checklist in an organisational design exercise: see Figure 10.5.

The rest of the book has been concerned with strategy and this chapter has already addressed structure and systems. This section will comment on the remaining four elements of the 7-S framework, as follows:

- *Style* here refers to the leadership style of top managers in an organisation, which are discussed in section 10.5.3. The important point to emphasise is that leadership style should fit other aspects of the 7-S framework: for example, a highly directive or coercive style is not likely to fit a matrix organisation structure.

- *Staff* is about the kinds of people in the organisation and how they are developed. This relates to systems of recruitment, socialisation and reward (see section 10.3.3). A key criterion for the feasibility of any strategy is: does the organisation have the people to match? A common constraint on structural change is the availability of the right people to head new departments and divisions.

Figure 10.5 The McKinsey 7 Ss

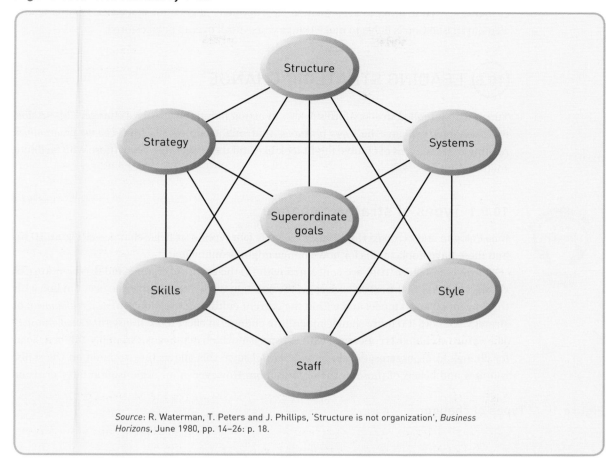

Source: R. Waterman, T. Peters and J. Phillips, 'Structure is not organization', *Business Horizons*, June 1980, pp. 14–26: p. 18.

- *Skills* relates to staff, but in the 7-S framework refers more broadly to capabilities in general (see Chapter 3). The concept of capabilities here raises not only staff skills but also issues to do with how these skills are embedded in and captured by the organisation as a whole. For example, how do the organisation's training schemes, information technology and reward systems transform the talents of individuals into the organisational capabilities required by the strategy?

- *Superordinate goals* refers to the overarching goals or purpose of the organisation as a whole, in other words the mission, vision and objectives that form the organisational purpose (see Chapter 4). Superordinate goals are placed at the centre of the 7-S framework: all other elements should support these.

The McKinsey 7-S framework highlights at least three aspects of organising. First, organising involves a lot more than just getting the organisational structure right; there are many other elements to attend to. Second, the 7-S framework emphasises fit between all these elements: everything from structure to skills needs to be connected together. Third, if managers change one element of the 7-S, the concept of fit suggests they are likely to have to change all the other elements as well in order to keep them all appropriately aligned to each other. Changing one element in isolation is liable to make things worse until overall fit is restored.

(10.5) LEADING STRATEGIC CHANGE

Turning an intended strategy into strategy in action invariably involves change. This section of the chapter explains the *types of change* that might be needed, what *change programmes* relating to these types of change might look like and the *leadership roles* of those who facilitate such change.

KEY CONCEPT

Types of strategic change

10.5.1 Types of strategic change

Julia Balogun and Veronica Hope Hailey[10] identify four types of strategic change (see Figure 10.6), and these have implications for how change might be managed.

The axes in Figure 10.6 are concerned with (a) the extent of change and (b) the nature of change. In terms of the *extent* of change, the question is whether change can occur in line with the current business model and within the current culture (see section 4.6) as a *realignment* of strategy? Or does it require significant culture change; in effect more *transformational* change? The nature of change is concerned with the speed at which it happens. Arguably, it is beneficial for change in an organisation to be *incremental* since this allows time to build on the skills, routines and beliefs of those in the organisation. However, if an organisation faces crisis or

Figure 10.6 Types of change

Source: Adapted from J. Balogun and V. Hope Hailey, *Exploring Strategic Change*, 3rd edition, Prentice Hall, 2007.

needs to change direction fast a '*big bang*' approach to change might be needed on occasion. Combining these two axes suggests four types of strategic change:

1 *Adaptation* is change that can be accommodated within the current culture and occur incrementally. It is the most common form of change in organisations.

2 *Reconstruction* is change that may be rapid and involve a good deal of upheaval in an organisation, but which does not fundamentally change the culture. It could be a *turnaround* situation where there is need for major structural changes or a major cost-cutting programme to deal with a decline in financial performance or difficult or changing market conditions.

3 *Revolution* is change that requires rapid and major strategic as well as culture change. This could be in circumstances where the strategy has been so bounded by the existing culture that, even when environmental or competitive pressures might require fundamental change, the organisation has failed to respond. This might have occurred over many years and resulted in circumstances where pressures for change are extreme – for example, a takeover threatens the continued existence of a firm.

4 *Evolution* is change in strategy that requires culture change, but over time. In some respects this is the most challenging type of strategic change since, for many in an organisation, there may be no pressing need for change.

Many of the tools of analysis in Chapters 2–4 can help identify the type of change required. For example, does the change require a substantial reconfiguration of the value chain (section 3.4.1), significant changes in the activities underpinning strategic capabilities (section 3.4.2) or major change to the current culture (section 4.6)? Care does, however, need to be taken in considering the significance of new strategies on required change. For example, a business may launch new products without requiring fundamental changes in the organisation's culture. On the other hand, some changes in strategy, even if they do not take the form of dramatic product changes, may require fundamental changes in culture; for example, the shift from a production focus for a manufacturer to a customer-led, service ethos.

10.5.2 Strategic change programmes

Adaptive change builds on and develops what currently exists in terms of culture and capabilities. In many respects it is therefore 'steady as you go'. However, the other three types of change may require particular and different approaches to change. This section therefore considers what may be involved in change programmes for these three types of change.

Reconstruction: turnaround strategy

There are circumstances where the emphasis has to be on rapid reconstruction, in the absence of which a business, for example, could face closure, enter terminal decline or be taken over. This is commonly referred to as a turnaround strategy, where the emphasis is on speed of change and rapid cost reduction and/or revenue generation. This may not involve significant culture change but does require the prioritisation of the things that give quick and significant improvements so typically it is a situation where a directive approach to change (see section 10.5.3 below) is required. Some of the main elements of turnaround strategies are as follows:[11]

- *Crisis stabilisation.* The aim is to regain control over the deteriorating position. This typically involves a reduction of labour and senior management costs, productivity improvement, the reduction of inventory, the tightening of financial control and the identification and elimination of non-profitable products or services. There is nothing novel about these steps: many of them are good management practice. The differences are the speed at which they are carried out and the focus of managerial attention on them. The most successful turnaround strategies focus on reducing direct operational costs and on productivity gains. Less effective approaches pay less attention to these and more to the reduction of overheads.

- *Management changes.* Changes in management may be required, especially at the top. This usually includes the introduction of a new chairman or chief executive, as well as changes to the board, especially in marketing, sales and finance, for three main reasons. First, because the old management may well be the ones that were in charge when the problems developed and be seen as the cause of them by key stakeholders. Second, because it may be necessary to bring in management with experience of turnaround management. Third, because, if new management come from outside the organisation, they may bring different approaches to the way the organisation has operated in the past.

- *Gaining stakeholder support.* Poor quality of information may have been provided to key stakeholders. In a turnaround situation it is vital that key stakeholders, perhaps the bank or key shareholder groups, and employees are kept clearly informed of the situation and improvements as they are being made.

- *Focusing on the target market(s) and core products.* Central to turnaround success is ensuring clarity on the target market or market segments most likely to generate cash and grow profits. A successful turnaround strategy involves getting closer to customers and improving the flow of marketing information, especially to senior levels of management, so as to focus revenue-generating activities on key market segments. Of course, a reason for the poor performance of the organisation could be that it had this wrong in the first place. Clarifying the target market also provides the opportunity to exploit additional revenue opportunities related to such markets and discontinue or outsource products and services that are not targeted on those markets, but consume management time for little return.

- *Financial restructuring.* The financial structure of the organisation may need to be changed. This typically involves changing the existing capital structure, raising additional finance or renegotiating agreements with creditors, especially banks.

Revolutionary strategic change

Revolutionary change differs from turnaround (or reconstruction) in two ways that make managing change especially challenging. First, the need is not only for fast change but also cultural change. Second, it may be that the need for change is not as evident to people in the organisation as in a turnaround situation; or that they see reasons to deny the need for change. For example, this situation may have come about as a result of many years of relative decline in a market, with people wedded to products or processes no longer valued by customers. Or it could be that the problems of the organisation are visible and understood by its members, but that people cannot see a way forward. Leading change in such circumstances is likely to involve:

- *Clear strategic direction.* In these circumstances the need for the articulation of a clear strategic direction and decisive action in line with that direction is critical. So this is the type of change where individual CEOs who are seen to provide such direction are often credited with making a major difference.

- *Combining rational and symbolic levers.* Very likely some of the hard decisions outlined above for turnaround will be taken: for example, portfolio changes, greater market focus, top management changes and perhaps financial restructuring. However, often these are also employed to send major symbolic messages of change. Most common here is the replacement of very senior executives or, perhaps, major changes in board structure signalling both internally and externally the significance of change at the very top. Similarly, the introduction of new managers, often at a senior level, may make sense in gaining the benefits of a fresh perspective, but also signals the significance of change. Consultants may also be used to provide a dispassionate analysis of the need for change but also to signal how meaningful the change process is.

- *Working with the existing culture.* It may be possible to work with elements of the existing culture rather than attempt wholesale culture change. This involves identifying those aspects of culture that can be built upon and developed and those that have to be changed.

- *Monitoring change.* Revolutionary change is likely to require the setting and monitoring of unambiguous targets that people have to achieve. Often these will be linked to overall financial targets and in turn to improved returns to shareholders.

Evolutionary strategic change

Managing change as evolution involves transformational change, but incrementally. It can be thought of in two ways. The first is in terms of the creation of an organisation capable of continual change. Trying to achieve this in practice is a significant challenge for management, not least because it requires:

- *Empowering the organisation.* Rather than top-down management, there is the need here for people throughout the organisation to accept the responsibility for contributing strategic ideas, for innovating, and for accepting change as inevitable and desirable. Clearly, then, there is a need for a high level of involvement in the change agenda.

- *A clear strategic vision.* It is the responsibility of top management to create the context within which new ideas can bubble up from below around a coherent view of long-term goals. This requires them to provide very clear guidelines – perhaps in the form of a clear vision and mission (see section 4.2) – around which those ideas can cohere. In so doing, they need to find the balance between the clarity of such vision that allows people to see how they can contribute to future strategy while avoiding specifying that strategy in such detail as to constrain people's enthusiasm to contribute and innovate.

- *Continual change and a commitment to experimentation* with regard to organisational processes throughout the organisation.

A second way of conceiving of strategic change as evolution is in terms of the movement from one strategy to a changed strategy, but over perhaps many years. Here, the principles that might guide managers are these:

- *Stages of transition.* Identifying interim stages in the change process can be important. For example, there may be insufficient readiness or insufficient management capability in change management to make major changes initially. It will therefore be important to establish these conditions before other major moves are taken.

- *Irreversible changes.* It may be possible to identify changes that can be made that, while not necessarily having immediate major impact, will have long-term and irreversible impacts. For example, a law firm or accountancy firm that wishes to manage an evolutionary approach to strategic change might legitimately see this as dependent on the skills and focus of its partners. Changing the criteria for appointment of partners to achieve this might therefore be crucial. The time horizons for the effects of such changes to take effect would be many years but, once made, the effects would be difficult to reverse.

- *Sustained top management commitment* will be required. The danger is that the momentum for change falters because people do not perceive consistent commitment to it from the top.

- *Winning hearts and minds.* Culture change is likely to be required in any transformational change. This may be more problematic than for revolutionary change because people may simply not recognise that there are problems with regard to the status quo. The need is for multiple levers for change to be used consistently: styles of managing change to allow people to see the need for change and contribute to what that change should be; the signalling of the meaning of change in ways that people throughout the organisation understand both rationally and emotionally; and levers that signal and achieve improved economic performance.

Illustration 10.3 shows two different types of change programme.

10.5.3 Strategic leadership: roles and styles

Leadership is the process of influencing an organisation (or group within an organisation) in its efforts towards achieving an aim or goal.[12] Without effective leadership of strategic change the risk is that people in an organisation are unclear about its purpose or lack motivation to deliver it. Strategic leadership is therefore central to strategic change. Whichever change programme is needed, there are likely to be three key roles that are especially significant in terms of leading strategic change:

- *Envisioning future strategy.*[13] The effective strategic leader needs to ensure there exists a clear and compelling vision of the future and communicate clearly a strategy to achieve that both internally and to external stakeholders. In the absence of top management doing this, those who attempt to lead change elsewhere in an organisation are likely to construct such a vision themselves. This may be well intentioned, but can lead to confusion, highlighting the importance of overall clarity on the purpose of strategic change.

ILLUSTRATION 10.3

Change programmes at IBM and Pace

Change programmes need to be tailored to context.

Values-based change at IBM

Sam Palmisano took over as CEO of IBM in 2002. His predecessor Lou Gerstner had made major changes but, as Palmisano explained: 'Then there was "a burning platform".' In 2002, there was a need for a continuation of change but 'instead of galvanising people through fear of failure, you have to galvanise them through hope and aspiration'. Palmisano believed it was impossible to do this in a company as complex as IBM by relying on structures and control systems. It had to be through values.

In July 2003 over a three-day period over 50,000 employees took part in an intranet discussion on company values: the 'ValuesJam'. Much of what was posted was highly critical. IBM talked a lot about trust but spent endless time auditing people; no one questioned the views of senior executives; mistakes were not tolerated or seen as part of learning. It was uncomfortable and some senior executives wanted to pull the plug on the exercise. But Palmisano insisted it continue and joined in, posting his personal views and acknowledging problems.

In many respects the values that emerged extended what IBM already espoused: 'dedication to every client's success', 'innovation that matters – for our company and the world', 'trust and personal responsibility in all relationships'. However, they were not being enacted, so the next step was to identify where the values were not being delivered. This was also rolled out to an online jam again, identifying examples of processes and routines contrary to the values.

Palmisano then instigated changes in control systems to bring them in line with the values. This included changes to the incentive scheme for managing directors of IBM businesses, through to providing funds to line managers to use at their discretion to generate business or develop client relationships. Price setting was also made more client-friendly, especially for products and services crossing IBM businesses, involving significant reworking of the IBM pricing routines.[1]

Turnaround at Pace

Pace manufactures products for the digital TV markets: in particular set-top boxes for customers such as BSkyB and Canal+. When Neil Gaydon took over as Chief Executive in 2006, the company was facing bankruptcy with a loss of £15m (~€16.5m; ~$22.5m) on sales of £175m and a bank facility that had just been withdrawn. By 2010 the company was reporting profits of £69.9m on revenues of over £1 billion.

Gaydon broadened the customer base. At the turn of the century 90 per cent of revenue came from just two customers. By 2010 Pace had more than 100 customers world-wide. In addition, he focused on key areas of market development; in particular on high definition television and on pay-TV operations which have a higher price level and offer better margins.

However, he also introduced a major reorganisation of the company. He significantly pruned management and organised the company into small teams focused on particular customers. Each team was given a lot of freedom, controlled its own profit and loss account and bonuses were linked to the teams' performance, incentivising everyone to get results. Pace, notorious for late deliveries and over-runs on R&D costs, significantly improved its reliability and cost control.

Reference:
1. Based on Paul Hemp, 'Leading change when business is good', *Harvard Business Review*, vol. 82, no. 12 (2004), pp. 60–70.

Questions

1 How would you characterise the types of change programme at IBM and Pace?

2 Compare the different approaches of Palmisano and Gaydon. Why were they different?

3 How do they compare to that of John Howie and Craig Lockhart at Faslane (see the case example).

- *Aligning* the organisation to deliver that strategy.[14] This involves ensuring that people in the organisation are committed to the strategy, motivated to make the changes needed and empowered to deliver those changes. There is, then, a need for leaders to build and foster relationships of trust and respect across the organisation. It may, however, also be necessary to change the management of the organisation to ensure such commitment, which is a reason that top teams often change as a precursor to or during strategic change.

- *Embodying change.* A strategic leader will be seen by others, not least those within the organisation, but also other stakeholders and outside observers, as intimately associated with a future strategy and a strategic change programme. A strategic leader is, then, symbolically highly significant in the change process and needs to be a role model for future strategy.

Roles in leading change

While there is often an emphasis on individuals at the top of an organisation, the leadership of change also involves others in and around the organisation.

Middle managers

A top-down approach to managing strategy and strategic change sees middle managers as implementers of top-management strategic plans. Here, their role is to ensure that resources are allocated and controlled appropriately and to monitor the performance and behaviour of staff. In the context of managing strategic change there are, however, three other roles they play:[15]

- *'Sense-making'* of strategy. Top management may set a strategic direction; but how it is explained and made sense of in specific contexts (e.g. a region of a multinational or a functional department) may, intentionally or not, be left to middle managers. In this sense they can play a *local leadership* role. If misinterpretation of that intended strategy is to be avoided, it is therefore vital that middle managers understand and feel an ownership of it.

- *Reinterpretation and adjustment* of strategic responses as events unfold (e.g. in terms of relationships with customers, suppliers, the workforce and so on); this is a vital role for which middle managers are uniquely qualified because they are in day-to-day contact with such aspects of the organisation and its environment.

- *Advisers* to more senior management on what are likely to be blockages and requirements for change.

Consultants

Consultants are often used to help formulate strategy or to plan the change process. They are also increasingly used as facilitators of change processes: for example, in a coordinating capacity, as project planners for change programmes, as facilitators of project teams working on change, or of strategy workshops used to develop strategy and plan means of strategic change. The value of consultants is threefold. First, they do not inherit the cultural baggage of the organisation and can therefore bring a dispassionate view to the process. Second, as a result, they may ask questions and undertake analyses which challenge taken-for-granted ways of seeing or doing things. Third, they signal symbolically the importance of a change process, not least because their fees may be of a very high order.

Styles of strategic leadership

There is no one best style of strategic leadership. Moreover, there is evidence[16] that successful strategic leaders are able to adjust their style of leadership to the context they face. This has become known as 'situational leadership'. Here this is explained, first by reviewing different generic approaches to managing change, next by considering more specific styles of leading change, then by considering how these may need to differ by context.

On the basis of many years' study of corporate change programmes, Michael Beer and Nitin Nohria observe that, broadly, there are two approaches to managing change which they describe as 'Theory E and Theory O'.[17]

- *Theory E* is change based on the pursuit of economic value and is typically associated with the top-down, programmatic use of 'hard' levers of change such as changes of structures and systems, financial incentives, often associated with portfolio changes, downsizing and consequent job layoffs.

- *Theory O* is change based on the development of organisational capability. The emphasis here is on culture change, learning and participation in change programmes and experimentation.

Within these two generic approaches to change there are several styles of change leadership: Table 10.1 summarises these.[18]

- *Education* involves persuading others of the need for and means of strategic change. Four phases of this style of change leadership have been advocated:[19]

  - Convince employees that change is imperative and why the new direction is the right one.

  - Since change is likely to be interpreted differently throughout the organisation, frame the changes in ways relevant to the different groups and functions that have to enact the change and gather feedback on how this is understood and communicated within those groups.

  - Ensure ongoing communication of the progress of change.

  - Reinforce behavioural guidelines in line with the change and reward the achievement of change goals.

  However, the assumption that reasoned argument in a top-down fashion will overcome perhaps years of embedded assumptions about what 'really matters' may be optimistic. There may be apparent acceptance of change without its actually being delivered. Such an approach to change can also take a long time and can be costly, for example in terms of training and management time.

- *Collaboration* in the change process is the involvement of those affected by strategic change in setting the change agenda; for example, in the identification of strategic issues, the strategic decision-making process, the setting of priorities, the planning of strategic change or the drawing up of action plans. Such involvement can foster a positive attitude to change; people may see the constraints the organisation faces as less significant and feel increased ownership of, and commitment to, a decision or change process. It may, therefore, be a way of building readiness and capability for change. However, there are

Table 10.1 Styles of leading change

Style	Description	Advantages	Disadvantages
Education	Gain support for change by generating understanding and commitment. This is likely to be accompanied by delegation of responsibility for change.	Spreads support for change. Also ensures a wide base of understanding.	Takes a long time. If radical change is needed, fact-based argument and logic may not be enough to convince others of need for change. Easy to voice support, then walk away and do nothing.
Collaboration	Widespread involvement of employees on decisions about both what and how to change.	Spreads not only support but ownership of change by increasing levels of involvement.	Time-consuming. Little control over decisions made.
Participation	Strategic leaders retain overall coordination and authority, but delegate elements of the change process.	Again, spreads ownership and support of change, but within a more controlled framework. Easier to shape decisions.	Can be perceived as manipulation.
Direction	Change leaders make the majority of decisions about what to change and how. Use of authority to direct change.	Less time-consuming. Provides a clear change direction and focus.	Potentially less support and commitment, and therefore proposed changes may be resisted.
Coercion	Use of power to impose change.	Allows for prompt action.	Unlikely to achieve buy-in without a crisis.

Source: Adapted from J. Balogun and V. Hope Hailey, *Exploring Strategic Change*, 3rd edn, 2008.

potential problems here too. People may come up with change solutions that are not in line with, or do not achieve the expectations of, top management or key stakeholders. There is, then, the risk of perpetuating the status quo or merely an adaptation of it. A strategic change leader who takes this approach may, therefore, need to retain the ability to intervene in the process, but this runs the risk of demotivating employees who have been involved in the change process.

- *Participation* retains the coordination of and authority over processes of change by a strategic leader who delegates *elements* of the change process. For example, particular stages of change, such as ideas generation, data collection, detailed planning, the development of rationales for change or the identification of critical success factors, may be delegated to project teams or task forces. Such teams may not take full responsibility for the change process, but become involved in it and see their work building towards it. The responsibility for the change is retained by the strategic leader who ensures the monitoring of progress and that change is seen to occur. An advantage is that it involves members of the organisation, not only in originating ideas, but also in the *partial implementation* of solutions, helping build commitment to the change. It may also be that the retention of the agenda and means of change by the strategic leader reduces the possibility of a negotiated compromise and means that more radical change can be achieved. The potential problem is that employees may see this approach as manipulation and become disenchanted and demotivated.

- *Direction* involves the use of personal managerial authority to establish clarity on both strategy and how change will occur. It is top-down management of strategic change where change 'solutions' and the means of change are 'sold' to others who are tasked with implementing them. The need here is for both clarity of strategic vision and the specifics of a change programme in terms of critical success factors and priorities. The approach may be needed if there is a need for fast change or control over the change agenda (for example to meet the expectations of dominant external stakeholders). The danger is that it can result in explicit resistance to change or people going along with the rhetoric of change while passively resisting it. It is also worth noting that even where top management people see themselves adopting participative styles, their subordinates may perceive this as directive and, indeed, may welcome such direction if they see major change as needed.

- *Coercion* is direction in its most extreme form. It is the imposition of change or the issuing of edicts about change. This is the explicit use of power and may be necessary if the organisation is facing a crisis, for example.

Styles of managing change are not mutually exclusive. For example, clear direction on overall vision might aid a more collaborative approach to more detailed strategy development. Education and communication may be appropriate for some stakeholders, such as financial institutions; participation may be appropriate for groups in parts of the organisation where it is necessary to build *capability and readiness*; whereas if there are parts of the organisation where change has to happen fast, *timing* may demand a more directive style.

Illustration 10.4. provides examples of different strategic leadership styles.

SUMMARY

- There are different *structural types* (e.g. functional, divisional and matrix), each with their own strengths and weaknesses.
- There is a range of different organisational *systems* to facilitate and control strategy.
- The structure and systems of organisations should contribute to a coherent *organisational configuration* summarised in the *McKinsey 7-S framework*.
- Translating intended strategy into strategy in action requires the *leadership of strategic change*. This may take different forms such as *incremental change, reconstruction (or turnaround), revolutionary and evolutuionary change*.

ILLUSTRATION 10.4

Leadership styles for managing change

Successful top executives have different leadership styles.

Don't noodle

Terry Lundgren, CEO of Federated Department Stores:

> 'I have always been a pretty good listener, and I am quick to admit that I do not have all the answers. So I am going to listen. But shortly after I listen, the second piece is to pull the trigger. I have all the input, and here is what we are going to do. People need closure on a decision. If you listen and then noodle on it, people get confused, and that's not effective leadership.'[1]

The promised land

James Strachan, former Chairman of the Audit Commission UK, reporting what a CEO had told him:

> 'All you have to do is to figure out precisely where you want to go and you need to be able to paint that "promised land" in technicolour. Second, you need to ask whether you have got the right people around you, particularly at the top: if not change them tomorrow – literally tomorrow. Third, you delegate; but you do so without actually absolving yourself of all responsibility. You still own the ultimate responsibility – the buck stops with you – but you significantly delegate to people to enable them to bring out the best in themselves. Last you praise their success to high heaven.'[2]

He then added:

> 'The lesson about change for me is that in times of change there is a lot of turbulence, confusion, worry and concern. This is all natural. So people naturally gravitate towards a leadership that tries to take this confusion and describe it in simple terms about why we are doing this, what the "promised land" that we are going to get to is and why all this agony is worthwhile. In terms of change, it is simplicity and conviction that rule.'

Coach but don't coddle

Allan G. Laffley, CEO of Procter & Gamble:

> 'My approach to leadership is to raise aspiration and then achieve great execution . . . communicate priorities clearly, simply and frequently . . . to a large degree our division leaders must define their own future. I play the role of coach; but coaching doesn't mean coddling.

> I expect our managers to make choices . . . to help managers make these strategic choices leaders must sometimes challenge deeply held assumptions. . . . Being a role model is vital . . . I know that I must be ready for moments of truth that alert the organisation to my commitment.'[3]

Be dedicated and collegiate

Sir Terry Leahy of Tesco has overseen one of the biggest retail transformations in the world. Yet he is

> disarmingly ordinary. . . . His speech is serious and straightforward. He's no showman . . . He talks only about Tesco; . . . it's like meeting a religious leader faithfully reciting a creed. . . . His co-workers respect him for his decision-making but he doesn't make his moves on a whim. . . . Everything is analysed, taken apart, discussed and put back together. . . . He's gathered around him senior managers who've been with him and the group for years. He's in charge but he's also collegiate.[4]

He also likes to talk and listen to people in the stores:

> What makes Leahy different is the extraordinary degree to which he chats with junior staff and absorbs their views and the attention he pays to customers.

References:
1. Interview by Matthew Boyle, in *Fortune*, 12 December 2005, vol. 152, no. 12, pp. 126–27.
2. *Lessons Learned: Straight Talk from the World's Top Business Leaders: Managing Change*, Harvard Business School Press, 2007.
3. *Leadership Excellence*, November 2006, vol. 23, no. 11, pp. 9–10.
4. Chris Blackhurst, 'Sir Terry Leahy', *Management Today*, February 2004, p. 32. Reproduced from *Management Today* magazine with the permission of the copyright owner, Haymarket Business Publications Limited.

Questions

1 How would you describe each of the styles illustrated here in terms of those explained in section 10.5.3?

2 What might be the benefits and problems of each of the leadership styles? In what circumstances?

3 Only some stakeholders are specifically mentioned in the examples. Does this mean that the style should be the same towards all stakeholders of the organisation? If not, how would they differ?

RECOMMENDED KEY READINGS

- The best single coverage of issues relating to organisational structures and systems is in R. Daft, *Understanding the Theory and Design of Organizations*, South-Western, 2009.
- J. Balogun, V. Hope Hailey, *Exploring Strategic Change*, Prentice Hall, 3rd edition, 2008, builds on and extends many of the ideas in this chapter. In particular, it emphasises the importance of tailoring change programmes to organisational context and discusses more fully many of the approaches to change reviewed in this chapter.

REFERENCES

1. A good review of new and old structural types can be found in G. Friesen, 'Organisation design for the 21st century', *Consulting to Management – C2M*, vol. 16, no. 3 (2005), pp. 32–51.

2. See L. Donaldson, *The Contingency Theory of Organizations*, Sage, 2001, or R. Whittington, 'Organizational structure', in *The Oxford Handbook of Strategy, Vol. II*, Oxford University Press, 2003, Chapter 28, for summaries.

3. This view of divisionalisation as a response to diversity was originally put forward by A.D. Chandler, *Strategy and Structure*, MIT Press, 1962. See R. Whittington and M. Mayer, *The European Corporation: Strategy, Structure and Social Science*, Oxford University Press, 2000, for a summary of Chandler's argument and the success of divisional organisations in contemporary Europe.

4. For a review of current experience with matrix structures, see S. Thomas and L. D'Annunzio, 'Challenges and strategies of matrix organisations: top-level and mid-level managers' perspectives', *Human Resource Planning*, vol. 28, no. 1 (2005), pp. 39–48, and J. Galbraith, *Designing Matrix Structures that Actually Work*, Jossey-Bass, 2009.

5. M. Goold and A. Campbell, *Strategies and Styles*, Blackwell, 1987.

6. The value of goals and performance targets has been debated vigorously: see L. Ordonez, M. Schweitzer, A. Galinksy and M. Bazerman, 'Goals gone wild: the systematic side effects of overprescribing goal setting', *Academy of Management Perspectives*, vol. 23, no. 1 (2009), pp. 6–16 and E. Locke and G. Latham, 'Has goal setting gone wild?', *Academy of Management Perspectives*, vol. 23, no. 1 (2009), pp. 17–23.

7. See R. Kaplan and D. Norton, 'Having trouble with your strategy? Then map it', *Harvard Business Review*, vol. 78, no. 5 (2000), pp. 167–76 and R. Kaplan and D. Norton, *Alignment: How to Apply the Balanced Scorecard to Strategy*, Harvard Business School Press, 2006.

8. E.C. Wenger and W.M. Snyder, 'Communities of practice: the organized frontier', *Harvard Business Review*, vol. 78, no. 1 (2000), pp. 139–46.

9. R. Waterman, T. Peters and J. Phillips, 'Structure is not organization', *Business Horizons*, June 1980, pp. 14–26.

10. *Exploring Strategic Change* by J. Balogun and V. Hope Hailey, 3rd edition, Prentice Hall, 2008, is a sister text to this book; this part of the chapter draws on their Chapter 3 on the context of strategic change.

11. Turnaround strategy is more extensively explained in D. Lovett and S. Slatter, *Corporate Turnaround*, Penguin Books, 1999, and P. Grinyer, D. Mayes and P. McKiernan, 'The sharpbenders: achieving a sustained improvement in performance', *Long Range Planning*, vol. 23, no. 1 (1990), pp. 116–25.

12. This definition of leadership is based on that offered by R.M. Stodgill, 'Leadership, membership and organization', *Psychological Bulletin*, vol. 47 (1950), pp. 1–14.

13. See D. Ulrich, N. Smallwood and K. Sweetman, *Leadership Code: the Five Things Great Leaders Do*, Harvard Business School Press, 1999.

14. This is emphasised by John Kotter, 'What leaders really do', *Harvard Business Review*, December, 2001, pp. 85–96.

15. See S. Floyd and W. Wooldridge, *The Strategic Middle Manager: How to Create and Sustain Competitive Advantage*, Jossey-Bass, 1996.

16. The discussion on different approaches of strategic leaders and evidence for the effectiveness of the adoption of different approaches can be found in D. Goleman, 'Leadership that gets results', *Harvard Business Review*, vol. 78, no. 2 (March–April 2000), pp. 78–90, and C.M. Farkas and S. Wetlaufer, 'The ways chief executive officers lead', *Harvard Business Review*, vol. 74, no. 3 (May–June 1996), pp. 110–12.

17. See M. Beer and N. Nohria, 'Cracking the code of change', *Harvard Business Review*, vol. 78, no. 3 (May–June 2000), pp. 133–41.

18. Different authors explain change styles in different ways. This section is based on the typologies used by J. Balogun and V. Hope Haley (see 10 above, section 2.4, pp. 31–36) and D. Dunphy and D. Stace, 'The strategic management of corporate change', *Human Relations*, vol. 46, no. 8 (1993), pp. 905–20.

19. For example see D.A. Garvin and M.A. Roberto, 'Change through persuasion', *Harvard Business Review*, February 2005, pp. 104–12.

CASE EXAMPLE

Managing change at Faslane

Thirty miles west of Glasgow is HM Naval Base Clyde (Faslane), the home of the UK's nuclear submarines that carry the Trident weapon system. It is a Ministry of Defence (MoD) installation, but managed by private sector Babcock Marine, part of Babcock International.

The Babcock Marine office overlooks Gareloch on which the naval base is situated and where the ships and the 148-metre-long Trident submarines are maintained. As well as the base's offices there is also accommodation for the sailors, all within a heavily guarded barbed wire perimeter fence. Over the peninsula is Coulport, also part of the base, where nuclear warheads are processed and loaded onto submarines.

John Howie was the Babcock Marine Managing Director from 2002 to 2006.

John, how did Babcock Marine get involved at Faslane?

Faslane had been run entirely by the MoD and the Royal Navy. By 2000 the MoD had decided they needed to significantly reduce the cost and improve operational effectiveness of their naval bases and that in-house MoD management would find that difficult given the restrictions they operated under as part of a wider civil service. So they established partnering arrangements with industrial firms. In 2002, we signed a contract initially for a five-year period to deliver £76 (~€83; ~$114) million of cost savings without affecting the service provided to the Navy. A percentage of that saving would come to us as profit; the bulk would go to the customer as cost reduction. Our profit was entirely a share of the savings, so no cost reduction, no profit; but the contract made sure we couldn't do that by prejudicing service levels.

Over 1,700 civil service posts and nearly 300 Royal Navy personnel and civil servants were seconded to us. In addition, there remained 1,000 other civil servants on site, security personnel, police and the MoD Guard

Source: Babcock Faslane.

Service, Royal Marines, together with the sailors, ships and the submarines. The population of Faslane and Coulport is about 7,500 people.

What was it like when you arrived?

The customer support ethos didn't feel right. Despite being a naval base, the staff saw buildings and infrastructure facilities as more important than supporting the Navy. The focus was from the waterfront inward rather than looking outwards to the ships and submarines. I think that was because the people who looked after the site were often civilians who had been here much longer than the Navy people who looked after ships and submarines and generally moved on after 2–3 years. The civilians had built up empires. So the challenge was to become focused on delivering services to the customer, the Navy.

Moreover, a public sector manager who's got wide-ranging responsibilities and a fairly large budget has no incentive to reduce costs. They don't share in any benefits and were brought up in a system where, if they hadn't spent their budget, next year it would be cut. So we believed that a big opportunity might come from changing the mindset: to see their job as to deliver with the minimum possible spend.

Another difficulty is that every significant decision of a civil servant could be questioned by an elected politician. That makes people naturally conservative. You also end up with lots of layers in the organisation; lots of people with limited autonomy who focus on doing things within their own control. It's procedural; a 'handle turning' exercise.

With political accountability it's also important to demonstrate an audit path for the decision you made. So speedy decision-making is secondary to being able to demonstrate why you made the decision.

What of the management here before Babcock?

The commodore in charge when this process started was willing to change in a way some of his predecessors hadn't been. He'd come to the same conclusion about the need to change from infrastructure focus to naval focus. He saw partnering as the opportunity to better manage the people. The commodore's management team were a mix of people who either believed change was necessary and were willing to give partnering a try or people who were likely to be personally disadvantaged by partnering and were less supportive.

What of the workforce?

There was a perception that because of the base's role supporting the nuclear deterrent, they were ring-fenced from radical changes. Their view was that the base was doing a good job so why would you want to change that? There was no perception of a need to save money. They'd also been through a whole raft of MoD change, not least large-scale outsourcing programmes. There was the feeling of flavour-of-the-month change

programmes. So the backdrop was a workforce forcibly transferred to a private company and fearful of what change would mean.

So how did you set about change?

We brought in people from Babcock who had lived through similar changes. What they didn't necessarily understand was how to run a naval base, but the MoD transferred people to us who knew how to do that. Our job was to manage them differently.

The initial aim was to get visibility about how money was being spent while focusing on things that matter to the customer. We looked carefully at structures and processes to figure out how they operated and ask how that could be done differently. For example, there was a process that required any change to be documented and passed through a series of review points. After all, in a nuclear naval base you have to be sure that changing something fundamental to safety can be done without unacceptable risk. At each stage of that process people were given 14 days to review it; and of course everyone looked at it on day thirteen. So the overall process took about 56 days. It also became clear that a number of the review points weren't adding value; it was: 'I'm letting you look at this because you might be interested', not because involvement was critical. By taking those stages out you free up people's bureaucratic burden. You also don't give them 14 days to review it; you give them two days. Now that 56-day process is six days; a simple example of process re-engineering.

All that sounds very mechanistic.

It's not like that. We are an organisation that doesn't own any physical assets other than the people who walk through the gate every day. So change is very much about people. And with 2,000 people you get access to a whole raft of ideas and change initiatives that we would never have thought of because we had never worked in this environment. So part of it was about removing shackles from people to come up with their own change ideas. But culturally that's a challenge, when for many there's no incentive to come up with a change when it might mean that people next to you get made redundant.

So how do you do it?

We had a management structure that wasn't right to deliver change. We had seven layers in it. It's now (2006) down to a maximum of four layers. We've reappointed all the jobs. We asked other companies which had been through large-scale changes: 'What should we learn from what you did?' The answer was: 'Implement the management structural changes early.' People tried to launch transformational change with the existing team, got two or three years into it, realised it wasn't working, and then changed the structure. We are doing it the other way round. We implemented all the low-level changes upfront because they're easy. That allowed us to deliver £14 million of saving in the first year against a target of £3 million. But once you get into more transformational change – about trying to deliver a strategy of being the best, most profitable organisation supporting the UK submarine fleet – we needed different skill sets. So we've changed the structure. The management team we had was about 250; it's now about half of that.

The problem is that as we get away from the changes which are relatively mechanistic we get into changes that are much more complex in nature.

It also seems a difficult political situation

The first thing is to understand who you need to have as allies, such as the Naval Base Commander. Our success was intertwined. I have a parent company to satisfy, while the Commodore has to manage the relationships with the wider MoD and the Navy Board. Beyond that you have to look at the wider stakeholders. If the commanding officers of the ships and submarines were saying 'we're getting a bad service' we'd have struggled. Or if the security people thought we weren't interested in national security. Another key stakeholder was the local community. We did a lot of work upfront with two local councils because the base represents 9.5 per cent of employment in the area and we've reduced by about 400 full-time equivalent posts. Some of those have been naval posts rather than local people. And 98 reductions have been voluntary redundancies. Fairly quickly, the meetings with the councils stopped because they became comfortable we were doing things the right way.

So, what has been achieved?

Year 1 the target was £3 million of savings; we delivered £14 million. Year 2 the target was £12 million; we delivered £16 million. By the end of Year 5 we had delivered around £100 million against our £76 million target; that's over 20 per cent reduction in annual running costs. By the end of Year 10 we should have saved £280 million; that's 38.2 per cent. And the Navy's view was that the service they received was better, attitude better, communication better, responsiveness better. So we have delivered both cost reductions and service improvement.

Craig Lockhart, part of the original Babcock management team, succeeded John Howie in 2006. He takes up the story in 2009.

We are in our second year of having a performance scorecard. We started to measure outputs. Everyone down to team leaders have become acutely aware that business performance is not something to be hidden. It has to be transparent. However, it wasn't just about measurement. Business planning had been top-down. As our journey developed we appreciated that it was a hearts and minds issue: that we had to get the entire workforce aligned around common objectives. We held 'the event in the tent' sessions and nearly 3,000 people went through day-long discussions where we allowed them to challenge and express their views about the transformation of Naval Base Clyde.

They got to ask real questions and started to see that they got real answers. If there was bad news we would tell them it was bad news. If it was good news we would tell them it's good news but it was always honest news. So, we started to get the trust of the workforce. Now we've got the trade unions talking about 'our company'. We followed it up with blank business plans. We said, 'We've given you the broad headings, the broad objectives from a company point of view, but what's important is where do you think you fit in.' They were tasked to generate their own team, their own departmental business plans.

By 2009 we were also producing a joint business plan with the customer. It's not a Babcock Marine business plan or an MoD business plan. It's a plan on behalf of Clyde; and by the end of the year the Commodore and his team of directors will co-locate with us. We will be working together.

In April 2010, Craig was able to announce* that Faslane would become the home base, not just for nuclear submarines but for the entire UK submarines fleet. Together with the associated submarines and nulear training schools, it could mean up to 2000 more jobs at the base by 2014.

* *Source: Helensburgh Advertiser*, 29 April 2010.

Questions

1 Which of the organisational systems explained in section 10.3 are evident in the Babcock management of Faslane? Do you consider them to be effective? Why?

2 In relation to sections 10.5.1 and 10.5.2 what is the type of change being pursued at Faslane?

3 Describe the change styles of John Howie and Craig Lockhart.

4 Assess the effectiveness of the change programme.

APPENDIX
EVALUATING STRATEGIES

Learning outcomes

After reading this appendix you should be able to:

- Employ three *success criteria* for evaluating strategic options:
  - *Suitability:* whether a strategy addresses the key issues relating to the *opportunities and constraints* an organisation faces.
  - *Acceptability:* whether a strategy meets the *expectations* of stakeholders.
  - *Feasibility:* whether a strategy could *work in practice*.

INTRODUCTION

Chapters 5 to 9 introduced an array of strategic options and choices. The strategist has therefore to decide between these options; to decide what the organisation is actually going to do. This can be a challenge. It is not unusual for managers in a business – or indeed a group of students analysing a case study – to generate a long list of options. How is a decision to be made between them? This appendix provides three key evaluation criteria summarised by the acronym **SAF**e that can be used to do this.

S: SUITABILITY

Early chapters explained how the strategic position of an organisation can be understood in terms of key drivers and expected changes in its *environment* (Chapter 2) and its *strategic capabilities* (Chapter 3) in the context of *historical* and *cultural influences* (Chapter 4). These factors provide opportunities, but also place constraints on the future direction of an organisation. **Suitability is concerned with assessing which proposed strategies address the *key opportunities and constraints* an organisation faces** through an understanding of the strategic position of an organisation: it is therefore concerned with the overall *rationale* of a strategy. At the most basic level, the need is to assess the extent to which a proposed strategy:

- exploits the opportunities in the environment and avoids the threats;
- capitalises on the organisation's strength and strategic capabilities and avoids or remedies the weaknesses.

So the concepts and frameworks already discussed in Chapters 2, 3 and 4 can be specially helpful in understanding suitability. However, there is an important point to bear in mind. It is

ILLUSTRATION

Ranking options for SRR Consulting

Ranking can usefully provide an initial view of the suitability of strategic options by comparing strategic options against the key strategic factors from the SWOT analysis.

Simon and Ruth were both IT specialists who returned to their companies after completing their MBAs. Raj, a friend of theirs, had been an IT consultant who did the same MBA course a year later. His MBA project looked at the feasibility of setting up an IT consultancy partnership with Simon and Ruth. SRR was established in 2008. Their strategy was initially to build on 'outsourcing' the IT needs of the organisations they worked for. Raj had worked on IT assignments for business start-ups for a consultancy: 'It was not big business for them and they were delighted to have me operate as an associate; in effect outsourcing that work.' Simon worked for a medium-sized local engineering business and Ruth for a retailer with a small chain of local shops. As Simon explained: 'Neither of our employers really needed IT specialists full-time: an outsourced facility made good economic sense.'

Ruth continues:

'Our first year went well. We provided a good service to our previous employers together with developing business with some other contacts. We are both the owners and the consultants of SRR and our overheads are pretty low so we have made a reasonable living. Our problem now is, where from here? We are keen to grow the business, not just because we would like a higher income, but because with our rather limited client base we are vulnerable. We have built on our IT expertise and the sectors we know, but we have reached something of a ceiling with regard to our personal contacts. We can see a number of possible options. There is an opportunity on the management development aspects of IT; how can IT be used to aid better management? Most of our clients don't understand this.

Our problem is that we are not trainers so we would need to develop those skills or hire someone who has them. Another option is to actively go out and develop new contacts. The problems here are that it means branching out into sectors unfamiliar to us and that will take our time – which won't be fee earning – so it would reduce our income at least in the short term. Linked to this is the possibility of going for much bigger clients. This might get us bigger fees, perhaps, but it would quite possibly mean competition with some big competitors. In the last year, our business has also been very local. We could stick with the same sectors we know but broaden the geographic area. The problem there, of course, is we are not known. Finally, we have been approached by another IT consultancy about the possibility of a merger. They operate in complementary sectors and do have training capabilities, but it is bigger than us and I don't know if we are ready to lose our own identity yet.'

Simon, Ruth and Raj had begun a ranking exercise to look at these options as shown below.

Questions

1 Are there other options or factors that you think Simon, Ruth and Raj should consider?

2 How could you improve the ranking analysis?

3 Consider the most favoured options in terms of acceptability and feasibility criteria.

Ranking analysis

Strategic options	Key strategic factors								
	Fit with technical competences	Fit with sector know-how	Builds on our known reputation	Increases non-fee-earning management time	Reached our 'contact ceiling'	Builds on client need	Higher fee income	Increased competition	Ranking
1. Develop new contacts	✓	✗	✓	✗	✓	?	?	?	3–1 (B)
2. Develop bigger clients	✓	?	✗	✗	✓	✗	✓	✗	3–3 (C)
3. Geographic market development	✓	✓	✓	✗	✓	✓	✗	✗	5–3 (B)
4. Develop IT training	✗	✓	✓	✗	✓	✓	✓	✓	6–2 (A)
5. Merger	✓	✓	?	✓	✓	?	?	✓	5–0 (A)

✓ = favourable; ✗ = unfavourable; ? = uncertain or irrelevant.
A = most suitable; B = possible; C = unsuitable.

likely that a great many issues will have been raised if the concepts and tools discussed in these early chapters have been employed. It is, therefore, important that the really important *key strategic issues* are identified from among all these.

A useful way of thinking through the suitability of a strategic option is to employ a *ranking* mechanism. Here, possible strategies are assessed against key factors relating to the strategic position of the organisation and a score (or ranking) established for each option. The Illustration opposite gives an example. One of the advantages of this approach is that it forces a debate about the implications and impacts of specific key factors on specific strategic proposals. It therefore helps overcome a potential danger in strategy evaluation; namely that managers are likely to interpret the impact of particular factors, or have preferences for proposed strategies, in terms of their own subjectivity.

More sophisticated approaches to ranking can assign weightings to factors in recognition that some will be of more importance in the evaluation than others. It should, however, be remembered that assigning numbers, of itself, is not a basis for evaluation; any scoring or weighting is only a reflection of the quality of the analysis and debate that goes into the scoring.

A: ACCEPTABILITY

Acceptability is concerned with whether **the expected performance outcomes of a proposed strategy meet the expectations of stakeholders.** These can be of three types, the '3Rs': *risk, return* and *stakeholder reactions*.

Risk concerns the extent to which the outcomes of a strategy can be predicted. For example, risk can be high for organisations with major long-term programmes of innovation, where high levels of uncertainty exist about key issues in the environment, or about market behaviour, or where there are high levels of public concern about new developments. Formal risk assessments are often incorporated into business plans as well as the investment appraisals of major projects. Developing a good understanding of an organisation's strategic position (Chapters 2–4) is at the core of good risk assessment. However, it is also useful to consider how sensitive a proposed strategy is to deviations in the assumptions underpinning it. Sensitivity analysis can help here. It allows each of the important assumptions underlying a particular strategy to be questioned and challenged. In particular, it tests how sensitive the predicted performance or outcome (e.g. profit) is to each of these assumptions. For example, the key assumptions underlying a strategy might be that market demand will grow by 5 per cent a year, or that a new product will achieve a given sales and contribution level, or that certain expensive machines will operate at 90 per cent loading. Sensitivity analysis asks what would be the effect on performance (for example, profitability) of variations on these assumptions. For example, if market demand grew at only 1 per cent, or by as much as 10 per cent, would either of these extremes alter the decision to pursue that strategy? This can help develop a clearer picture of the risks of making particular strategic decisions and the degree of confidence managers might have in a given decision.

The second R is **returns**. These are **the financial benefits which stakeholders are expected to receive from a strategy.** In the private sector, typically these are shareholders and lenders; in the public sector the equivalent is funders, typically government departments. Measures of return are a common way of assessing proposed new ventures or major projects within businesses.

So an assessment of financial and non-financial returns likely to accrue from specific strategic options could be a key criterion of acceptability of a strategy – at least to some stakeholders. Three commonly used bases of financial analysis are:

- Forecasting the *return on capital employed (ROCE)* for a specific time period after a new strategy is in place. The ROCE (typically profit before interest and tax – PBIT, divided by capital employed) is a measure of the earning power of the resources used in implementing a particular strategic option.

- Estimating the *payback period* is a cash flow measure. This is the length of time it takes before the cumulative cash flows for a strategic option become positive. This measure has the virtue of simplicity and is most often used where the difficulty of forecasting is high and therefore risk is high. In such circumstances, this measure can be used to select projects or strategies that have the quickest payback.

- Calculating *discounted cash flows (DCF)*. This is a widely used investment appraisal technique using common cash flow forecasting techniques with the purpose of identifying which proposed projects are likely to achieve the best cumulative cash flow. The resulting measure is the net present value (or NPV) of the project, one of the most widely used criteria for assessing the financial viability of a project. While on the face of it the project with the best NPV should be selected, given that a DCF is only as valid as the assumptions built into it, a) sensitivity testing of assumptions is important and b) it may be more prudent to regard any project with a positive NPV as worthy of further consideration and evaluation.

Whichever approach is used it is important to remember:

- There are no absolute standards as to what constitutes good or poor return. It will differ between industries, countries and between different stakeholders. So it is important to establish what return is seen as acceptable by which stakeholders. Views also differ as to which measures give the best assessment of return, as will be seen below.

- Be wary of the apparent thoroughness of the various approaches to financial analysis. Most were developed for the purposes of investment appraisal. Therefore, they focus on discrete projects where the additional cash inflows and outflows can be predicted with relative certainty: for example, a retailer opening a new store has a good idea about likely turnover based on previous experience of similar stores in similar areas. Such assumptions are not necessarily valid in many strategic contexts because the outcomes are much less certain.

- Financial appraisals tend to focus on direct *tangible* costs and benefits rather than the strategy more broadly. However, it is often not easy to identify such costs and benefits, or the cash flows specific to a proposed strategy, since it may not be possible to isolate them from other ongoing business activities. Moreover, such costs and benefits may have spillover effects. For example, a new product may look unprofitable as a single project. But it may make strategic sense by enhancing the market acceptability of other products in a company's portfolio.

- Financial analysis is only as good as the assumptions built into the analysis. If assumptions about sales levels or costs are misguided, for example, then the value of the analysis is reduced, even misleading. This is one reason why sensitivity testing based on variations of assumptions is important.

Reaction of stakeholders

The third R is the likely *reaction* of stakeholders to a proposed strategy. Section 4.5.2 and Figure 4.4 showed how *stakeholder mapping* can be used to understand the political context and consider the political agenda in an organisation. It also showed how stakeholder mapping can be used to consider the likely reactions of stakeholders to new strategies and thus evaluate the acceptability of a strategy.

F: FEASIBILITY

Feasibility is **concerned is concerned with whether a strategy could *work in practice*:** therefore whether an organisation has the capabilities to deliver a strategy. An assessment of feasibility is likely to require two key questions to be addressed: a) do the resources and competences currently exist to implement a strategy effectively? And b) if not, can they be obtained? These questions can be applied to any resource area that has a bearing on the viability of a proposed strategy. However, typically there are three key issues.

Financial feasibility

A central issue in considering a proposed strategy is the funding required for it, so *cash flow analysis and forecasting* required for evaluating the acceptability of possible strategies is relevant here. The need is to identify the cash required for a strategy, the cash generated by following the strategy and the timing of any new funding requirements. This then informs consideration of the likely sources for obtaining funds.

People and skills

Chapter 3 showed how organisations that achieve sustainable competitive advantage may do so on the basis of competences that are embedded in the skills, knowledge and experience of people in that organisation. Indeed, ultimately the success of a strategy will likely depend on how it is delivered by people in the organisation. Three questions arise: do people in the organisation currently have the competences to deliver a proposed strategy? As explained in Chapter 10, are the structures and systems to support those people fit for the strategy? If not, can the competences be obtained or developed?

Strategic change

As Chapter 10 also explains, a strategy's success will also depend what the implications are for the nature and extent of strategic change and whether management can put into place an effective programme of change to achieve this.

GLOSSARY

Acceptability expected performance outcomes of a proposed strategy to meet the expectation of the stakeholders (p. 263)

Acquisition when one firm takes over the ownership ('equity') of another; hence the alternative term 'takeover' (p. 210)

Backward integration develop activities that involve the inputs into a company's current business (p. 142)

Balanced scorecards performance targets set according to a range of perspectives, not only financial (p. 241)

Barriers to entry factors that need to be overcome by new entrants if they are to compete in an industry (p. 28)

Blue Oceans new market spaces where competition is minimised (p. 40)

(Boston Consulting Group) matrix uses market share and market growth criteria to determine the attractiveness and balance of a business portfolio (p. 150)

Business-level strategy the plan of how an individual business should compete in its particular market(s) (p. 6)

Business model describes how an organisation manages incomes and costs through the structural arrangement of its activities (p. 192)

Buyers the organisation's immediate customers, not necessarily the ultimate consumers (p. 29)

CAGE framework emphasises the importance of cultural, administrative, geographical and economic distance (p. 173)

Collective strategy how the whole network of an alliance, of which an organisation is a member, competes against rival networks of alliances (p. 218)

Competences the ways in which an organisation may deploy its assets effectively (p. 5)

Competitive advantage how a strategic business unit creates value for its users which is both greater than the costs of supplying them and superior to that of rival SBUs (p. 111)

Competitive strategy how a strategic business unit achieves competitive advantage in its domain of activity (p. 111)

Configurations the set of organisational design elements that interlink together in order to support the intended strategy (p. 242)

Conglomerate (unrelated) diversification diversifying into products or services that are not related to the existing business (p. 136)

Core competences the linked set of skillls, activities and resources that, together, deliver customer value, differentiate a business from its competitors and, potentially, can be extended and developed (p. 54)

Corporate entrepreneurship refers to radical change in an organisation's business, driven principally by the organisation's own capabilities (p. 209)

Corporate governance concerned with the structures and systems of control by which managers are held accountable to those who have a legitimate stake in an organisation (p. 82)

Corporate-level strategy concerned with the overall scope of an organisation and how value is added to the constituent businesses of the organisation as a whole (p. 6)

Corporate social responsibility (CSR) the commitment by organisations to behave ethically and contribute to economic development while improving the quality of life of the workforce and their families as well as the local community and society at large (p. 87)

Cost-leadership strategy this involves becoming the lowest-cost organisation in a domain of activity (p. 112)

Critical success factors (CSF) those factors that are either particularly valued by customers or which provide a significant advantage in terms of costs. [Sometimes called key success factors (KSF)] (p. 40)

Cultural systems these aim to standardise norms of behaviour within an organisation in line with particular objectives (p. 241)

Cultural web shows the behavioural, physical and symbolic manifestations of a culture (p. 98)

Differentiation involves uniqueness in some dimension that is sufficiently valued by customers to allow a price premium (p. 116)

Diffusion the process by which innovations spread amongst users (p. 194)

Disruptive innovation this creates substantial growth by offering a new performance trajectory that, even if initially inferior to the performance of existing technologies, has the potential to become markedly superior (p. 200)

Diversification increasing the range of products or markets served by an organisation (p. 135)

Dominant logic the set of corporate-level managerial competences applied across the portfolio of businesses (p. 140)

Dynamic capabilities an organisation's ability to renew and re-create its strategic capabilities to meet the needs of changing environments (p. 52)

Economies of scope efficiency gains made through applying the organisation's existing resources or competences to new markets or services (p. 139)

Exploring Strategy Model this includes understanding *the strategic position* of an organisation (context); assessing *strategic choices* for the future (content); and managing *strategy in action* (process) (p. 9)

Feasibility whether a strategy can work in practice (p. 265)

First-mover advantage where an organisation is better off than its competitors as a result of being first to market with a new product, process or service (p. 198)

Focus strategy this targets a narrow segment of domain of activity and tailors its products or services to the needs of that specific segment to the exclusion of others (p. 119)

Forward integration developing activities concerned with the output of a company's current business (p. 142)

Functional structure this divides responsibilities according to the organisation's primary specialist roles such as production, research and sales (p. 233)

Global–local dilemma the extent to which products and services may be standardised across national boundaries or need to be adapted to meet the requirements of specific national markets (p. 169)

Global sourcing purchasing services and components from the most appropriate suppliers around the world, regardless of their location (p. 167)

Global strategy this involves high coordination of extensive activities dispersed geographically in many countries around the world (p. 161)

Governance chain this shows the roles and relationships of different groups involved in the governance of an organisation (p. 83)

Industry a group of firms producing products and services that are essentially the same (p. 25)

Inimitable capabilities those capabilities that competitors find difficult to imitate or obtain (p. 57)

Innovation the conversion of new knowledge into a new product, process or service *and* the putting of this new product, process or service into actual use (p. 187)

International strategy a range of options for operating outside an organisation's country of origin (p. 161)

Key drivers for change the environmental factors likely to have a high impact on the success or failure of strategy (p. 21)

Leadership the process of influencing an organisation (or group within an organisation) in its efforts towards achieving an aim or goal (p. 248)

Managing strategy in action this is about how strategies are formed and how they are implemented (p. 13)

Market a group of customers for specific products or services that are essentially the same (for example, a particular geographical market) (p. 25)

Market development this offers existing products to new markets (p. 138)

Market penetration this implies increasing share of the current markets with the current product range (p. 136)

Market segment a group of customers who have similar needs that are different from customer needs in other parts of the market (p. 38)

Matrix structure this combines different structural dimensions simultaneously, for example product divisions and geographical territories or product divisions and functional specialisms (p. 236)

McKinsey 7-S framework this highlights the importance of fit between strategy, structure, systems, staff, style, skills and superordinate goals (p. 242)

Merger the combination of two previously separate organisations, typically as more or less equal partners (p. 210)

Mission statement this aims to provide the employees and stakeholders with clarity about the overriding purpose of the organisation (p. 79)

Multidivisional structure this is built up of separate divisions on the basis of products, services or geographical areas (p. 235)

Objectives statements of specific outcomes that are to be achieved (often expressed in financial terms) (p. 80)

Open innovation this involves the deliberate import and export of knowledge by an organisation in order to accelerate and enhance its innovation (p. 191)

Operational strategies these are concerned with how the components of an organisation effectively deliver the corporate- and business-level strategies in terms of resources, processes and people (p. 7)

Organic development this is where a strategy is pursued by building on and developing an organisation's own capabilities (p. 209)

Organisational culture the taken-for-granted assumptions and behaviours that make sense of people's organisational context (p. 95)

Outsourcing activities that were previously carried out internally are subcontracted to external suppliers (p. 144)

Paradigm the set of assumptions held in common and taken for granted in an organisation (p. 96)

Parental developer an organisation that seeks to use its own central capabilities to add value to its businesses (p. 150)

Performance targets these focus on the *outputs* of an organisation (or part of an organisation), such as product quality, revenues or profits (p. 240)

PESTEL framework this categorises environmental influences into six main types: political, economic, social, technological, environmental and legal (p. 21)

Planning systems these plan and control the allocation of resources and monitor their utilisation (p. 238)

Platform leadership this refers to how large firms consciously nurture independent companies through successive waves of innovation around their basic technological 'platform' (p. 191)

Porter's Diamond this suggests that locational advantages may stem from local factor conditions; local demand conditions; local related and supporting industries; and from local firm strategy structure and rivalry (p. 165)

Porter's five forces framework this helps identify the attractiveness of an industry in terms of five competitive forces: the threat of entry; the threat of substitutes; the power of buyers; the power of suppliers; and the extent of rivalry between competitors (p. 25)

Portfolio manager he or she operates as an active investor in a way that shareholders in the stock market are either too dispersed or too inexpert to be able to do so (p. 148)

Product development organisations deliver modified or new products, or services, to existing markets (p. 137)

Rare capabilities those capabilities that are possessed uniquely by one organisation or by a few (p. 56)

Related diversification diversifying into products or services that are related to the existing business (p. 135)

Resource-based view (RBV) of strategy this states that the competitive advantage and superior performance of an organisation is explained by the distinctiveness of its capabilities (p. 50)

Resources assets possessed by an organisation, or that it can call upon (e.g. from partners or suppliers) (p. 51)

Returns the financial benefits that stakeholders are expected to receive from a strategy (p. 263)

Risk the extent to which the outcomes of a strategy can be predicted (p. 263)

Rivals organisations with similar products and services aimed at the same customer group (NB not the same as substitutes) (p. 30)

Scope indicates how far an organisation should be diversified in terms of products and markets (p. 134)

S-curve the shape of the curve reflects a process of initial slow adoption of an innovation, followed by a rapid acceleration in diffusion, leading to a plateau representing the limit to demand (p. 195)

Staged international expansion model this proposes a sequential process whereby companies gradually increase their commitment to newly entered markets as they build market knowledge and capabilities (p. 168)

Stakeholder mapping this identifies stakeholder expectations and power, and helps in the understanding of political priorities (p. 91)

Stakeholders those individuals or groups that depend on an organisation to fulfil their own goals and on whom, in turn, the organisation depends (p. 78)

Statements of corporate values these communicate the underlying and enduring core 'principles' that guide an organisation's strategy and define the way that the organisation should operate (p. 80)

Strategic alliance where two or more organisations share resources and activities to pursue a strategy (p. 218)

Strategic business unit (SBU) this supplies goods or services for a distinct domain of activity (p. 110)

Strategic capabilities the capabilities of an organisation that contribute to its long-term survival or competitive advantage (p. 51)

Strategic choices these involve the options for strategy in terms of both the *directions* in which strategy might move and the *methods* by which strategy might be pursued (p. 12)

Strategic customer the person to whom the strategy is primarily addressed because they have the most influence over which goods or services are purchased (p. 39)

Strategic groups organisations within an industry or sector with similar strategic characteristics, following similar strategies or competing on similar bases (p. 36)

Strategic position this is concerned with the impact on strategy of the external environment, the organisation's strategic capability (resources and competences), the organisation's goals and the organisation's culture (p. 11)

Strategy the long-term direction of an organisation (p. 2)

Strategy canvas this compares competitors according to their performance on key success factors in order to develop strategies based on creating new market spaces (p. 40)

Strategy statements these should have three main themes: the fundamental *goals* that the organisation seeks, which typically draw on the organisation's stated mission, vision and objectives; the *scope* or domain of the organisation's activities; and the particular *advantages* or capabilities it has to deliver all of these (p. 7)

Substitutes products or services that offer a similar benefit to an industry's products or services but by a different process (p. 28)

Suitability assessing which proposed strategies address the *key opportunities and restraints* an organisation faces (p. 261)

Suppliers those who supply the organisation with what it needs to produce the product or service (p. 30)

SWOT the strengths, weaknesses, opportunities and threats likely to impact on strategy development (p. 65)

Synergy the benefits gained where activities or assets complement each other so that their combined effect is greater that the sum of parts (p. 140)

Synergy manager a corporate parent seeking to enhance value for business units by managing synergies across business units (p. 148)

Three horizons framework this suggests that every organisation should think of itself as comprising three types of business or activity, defined by their 'horizons' in terms of years (p. 3)

Threshold capabilities those capabilities that are needed for an organisation to meet the necessary requirements to compete in a given market and achieve parity with competitors in that market (p. 53)

Tipping point this is where demand for a product or service suddenly takes off, with explosive growth (p. 195)

Value strategic capabilities are of value when they provide potential competitive advantage in a market at a cost that allows an organisation to realise acceptable levels of return (p. 54)

Value chain the categories of activities within an organisation which, together, create a product or a service (p. 59)

Value curves a graphic depiction of how customers perceive competitors' relative performance across the critical success factors (p. 40)

Value innovation the creation of new market space by excelling on established critical success factors on which competitors are performing badly and/or by creating new critical success factors representing previously unrecognised customer wants (p. 40)

Value network inter-organisational links and relationships that are necessary to create a product or service (p. 59)

Vertical integration entering into activities where the organisation is its own supplier or customer (p. 141)

Vision statement concerned with the desired future state of the organisation (p. 80)

Yip's globalisation framework this sees international strategy potential as determined by market drivers, cost drivers, government drivers and competitive drivers (p. 161)

INDEX OF NAMES

GENERAL INDEX

Note: Page numbers in **bold** refer to definitions in the Glossary.

PUBLISHER'S ACKNOWLEDGEMENTS

We are grateful to the following for permission to reproduce copyright material:

Figures

Figures 2.2 and 5.8 adapted from *Competitive Strategy: Techniques for Analyzing Industries and Competitors*, The Free Press (Michael E. Porter 1998) Adapted with the permission of the Free Press, a Division of Simon & Schuster, Inc. Copyright © 1980, 1998 by The Free Press. All rights reserved; Figures 3.3 and 3.4 adapted from *Competitive Advantage: Creating and Sustaining Superior Performance* (Michael E. Porter 1998) Adapted with the permission of The Free Press, a Division of Simon & Schuster Inc. Copyright © 1985, 1998 by Michael E. Porter. All rights reserved; Figure 4.2 adapted from David Pitt-Watson, Hermes Fund Management, reproduced with permission; Figure 4.5 adapted from *Turnaround: Managerial Recipes for Strategic Success*, Associated Business Press (Grinyer, P. and Spender, J.C. 1979), p. 203, reprinted by permission of Peter H. Grinyer and J.C. Spender; Figure 5.2 from *Competitive Advantage: Creating and Sustaining Superior Performance*, The Free Press (Michael E. Porter 1985,) p. 12, Reprinted with the permission of The Free Press, a Division of Simon & Schuster, Inc. Copyright © 1985, 1998 by Michael E. Porter. All rights reserved; Figure 5.5 adapted from The US airlines relative positioning, *Tourism Management*, vol. 26, no. 1, 62, fig. 1 (Gursoy, D., Chen, M. and Kim, H. 2005), Copyright © 2005, with permission from Elsevier; Figure 5.6 adapted from *The Essence of Competitive Strategy*, Prentice Hall (Faulkner, D. and Bowman, C. 1995) reproduced with permission from Pearson Education Ltd.; Figure 5.7 adapted from *Hypercompetition: Managing the Dynamics of Strategic Manoeuverings*, The Free Press (D'Aveni, R. 1984), p. 50, Adapted with the permission of The Free Press, a Division of Simon & Schuster, Inc. Copyright © 1994 by Richard D'Aveni. All rights reserved; Figure 6.2 adapted from *Corporate Strategy*, Penguin (Ansoff, H.I. 1988), Ch. 6, With permission of The Ansoff Family Trust; Figure in Note 1 of Chapter 6 References from *The New Corporate Strategy*, John Wiley & Sons, Inc. (Ansoff, H. 1988) Copyright © 1988. Reproduced with permission of John Wiley & Sons, Inc. and The Ansoff Family Trust; Figure 7.1 from http://finance.yahoo.com/echarts, reproduced with permission of Yahoo! Inc. © 2011 Yahoo! Inc. Yahoo! and the Yahoo! logo are registered trademarks of Yahoo! Inc.; Data in the figure reproduced with permission from NASDAQ OMX Group, Inc.; Figure 7.3 adapted from *The Competitive Advantage of Nations* (Porter, M. 1998) Adapted with permission of The Free Press, a Division of Simon & Schuster Adult Publishing Group. Copyright © 1990, 1998 by Michael E. Porter. All rights reserved; Figure 7.4 adapted from Changing patterns of international competition,*California Management Review*, vol. 28, no. 2, pp. 9–39, fig. 5 (Porter, M. 1986), Copyright © 1986, by The Regents of the University of California. Reprinted by permission of the University of California Press; Figure 7.5 from In the eye of the beholder: cross cultural lessons in leadership, *Project GLOBE, Academy of Management Perspectives*, February, pp. 67–90 (Figure 4: USA vs China, p. 82) (Javidan, M., Dorman, P., de Luque, M. and House, R. 2006), The Academy of Management Perspectives by Academy of Management. Copyright 2006 Reproduced with permission of ACADEMY OF MANAGEMENT (NY) in the format Textbook via Copyright Clearance Center; Figure 7.6 from Global gamesmanship, *Harvard Business Review*, May (MacMillan, I., van Putter, S. and McGrath, R. 2003), Reprinted by permission of Harvard Business Review. Copyright © 2003 by the Harvard Business School Publishing Corporation, all rights reserved; Figure on p. 197 from Alexa Internet, www.alexa.com; Figure 8.2 adapted from A dynamic model of process and product innovation, *Omega*, vol. 3, no. 6, pp. 142–60 (Abernathy, J. and Utterback, W. 1975), Copyright ©1975, with permission from Elsevier; Unnumbered Figure 2 in Chapter 8 Case Example from *Skype Journal* (Phil Wolff), 08/03/2010, reproduced with permission; Figure 8.4 adapted from *The Innovator's Solution*, Harvard Business School Press (Christensen, C. and Raynor, M.E. 2003), Copyright © 2003 by the Harvard Business School Publishing Corporation, all rights reserved; Figure 8.5 from *The Entrepreneurial Mindset*, Harvard Business School Press (MacMilan, I. and McGrath, R.G. 2000), p. 176, Copyright © 2000 by the Harvard Business School Publishing Corporation, all rights reserved; Figure 9.2 from *Managing Acquisitions*, The Free Press (Haspeslagh, P. and Jemison, D. 1991), reproduced with permission from the authors; Figure 9.4 adapted from Strategic Alliances: Gateway to the New Europe, *Long Range Planning*, vol. 26, p. 109 (Murray, E. and Mahon, J. 1993), Copyright © 1993, with permission from Elsevier; Figure 10.5 from Structure is not organization, *Business Horizons*, June, p. 18 (Waterman, R., Peters, T. and Phillips, J. 1980), McKinsey & Company, reproduced with permission; Figure 10.6 adapted from *Exploring Strategic Change*, Prentice Hall (Balogun, J. and Hope Hailey, V. 2008), reproduced with permission from Pearson Education Ltd.

Tables

Table 3 in Chapter 2 Case Example from *Strategies for growth in an increasingly consolidated global beer market* (Euromonitor International 2010) reproduced with permission; Table 10.1 adapted from *Exploring Strategic Change*, 3 ed., Prentice Hall

284 PUBLISHER'S ACKNOWLEDGEMENTS

(Balogun, J. and Hope Hailey, V. 2008) reproduced with permission from Pearson Education Ltd.

Text

Illustration 1.2 from www.nokia.com, reproduced with permission; Illustration 1.2 from www.ucc.ie, reproduced with permission; Illustration 3.1 from www.smt.sandvik.com/sandvik © AB Sandvik Materials Technology, reproduced with permission; Illustration 4.1 from http://www.savethechildren.org.uk/en/what-we-stand-for.htm, reproduced with permission; Illustration 4.2 from *The Times*, p. 2, 16/09/2008, © The Times/ N I Syndication; Illustration 6.3 from Extracts from 2009 Berkshire Hathaway, Inc.'s Annual Report, The material is copyrighted and used with permission of the author.

The Financial Times

Box 5.2 from Volvo takes a lead in India, *Financial Times*, 31/08/2009 (Leahy, J.)

Photographs

Alamy Images: Picturesbyrob 44; Getty Images: 16, 72; iStockphoto: 227; Press Association Images: Kin Cheung / AP 182; Rex Features: Steve Bell 155, Steve Forrest 204, Lehtikuva OY 129; Shutterstock.com: 105.

In some instances we have been unable to trace the owners of copyright material, and we would appreciate any information that would enable us to do so.